KW-326-371

Department of Education and Science
Welsh Office
Department of Education for Northern Ireland

Assessment of Performance Unit

Language Performance in Schools

Review of APU Language Monitoring 1979–1983

T. P. Gorman
J. White
G. Brooks
M. Maclure
A. Kispal

A report submitted to the Department of Education and Science, the Welsh Office and the Department of Education for Northern Ireland by the Language Monitoring Research Team at the National Foundation for Educational Research

London
Her Majesty's Stationery Office

© Crown copyright 1988
First published 1988
ISBN 0 11 270630 4

Contents

List of Tables

List of Figures

List of Illustrations

Acknowledgements

The Language Monitoring Team at the National Foundation for Educational Research would like to thank, on behalf of themselves and the APU, the large number of people who played a part in enabling the surveys reported here to take place. We wish to express our thanks in particular to members of the APU Language Steering Group, to the Monitoring Group at the NFER, and to our colleagues in the Science and Mathematics Monitoring teams who contributed to Chapter 6.

We are also grateful to the members of the Monitoring Services Unit at the NFER, under the supervision of Mrs. Barbara Bloomfield. The statistical analysis of the results was guided by Mr. Barry Sexton, project statistician until January 1985, Mr. Cres Fernandes, project statistician from February 1985, and their colleagues, especially Mrs. Lesley Kendall.

The report was read in draft form by the Language Steering Group, the APU Statistics Group and the APU Consultative Committee. Their suggestions and advice have contributed to the coherence of the final draft.

The formidable task involved in typing successive versions of the report was undertaken with patience and skill by the secretarial staff of the Project: Mrs. Betty Peasgood, Mrs. Dorothy Merritt and (in the early stages) Mrs. Margaret Mason.

The assistance of teachers in reviewing and pre-testing materials and assessing written work is an integral part of the monitoring programme. We wish to acknowledge the invaluable contribution made by the members of the panels of markers responsible for the marking of pupils' work obtained in the surveys of writing and oracy performance. Those who took part in the marking of the 1983 surveys are listed in Appendix 1.

Finally we would like to acknowledge the help of the head teachers and members of staff in schools throughout the country whose co-operation enabled the ten surveys to be carried out. Above all, we are grateful to the pupils who participated in the surveys.

An introduction to the assessment framework

This report highlights some of the findings that have emerged from the surveys of language performance sponsored by the Assessment of Performance Unit (APU) between 1979 and 1983. Since 1979 ten national surveys have been carried out, five involving pupils aged 11 and five involving pupils aged 15.

for monitoring are aged 11 and 15. Eleven is typically the age at which children in the UK finish primary schooling, while 15-year-olds are nearing the end of their compulsory schooling. The secondary surveys thus take place before most children sit their first public examinations (GCE or CSE) in a range of subjects.

1.1 Background information on the APU

The Assessment of Performance Unit (APU) was set up in 1975 within the Department of Education and Science. It aims to provide information about general levels of performance of children at school and how these change over the years.

The terms of reference of the APU are as follows:

To promote the development of methods of assessing and monitoring the achievement of children in school, and seek to identify the incidence of underachievement. Associated with these terms of reference are the following tasks:

1. To identify and appraise existing instruments and methods of assessment which may be relevant for these purposes.

2. To sponsor the creation of new instruments and techniques of assessment, having due regard to statistical and sampling methods.

3. To promote the conduct of assessment in co-operation with local education authorities (LEAs) and teachers.

4. To identify significant differences of achievement related to the circumstances in which children learn, including the incidence of underachievement, and to make the findings available to those concerned with resource allocation within government departments, LEAs and schools.

In its monitoring programme the APU has been concerned to reflect the breadth of curriculum in schools and to display the wide range of pupil performance in language, mathematics, science and foreign languages.

Pupils are randomly selected from schools in England, Northern Ireland and Wales using a light sampling strategy, and according to background variables such as region, location, school size and type. The pupils chosen

1.2 The background to the surveys

(i) Reading and writing

Prior to the establishment of the APU there had been a number of national surveys of reading performance which involved pupils at these two age levels. The texts used in earlier surveys were sentence-completion tests in which pupils were asked to complete a series of incomplete, uncontextualised sentences. The limitations of these tests and of the evidence they provided about reading performances have been commented on in previous survey reports.

The members of the Bullock Committee whose report, *A Language for Life*, was published in 1975, reviewed the evidence from previous national surveys and concluded that there was a need for tests which would indicate the extent to which reading proficiency has been developed to serve personal and social needs. They proposed that new instruments of assessment should be developed which would 'embrace teaching objectives for the entire ability range'. They also recommended that the tests should draw on a variety of sources to ensure an extensive coverage of the area to be assessed, in contrast to the inevitably narrow focus of assessment afforded by a single test (DES, *A Language for Life*, HMSO, 1975, chapter 3).

In order to assess whether pupils' reading performance was adequate to the demands of schooling and purposes outside it, a number of theoretical and practical issues needed to be considered. These included questions such as the following:

– how are tests to be devised so as to represent the numerous reading activities that children might be engaged in?

– what account, if any, should be taken of the many inconclusive attempts to differentiate so-called 'sub-skills' in reading?

- to what extent is it appropriate in tests of reading to require pupils, particularly younger pupils, to provide extended answers in writing?

Similarly, in order to put into effect the Bullock Committee's proposal for the national monitoring of writing performance, problems such as the following had to be addressed:

- what features of writing should be assessed?

- by what criteria should one measure them?

- how can reliability be assured?

A number of these questions were considered by the Language Working Party (subsequently the Language Steering Group) which was convened by the APU to formulate a working set of guidelines.

The Group comprised teachers, HMIs, advisers and academics. In collaboration with the research team, appointed in 1977, the Steering Group made proposals relating to aspects of reading and writing for inclusion in the monitoring programme. In considering the range of tasks that pupils might be asked to undertake the Group adopted a functional perspective. The guiding questions asked were: What do children read and why? and What do children write and why? The resulting set of proposals was published in the pamphlet *Language Performance* (DES, 1978).

Two important components of the assessment programme for reading and writing included, firstly, information about attitudes and preferences and, secondly, the collection of written work from everyday classroom situations. Thus, in addition to asking pupils to engage in a variety of literacy activities, the team sought to investigate whether pupils saw reading and writing as a source of pleasure, and what kinds of voluntary reading they preferred. The assessment of pupils' writing was supplemented by reference to their own views about themselves as writers, and by reference to the kinds of writing they were accustomed to do in the classroom.

A decision was taken to assess reading and writing separately in the first survey, as it was recognised that some pupils are able to read but find it difficult to express an understanding of what they have read in extended written form. Increasingly however, as it has been demonstrated that the number of pupils in this category is small, it has been possible to draw more upon the interaction of reading and writing in the construction of assessment measures.

(ii) The assessment of oracy

The assessment of pupils' spoken language was not undertaken until 1982, its later beginning a reflection in part of the caution with which the topic was surrounded. Some members of the Steering Group expressed doubts as to the feasibility of monitoring oracy at all:

- was oracy actually a part of the school curriculum in the way that reading and writing were?

- could teachers arrive at anything like a consensus judgement about aspects of oral language?

- would it be possible to make assessments of spoken language interactions from tape recordings, and if not, how were pupils' performances to be compared with one another?

- to what extent would the presence of an assessor radically alter the nature of pupils' talk?

On the basis of extensive pilot work in schools and discussions with teachers these doubts were sufficiently allayed to enable the monitoring programme to go ahead.[1] In the opinion of many teachers and researchers it was important to give tangible expression to the strong groundswell of opinion, from the Bullock Report and before it, concerning the significance of spoken language in the educational experience of children.

1.3 The design of the APU surveys

The design of the APU surveys is such that any one pupil can only complete one or two tests out of the total range of tests. If these were now to be taken by any one pupil, he or she would need about three school weeks to complete the full set of tests (at either primary or secondary level). Such variety is required in order to reflect something of the complexity and range of the language curriculum.

A diagrammatic representation of the survey procedures is given below to illustrate the components of the programme, and their interconnections. Unless otherwise stated, the diagram refers to surveys at both age levels.

Total Sample	1983	1982	1981	1980	1979
Reading					
Writing					
Reading & Writing					

Sub-Sample	1983	1982	1981	1980	1979
Attitudes to Reading					
Attitudes to Writing					
Listening and Speaking					
Work Sampling (Age 15)					
Work Sampling (Age 11)					

---

[1] For a full discussion of the theoretical and practical issues in the assessment of oracy, see *Language Performance in Schools: 1982 Primary Survey Report*. London: DES, 1984, and *Language Performance in Schools: 1982 Secondary Survey Report*. London: DES, 1984.

1.4 The assessment of reading

Many studies have been undertaken which have attempted to isolate factors that might be said to underlie reading and to differentiate between reading 'sub-skills'; but no model of the reading process is generally accepted as an adequate representation of the processes by which readers understand what they read. As such comprehension is as complex as thinking itself, this lack of agreement is to be expected.

The reading test materials used in the APU test differ in form from those employed in previous national surveys and from most conventional tests of reading comprehension. The procedure of using single unrelated sentences as a basis for assessing pupils' reading performances is avoided, as is the procedure of using short unrelated passages or paragraphs for comprehension. Wherever possible the tests have some coherence in content and structure.

Most of the materials which pupils were asked to read in the different surveys fell into three broad categories: *works of reference, works of literature* and *reading materials* similar to those pupils read *for practical purposes in daily life.*

Works of reference

In each survey there were a number of test booklets which contained readings which were thematically related. The booklets generally included a page of contents and an index and other cues, such as page or chapter headings, which pupils need to use when reading reference materials. In most cases, the booklets also included relevant illustrations devised to supplement the text. These included charts, diagrams, tables and maps.

As stated above, the booklets were coherently organised in terms of content and structure. In a number of booklets pupils were gradually exposed to information of greater detail and complexity. This structure was, in turn, reflected in the types of question asked at each stage. For example, in most booklets based on reference materials, a number of questions were asked towards the end of the booklet which required pupils to relate and integrate information derived from different sections.

Works of literature

Each of the surveys also included a number of tasks in which pupils were asked to read works of literature. Wherever possible, the work included was complete in itself, in the form, for example, of a short story or poem. In a limited number of cases (for instance in a booklet focusing on the description of different places or settings), the reading material was made up of extracts from different sources, and these differences formed the subject of questions about the variety of approaches taken to a common theme.

Everyday reading materials

Some tests comprised reading materials that were similar to those that pupils would encounter outside school. These included extracts from periodicals such as comics, magazines or newspapers and sub-sections of these such as classified advertisements. Other reading materials included forms (to be read and filled in), sets of instructions, notices, signs and labels and listings of different kinds. For example, one test was presented in the form of a travel brochure which included information about the geographical, historical and economic setting of a fictional town and a full description of the amenities, set out in different sections. The brochure also included a map and a booking form. A second test was presented in the form of a magazine.

Forms of response

Attempts were made to obtain different types of response to the questions asked about the reading tests. The majority of questions required a written response but pupils were also asked to complete forms, fill in tables, label diagrams and design posters. In some tasks, also, they were asked to make notes on what they had read and to prepare a summary of this.

The guiding principle adopted in devising questions was that they should be similar to those that an experienced teacher would be likely to ask pupils taking account of the *subject matter,* the *form* and *function* of the reading material, and the *context* in which it was likely to be encountered. In this aspect of the work, the team was greatly aided by the practical advice and training offered by many teacher liaison groups.

1.5 The assessment of writing

The model of writing adopted for APU assessment assumes that the ability to write develops out of a child's general desire to communicate. To communicate effectively they have to learn to assemble and order their ideas and to use the linguistic resources available to them in order to create writing appropriate to the topic and to their purposes. Pupils also need to learn to adjust what they write to reflect what is known about the reader(s). For example, they need to be able to recognise and to meet the informational needs of a general audience as distinct from those of a known reader. Learning to write also involves learning to use the surface features of written expression such as those relating to spelling, punctuation and the general control of the orthographic system.

The range of writing tasks

Previous reports on the APU surveys have given information about the initial guidelines suggested by the Language Steering Group with reference to the range of writing tasks that pupils at the two age levels might be asked to complete. The initial proposals were discussed with groups of teachers. In these discussions, three main issues were considered: firstly, for what general purpose or purposes pupils would wish or need to undertake such tasks; secondly, what forms of writing or types of discourse might be produced in relation to such categories; and thirdly, what readership could be most appropriately specified for each task.

In each survey a series of ten different writing booklets was designed. Although there was some variation from survey to survey, in most cases each booklet comprised four parts: a short writing task common to all booklets; one of ten different longer writing tasks; a text-based exercise such as editing or note-making; and a final section comprising short questions about the pupils' writing preferences and experience in writing.

The tasks varied in terms of the freedom given to the pupil to define the subject matter and form of the writing. In some cases both topic and form were defined fully. In others the selection of both was left to the writer. Again, some tasks were designed to draw on writers' first-hand experience. Others were based on given material.

In successive surveys over 50 different writing activities were introduced at each age range. These were intended to reflect the range of activities that pupils encountered across the curriculum.

In 1982, and in subsequent surveys, pupils were asked to complete a separate questionnaire relating to attitudes to writing. As with the questionnaire relating to attitudes to reading, pupils responded in two ways. They were asked to write extended answers in response to some open-ended questions explaining and illustrating their attitudes to writing and their view of themselves as writers. In another section of the questionnaire they were asked to say whether they agreed or disagreed with statements, made originally by pupils of the same age, reflecting different attitudes and views about writing.

Different contexts of assessment: work written in classroom conditions

Not all writing activities are amenable to assessment under test conditions. For example, some of the writing which children carry out in schools in subject areas involves collaborative activities which require time and resources to complete. Such writing, including the writing of plays or poetry, cannot generally be produced 'on demand'. Some types of writing depend on a variety of starting points, such as outside interviews or visits. For these reasons, the feasibility of systematically gathering work obtained under such conditions was investigated in two pilot surveys, one for each age group. Selected pupils were asked to provide specified types of writing produced in the weeks preceding the surveys. Information about the genesis of each piece of writing was obtained by

means of a 'Context Questionnaire'. This provided information of different kinds, such as whether the work was done in the course of group work or as an individual initiative. Teachers were also asked to outline the procedures leading up to the writing, and to say whether any framework for the writing was suggested, in the form of an outline plan or notes. The time taken for writing was recorded and information was obtained about whether or not the work had undergone revisions.

Work sampling was incorporated with the main assessment programme from November 1982.

Methods of assessment

Complementary methods of marking were used to assess the written work of pupils, holistic marking and analytic marking. The first method involved impression-marking by panels of 40 teachers and each script was double-marked. The evidence from holistic marking was used as a basis for relating and comparing the performance of *groups* of pupils.

The separate and second method involved the double-marking of scripts analytically. A smaller panel of teachers was involved.

In analytic assessment, each task is assessed in relation to categories designated as *Content, Organisation, Knowledge of stylistic conventions, Knowledge of grammatical conventions* and *Knowledge of orthographic conventions.*[1] Such assessment provides evidence about the specific task-related difficulties that pupils encounter. The application of the analytic schemes is illustrated in the following chapters.

The following chart summarises the procedures applied in the assessment of writing:

Assessment of writing

Holistic scoring	*Analytic scoring*
Stage 1	Stage 2
Overall impression (Scale 1–7)	Focused assessment to apply analytic criteria
	(a) Content
	(b) Organisation
Double-marking of scripts	(c) Knowledge of stylistic conventions
Panel of 40 teachers	(d) Knowledge of grammatical conventions
All scripts	(e) Knowledge of orthographic conventions
	Scale 1–5
	Panels of 4–6 teachers
	Random sub-sample of scripts across tasks
	Double-marking of scripts

---

[1] These categories and their application have been discussed in all published reports. See particularly *Language Performance in Schools: 1982 Secondary Survey Report.* London: DES, 1984.

1.6 The assessment of speaking and listening (oracy performance)

At the start of the assessment programme the research team was asked to investigate the feasibility of assessing listening and speaking (oracy) in the context of a national monitoring programme. After investigation, the team recommended that such assessment was feasible. Work began on the development of materials to assess aspects of speaking and listening in 1980. Oracy assessment was incorporated in the main surveys from May 1982.

The tasks selected

As was the case with the assessment of reading and writing, pupils were asked to carry out activities involving listening and speaking which were similar to those that they might encounter in school or everyday life. In selecting and developing tasks the following issues were kept in mind: for what purposes do pupils tend to use sustained talk in the classroom and outside it and to whom do they address such talk?; and for what purposes and in what context do they listen to and interpret such talk?

From among the numerous possibilities that suggested themselves, tasks of the following kinds were selected for inclusion in the national surveys carried out in 1982 and 1983.

The interpretation and production of sustained talk
Examples of tasks and communicative purposes (1982/1983 surveys)

General purpose	Task	Audience
Describing and specifying	Describing pictures for identification.	P
	Description of a place and explanation of interest.	P/A
	Description of a sequence of pictures.	P
Informing/ Expounding/ Summarising	Interpretation of an account of a process (with diagrams).	PP
	Exposition of the gist of the account to others.	
	Interpretation of an account of an experiment. Exposition of the process to others.	PP
Instructing/Directing	Practical interpretation of rules of a game. Instructing pupil to play the game.	P
	Constructing a model following a sequence of instructions.	A
	Instructing others how to carry out an experiment.	PP
Reporting	Report of something learned and explanation of interest.	P/A
	Report on a favourite book and explanation of interest.	P
	Report of the results of an experiment.	PP
Narrating	Interpretation of a story, retelling to others	PP
	Interpretation of anecdote narrating personal experience.	A
	Telling a story based on a sequence of pictures.	P/A
Arguing/Persuading	Interpretation of opposing arguments, restatement of gist of argument and explanation of viewpoint.	PP
	Explanation of choice of career – argument/justification of point of view.	P
Focused questioning	Several tasks required this, e.g. in obtaining further information about an object described or a process outlined.	PP
Collaborative discussion/ Evaluation of evidence	Interpretation and discussion of evidence to decide on proposed action.	PP
	Interpretation and discussion of arguments to reach a consensus.	PP
	Interpretation and discussion of evidence to reach agreement.	PP
Speculating/ Advancing hypothesis	Speculating on the reasons for an experimental finding.	P/A
	Speculating on the characteristics of a hidden object and production of a diagram.	P

P pupil's friend   PP other pupils   A assessor

The majority of the tasks listed above have different components involving both the interpretation and the production of sustained talk. This task structure reflects the fact that in normal life, *in classroom activities, listening and speaking are not generally dissociated artificially.*

A number of tasks also involve a sequence of language activities as is illustrated below. For example, a task might involve children in interpreting an account of an experiment and instructing another pupil how to carry it out. The second pupil, in turn, would describe the results of the experiment and both pupils might report on what was perceived. Such activities follow a normal communicative sequence.

In some cases also the oracy tasks incorporate activities that involve the use of language in reading or writing, as a prelude to talk or as a consequence of it.

Methods of assessment

As in writing, two main approaches to assessment were used in the oracy programme. In the first place, on-the-spot assessors assigned impression marks to the relevant components of the tasks on a 7-point scale. They also assessed aspects of the pupils' non-verbal behaviour (such as eye-contact and general orientation to listener) which were relevant to effective communication.

With respect to certain tasks, such as those that involved giving or interpreting instructions, assessors would also take note of the extent to which specific instructions had been accurately conveyed, using a check-list for this purpose.

The recordings made of each performance were then double-impression-marked by a panel of teachers. The results were used for the same general purposes as the impression marks assigned in writing assessment; namely, for providing evidence relating to the relative performances of groups of pupils, such as boys and girls.

A randomly selected sample of taped records was then marked analytically by a third panel of teachers with reference to general and task-specific criteria. These criteria are detailed in the following chapters. Again, the main purpose of the analytic assessment was to provide evidence relating to the task-specific difficulties or achievements of pupils. The following chart summarises the methods of assessment used:

Assessment of speaking

On-the-spot assessment *Stage 1*	*Impression-marking* *Stage 2*
Overall impression (Scale 1–7)	Initial impression-marking (Scale 1–7)
Orientation to listener (Scale 1–5)	Panels of 12–20 teachers
Task-specific features (check-list)	All taped records
	Double-marking of taped records

Analytic marking
Stage 3

Focused assessment of task-related criteria

(a) Propositional/semantic content

(b) Sequential structure

(c) Lexico-grammatical features (syntax, lexis)

(d) Performance features (self-correction, hesitation, tempo, etc.)
Scale 1–3, 1–5

Panels of 8–10 teachers

Random sub-samples of taped records

Double-marking of taped records

Integrated tasks

Practical constraints relating to the amount of time that any one pupil could be involved in assessment dictated that each pupil was asked to complete one or, at most, two examples of the wide range of test materials developed for use in the surveys. In principle, however, there is no reason why assessments of performance in reading, writing, listening and speaking should be conducted as discrete and separate activities. It was indeed thought essential that a number of tasks involving language use in more than one mode should be developed. Early in the test development programme, therefore, a number of composite tasks involving reading and writing were developed. Subsequently, some tasks involving discussing, reading and writing were also constructed.

In the second phase, which will extend from January 1985 to December 1989, further analyses of existing data will be carried out. The studies will include analyses of pupils' performance at different levels of attainment, the comparative performance on selected materials of pupils aged 11 and 15, and analyses of the possible effect on performance of a number of variables such as the sex of the pupil. Such data as are available about school resources will also be studied in this context. Increased emphasis will be given to a number of projects that involve the dissemination of the findings to various audiences through conferences and courses and by means of booklets and audio-visual materials prepared for the use of teachers. Primary and secondary surveys will be undertaken in 1988.

An overview of pupils' performance

Synopsis

Reading performance

The incidence of illiteracy among school pupils in the age groups assessed is very low, in the sense that relatively few are unable to decode words that they are familiar with. Many pupils nevertheless misunderstand what they read, and such misunderstanding stems from different causes.

We noted, for example, a tendency for lower-performing pupils to impose a literal interpretation on what they read, with a consequent failure to interpret a writer's unstated assumptions or beliefs. We noted also a failure on the part of many pupils to understand the implications of variations in the style and tone of what was written, particularly in works of literature. In dealing with reference materials many pupils had difficulty in locating and selecting evidence that was relevant to issues in question, and in reconstructing such information and presenting it in a form appropriate to the purposes they had in mind. Good readers, in contrast, are generally willing to modify their initial interpretations of what they read, as they read, and to integrate information given at different points in the manner required by the tasks set.

Writing performance

A tiny minority of children are non-writers in the sense of being unable to construct legible, comprehensible messages, however short. For the majority of children assessed, making progress in writing has more to do with becoming familiar with a greater range of written discourse and being encouraged to write for specific purposes. The analytic criteria for content and organisation showed most variation between tasks, indicating that there are certain kinds of writing which children are more familiar with than others. For example, story writing and reporting on recent experiences are two kinds of activities for which children can assemble subject matter fairly readily, and, in the case of stories, also have available a standard organisational structure.

Although the results show that 15-year-olds have command of more types of discourse than the 11-year-olds, it appears that neither age group is particularly confident in the uses of writing that have to do with the development of hypotheses, speculation or enquiry. Similarly, for both age groups the category of appropriateness and style

proved to be harder to score high marks on than was the case for content and organisation. Problems in this category had to do with writing in other than informal registers, and writing in styles that were varied and precise. There seem to be obvious parallels to be drawn between aspects of writing which pupils find difficult and aspects of reading performance where they also appear to be experiencing problems.

Oracy performance

The majority of 11- and 15-year-olds performed satisfactorily on the tasks used to assess speaking and listening. The tasks which pupils found slightly more difficult were those which were less familiar, or which required the recasting of previous experience, or which imposed considerable cognitive demands. Both on these and simpler tasks the great majority of pupils were able to take into account the needs of their listeners.

In this section of the chapter we will review broadly some of the findings of the surveys of performance with particular reference to tasks that have been analysed in detail and reported on. In doing so, we will make a number of generalised statements about aspects of performance that the majority of pupils appear to have mastered. Subsequently, we will comment on aspects that a minority of pupils have mastered or that appear to cause difficulties to a substantial number of pupils. The references given in brackets refer to chapters and sections in the published reports. They are referred to as follows:

Year	Primary level	Secondary level
1979	PR1	SR1
1980	PR2	SR2
1981	—	—
1982	PR3	SR3
1983	This report	

2.1 Reading performance at age 11

This first point to note is that very few pupils aged 11 are unable to read in the sense that they are unable to decode written language. The results of the surveys show that only one pupil in 100 responded with a success rate of 10 per cent or less to questions asked about what they had read. Being able to decode familiar written words, however, does not mean that pupils can understand the range of meanings a writer intends to convey, as will be apparent from the following commentary. Having said that, the following generalisations can be made.

When dealing with either expository or literary materials most pupils (80–90 per cent) were able to locate explicitly stated information and to interpret it accurately (cf. PR2, 2–26; 2–39; 2–59).

Pupils also found it comparatively easy to establish the main theme or idea of a paragraph or a short passage, if it was clearly asserted (cf. PR1, 2–44; 2–43). If pupils were asked to extract the gist of a passage from paragraphs which did not contain a single topic sentence clearly asserting the main idea, approximately two-thirds were normally able to do this correctly. One reason for this is that to identify the main idea of a particular paragraph requires the pupil to understand the structure of the passage as a whole and the way in which the information in it is sequenced and related. It frequently requires considerable insight to understand the relative importance of different ideas raised but this is necessary before the underlying theme of a particular passage can be deduced or inferred.

Most pupils (80–90 per cent) were able to extract sufficient information from what they read to confirm or reject a proposition if this was phrased in a way that was identical or very similar to something written in the original text (PR2, 2–33; 2–42; 2–45; 2–56).

The majority of the test booklets containing expository materials were designed in the form of a short booklet with a page of contents, section or chapter headings and an index. Approximately 85 per cent of pupils were able to use an index competently in locating information given in different sections of a booklet (cf. PR1, 2–48; PR2, 2–46). When asked to carry out slightly more complex cross-referencing, for example when two passages needed to be compared for similarities or dissimilarities, 70 per cent of the pupils successfully accomplished what was required (PR1, 2–47).

Over 70 per cent of pupils also showed themselves to be competent at using a page of contents, and a bibliography (approximately 65 per cent), and at executing straightforward referential tasks on them, as is indicated subsequently in this report (cf. Chapter 3).

Most pupils also showed themselves able to interpret evidence provided in simple tables of statistics relating to a passage of text. For example, in the 1980 primary survey just under 90 per cent of pupils correctly answered at least one question relating to a table giving information on the planets (PR2, 2–42).

Similarly most pupils at primary level demonstrated the ability to interpret information presented in maps or diagrams, if this information was unambiguously presented. In general, pupils were able to interpret materials presented in a wide variety of formats and graphical layouts.

In reading short stories or passages of literature nine out of ten pupils were able to follow and recall the sequence of narrative events, to recognise main characteristics of different characters and to draw conclusions about their motivation. For example, one booklet included a very short story depicting an imaginary meeting between an astronaut and a young Martian. The questions asked about the story concerned the emotional responses of the Martian to the arrival of the astronaut and to the events that followed. None of the questions asked could be answered simply by reference to explicit assertions in the passage.

In reading a simply written poem, nine out of ten pupils showed an ability and willingness to respond to imaginative description or depiction. When reading poetry or prose over 80 per cent could deduce the meaning of an unknown word if the text provided sufficient contextual background (cf. PR1, 2–62; PR2, 2–26). When asked to select particular words that contributed to an imaginative effect or mood in a poem, seven out of ten pupils were able to point to such words or phrases (PR1, 2–68). Most pupils were able to point to such words or phrases used metaphorically though the results varied according to the context and the familiarity of the concepts related. For example, 66 per cent recognised the point and meaning of the metaphor used in a descriptive statement beginning 'The line snaked through our hands . . . pulling the bows of the boat into the air' (PR1, 2–63).

Again, depending on the context, between 40 and 60 per cent of pupils showed themselves able to detect stylistic effects of some subtlety as, for example, when a writer attempted to evoke a particular 'mood' or 'atmosphere' through a series of descriptive statements (cf. PR2, 4–64; PR2, 2–71).

In reading argumentative prose or expository prose explicitly presenting a particular point of view over 80 per cent of the pupils were able to form an opinion about the topic discussed and to justify it.

After reading a number of versions or accounts of an incident between 70 and 90 per cent of primary pupils were able to identify points of conflicting evidence and draw their own conclusions with reference to the information given.

2.2 Reading performance at age 15

Fifteen-year-old pupils can successfully undertake all the activities referred to above, but with higher levels of performance and in relation to more complex reading material in a wider range of formats. For example, 90 to 97 per cent can locate explicitly stated information on a clearly specified topic about which evidence is given unambiguously in a single source (cf. SR1, 2–71).

In addition, they are more able to distinguish between different styles of writing such as those that are intended to persuade and those that are intended to inform (cf. SR1, 2–77).

Some differences between primary and secondary level

In interpreting literature, secondary pupils display more insight into human character and motivation and are more able to understand the broader implications or underlying themes in what is written than primary pupils. Both primary and secondary pupils in the 1980 surveys, for example, were asked to read and respond to a short story, *The Flying Machine* by Ray Bradbury. The main focus of the story concerns the actions of an emperor who is supposedly confronted by an early version of a flying machine and its inventor. His response, in ordering the death of the flyer and the destruction of the machine, can be interpreted in different ways, as being cruel or altruistic (though the writer never implies the former).

At a more general level the story can be taken to relate to the possible socially destructive effects of developments in science and technology. In interpreting the emperor's actions older pupils were much more inclined than younger ones to assume that these were motivated by a general concern for the good of the people rather than by jealousy of the flyer and envy of the machine. At primary level an interpretation of the emperor's actions as altruistic was associated with a test score that was close to the average for the age group, whereas at secondary level such an interpretation was associated with a significantly lower score. As would be expected, secondary pupils were generally more aware of the social, political and moral issues raised in the narrative. On average, for common questions, the level of success of secondary pupils was approximately 20 per cent higher than for younger pupils.

What pupils found it difficult to read

We have noted elsewhere that the difficulty of a reading task or activity may be affected by the type of meaning to be extracted (i.e. the *focus* of the question), the amount of material to be referred to and assimilated (the *scope* of the question) and the strategies that need to be applied. For example, questions may relate to the ideas conveyed (the propositional meaning), which may be explicitly asserted, implied or presupposed in what is said. Questions may also relate to the affective meaning or emotive connotation of what is said, including the tone adopted by a writer in conveying a message, for example, whether this is polite or familiar. Questions may also relate to aspects of meaning that do not derive directly from language of the text but from the shared background knowledge assumed by the writer concerning the nature of human action and motivation.

In general, therefore, what determines the difficulty of any task or series of tasks is not simply the complexity or density of the material to be read, though this is a

relevant factor, but the question pupils are attempting to answer, and the form in which their response has to be presented.

For example, when pupils at primary level were asked to answer questions relating to certain features of different types of whales, such as size and colour, the great majority had no difficulty in doing this, even though the material to be read was technically very complex. The evidence that had to be extracted was nevertheless relatively easy to locate and explicitly asserted (PR1, 2–46).

The results of the reading surveys have indicated a number of ways in which pupils who can read nevertheless misunderstand what they read, or find some types or applications of reading difficult to accomplish. We will refer briefly here to some of the more common causes and effects of such a lack of understanding, illustrating these with reference to particular questions.

When pupils are reading a text, they construct an interpretation of what they read which appears to make sense, given their understanding of the intentions of the writer and the purpose of what is written. However, one recurrent source of error for a minority of pupils stems from a tendency for them to impose a literal interpretation on what they read. Instances of consistent misinterpretation from such a cause were found in the analyses of pupils' responses to short stories at both primary and secondary level. For example, one of the stories used at primary level, *King Lion*, depicted how a tyrannical lion was outwitted and led to his death by a clever ground squirrel. The lion professes to be concerned about the welfare of the animals he dominates. We infer, however, from his words and actions precisely the opposite. A small number of pupils – not more than 10 per cent – misinterpreted this intent. Their interpretation of the story in general was coherent and consistent with the literal interpretation of what was written.

In the discussion of secondary pupils' interpretation of reading in this report, other examples are given of cases in which pupils failed to understand the underlying meaning of what they read. No more than 50 per cent of pupils, for example, showed an understanding of the satirical viewpoint expressed in the opening section of *Brave New World*. Pupils assumed that the author was generally in favour of 'the principle of mass production', failing to recognise the ironic implication of what was written.

The difficulty that some pupils have in interpreting non-literal meaning can be related to a failure to understand the implications of the style and tone of language, such as that attributed to fictional characters. For example, in *The Landlady* by Roald Dahl (discussed in the report on the 1979 secondary survey), the author provides implicit information about the naive self-confident outlook of the main character through his description of the character and his way of speaking; but fewer than 25 per cent of the pupils were able to point to examples of ways in which the writer described the situation in words that the main character might have used e.g. 'The big shots up at Head Office were absolutely fantastically brisk all the time'.

A similar phenomenon, that is a lack of familiarity with registers or styles of language associated with particular situations, can be illustrated from the fact that only 60 per cent of pupils in the 1980 primary survey appreciated that a letter supposedly giving an account of a sighting of a UFO was one that might have been written to a newspaper. The content, style and layout of the letter were such as to indicate this unambiguously to an experienced reader. On a related point, a substantial number of pupils were unable to estimate the approximate age of the writer from its style and content.

In the APU surveys, we have been concerned not simply to assess pupils' 'comprehension' of what they read, but to see how they can make use of reading for different applications and for practical purposes. For this reason, in a number of instances, pupils were asked to interpret written materials and to record their response in a structured form, as would be frequently required in school. In the 1980 secondary survey report, for example, the results of two tasks were discussed which involved the interpretation of expository material on the theme of diamonds and their production. One exercise required pupils to read selectively and to extract and record evidence about five diamonds with respect to three issues (country of origin, colour and present location). Less than 10 per cent of the pupils noted all the available evidence relating to the different diamonds and recorded this in an economical format. In many cases (over 50 per cent of the 598 scripts examined) pupils reproduced evidence, in part, which had no bearing on the points at issue. However, when a second group of pupils was given the same question but provided with a framework in which to locate information, between 60 and 80 per cent of the pupils answered appropriately. We concluded that pupils' main difficulties did not stem from an inability to read and understand the material but from the requirement that they should select and reconstruct the information given and present *salient* features of content in a clearly *structured* and *succinct* form (SR2, 2–71).

In a further exercise pupils were asked to read through a difficult passage relating to diamond production and to summarise the main points in note form with respect to four headings. Just under 20 per cent of the pupils were judged to have made adequate reference to the main points in the passage and to these points exclusively, and, in doing so, to have used a form of layout which reflected and clarified the main divisions in content (SR2, 2–76f).

In the commentary on the pupils' oracy performance we have similarly noted the difficulty that pupils seem to have in recasting information into a significantly different form, even within the same language mode. A similar phenomenon was found in reading at primary level. In one booklet on the theme of *Chief Sitting Bull*, pupils were

asked to select, re-order and re-present information related to the topic in general. Over nine out of ten pupils were able to make an appropriate selection, but they found it more difficult to re-order the information in relation to a timeline, to select the more significant events in Chief Sitting Bull's life and to summarise these succinctly. They found it most difficult to reconstruct aspects of the historical background using information gathered from different sections. There was, again, a tendency to concentrate on comparatively trivial issues and to give disproportionate attention to them.

It was suggested earlier that problems of interpretation may arise when pupils are obliged to interpret the unspoken assumptions, intentions or beliefs of a writer, particularly when these express views and feelings of some complexity. In the interpretation of literature, in particular, difficulties of interpretation arise when pupils are asked to make inferences about complex human actions and motivations. For example, in the story referred to earlier, *The Flying Machine*, the writer depicts the Chinese Emperor, Yuan, on first sighting the flying machine. He is described as looking reflectively at the Great Wall of China which had 'protected his people from enemy hordes and preserved peaceful years without number'. The story continues: 'The Emperor glanced in all directions while the flying man soared down the morning wind. He saw a farmer in his fields, watching the sky and he noted where the farmer stood.' Pupils were asked 'Can you think of a reason why the emperor should have noticed where the farmer stood?' Just over a third of the primary pupils were able to do so. To answer appropriately they would have had to have in mind a number of possible scenarios, one of which would involve the emperor destroying evidence about the event, as indeed happens in the story.

From what has been written above it may be inferred that the number of pupils who have not attained a stage of basic literacy on leaving primary school is extremely small. (It will be remembered that pupils in Special Schools or Special Units in schools were not included in the assessment.) The evidence would appear to show that the proportion does not exceed 1 per cent of the school population. By the time pupils have reached the end of secondary school the proportion of those who are unable to read in the sense that they are unable to decode written words is minimal. However, it is not sufficient for pupils to have learned to read in this formal sense if their personal, social and academic needs are to be met adequately.

Pupils need to become familar with a wide range of reading materials and with the application of different reading strategies so that they can use the materials for different purposes. They may also need to modify their attitudes and approaches to reading in certain respects. To give two instances: it does not seem speculative to say that high performance in reading, and particularly in the interpretation of literature, generally requires both an openness to consider various possible interpretations of what is written and a willingness to modify and revise one's initial interpretation on the basis of subsequent evidence. This point is taken up and elaborated in subsequent chapters relating to reading.

Summary statement on reading performance

Almost all pupils aged 11 and 15 are able to read in the sense of being able to decode items of written language; the proportion who cannot do so does not exceed 1 per cent.

Most 11-year-olds (at least 50 per cent) can follow and recall sequences of events in short stories and poems; they can identify the main attributes of characters and make deductions about motives.

80 per cent to 90 per cent are able to locate explicitly stated information and interpret this accurately whether the material is expository or literary.

85 per cent can use an index and bibliography to locate information, and perform straightforward referencing tasks.

- can interpret evidence presented in simple tables of statistics related to texts

- can read information from a variety of graphical layouts if the presentation is clear.

At least 80 per cent can establish the main theme or idea of a paragraph if this contains a single topic sentence.

- can confirm or reject a proposition phrased in a similar way to original text

- are able to form an opinion about a topic discussed and justify it

- can deduce the meaning of an unknown word in a literary text using contextual clues.

70 per cent are able to carry out cross-referencing tasks using index, table of contents etc.

- can locate words or phrases contributing to effect or mood

- are able to identify points of conflicting evidence from different accounts of an event and draw their own conclusions.

Approximately 60 per cent are able to establish the main idea of a paragraph or passage where this does not contain a single topic sentence.

Between 40 per cent and 60 per cent are able to explain metaphoric usage and interpret stylistic effects of some subtlety.

Pupils aged 15 achieve higher levels of performance in relation to more complex material in a wider range of formats. (On common questions the difference in success rates between 11- and 15-year-olds may be as high as 20 per cent.) Fifteen-year-olds are generally able to distinguish between functions of language (e.g. persuade vs. inform); they are more able than 11-year-olds to understand the broader social, political, moral implications of what is written, showing more insight into questions of character and motivation in fictional texts.

Difficulties in reading for both age groups result not simply from the density of material, but from the nature of the question posed (its scope and focus), together with the form of response required. Thus, pupils find it difficult:

- to recast information in a different mode

- to read selectively for salient points and record these succinctly without irrelevancies

- to assess the satirical or ironical tone of a passage, or understand the attribution of particular viewpoints to fictional characters.

Pupils' lack of familiarity with different registers makes it difficult for them to contextualise some forms of writing or to estimate the age/status of authors.

Difficulties of this kind suggest that pupils need more help in applying their reading skills for a wider range of practical purposes, and that they need to develop a more questioning approach to what they read.

2.3 Writing performance: results from impression-marking

In the course of the surveys of writing pupils were asked to undertake a very large number of tasks. We will comment specifically on pupils' performances on tasks used in the 1979 and 1983 surveys, the first and last surveys in the five-year series, though reference will be made to tasks introduced into surveys in other years where it seems relevant to do so.

It will be recognised that the distribution of raw scores in any one survey can only serve to provide a general indication of levels of performance on different writing tasks. It does not provide a basis for comparing the performance of pupils on different tasks in different years. For reporting purposes, before summary statements are made relating performance to background variables, such as sex or region, the raw scores are scaled and adjusted to take account of the relative leniency of markers and the relative difficulty of the tasks (cf. PR1, Appendix 2). Readers should note that the data used in this chapter has not been scaled in this way.

Distribution of general impression marks: age 11

In 1983, the overall distribution of raw scores on the 7-point scale was as follows. These were generally reflective of the distribution of scores in the majority of primary surveys, though there was some fluctuation from year to year.

Table 2.1 *Distribution of general impression scores for writing, all tasks, age 11, 1983 (%)*

Score	1	2	3	4	5	6	7
Boys	4	13	30	30	15	6	2
Girls	1	7	23	34	21	10	3
TOTAL	3	10	26	32	18	8	3

An arbitrary distinction may be made between tasks on which the great majority of pupils (70 per cent or more) obtained impression scores of 4–7; those in which between 50 and 70 per cent obtained a score of 4 or more; and those on which fewer than 50 per cent were assigned marks in this range.

In the 1979 survey between 50 and 70 per cent of 11-year-olds were assigned average or higher scores on all tasks, except one in which they were asked to give an account of the sighting of a strange object on the basis of a given narrative and with reference to a set of instructions providing details of what was to be reported on. A higher proportion, 70 per cent, of pupils were assigned marks of 4 or more on the task. This may be accounted for by the fact that detailed information was provided relating to the content and structure of the task, thus making it an easier task on some dimensions.

In the 1983 survey a generally similar pattern of results was found. Between 60 and 70 per cent of pupils achieved a raw score of 4 or better on the majority of tasks. There were two exceptions. Just over 70 per cent of the pupils who gave a descriptive account of a strange animal or grown-up or an eye-witness account of a series of events they had witnessed were assigned scores of 4 or more; by contrast one task proved to be relatively difficult. This involved the pupils outlining how they would carry out an experiment (to establish how much water flowed from a dripping tap over a period of time). For that task less than 50 per cent of the pupils were assigned a mark of 4 or over on the general impression scale.

Figure 2.1 shows the proportion of pupils assigned a mark of 4 or more on writing tasks used in the 1979 and 1983 primary surveys. The order of the tasks *within* sections does not indicate a gradation of difficulty.

Distribution of general impression marks: age 15

At *secondary* level a higher proportion of pupils tended to be assigned a mark of 4 than was the case at primary level. There were no tasks in the 1979 or 1983 surveys on which fewer than 50 per cent of the pupils were assigned general impression scores of 4 or more and relatively few on which less than 60 per cent were assigned such ratings.

The overall distribution of scores on the general impression scale for the 1983 survey is shown below.

Table 2.2 *Distribution of general impression scores for writing, all tasks, age 15, 1983 (%)*

Score	1	2	3	4	5	6	7
Boys	3	10	24	27	20	11	4
Girls	1	4	16	27	27	18	8
TOTAL	2	7	20	27	24	15	6

The data given serves to conceal the fact that there is a consistent significant difference between the distribution of scores for boys and girls in relation to each of the tasks. In 1983, for example, approximately 80 per cent of girls in the sample, as opposed to just over 60 per cent of the boys, were assigned scores of 4 or more. A similar pattern was found in the 1979 survey except for the fact that the proportion of boys assigned a score of 4 or more was lower in that year.

In general, however, there is relatively little variation between tasks in terms of the distribution of scores on the general impression scale. This is to be expected, as these distributions reflect judgements that are unrelated to any *specific* aspects of writing performance. It is more illuminating to analyse the differences between tasks in

Figure 2.1 *Proportion of pupils achieving a raw score of 4 or above (general impression scale) on tasks in the 1979 and 1983 primary writing surveys*

70%+	Description of a memorable person or animal
	Narrative report based on given material
	Report of an eye-witness account
50%–70%	Story completion (given a situation)
	Story based on a well-known tale
	Autobiographical account of past experience
	Autobiographical account of an early memory
	A letter of request
	An account of an activity to be undertaken
	An account of something learnt
	A persuasive argument
	Personal letter to a friend
	Interpretation of poems
	Comparative description of two moths
	Explanation of a rule or regulation
<50%	Plan for a scientific experiment

Figure 2.2 *Proportion of pupils achieving a raw score of 4 or above (general impression scale) on tasks in the 1979 and 1983 secondary writing surveys*

>80%	A short story for younger readers
70%–80%	Explanation of rule or regulation
	Notes for a household manual
	Comparative description of two insects
	Comparative interpretation of two poems
	Response to a poem
	Persuasive argument
	Account of a skill on which the pupil is an expert
	Reflective discussion of a social issue
	Free response to a picture
	Autobiographical account of a journey
	An eye-witness report
	Autobiographical account of a past experience
60%–70%	Account of something learnt
	Letter of application for a job
	Comparative description of two dogs

terms of the distribution of analytic marks, as these serve to indicate which aspects of the writing tasks were found to pose greatest difficulty to pupils.

2.4 Writing performance: results from analytic marking

Distribution of analytic ratings

The distribution of analytic marks is informative, because the marks are indicative of the difficulties posed by specific components of different tasks. (The analytic criteria relating to the assessment categories of Content, Organisation and Knowledge of Stylistic, Grammatical, and Orthographic conventions have been described in previous reports. See, for example, SR3: Appendix 6.) Briefly, for students to be assigned a rating of 4 or more in relation to the analytic criteria the following circumstances need apply:

Content

A mark of 4 would be given if the pupils were judged to have coped with the topic adequately; for those given a mark of 5, the treatment of the subject matter would be judged to be wholly apt and presented with some degree of originality.

Organisation

A mark of 4 would indicate that the students were judged to have made a successful attempt to organise and sequence what they had to say. A mark of 5 would indicate that the organisation was judged to be entirely coherent and suitable to the type of discourse.

Appropriateness and style

Pupils would be given a rating of 4 if it was judged that they had successfully made appropriate choices of language at word and sentence level taking account, where relevant, of subject matter, the readership envisaged and the underlying purposes of the writer. Such a rating would indicate that a writer was judged to have made no more than three errors in the use of stylistic conventions in a 20-line stretch of writing. A rating of 5 would indicate that a pupil was judged to have produced a stylistically flawless piece of work.

Knowledge of grammatical conventions

In APU assessment this category is defined primarily with respect to the way pupils use such conventions to produce writing that is unambiguous. These conventions include the devices available for showing the relations between components of sentences, and clause relations and boundaries (for example, grammatical punctuation) as well as the conventions used to establish cohesion or relatedness between different parts of a sentence or between clauses

in succession (for example, in the management of tenses). A mark of 5 would indicate that no grammatical errors were evident and a mark of 4 that there were judged to be no more than three such errors in the first 20 lines of the text.

Knowledge of orthographic conventions

A mark of 4 would indicate that a pupil was judged to have made no more than two to three errors in ten lines of continuous writing relating to conventions of spelling, word boundaries, the appropriate use of capital letters and of a variety of non-grammatical punctuation marks. A mark of five would indicate that there was no more than one error in the same amount of writing.

Variations in performance with respect to each of these categories are discussed below. Reference is made to those tasks in which a contrastive pattern is evident as we pass from one category to another.

Results from analytic marking, age 11

Features of performance for content and organisation, pupils aged 11

The tasks on which pupils scored most highly for content and organisation in the 1979 and 1983 surveys were as follows:

Story completion
Personal letter to a friend
Autobiographical account of past experience
An account of interesting learning
A description of a memorable person or animal

On these tasks between 45 and 53 per cent of 11-year-olds scored marks of 4 or 5. By contrast fewer pupils scored top marks on these tasks:

A plan of an activity to be undertaken
An explanation of a rule or regulation
Interpretation of poems
A persuasive argument
Plan for a scientific experiment
Comparative description of two moths

On this group of tasks the proportion of pupils scoring marks of 4 or 5 ranged from 10 to 30 per cent.

From these results, we can highlight certain factors making for ease or difficulty in the management of content and organisation. Being able to draw on first-hand experience, or being free to define their own subject matter, is of assistance to pupils, but, as the contrast between performance on story or anecdotal writing and the writing of plans or arguments suggests, the shaping of personal experience is easier when the writer has a repertoire of spoken or written examples of a similar kind to draw upon. In such cases both the sequence of episodes and the language used will have been to some degree rehearsed.

In describing a rule or regulation, pupils' main difficulty lay in expounding reasons for adopting a particular stance towards it; the descriptive component of the task was less problematic. The point is made in later chapters of this report that pupils have more practice in writing 'factual' accounts than in using writing as a means of questioning or speculating about a given state of affairs. Pupils found difficulty with writing *comparative* descriptions however. This was evident in the tasks requiring comparative description of two poems and comparison of two pictured moths. In both cases pupils needed to select specific features for the purpose of distinguishing one poem or specimen from the other and the selection was best made from an overview of the data. Many of the descriptions or commentaries were inadequate in the sense that they lacked a general framework in relation to which salient features could be selected, described and ordered.

Features of performance for appropriateness and style, pupils aged 11

It proved in general to be harder for pupils to score highly on this category than for content and organisation. There were only two tasks on which more than 50 per cent of pupils scored marks of 4 or 5, and these were:

A personal letter to a friend
A letter of request to a disc jockey.

Other tasks which showed an aggregate of top scores obtained by between 20 and 40 per cent of pupils were nevertheless tasks on which a minority of pupils (about 3 per cent) achieved full marks, and on which approximately one-third of pupils' scripts were assessed as below average in stylistic terms. These were as follows:

An explanation of a rule or regulation
An account of interesting learning
A plan for a scientific experiment
A persuasive argument
An interpretation of poems

In both 1979 and 1983, a letter of request to a disc jockey was the task on which the highest proportion of pupils received a rating of 5 in relation to this category. We can deduce from this fact, and the fact that high scores were also obtained for style by pupils writing a personal letter to a friend, that performance is likely to be higher on tasks on which it is permissible for pupils to use a style of address that is relatively informal or familiar – in contrast to what would normally be expected in a letter written to unknown adults. The letter of request to the disc jockey was generally, and appropriately, interpreted as calling for the use of a familiar style of writing including the use of first names, as well as a jocular tone, reflecting the communicative style associated with request programmes.

Pupils' efforts to recollect and report on a number of interesting things that they had learnt also tended to give rise to a more informal or anecdotal style of writing, but in many cases the use of colloquialisms and markedly informal usage was judged to be stylistically unacceptable in this context. A degree of verbal precision in specifying what was learnt and in explaining why it was found to be interesting was also required for the writing to be given higher ratings.

In rhetorical terms, the task that involved describing and commenting on a rule or regulation had three main components: the description of the rule, the expression of pupils' views with respect to it, and an explanation as to why the rule should or should not be retained. The last requirement imposed stylistic demands of some complexity. The giving of explanations normally calls for the use of complex sentences including subordinate clauses as well as clauses linked by adverbials. The use of hypothetical instances (i.e. what would happen if the rule were not in existence) tended to pose problems in the handling of both stylistic and grammatical features, particularly with regard to tense sequences. Again, in this component a more formal, or at least non-personal style of address was generally entailed. As in the case of arguments, a greater degree of verbal specificity or precision in the selection of words and phrases is expected in the context in which a point of view is being formally advocated than in more informal communications.

There were specific difficulties also associated with the development of argumentation, some of which are elaborated later. In part, these stemmed from the need to take account of the supposed viewpoint of a third party and to maintain a tone appropriate for persuasive as opposed to one-sided communication.

Finally, the results on the task involving the planning of an experiment showed that pupils were, for the most part, unfamiliar with styles of writing associated with impersonal reporting. However, their main difficulties again tended to be associated with the need to say what might happen under different hypothetical circumstances, as is necessarily required in planning.

Features of performance for knowledge of grammatical conventions, pupils aged 11

Previous reports have drawn attention to a characteristic of 11-year olds' writing with respect to the assessment of grammatical conventions: namely, the run-on sequence. Some tasks more than others appear to produce writing which lacks essential punctuation. When tasks are set in such a way that subject matter can be dealt with as fairly discrete items, or when secondary source material provides an available model for sentence division, typical 'errors' in grammatical punctuation can be easily avoided. Examples of such tasks were:

A letter of request
A narrative report based on given material
An account of interesting learning

On these tasks between 45 and 60 per cent of pupils scored marks of 4 or 5. Fewer pupils (approximately 25 per cent) scored so highly on these tasks:

    A plan for a scientific experiment
    A comparison of poems

In writing about how they would conduct their experiments, pupils opting to use hypothetical/conditional verb tenses often failed to sustain them. In the case of comparison of poems, there were problems associated with explaining, exemplifying or qualifying statements, and also the temptation to 'tell the story' of the poem(s) brought into the writing the run-on sentences noted elsewhere in children's narrative prose.

Features of performance for knowledge of orthographic conventions, pupils aged 11

The variations in performance in terms of this assessment category can be largely explained by two considerations. One is the fact that if pupils are provided with source material to which they can refer in writing, the incidence of orthographic errors, more particularly with regard to spelling, is likely to be reduced. Secondly, the incidence of orthographic errors is lessened when pupils are dealing with everyday incidents or describing situations which allow them to call on vocabulary used in everyday circumstances.

These features were evident in three tasks in particular, namely:

    A narrative report based on given material
    An autobiographical account of an early memory
    A plan for a scientific experiment

On these tasks between 40 and 60 per cent of pupils obtained marks of 4 and 5. By contrast, other tasks showed a relatively low incidence of high marks:

    Comparative description of two moths
    A letter of request

On these tasks the proportions of pupils obtaining marks of 4 and 5 were 10 and 13 per cent. Analysis showed that orthographic errors stemmed from confusions regarding the use of apostrophe (wrongly inserted in *its*), and conventions of capitalisation (Moth A and Moth B). Similar types of orthographic error were noted in assessing the letter of request, concerning titles of records and names of musicians.

None of the tasks referred to so far serve to reflect the relatively high incidence of orthographic errors associated with the use of direct speech. This feature can be best exemplified with reference to the task introduced in the 1980 primary survey which involved dramatised argument (**The Balloon Game**). Only 1 per cent of the pupils completing that task obtained a rating of 5 with respect to their knowledge of orthographic conventions (cf. PR2, 4–58).

Results from analytic marking, age 15

Features of performance for content,[1] pupils aged 15

The majority of tasks produced distributions which showed that approximately two-thirds of 15-year-olds' writing was assessed as 4 or 5 in relation to this category. The contrast with performance at primary level will be noted. With a majority of pupils achieving high scores it is perhaps more revealing to contrast the proportions of grade 5s on certain tasks. In 1979, between 40 and 50 per cent of pupils were awarded a grade of 5 on the following tasks:

    A story for young children
    An account of a skill on which the pupil is an expert
    An autobiographical account of a past experience
    A report of a series of events

A second group of tasks, while still showing a majority of pupils scoring above average, contained a smaller incidence of marks in the highest category. Approximately 20 per cent of pupils scored maximum marks on these tasks:

    An application for a summer job
    A persuasive argument
    Comparative description of two dogs

A similar pattern emerged with the tasks used in the 1983 survey: the highest performances with respect to content were obtained in relation to the children's story, followed again by an account of a skill in which the pupil is an expert. Again, the least successful performance in relation to this category was judged to be found in the letter of application for a job. Lower performance, at least in terms of the incidence with which the highest mark of 5 was given, also occurred on these tasks, on each of which fewer than 20 per cent of the sample were awarded a mark in the highest category:

    A response to two poems
    A comparative description of two insects
    A discussion and explanation of a rule
    A reflective discussion relating to recreational facilities

As these results indicate, performance tends to be higher if pupils are drawing on their personal past experiences, relating events that they have witnessed or giving an account of an activity on which they can speak with authority. The fact that the highest levels of performance were achieved in the context of telling a short story is reflective of their own exposure over a number of years to writing in this genre. Although 15-year-olds may be judged to have fulfilled the demands of this category better than 11-year-olds, their ease or difficulty in doing so relates to similar features of the tasks set.

---

[1] Note that at secondary level *content* and *organisation* are assessed separately.

Features of performance for organisation, pupils aged 15

Marks for organisation tended to follow those for content, although over all tasks slightly fewer pupils scored marks in the top two bands (over half, but less than the two-thirds noted in this group for content).

In 1979, the tasks on which the highest proportion of pupils achieved full marks included those already listed as the 'easiest' for content, together with two other tasks:

Notes for a housework manual
Personal response to a single poem

On these tasks at least one-third of pupils' writing was awarded 5 for organisation. By contrast, 20 per cent of writing achieved this rating in relation to the job application letter, the persuasive argument and the comparative description of two dogs.

In the 1983 survey, the highest proportion of top scores again occurred in relation to the same tasks: the children's story, the account of a skill, the notes for a manual and another 'personal response' task (writing about a coloured picture postcard).

In 1983, pupils were least able to score top marks on the following tasks:

A comparative description of two insects
A comparative response to two poems
Explanation of a rule or regulation
Discussion of possible improvements to recreational
    facilities
An application for a summer job

As was noted in the context of results from the primary surveys, pupils find organisational matters more difficult when a comparative element is introduced into the writing. (Some of these problems are discussed later in this report, Chapter 7.) Difficulties encountered in the writing of a letter of application have been discussed in a previous report (SRI, 4–93) and can perhaps be generalised to other tasks in which the organisation of material has no evident chronology, but in which information has to be grouped according to implicit demands of relevance or emphasis, as was required in the **Rules** task and the discussion of recreational facilities.

Features of performance for appropriateness and style, pupils aged 15

In the 1979 survey, scores in relation to this category were higher for the story for younger children, the auto-biographical account of past experience and the instructional notes for the household manual, with over 70 per cent of pupils scoring marks of 4 or 5 for appropriateness and style. On these tasks, between 25 and 40 per cent of pupils scored top marks. By contrast fewer pupils (10 to 15 per cent) scored marks of 5 on these tasks:

A letter of application for a job
A persuasive argument

An explanation of a rule or regulation
A comparative description of two dogs

In 1983 a similar pattern was apparent for those tasks that were repeated, with the highest incidence of grade 5s noted in relation to the children's story and the lowest in association with tasks involving argumentative writing, the relatively formal letter of application and the comparative discussion of two poems. On these tasks, although upwards of 40 per cent of pupils achieved marks in the higher score bands, the percentage in the highest band was less than 10 per cent.

Both the task involving the expression of a strong opinion and that relating to desired improvements to recreational facilities involved pupils in producing a series of reasoned arguments, usually accompanied by counter-arguments, indicating the inadequacy of views other than those advanced. The stylistic features associated with such argumentation are discussed elsewhere (cf. SR3, 4–6, SR1, 4–61 and Chapter 8 of this report). A number are associated with the difficulty of advancing a strongly held viewpoint while at the same time taking account of the supposed views and attitudes of an uncommitted reader. The use of terms and strategies typical of assertive talk is frequently apparent, as is the over-use of a limited number of connecting words (most commonly *because*) whether or not these are appropriate, as well as the repeated use of connectives such as *also*, *and* and phrases such as *another thing* to loosely associate sequences of clauses.

The relative difficulty that pupils had in writing letters of application in an appropriate style stemmed in part from the requirement that the letters had to be written in a formal style of address. At the same time pupils have to sustain a tone of polite but not obsequious enquiry. However, pupils found it comparatively easy to handle the grammatical structures required for completing this task as contrasted with the required stylistic conventions (see below).

Letters of application typically comprise a series of declarative statements, not necessarily inter-linked, which means that the handling of grammatical structure generally poses few problems. At the same time a succession of statements introduced by I and similar in grammatical form is stylistically uninteresting, and would be likely to be judged as such by assessors.

The stylistic demands involved in writing a set of instructions for a household manual were simplified by the fact that pupils tended to be familiar with a number of 'registers' or styles of writing associated with giving directions to the uninstructed; nor was it necessary for them to take account of the personal views or attitudes of the reader who could be assumed to be eager to learn. Pupils also tended to have an assumed control over the words and phrases, sometimes technical, that were required to specify the processes involved in carrying out the activities they described. Recurrent stylistic problems did occur in this task, however, in the maintenance of consistency of address; and more particularly in the choice between an 'impersonal' form of address (characterised, for example, by the use of stative verbs and passive forms), the use of imperative forms in a series of directives, or a more familiar style, characterised by the use of the second person pronoun *you* (cf. SR1, 4–90).

The pupils' confident grasp of the complex stylistic conventions involved in story-telling for younger readers has been noted earlier. The scores given for the short stories also reflected the relative ease with which they modified their style and tone to be appropriate to a younger audience. For the most part, their work directly reflected the styles of writing associated with traditional fairy tales or with the genre of 'nursery-land' fiction associated with the name of Enid Blyton (SR2, 4–72f).

Features of performance for knowledge of grammatical conventions, pupils aged 15

In both 1979 and 1983 the highest levels of performance with respect to this category of assessment were reflected in three tasks, which were as follows:

Letter of application for a job
Story for a younger reader
Notes for a household manual

On these tasks, approximately 80 per cent of pupils achieved marks of 4 or 5, with the highest proportion of top scores occurring in relation to the letter of application. (The particular ease of such writing has been discussed above.) Similarly, those pupils who actually wrote 'notes' for the household manual, rather than continuous prose paragraphs, avoided some problems of grammatical interlinking, and thereby contributed to higher scores on this topic. Interestingly, the story for younger children contrasted with other narrative tasks in each survey, in as much as it was less associated with problems of grammatical punctuation of the type discussed earlier. The explanation for this must partly lie in the obvious familiarity 15-year-olds show with writing of this genre, and also because stories for younger children typically make use of shorter sentence types than other narrative writing.

Although in general terms around three-quarters of the age group achieved high marks for knowledge of grammatical conventions, the score distribution on some tasks suggested that task-specific features were causing difficulties. Thus, in the 1979 survey, only two-thirds of the pupils scored marks of 4 and 5 for grammar on the persuasive argument, the report of a series of events and the comparative description of dogs. In the 1983 survey the task involving a comparative description of insects produced lowest scores for grammar, with 50 per cent of pupils achieving marks of 4 and 5. Three other tasks showed that within the group of pupils obtaining marks of 4 and 5, a minority of these scores were in the highest category. These tasks were:

An explanation of a rule or regulation
A comparative discussion to two poems
An autobiographical account of a journey

The grammatical demands posed by these tasks are in various ways complex, in so far as explanatory/comparative writing involves the co-ordination and careful sequencing of materials. In this respect, the account of the journey (a 'traveller's tale') contrasts with the other narrative task mentioned earlier (the story for children): it appears that without the special conditions associated with structuring writing for a younger audience, the grammatical problems typical of narrative writing are more in evidence.

Features of performance for knowledge of orthographic conventions, pupils aged 15

In general, about 60 per cent of pupils scored marks of 4 and 5 across all tasks. Compared with distribution patterns across other analytic categories, there appeared to be less variation between the proportions in band 4 as against band 5 scores; nor was there a very substantial difference between tasks. However, in both the 1979 and 1983 surveys, proportionately fewer pupils scored marks of 5 on the persuasive argument in relation to scores on other tasks in each survey. Tasks on which 30 to 40 per cent of pupils' writing was assessed as 5 tended to be those which drew on everyday vocabulary, such as writing about a familiar environment, or on a well known 'technical' field, as was required in describing a skilled performance, or writing notes for a household manual. Because of the vocabulary range employed by many writers in composing a story for a younger audience, it was not surprising to find high scores on this task as well.

General comments on the results of analytic marking

The preceding discussion, which relates primarily to the results obtained in the first and last years of the surveys, needs to be considered in the context of more extended commentaries on writing performance contained in previous reports, and in Chapters 7, 8 and 9 of this report. On the basis of all such findings it is possible to make a number of generalisations.

On the analytic category of *appropriateness and style,* higher performance was associated with tasks on which it was possible to use a style of address that was relatively informal or familiar, although there was a problem that informality would work against the use of precise, specific vocabulary or a varied prose style. On average, across tasks, approximately 5 per cent of the pupils at primary level were assigned the highest rating of 5 on the analytic scale relating to the stylistic conventions and between 35 and 40 per cent a rating of 4, showing that they were judged to have an effective control of those aspects of the writing process entailed in selecting language appropriate to subject matter, readership and the writer's overall intentions. At secondary level, approximately 15 per cent of pupils were assigned the highest rating and 50 to 60 per cent a rating to 4 in relation to this category of assessment. In Chapter 12 we have referred to some of the pedagogical implications of this finding.

At primary level, at least 95 out of every 100 pupils whose work was assessed analytically were judged to have obtained sufficient control over the handling of *orthographic and grammatical conventions* in written English to be able to communicate in writing. That is, they had sufficient control of features such as word-division, spelling and capitalisation, and of grammatical and non-grammatical punctuation, for their work to be understood on first reading. However, the written work of approximately 20 to 25 per cent was found to contain numerous errors in the handling of such conventions, while approximately 30 per cent had a confident control over such features (these would be awarded ratings of 4 or 5 in relation to these analytic categories).

At secondary level, between 50 and 60 per cent of pupils were judged to be proficient for most purposes in the use of orthographic conventions and a somewhat higher proportion (70 to 80 per cent) in the handling of grammatical conventions. These would be awarded marks of 4 or 5 on the analytic scales. Approximately 30 per cent of the older pupils (as contrasted with just under 10 per cent of the younger ones) were judged to have attained a flawless control of orthographic conventions.

The analytic assessment categories of *content* and *organisation* showed the greatest amount of variability between tasks. Some ways of developing substantial subject matter in an appropriate format are obviously more familiar to 11- and 15-year-olds alike. Pupils achieved most success on topics drawing upon well assimilated 'knowledge' (whether this was of a previously experienced or imagined state of affairs), which could be deployed in narrative or reporting modes. Secondary pupils managed instructional writing better than primary pupils, but both age groups seemed under-confident in the use of writing to develop hypotheses, comparisons or speculations.

2.5 Performance in speaking and listening

Just over 4,000 pupils aged 11 and 15 took part in the four oracy surveys of 1982 and 1983. Full discussions of the 1982 surveys are included in the 1982 Primary Report and 1982 Secondary Report, and analyses of the individual tasks used in the 1983 surveys are given in Chapters 5 and 6 of this report. The overall picture gained from the 1983 surveys is summarised in Tables 2.3 and 2.4, which show the distribution of raw scores across all the tasks used at ages 11 and 15 respectively.

Table 2.3 *Distribution of general impression scores for oracy, all tasks, age 11, 1983 (%)*

Score	1	2	3	4	5	6	7
Boys	2	8	19	30	25	12	5
Girls	2	7	19	30	25	12	5
TOTAL	2	8	19	30	25	12	5

Table 2.4 *Distribution of general impression scores for oracy, all tasks, age 15, 1983 (%)*

Score	1	2	3	4	5	6	7
Boys	6	12	20	26	18	11	7
Girls	7	16	24	23	16	10	4
TOTAL	6	14	22	24	17	10	5

At age 11 the distribution of scores is very normal (in the statistical sense), and the distributions for boys and girls are very similar. At age 15 the distribution overall and for boys is also very close to normal, and the slight skewing of the distribution of girls' scores does not amount to a statistically significant difference.

More detailed comment can be made on the basis of the distribution of scores on particular tasks, at both ages and for both survey years. To do this, the following approach is adopted. On some tasks the great majority of pupils (70 per cent or more) were judged to have performed satisfactorily, i.e. were awarded a raw score of 4 or more (on the 1–7 scale used for general impression marking). On other tasks, 50 per cent or more of pupils were given a 4, and on these same tasks it was always the case that at least 70 per cent achieved a 3 or better. On a small number of tasks, fewer than 50 per cent were given a mark of 4 or better.

These three groups of tasks can be considered to be those on which a high, medium or low proportion of pupils achieved satisfactory marks, and the discussion will be organised in terms of this distinction. It should be noted that the categories are distinguished in terms of tasks rather than pupils, and therefore do not correspond directly to 'high', 'medium' and 'low' attainers.

It should also be noted that there is no compelling theoretical justification for defining the three groups of tasks in this way. Alternative boundaries between categories, and/or more categories, could have been defined. To have had more categories might have suggested a degree of discrimination between tasks which is not warranted at this stage, but the two boundaries used do begin to suggest some of the task characteristics which make for higher or lower performance. The three groups of tasks are set out, and described in functional terms, for both age levels in Table 2.5.

The classifications in Table 2.5 are based on raw scores. A little more detail can be given on the basis of analytic marks. The pupils involved in the surveys at both ages were in general able, while performing the tasks, to

- organise what they wished to say clearly
- avoid undue hesitation and pausing
- employ appropriate vocabulary and syntax
- adopt standard English usage and a widely intelligible accent.

That is, they were able to take detailed account of their listeners' needs.

Moreover, they were able to respond to the task demands with sufficient consistency for three panels of markers in each survey to reach substantial levels of inter-marker agreement.

Some further discussion can be given of the distribution of tasks between the 'high', 'medium', and 'low' categories. First, an explanation is in order at this point about the tasks in the low-performance group. In the context of the national monitoring programme, it would clearly have been bad practice and policy to have included many tasks which the majority of pupils found it difficult or impossible to carry out successfully. Such tasks were weeded out at the field-testing or pilot-survey stage.

Two tasks which typically produced poor performance at age 15 were retained in the surveys, however. They represented attempts to sample oral skills which it was thought would be valuable for older pupils to possess.

The first of these involved acting as chairperson in a group discussion. Both in **Teenagers** and in **Clones** it was found that the discussion was better if the assessor did not act as chairperson, even though pupils' performance in that role suggested a lack of familiarity with it.

Table 2.5 *Speaking and listening tasks on which high (70% +), medium (50%–70%) or low (<50%) proportions of pupils achieved a raw score of 4 or better**

age 11	age 15
HIGH	
Following instructions to produce a model (**Paper Folding**)	From a spoken description, identifying an object among a set of similar objects (**Bridges, Ships, Beetles, Gulls**)
Instructing a friend to play a game (**Board Game**)	Relaying simple information heard on tape (**Spiders**)
Instructing another pupil to carry out an experiment (**Tracks**)	Reporting something learnt and explaining its interest (**Recent Learning**)
Speculating on the reasons for a finding (**Tracks**)	Describing a place and explaining its interest (**Description of a Place**)
Reporting the results of an experiment (**Tracks**)	Stating ages at which certain rights are acquired (**Teenagers**)
Re-telling a story heard on tape (**King Lion**)	Contributing to small group discussion on teenagers' position in society (**Teenagers**)
Answering questions on a story or anecdote heard on tape (**King Lion, Brownies**)	
Narrating a personal anecdote (**Brownies, Transition**)	
Describing pictures (**Pictures**)	
Telling a story based on a sequence of pictures (**Pictures**)	
Summarising the plot of a book (**Book Club**)	

Age 11	Age 15
MEDIUM	
From a spoken description, identifying an object among a set of similar objects (**Bridges**)	Relaying more complex information heard on tape (**Brain, Clones**)
Relaying simple information heard on tape (**Spiders**)	Describing a job (**Jobs**)
Describing a job (**Jobs**)	Arguing to justify points of view (**Jobs**)
Arguing to justify a point of view (**Jobs, Sleuth**)	Describing objects for identification (**Bridges, Ships, Beetles, Gulls**)
Describing objects for identification (**Bridges**)	Planning an experiment collaboratively (**Woodlice**)
Summarising written information (**Island**)	Producing scientific speculation collaboratively (**Tin**)
Discussing to reach agreement (**Island**)	Enquiring about and explaining differences between two maps (**Map**)
Describing experimental observations (**Tracks**)	Contributing to small group discussion on an ethical issue (**Clones**)
Inventing a scenario for an imaginary crime (**Sleuth**)	
Predicting events (**Transition**)	
While listening to a tape, making notes for relaying (**Spiders**)	
LOW	
Discussing reasons for scientific problems (**Roses, Ivy**)†	Reporting part of a lengthy discussion (**Teenagers**, *unsupervised version*)
Reaching agreement on sequence of pictures for story (**Pictures**)†	Reporting a plan for an experiment (**Woodlice**)†
	Reporting new route across map (**Map**)†
	Chairing small group discussion (**Teenagers, Clones**)

Notes:
* The criterion for classification of a task was not in every case the proportion of pupils scoring 4 or better. On some discrete-item tasks it was the percentage of questions answered correctly (e.g. **King Lion**) or of instructions conveyed or obeyed correctly (e.g. **Board Game, Paper Folding**); for the listener's role in description for identification tasks (e.g. **Bridges**), it was the percentage of correct identifications.

† These elements were included only in piloted versions of the tasks and not in the surveys.

Linked with the chairperson's role in the **Teenagers** task was the other retained task on which performance tended to be poor, namely reporting part of the discussion. In the unsupervised version of **Teenagers**, the assessor left the room, and no on-the-spot assessment was made of the discussion itself. It was therefore arranged that, on returning to the room, the assessor would ask the chairperson to report the group's conclusion on one of the questions on which the group had been asked to base their discussion. In most instances, that report was very brief, and in most of the cases where it was compared to that portion of the taped discussion to which it was supposedly relevant it bore very little resemblance to the original conclusion.

Both of these skills would seem valuable, but our evidence suggests that they need practice to develop. For that reason they would fit well into a continuous assessment framework within a planned programme of oral work within a school. Further comments on the implications of this suggestion will be found in Chapter 13.

It also seems true that the two tasks in the low-performance group are both more difficult for and less familiar to 15-year-olds.

Inspection of the other two categories of task at age 15 suggests the confirmation of an intuitive grouping into simpler and more complex. The first two sets of tasks on which 70 per cent or more of 15-year-olds achieved a 4 or better involve attentive listening, either to simple material (**Spiders**, web) or for a straightforward purpose (**Bridges**, identification, etc.). The rest of the tasks in this group (from **Recent Learning** down to **Teenagers**) involve the pupils speaking from directly relevant personal experience, and in a way which does not require them to recast the experience in any fundamental way.

The 'medium' tasks at age 15, on the other hand, do seem more difficult. Where listening is involved, either the information is more complex (**Brain, Clones**), or the pupils have to make notes (**Spiders**, general information). In the predominantly speaking tasks, it seems necessary for the pupils to 'angle' or transform their experience in some way. In the describer's role in **Bridges**, etc., for instance, the pupils have to pick and choose what seems to them to be the most relevant aspects of the visual information, and bring reasonably precise vocabulary to bear in a task where the vocabulary is not provided. The rest of the tasks in that group (**Jobs**, and **Woodlice** down to **Clones**) all seem to require exploratory and tentative talk, of a kind which is clearly important for learning, however. All the tasks in this group seem to be ones which stretch the pupils.

With a few exceptions to be mentioned shortly, the distinction between tasks which seem less or more complex appears to hold also at age 11. The first three tasks listed (from **Paper Folding** to **Tracks**, instructing) require straightforward responses to relatively simple listening. The listening demands of re-telling a story, and of answering questions about a story or anecdote, also seem moderate. And narrating an anecdote, describing pictures, and telling a story from pictures all seem to fall within 11-year-olds' normal range of directly usable experience.

The tasks that seem out of place in this high-performance group are summarising the plot of a book and the two parts of **Tracks**, namely speculating and reporting.

In the medium group, all but one of the tasks do seem more difficult. Again they mostly require the recasting of experience in less familiar ways; and some might still be found difficult by adults, especially predicting events, summarising written information, and arguing competitively.

The only task in this group which from an adult perspective seems much simpler than the rest is **Spiders**. No obvious explanation of this finding, or of the three 'out-of-place' tasks in the high-performance group, suggests itself.

When tasks which were presented at both ages are inspected, it is heartening to note that identifying an object from a spoken description and relaying simple information both move up from the medium group to the high group. In both these tasks, however, the information was largely given within the task, and greater maturity and experience would be a parsimonious explanation of the improvement in performance.

On two other tasks used at both ages, describing a job and arguing competitively, the information had to be provided largely by the pupils themselves, and both tasks remained in the medium groups at age 15. This may well be because the two sets of markers had (justifiably) different ideas of what was reasonable to expect of pupils of the two ages on these tasks. An alternative explanation, however, would be that pupils had not had sufficient practice in either of these forms of talk to make progress suitable to the difference in age. In either case greater practice and experience, and appropriate teaching, might well be profitably invested. And this in turn underlines the need for teachers to be suitably equipped to provide the circumstances in which pupils could improve.

3

Reading at age 11

Synopsis

This chapter discusses 11-year-olds' interpretation of expository writing for reference purposes, including the use of maps, charts, tables, graphs, as well as extended passages of writing. The performance of pupils on four booklets was investigated with particular attention focused on high and low performers.

The responses on tasks in all four booklets revealed that the majority of pupils were able to extract explicitly stated information from the data in whatever format it was presented. Retrieval of implied information proved more difficult for low performers, who, if possible, drew upon prior knowledge or on personal expertise on the subject to answer questions. Similarly when asked to form a judgement or express an opinion on information presented, low performers frequently derived their responses from personal experiences and prejudices external to the text.

The responses of high performers were more text-related. For example, the high-scoring group was able to perform quite sophisticated deductions, not only in the retrieval of implied information but also in the separation of evidence from speculation and in drawing conclusions from the data consolidated from the various sources.

A high percentage of pupils was able to consult tables and charts successfully. High scorers demonstrated flexibility in the use of their contents, being able to manipulate the figures in complex ways.

Most pupils were able to select – from an extended piece of writing – facts relating to a given topic. High performers were also successful in condensing, reordering and paraphrasing the information according to the specifications of the task. The tasks connected with this booklet were interdependent and effort could be minimised by referring back to work done on the first and second exercises: the responses of low performers revealed a reluctance to exploit the work already done, while high performers appeared to make use of the information they had gathered in the course of previous tasks with greater frequency.

3.1 Introduction

The interpretation of expository writing and materials for reference

In addition to investigating pupils' reading of fictional and literary materials, a number of booklets employed over the five years of surveys tested the pupils' interpretation and use of documentary or expository writing mainly for purposes of reference. Since these booklets have not received attention in past reports, four of them: **Bicycles**, **Whales**, **Accident** and **Chief Sitting Bull**, will be discussed in greater depth here. Of these, two booklets were commented upon in previous reports: **Whales** (1979) in Primary Report no. 1, and **Accident** (1982) in the 1982 Primary Report.

In these tests pupils were required to refer to, interpret, select, reorganise and explain information working primarily from non-literary, non-fictional sources. In keeping with the 'documentary' nature of these booklets, many authentic charts, diagrams and tables were included. The accompanying tasks reveal both the ability to make practical use of the information presented in this form and the ability to explain it.

The findings are to be discussed with special attention paid to high and low performance represented by the top and bottom 20 per cent of the sample. This approach highlights those aspects of the tasks that pose specific difficulties to pupils in this age group.[1]

The numbers of pupils falling into these categories for each booklet are as follows:

	Low performers	High performers
Accident	63	75
Bicycles	68	65
Whales	69	80
Chief Sitting Bull	121	139

3.2 Bicycles

The first text to be considered consisted of five sections, each concerned with a different aspect of a common

---

[1] Information about the performance of the pupils falling into neither of these groups, and the performance of the population as a whole, is given in the Annex to this chapter.

theme: bicycles and cycling. Each section contained a text, table or chart followed by questions or tasks. The materials consisted of different types of writing, extracts from magazines, government publications and newsletters - common sources of information not often encountered in the classroom.

The booklet required the application of a number of study skills:

- the ability to understand and report assembled information

- to interpret, analyse and reorganise it

- to adapt it to hypothetical analogous situations

- to draw conclusions, detect bias, form personal opinion.

The passage below provides a convenient starting point for discussion because it was accompanied by a number of easy and difficult questions and is therefore very informative in terms of discriminating between different levels of attainment.

Illustration 3.1   Bicycles

Bicycles for older children

★ How should you buy a bike?
We found that most of the bikes we bought needed some kind of adjustment before they were fit to go on the road. Most of the bikes had grease on the wheel rims, which had to be cleaned off before the bikes' brakes would work properly. Three-quarters of the bikes needed to have nuts and bolts tightened, and nearly half needed their brakes adjusting. So check the bike yourself before it's ridden. We list below the things you should check – these are especially important if you buy a second- hand bike:

● Feel over the frame for bumps, ripples and cracks; look at it carefully from different angles for distortion. Pay attention to the front forks – these are liable to get bent backwards. Reject any frame you have doubts about, it could be dangerous.
● Lift the back wheel off the ground and push the pedal round – there shouldn't be any noise above normal running noise, nor should the cranks be bent or touch the chain guard. Pull the pedals gently towards you away from the frame and push then back – there should be hardly any movement.

● Spin the wheels – they should turn easily without wobbling too much, and should be clear of the brakes. When a properly- balanced front wheel stops spinning, the valve should be at the bottom.
● Apply each brake in turn hard, and try to push the bike forward. It shouldn't move, nor should there be any movement in the bearings between the handlebars and front forks.
● Check that the gears work – either by getting the child to have a test ride, or by putting the bike upside down and turning the pedals by hand.
● Check that the brake levers and gear controls are positioned so the rider can operate them comfortably.
● Look for signs of rust. Avoid a bike with lots of chips in it or that's been repainted anywhere - the rust may still be underneath.
● Check that the handlebar grips and handlebar end-plugs are firmy secured.
● Shake the bike and listen for rattles. Check that nuts and bolts aren't loose.

Which type of bike?
Small - wheel bikes: These usually adjust easily to accommodate a large range of sizes of people. We found, though, that there was more adjustment in the saddles than in the handlebars so taller people tended to have an awkward riding position. Small-wheel bikes are not usually as fast as large wheel ones, but are quite manoeuvrable.

Fun bikes: Often call "choppers" (though strictly, Chopper is the Raleigh brand name). They're usually meant to give the impression of an exotic motorcycle – with high-rise handlebars, a banana – or bench-seat, and the front wheel often smaller than the rear wheel. Some children find them difficult to manoeuvre. They tend to be too heavy.

Touring bikes: These have straight handlebars and large wheels. They don't have as much adjustment in the saddle and handlebars as small-wheel bikes, but are faster.

Drop-handlebar bikes: Often called racers or sports bikes. The riding position makes you more streamlined and able to exert more effort, but some children found it took getting used to. We also found that some children's hands weren't strong or large enough to operate the brakes properly. Drop-handlebar bikes tend to be lighter than other types, and have a "racing" saddle which is longer, thinner and harder than a conventional, mattress saddle (not the acme of comfort, but better for serious pedalling). Most of the boys in our survey wanted a drop-handlebar bike next time. There are few girls' drop-handlebar bikes on the market.

Four questions similar to the one below were designed to test the direct transference of information.

What checks should you make on the:
Frame ....

Low scorers appeared to have proportionally fewer difficulties with this basic task than with others. Answers from those pupils with low scores which were considered unacceptable were in most cases not the result of mis-selection of data. They consisted of statements derived from personal experience or knowledge, restatement of the question or fabrication. Typically, no reference to the text was evident. For example, in reply to the question 'What checks would you make on the gears?', the following suggestions were offered.

> 1) That they need 'oiling' and that they are not stiff.
> 2. be shore the gears work properly
> 3. Make shore that your haldle bares are up at the normal Place if it isnt your Gears Wont work.

Another of the questions that most pupils answered appropriately was 'If you were given a free choice which type of bike would you buy? Explain why'. In this case the pupil could state a preference reached either on the basis of personal knowledge or from knowledge gathered entirely from the text. The value lay in the information it imparted about pupils' use of and attitude to the information provided in the test. Since numerous possible replies are invited by such a question, markers were allowed considerable freedom in interpreting the responses, and on condition that the bicycle was clearly identified and the choice made properly justified any choice was to be accepted. Consequently few pupils could fail on this question, but those who did did not meet both of these requirements. The first three of the following examples display a lack of specificity and do not clearly describe the desired model. The last two offer complementary phrases devoid of explanatory content.

Which type of bike? If you were given a free choice which type of bike would you buy? Explain why.

Manoeuvrable type.

A quite big one. Becuse it can last you till you get older.

Nice one because, it will look lovely.

The top bike I would get. it is beather.

The most interesting characteristic of low performers is their reluctance to make use of material given in the text. This appears to be true of low scorers in general, not simply with respect to this particular question. The responses below for example, all of which were recorded as acceptable, reveal a heavy reliance on personal knowledge.

Which type of bike? If you were given a free choice which type of bike would you buy? Explain why.

A BMX because they can do Jumps and other good things.

bmx becouse thers padding on the frame and handle bars

BMX becouse thay are stonger the spocks are stronger than the others.

The BMX, not mentioned in the booklet, proved to be the most popular choice of the low-scoring group. This group made the reasonable assumption that the question was answerable without specific reference to the text and their answers reveal that even in 'test' conditions many low performers prefer to have recourse to their own knowledge rather than to the material offered.

This tendency to overlook the text contrasts sharply with the approach shown in the responses offered by high scorers. These rarely named a model which did not feature in the text; their explanations were also more text-bound and drawn from aspects of the descriptions which appealed to them.

Which type of bike? If you were given a free choice which type of bike would you buy? Explain why.

I wood buy a small wheel bike because the saddle is easier to put up and has room to put a basket on the back.

dropped handlebar. They can go fast and they are not as heavy as choppers.

The questions to be discussed next necessitated detailed examination of the text and consistently discriminated between the high performers and other pupils.

Who is this report written for – children or their parents?
....
How can you tell? ....

Despite the fact that pupils were given two opportunities to consider basically the same question, the success rate was low. This is presumably because:

1. the answer is implicit in the text; parents are not directly addressed

2. both the title and the subject matter suggest that the article would attract the child reader.

The intended readership is indicated by lexical clues scattered throughout the passage, e.g. '. . . the best way to fit a child to a bike is to take the child to the shop.'

Failure to answer this question correctly, therefore, cannot be attributed to a lack of reference to the text, but to a lack of awareness of relevant aspects of lexis and style. In comparison to the 39 per cent overall success rate on this question, 66 per cent of the high-scoring group answered it correctly. Their responses demonstrated that they had the ability to detect and interpret the clues and to readjust their initial understanding of the text to integrate the new information.

A comparison of the incorrect answers of the two groups is very informative. While 50 per cent of low scorers maintained that the article was written exclusively for children, only 7 per cent of high scorers concurred. The remainder of the high-scoring group – 93 per cent – suggested that it was addressed to both parents and their children and this response, taking wider implications into account, is not unfounded.

The follow-up question: 'How can you tell?' provided the pupil with a second opportunity to check the answer to the previous question against the text. Of the 24 per cent of low scorers who had correctly replied that the article was addressed to parents, none provided an acceptable explanation of how the conclusion was arrived at. Typically, replies consisted of reasons invented by the pupils rather than deduced from the text, e.g.

How can you tell?

Because it is important to no about a Bik

Similarly incorrect answers were equally well justified by appeals to common sense.

Who is this report written for – children or their parents?

Children

How can you tell?

becuse children play on there bicks more than parent.

10 per cent of the sample were judged to have given an appropriate response and of the top 20 per cent over one-third put forward an adequate and often sophisticated explanation derived from the article. These fell into three groups:

1. those who cited directly from the article, e.g.

   How can you tell?

   because the report says 'if you buy a bike to fit a small child.'

2. those who offered a brief synopsis of the purpose of the article, e.g.

   I can tell because it tells the parent about how children feel about the bikes and the information is for parents.

3. Those who paraphrased the function of significant nouns and pronouns, e.g.

   When refering to children it says he instead of you.

The last group demonstrated not only that they had understood the essence of the matter but that they were able to formulate an applicable generalisation.

The other exercises in this booklet were less conventional in format than the one discussed above in that they did not consist of text and questions alone. The results, therefore, are to some degree a function of reading ability and familiarity with the test method and disclose much about the flexibility of pupils in handling different types of tasks.

In the first exercise, entitled 'The Joys of Cycling', pupils were asked to identify the pros and cons of cycling and to underline them in two distinct ways. Of greater note than the responses themselves is the omission rate. 39 per cent of all pupils left the exercise blank.

The high omission rate cannot be attributed to the time factor or the difficulty of the exercise. Some pupils had difficulty in understanding what was required. Whereas all of the high attainers completed the task, almost one half (44 per cent) of the low-scoring group did not attempt it. While some of them were deterred altogether, others failed to grasp what was expected and proceeded to underline various sentences throughout the booklet. Others underlined every sentence in the passage and showed either that they had misunderstood the question or that they were unable to distinguish between neutral and biased statements. In all, 40 per cent of the sample were recorded as not following the instructions.

Interestingly, those low attainers who did as requested performed relatively well. On average they identified six of the nine items. This may imply that the knowledge required to interpret the instructions is greater than that necessary to complete the exercise successfully.

Another exercise in the booklet required the same mode of response and yielded more interesting results because it possessed a greater discriminatory power between low and high performers. The task itself was quite complex and involved the interaction of two texts.

Illustration 3.2 Bicycles *Cycling Safety Code*

Read through these notes on cycling safety. Then look at the extract from "The Diary of a wheel-based fiend" on the opposite page.

When you have done this, underline all the bits in the passage where the "wheel-based fiend" has forgotten or ignored the simple rules for safe cycling. (The first one is underlined for you as an example.)

CYCLING SAFETY

On our busy roads it is essential for the safety of all that cyclists know how to behave correctly. In 1973, 4757 cyclists were either killed or seriously injured and 15204 were less seriously injured. Nearly half of these casualties were under 15 years old, and many of these accidents could have been avoided if the cyclists had remembered some simple rules. These can be found in the Highway Code and are called Extra Rules for Cyclists.

1. Make sure your cycle is in good condition - particularly the brakes, tyres, lamps and rear reflector - before you ride it.
2. Do not start off, turn right or left, or pull up without first glancing behind to see it is safe. Give a clear signal of what you mean to do.
3. Do not ride more than two abreast. Ride in single file on busy or narrow roads.
4. On busy roads, if you want to turn right, it is often safer to pull well into the left side of the road and wait for a safe gap in the traffic in both directions before you start to cross.
5. While riding:
   a) always hold the handlebar and keep your feet on the pedals,
   b) do not hold on to another vehicle or another cyclist,
   c) do not carry a passenger unless your cycle has been built or altered to carry one,
   d) do not ride close behind another vehicle,
   e) do not carry anything which may affect your balance,
   f) do not lead an animal.
6. If there is an adequate cycle path beside the road, ride on it.

Illustration 3.2 Bicycles contd.

Diary of a wheel-based fiend

Here we go pedalling down Paradise Street . . . Thick with traffic, belching exhaust fumes – not my idea of paradise at all. See young Moggie ahead and cling to back of milk van to catch up with him. Riding two abreast down the street, swapping gossip, telling stories. Have you heard the latest . . .? Pa-pa-pa-pa. Why are car drivers so impatient. I'm a road user too!

See newsagents across street and do my specialised super-wheelie right wheel turn. Lorry driver behind jams on brakes. Stock up with magazines, crisps and cans of 7-up. Decaffeinated. Remount and glide away smoothly from kerb clutching large carrier . . . skillfully avoiding elderly lady in Mini who drives with her eyes shut . . . execute second level wheelie-stunt with feet on handlebars in public spirited attempt to wake her up. It does!

Hazard ahead. Little brother and dog walking along pavement. Shut eyes in hope this will mean he won't see me. But he does . . . Passenger boarding. If he only wouldn't wriggle so much! Wriggling Ricky strikes again . . . while that terror of the highway, Tammy the terrier, runs alongside. Will reckless Ricky manage to keep hold of his lead? At bottom of hill, unwind dog's lead from pedal, unload small brother still clutching dog's lead, and point him in direction of home.

Take to the road again, the long brown road before me . . . meander down Mill Street, whizz down White-hall Road, halt at High Street. What a bike! Tyres worn down to rim, (you can skid so well in the wet), brakes not what they ought to be . . . Execute Mark II specialised wheelie-right turn and roll along footpath. Pedestrians deliberately try to obstruct me . . . before they run for cover. Now for hyping-up in preparation for ultimate stunt. Backward facing, forward moving wheelie-turn executed in quick motion. Almost collide with a couple of policemen outside Marks and Spencers. Angry noises. Stern words. Names taken. Parents to be contacted. Action may be taken.

When incident is over streak home like lightning, planning a new stunt – the Mark III wheelie-based Omega – the ultimate stunt.

The test entailed the analysis of the first person narrative in terms of the code printed alongside. Pupils were requested to apply the rules to their assessment of the cycling behaviour of the 'wheel-based fiend' and to determine in what ways the cyclist contravened them. (The infringements were to be underlined in the booklet.)

As with the last exercise described, very few low attainers tackled this task – presumably because of the unfamiliar mode of response, a lack of time or the difficulty of the exercise. The 18 per cent who did register some response did not perform as well as they had on 'The Joys of Cycling' – not one underlined more than four of the 11

transgressions. Furthermore, no pattern emerged in their correct responses. On the contrary, there is a noticeable absence of pattern, accompanied by a sprinkling of superfluous underlinings. For example '. . . little brother and dog walking along pavement' was twice labelled as being an offence against the code. The difficulty of this exercise is reflected in the low facility value of the items (23 per cent to 53 per cent) and the high omission rate even among pupils of average attainment. High scorers, nevertheless, performed well on this task.

Almost 100 per cent of the top band undertook and completed the assignment and their results reveal a competent and confident approach. 13 per cent were recorded as correctly ringing all 11 items and none of the remaining 87 per cent found less than half.

An interesting feature emerged in the nature of the contraventions most frequently noted. While 77 per cent noticed that 'riding two abreast down the street' is an infringement of rule 3, 100 per cent correctly marked certain sections relating to the performance of stunts. These types of offences were noted with greater frequency despite the fact that the code omits direct reference to stunts. Tricks of this nature e.g. 'super-wheelie right wheel turns' are not explicitly forbidden but contravene rules such as No. 4. on right turns. This would imply that pupils did not rely entirely on the code printed before them, but judged the cyclist's behaviour by what they knew about sensible cycling from personal experience.

The ability to interpret and use tabulated information was tested by means of an RSPA table of child fatalities in various types of road accident.

When asked to extract and manipulate the figures in individual categories, the majority responded with accuracy. 47 per cent of the low-scoring group and 95 per cent of the high scorers correctly answered the following questions.

How many 11-year-olds were killed from running into the road?

How many 10-year-olds were killed hanging on to moving vehicles?

How many children aged 8 to 13 were killed because they crossed the road without looking?

How many cyclists between the ages of 8 and 13 were killed because they failed to stop at major roads?

Problems were encountered when they were asked to provide a summary explanation of the contents of the table.

Many definitions were very detailed and some expounded upon the moral implications and didactic value of the information. Although included in the preceding statement few pupils mentioned all three factors constituting the information represented by the table: namely that the table depicts the number of road *accidents* resulting in *child mortality*. 7 per cent of low performers offered this full explanation as opposed to 45 per cent of the high performers. Broadly, this shows that pupils of this age

Illustration 3.3 Bicycles *RSPA table*

This table was supplied by the Royal Society for the Prevention of Accidents. It refers only to fatal accidents – ones where someone dies. There were another 54,000 severe and minor accidents involving children in these age-groups, as well.

CIRCUMSTANCES OF FATAL ACCIDENT	Age-8	9	10	11	12	13	Total
Pedestrians							
Playing near delivery vehicles						1	1
Hanging on to moving vehicles	1		2	1	1	1	6
Losing control of toys	1						1
On footpath, verge	1	1	1	1	3	2	9
Zebra crossing with centre refuge	1		1			1	3
Zebra crossing without centre refuge	1	3	2	3			9
Running into road	23	18	14	14	10	5	84
Running across road to join relatives, friends, etc.							
Crossing road masked by moving vehicles			1		1		2
Crossing road masked by stationary vehicles	6	6	3	3	3	3	24
Alighting from bus (school/psv)	1	3	4	2	2	3	15
Playing in street	1				1		2
Crossing road to/from ice-cream van				1			1
Crossing road without looking (not running)	9	8	4	4	7	7	39
Crossing road masked by hedge, fence, concealed entrance							
Passengers	10	7	11	13	7	12	60
Others		1	2	1		4	8
Cyclists							
turning right						1	1
Cyclists failing to stop at major roads	1	4	1	4	1		11
Cyclists losing control				5	2	3	10
Cyclists colliding with vehicles turning/overtaking	1	3	6	4	2	4	20
Cyclists with faulty equipment					1	1	2
TOTALS	57	54	53	57	42	51	314

are competent interpreters of tabulated information while being less able to compose an explanatory abstract of the same material.

This is true of high attainers, but the picture is somewhat more complicated among low scorers. While 47 per cent successfully located figures in response to the four questions above, they were far less able to use the table for more complex purposes. For instance, only 5 per cent correctly combined the figures in five boxes to calculate 'How many 11-year-old cyclists were killed?' Even fewer were able to interpret the information backwards in response to a question 'What was the way most cyclists were killed?' Finally, few low attainers appeared to be aware of the function of the totals column – only 16 per cent correctly reported the sum of all child fatalities.

Nevertheless, the impression that is given by the responses about the use of tabulated information is not a discouraging one. Most 11-year-olds seem well able to use the information to the degree required by the task. Low attainers also demonstrated a certain familiarity with elementary interpretative tasks, but they had not yet developed a full flexibility in using material of this nature. Giving an explanation of the content constitutes another skill, independent of accurate interpretation of the table. It demands the ability to provide a verbal generalisation of material presented largely in a non-verbal form. This is patently a more complex skill, acquired only by a minority of high-attaining 11-year-olds.

The ability to provide such explanations, to explain the purpose or 'gist' of tabulations was investigated in greater detail in the **Whales** booklet, discussed below.

3.3 Whales

This test consisted of two booklets. The reading booklet took the format of an illustrated information book – comprising five one-page 'chapters' relating facts on different aspects of the whale as well as a short extract from a children's story 'Dolphin's Island'.

It had been used in earlier surveys (and was released with the report on the 1979 primary survey). However, the answer booklet in the version under discussion differed in content and emphases from the original version.

In the first question to be discussed, pupils were asked to locate explicit information about whales, given primarily in pictorial form. The pupils were instructed to match two pictures of different whales against the illustrations in the information booklet and identify them accordingly. 73 per cent of the sample correctly named both whales, 89 per cent named one. Low performers' scores were comparable to scores obtained for similar question types when interpreting a passage of prose. 48 per cent identified both whales, 60 per cent only one. High performers predictably found this question exceptionally easy as indicated by their success rate 84 per cent and 100 per cent respectively. The fact that the sources of information were illustrations did not appear to affect pupils' performance noticeably in this case.

The greatest difficulties pupils faced arose in connection with tasks relating to the Table of Contents, the Index, the Glossary and the booklist. Pupil performance on these tasks tended to reflect the findings reported earlier on the discussion of the RSPA Table of Accidents section in the **Bicycles** booklet.

Illustration 3.4 Whales

Table of Contents and Index

At the beginning of the 'Whales' booklet there is a CONTENTS PAGE.

What does this page tell you?

13. --

----

14. Which page would you turn to if you wanted to know more about:

Whalebone whales	page(s) ...
Toothed whales	page(s) ...
How whales manage to live in water	page(s) ...
Small whales like dolphins and porpoises	page(s) ...

15. At the back of the 'Whales' booklet there is an INDEX PAGE

16. What does the index page tell you?

----

17. How is it arranged?

----

18. Which page would you turn to in order to find out:

About seals	page(s) . . .
About Killer whales	page(s) . . .
About toothed whales	page(s) . . .
What rorquals are	page(s) . . .
What krill is	page(s) . . .
What plankton is	page(s) . . .
How whales communicate	page(s) . . .
How big whales are	page(s) . . .

A high percentage of pupils were able to consult and utilise these tables effectively; when asked to cite page numbers for 12 given subjects, 70 per cent did so with complete accuracy. On average those low scorers who responded quoted five correct page numbers. They found it very difficult to explain the function of the Contents and Index pages (questions 13 and 16). Only 9 and 18 per cent of all low attainers gave acceptable definitions or descriptions of the purpose of the Index and Contents pages. Amongst high scorers 48 per cent and 57 per cent answered these questions correctly. By far the commonest characteristic of high scorers was that they saw no clear distinction between the two tables. As a result their two definitions often differed only minimally or not at all, e.g.

At the beginning of the "Whales" booklet there is a CONTENTS PAGE.
What does this page tell you?

13. ...It tells you where you can find the things that you want?

16. What does the index page tell you?

...It tells you where things are.

Others suggested that the functions of the two were essentially the same, the Index being a more detailed version of the Contents page e.g.

At the beginning of the "Whales" booklet there is a CONTENTS PAGE.

13. Its gives you a page number and below it whats on that page...

16. What does the index page tell you?

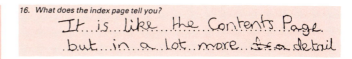

It is like the Contents Page but in a lot more ~~is a~~ detail

The incorrect responses of low scorers revealed that many had no notion of the meaning of these two terms. Almost 50 per cent of these responses were whale-related definitions and bore no relation to books or their organisation. Although many low scorers demonstrated correct use of the tables, they were not able to describe their purpose and offered inaccurate explanations. The example below illustrates this feature – a low scorer who knew exactly how to use this body of knowledge but offered an explanation which revealed a different level of interpretation of its purpose.

At the beginning of the "Whales" booklet there is a CONTENTS PAGE.
What does this page tell you?

13. Some facts about what have whales are adaped with sea

14. Which page would you turn to if you wanted to know more about:

Whalebone whales	page	...3......
Toothed whales	page	....3....
How whales manage to live in water	page	...2......
Small whales like dolphins and porpoises	page	....6.....

The same tendency was found in the use of explanation of the index.

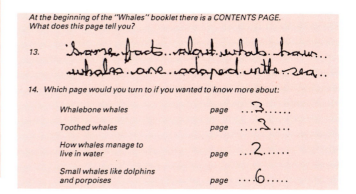

What does the index page tell you?

..all kind of thing like ....whales.............

Which page would you turn to in order to find out:

About seals	page(s)	.......4.....
About Killer whales	page(s)	......4.5...
About toothed whales	page(s)	.....3,45..
What rorquals are	page(s)	........5.....
What krill is	page(s)	......1,3...
What plankton is	page(s)	........3.....
How whales communicate	page(s)	.......2.....

In brief, only about 10 per cent of the pupils provided accurate definitions of both the Contents page and the Index.

The following question asked 'How is it (the index) arranged?' In responding, 96 per cent of the high-scoring group and 15 per cent of the low scorers correctly identified the alphabetical order of the entries. Many of the low-performing pupils did not appear to look for a system of organisation determining the sequence of items in the list, but preferred to deal with the external structure. 36 per cent of these answers concerned visual layout and appearance, e.g.

27

How is it arranged?

It is arranged in to two colmns

nicely

in roose besed the naime ther are munbers

It is arranged in two straight lines

This implies that many children are unfamiliar with books, their sections and functions. They can use these tables but do not know why or how.

Glossary

Although an example glossary was provided alongside the questions, only 34 per cent of the sample produced an acceptable description of what a glossary is. High attainers, in contrast to the rest of the sample, scored remarkably well on this question. 75 per cent of their definitions were judged as acceptable. This increase can be attributed to the very wide variety of definitions allowed. Explanations ranging from broad generalisation e.g. (I) to a detailed and precise description e.g (II) were accepted.

I. *What do you think a glossary is?*

.... a .... kid(;... of ...... Dictonary ......

....

II. *What do you think a glossary is?*

a selection of words used in a book which you may not know

By contrast, definitions for the Table of Contents and the Index were required to illuminate a relatively fine distinction and therefore needed to be exact.

Low performers, on the contrary, achieved a considerably lower score on this question than on the other questions asking for descriptions or definitions. Only 3 per cent were judged to have given an accurate answer. 30 per cent of the group, working by analogy, supposed that the term 'glossary' belonged to the list of specialised whale-related words and proceeded to create various ingenious definitions.

What do you think a glossary is?	*the pleace wear they ceep the blubber*
When would you use it?	*for clothes*
What do you think a glossary is?	*a thin layer of whale skin to kip them warm*
When would you use it?	*all of the time*
What do you think a glossary is?	*It is a thing to sharpen your knife*
When would you use it?	*when your knife is blunt*
What do you think a glossary is?	*food*
When would you use it?	*meal times*

Very few – 12 per cent – established a connection between the word and the function of the table itself and 9 per cent of these were mistaken in their proposals.

Success or failure on this question affected the outcome on the next question 20. Those pupils who had invented inaccurate definitions were obliged to think of equally inaccurate uses for glossaries (see examples above). 72 per cent of the pupils in the high-scoring group gave accurate explanations of when or why a glossary would be required.

List of books for further reading

Pupils were asked to select from the list on the following page the books they would refer to if interested in these subjects:

1. Whales that live in the Arctic

2. How Eskimos catch whales

3. Whales and other mammals

4. Fish

Illustration 3.5   Whales *Books for further reading*

Berill J.	*Wonders of the Antarctic.* World's Work Ltd.
Buckles M. P.	*Mammals of the World.* Bantam Press.
Clarke A. C.	*Dolphins Island.* Victor Gollancz.
Cousteau J. Y.	*The Ocean World of Jaques Cousteau – Oasis in Space.* Angus Robertson.
Cousteau J. Y. and Dide P.	*The Whale, Mighty Monarch of the Sea.* Cassells.
Hoke M.	*Arctic Mammals – a first book.* Franklin Watts Ltd.
Hughes J.	*A Closer Look at the Eskimoes.* Hamish Hamilton.
Rockett B. W.	*Whales and Dolphins.* Puffin Explorer 18, Penguin Books.
Tinburgen N.	*Animal Behaviour.* Life Nature Library. Time – Life International.
Tyler J.	*The Children's Book of the Seas.* Osbourne Publications.
Vevers G.	*Life in the Sea.* Bodley Head.
	A Guide to the Mammals of Britain and Europe. Elsevier Press.

The scores varied from 48 per cent to 83 per cent on the four items. In comparison to their performance on table-interpretation tasks, low attainers performed poorly on this section. Of the entire group only 12 per cent suggested two appropriate titles and 15 per cent made one suitable suggestion. Some had clearly misunderstood either the objective of the task or the purpose of the booklist because they reacted to the sub-headings as if they were questions, e.g.

Whales that live in the Arctic	*Yes*
How the Eskimos catch whales	*By stick*
Whales and other mammals	*live on milk*

The average score of the low-performing group was affected by the high omission rate. 45 per cent of the group omitted the final questions.

With the exception of 6 per cent blank respondents, no member of the high-scoring group suggested fewer than two applicable book titles and the majority (57 per cent) gained full marks on this task. Items 2 and 4 were answered with noticeable success: the second, because the key word 'Eskimos' undoubtedly aided selection of the appropriate book; the fourth, because there were three applicable titles to choose from.

In summary, the results indicate that most pupils, including about half of the low-scoring group, competently answer questions involving the interpretation of tables. On average low scorers are able to pick out relevant items or numbers with near to 50 per cent accuracy, while high performers frequently do so with complete accuracy. However, pupils generally found it difficult to explain clearly the function of each of these listings. It is interesting to note that low attainers formulated comparatively better definitions when given the opportunity to use the table or list concerned at some point. This factor did not appear to affect the performance of the top group.

3.4 Accident

The next booklet to be discussed focuses on the interpretation and use of the documentary material itself, rather than concerning the purpose or organisation of the tables and diagrams included.

Accident was completed by primary school pupils in 1982 and 1983. It consisted of five personal accounts of a road accident. These take the form of a newspaper article, a letter, an interview and two police reports which together create a full but inconclusive picture.

The answer booklet, assigning the pupil the role of investigator, guides the pupil through increasingly complex tasks towards drawing a conclusion. Much of the booklet requires table-filling, involving the selection of relevant details and their presentation in brief table or note form, very much in the fashion of an actual police report. In addition to selecting and transferring information, the pupil is required to sort and synthesise the conflicting accounts, bearing in mind that they are coloured by the individual perceptions or biases of the protagonists and witnesses. The pupils found 16 of the 30 questions relatively easy to answer; these were questions with facility values of 70 per cent or above. The greater part of the test, therefore, did not present the majority of pupils with too many difficulties. As would be expected, least difficulty was encountered with questions relating to factual, asserted information, e.g. the time and location of the accident, and the identification of those involved. Points of conflicting evidence were also located with great ease and written in the table provided. Among the low-scoring group, however, even questions asking for explicitly stated information elicited a substantial number of incorrect responses. This was not because they were unable to interpret evidence that appeared to be conflicting. The majority of incorrect answers were marked down for their lack of specificity, for example:

REPORT ON ACCIDENT

Please write down the date and time the accident took place:

___Yesterday___

Where did the accident take place? (give as much detail as possible).

The accident took place when David went to get a ice cream The accident happend when we went to cross the road.

Another task required the pupil to prepare a sketch map on the basis of the information given. This called for the ability to translate the verbal description of the sequence of events into a visual medium. 52.9 per cent of the sample offered an acceptable, if not very enlightening, visualisation – usually a picture. Very few pupils (9.4 per cent) were recorded as conveying no relevant information at all, while 29.9 per cent were considered to have given a clear diagrammatic explanation, illustrating the relative positions and movements of David, Michael, the ice-cream van, the Biggs' home and the car. Only 12 per cent of the low scorers fell into this last category. 64 per cent of their pictures were classed as adequate. This implies that the greater part of this group did grasp the essence of the incident from the written accounts but they were not able to visualise it or to represent its salient components graphically. A much larger proportion of high scorers (48 per cent) displayed this ability by producing accurate and informative illustrations or sketch maps.

ICE CREAM DISASTER !

A trip to buy an ice cream ended in near tragedy for nine-year old David. David Biggs (9) is recovering in Park Gate General Hospital today after being knocked down by a youth on a motor cycle in Leek Street yesterday. When questioned at her home at 59, Leek Street, Mrs. Biggs (33) said although she was relieved that David has suffered no more than a broken leg as a result of the incident, she felt that the police should enforce speed limits more strictly in built up areas. "David", she said, "is a sensible boy and wouldn't run across the road without looking. The motor cycle was going much too fast."

Mrs. Biggs also wanted to extend her thanks to the anonymous driver of a white car who saw the accident and stopped to help her.

The rider of the motor cycle, Michael Fenton (17), of 2, Lidgett Lane, was unhurt but told our reporter that David has walked out into the road out into the road in front of him. He had not been exceeding the speed limit. His motorbike had been a present for his seventeenth birthday only a week before and was now a total wreck.

Examples of the three categories of sketches can be seen below:

Illustration 3.6   Accident *Pupils' sketches. Graded on a scale of 0–2*

Inadequate information. Grade 0.

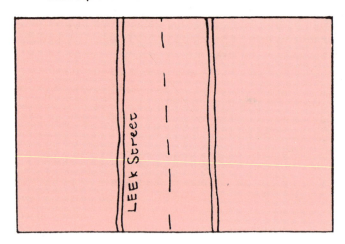 

Accurate and informative. Grade 1.

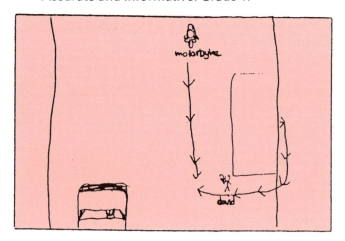 

Adequate information. Grade 2.

 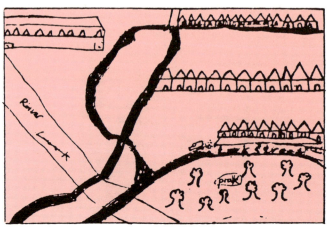

The most difficult exercise in the test, yielding facility values from 4.5 per cent to 37 per cent, required pupils to supply reasons why they might suspect the reliability of each account.

Confidential section

Who do you believe?

Good investigators don't believe everything they are told, or read. They have suspicious minds. They like to be able to check their facts.

Can you think of a good reason not to believe, or not *to rely on the following people's accounts of the accident? You must say* why *you think so.*

The requirements of this task are:

1. reading and synthesis of the accounts

2. making deductions from the evidence amassed

3. giving a justification for the deductions

The performance of the entire sample declined on this task with 2.4 per cent of low scorers' answers being regarded as acceptable. The following characteristics were found in their responses.

1. The tendency to answer the question 'do you believe X?' instead of 'Can you think of reasons not to believe X?' The recurrence of this type of response is possibly due to the fact that the question at the top of the page may have misled those who read no further.

2. Lack of objectivity; e.g.

David
I believe Davida because it has more sense than Michael's If his mother said he was a sensible boy then I believe David

3. Failure to draw general assumptions from the accumulated evidence, often attributing suspicion to a single disputed fact as if it constituted proof; e.g.

Mrs Biggs
Mrs Biggs Sed David baught a ice cream. But Mr Ford sed it was a lollipop.

4. the making of unfounded allegations and jumping to unsupported conclusions; e.g.

Mr Ford (the man in the ice-cream van)
because he realy didn't like the boy en he was always cheaky

High attainers performed somewhat better on the exercise but not all questions were answered correctly by the majority of pupils. 65 per cent of their responses explaining the unreliability of the witnesses were judged to be accurate as opposed to only 22 per cent of their answers concerning the trustworthiness of the protagonists. The two questions entail different skills. The items relating to the witnesses can be answered with reference to explicitly and implicitly stated information. However, in order to judge the reliability of David's and Michael's testimonies, it is necessary to speculate about their motives, which are neither discussed nor alluded to. It is apparent that one of the two protagonists is responsible for the accident, but the evidence is inconclusive and both appear equally culpable. Although it transpires that only one is concealing the truth, both could be suspected of doing so, to protect their own interests. Relatively few (35 per cent) of the high-scoring group displayed the investigative ability needed to arrive at this conclusion. Many high performers stopped short of drawing the final conclusion, suggesting guilt but not the intention to conceal liability for the accident.

DAVID
Should not have been wondering wether his father was home or not. He should have been concentrating on the road.

MICHAEL
He saw the Ice Cream Van so he could of slowed down to make sure that no body ran out infront of him and if They did he might of been expecting it, so avoided it. He could of been showing off on his new motor bike.

Otherwise many high scorers displayed features common to the low performers on these two items. High performers were able, for the most part, to make deductions drawing upon all the sources of information provided, but only a third of them possessed the skills to complete the chain of conclusions and speculations necessary to reach a final verdict.

Throughout the answer booklet the pupils were guided towards making an eventual judgement. However, until the final section of the booklet the evidence provided was inconclusive. When asked 'Whose fault was it?' equal proportions of pupils opted for the child and the motorcyclist (37 per cent and 30 per cent respectively). 14 per cent refused to give a verdict, suggesting that it was impossible to tell or that neither or both were equally to blame.

The main interest of this question derives largely from its relation to the subsequent task, in which the pupil was asked to make a final judgement taking new evidence into account.

31

New evidence has come to light as a result of your enquiries.

Item 1: Mrs. Mohammed Johnson is a friend of Michael's mother.

Item 2: Michael's insurance company won't pay the full cost for replacing his bike if the accident was his fault.

Item 3: Michael was stopped by the police twice last week and warned about not wearing a crash helmet.

Item 4: Tracey Graham (12) who lives at the bottom of Leek Street says she nearly got knocked down by a motorbike racing down the street at about 4 p.m. on Thursday, June 24th.

Item 5: The police report on the skid marks on the road show that the motorbike was travelling at about 40 miles an hour when the accident took place.

The new evidence incriminates Michael and 58 per cent correctly inferred this. It is, however, revealing to compare the verdicts of low and high performers before and after access to the new evidence.

Table 3.1 *Comparison of high and low performers' verdicts, Accident*

VERDICT	Low performers			High performers		
	Michael	David	Both/ neither	Michael	David	Both/ neither
Before evidence	53%	30%	17%	38%	34%	28%
After	60%	10%	30%	89%	2%	8%

While high scorers generally concurred that Michael was the offender after examination of the new evidence, only 60 per cent of the low attainers arrived at this conclusion.

The most notable of these results is the very slight increase in the number of low scorers who corrected their verdicts consequent to the new data. For the most part, low performers did not appear to re-assess their opinions to the same extent as the high-scoring group. 10 per cent still maintained that their initial impressions were right, normally claiming that David's behaviour as a pedestrian was at fault.

I still blame David because I still think he should not have ran out. If he had not have ran out he would not have been ran down. I do believe that Michael could have been going forty but if David hadn't of ran out he wouldn't have been knocked down. I think the ice-cream man was telling lies. Mrs. Johnson was telling lies too.

A substantial number of low scorers appeared to allow their own perceptions of the incident to supersede the

evidence. Others, who fell into the 'both/neither' category, were prepared to alter their view but took pains to justify their original verdict.

I must have been wrong. The new evidence means that it was the fault of Michael as well as David. The fault's to them both. I didn't know that Michael had a bad record on his motorbike.

Closer examinations of the answer booklets revealed that these changes were made by those pupils who had worked their way systematically through the tasks and reached their first decision (even if wrong) by a careful and reasoned analysis. These pupils were more likely to take account of the implications of the new evidence and confirm or reject their judgements than those who had arrived at the initial decision through somewhat muddled thinking.

I would say it was David's Fault because he never let the motorbike go past.

I would now say that it was Michael's Fault because of the new evidence mainly because of the skid marks and the other person nearly being knocked over. My conclusion is that it was Michael's fault.

If you were asked 'Whose fault was it?', what would you say?

I would say I do not no whose it is.

Please write down your conclusions – and the reasons for them – in the space below.

The motorbike is most important thing.

I think it was Mr. Ford he should not of parked there in the first place.

I would put the blame on Mr. ford. He should not of parked there in the first place and david did have an ice cream. It was a dull day and the day was a Thursday. He went behind the ice cream van not in front and he did not use the green cross code. Mr. ford should have parked somewhere els but in a safe place.

The new evidence has not shed any light on the matter as far as the last two pupils are concerned. Two possible reasons for a failure to answer the question correctly were 1. the inability to synthesise and assimilate the quantity of information gathered from six different sources and 2. the failure to recognise the overriding importance of the final police reports and to notice the weight of evidence against him.

Whilst most pupils were persuaded of Michael's guilt by the police, only 29 per cent justified their decision by reference to the *single* convincing factor: the skid marks. Although the other facts implicate Michael, they do not relate to the particular incident in question. 13 per cent of the low-scoring group who made the correct verdict gave special importance to the skid marks whereas 38 per cent of the high attainers did so. The pupil below, for example, provided not only the correct verdict but also explained how she interpreted the evidence to arrive at this conclusion.

Item five is the most important because of the marks on the road.

They also show that Michael was speeding, so I am inclined to believe David and his mother now.

Few pupils realised that the skid marks constituted the single most decisive piece of proof that Michael had broken the speed limit. Low performers largely failed to demonstrate the ability to differentiate between evidence and proof and attributed their verdicts either to the whole mass of evidence or to a 'clue' picked at random. As a result of high performers' apparent awareness of the need for proof before casting a verdict with any degree of certainty, they tended to reach a conclusion at a later stage than low performers, many of whom had firmly made up their minds earlier in the investigation. This also accounts for the difference in willingness to reconsider initial opinions. High performers were more able to interpret and integrate new evidence into their perception of the incident than were low performers. At the last stage of the test 51 per cent of the high group reassessed and corrected their verdicts. Low scorers tended to adhere to their initial opinions and to overlook any contradictory evidence.

3.5 Chief Sitting Bull

The material (a booklet on the topic of the Red Indians of North America) was presented in short illustrated and assorted paragraphs relating to various historical, biographical and anthropological aspects of Indian life in the latter half of the nineteenth century. The questions asked, however, primarily concerned the life of a single individual – Chief Sitting Bull. Pupils were required to select, re-order and re-work relevant information scattered throughout the booklet.

The tasks in the answer booklet guide the pupil through the three steps: selection, re-ordering and rewriting. Although it is possible for a pupil to write an adequate life-history of Sitting Bull based on the text, each task is somewhat dependent on the successful completion of the former.

The answer booklet commences with an instruction to the pupil to circle all sections of the data relating to Chief Sitting Bull. This was accomplished with notable success – an average of 91 per cent of the sample correctly picked out all six sections.

The pupils were then asked to insert the major incidents of Sitting Bull's life on a timeline provided. Below is an example of a successfully completed line.

The completion of the line involves the translation of full length discourse into a diagrammatic outline. In this it

differs from more conventional chart or table-related work. It is not a simple undertaking because pupils are required to re-order and condense all the information selected in the previous exercise. The facility values on the eight items to be included range from 9.4 per cent to 79.4 per cent.

Illustration 3.7 Chief Sitting Bull. *Timeline task. High scorer*

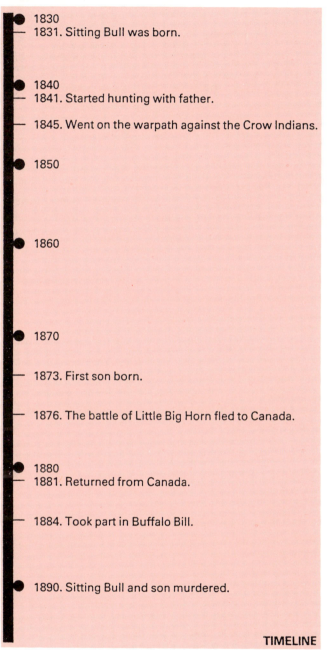

- 1830
- — 1831. Sitting Bull was born.
- 1840
- — 1841. Started hunting with father.
- — 1845. Went on the warpath against the Crow Indians.
- 1850
- 1860
- 1870
- — 1873. First son born.
- — 1876. The battle of Little Big Horn fled to Canada.
- 1880
- — 1881. Returned from Canada.
- — 1884. Took part in Buffalo Bill.
- 1890. Sitting Bull and son murdered.

TIMELINE

The most obvious dates to enter on the line were those of the Chief's birth and death and these were inserted by 59 per cent and 79 per cent of the sample respectively. (The fact that Sitting Bull's date of death was repeated twice in the text may account for the 20 per cent difference in the scores incurred.) 44 per cent and 56 per cent of all low attainers marked these dates while 98 per cent and 100 per cent of the high-scoring group did. Whereas this question required the simple transference of data to an appropriate slot on the line, the timing of other events in the Chief's life was left undated in the text and paraphrased in a way that made some calculation necessary (see extract). Although the mathematics involved was extremely simple, only 9 (low scorers) and 22 (high scorers) per cent of the sample successfully dated and marked these two events.

> Education? There was no 'school' for Indian children. Children learned by helping and watching their parents and relatives. Boys went out with the male members of their families and learnt to ride and shoot. The famous chief, Sitting Bull, for example, was hunting with his father by the time he was ten years old. At the age of fourteen he went on the warpath against the Crow Indians. Late in his life he remembered how he first saw that the lands belonging to his people were being taken by the white farmers.

Given this information and having been told that he was born in 1831, only 8 per cent of the low-scoring group correctly calculated the dates and inserted them on the timeline. 76 per cent of the high attainers correctly entered them in place. This result can be explained in part with reference to the preceding exercise (Exercise 1).

In that exercise 40 per cent of all low performers had failed to ring the appropriate section in the booklet – hence the omission on the timeline.

As expected, pupils rightly tackled the second exercise with the intention of using only those portions of the text they had encircled and henceforth disregarded the other, apparently irrelevant, sections. This would be likely to lead to relevant information being disregarded in the second exercise.

However, 60 per cent of the low-performing group who *had* ringed the section relating to Sitting Bull's youth still did not mention those events on the timeline.

Of the 56 per cent who had not included the birth and death dates, only 49 per cent had also failed to mark them in the text.

Failure to complete exercise 2 correctly cannot necessarily be attributed to failure in exercise 1 because most low performers did not appear to transfer information from one exercise to the next. A significant proportion of low performers found it difficult to complete other aspects of the exercise, also. Some (4 per cent) wrote on the page evidently unaware of the presence of the time-graduated line; other (24 per cent) inserted events – but in the wrong place. Low performers also had a tendency to write much more than necessary; sometimes a paragraph of superfluous descriptive detail was added to accompany a single date (see example).

This implies that these pupils were not familiar with the function of the line as an annotated diagram summarising major events over a period of time. The results seem to

indicate that many low performers glimpsed a date in the booklet and transferred it and the adjoining sentence directly from the text to the answer sheet. High performers, on the other hand, characteristically provided a succinct, non-verbose caption for each event as was appropriate to the task (see first example).

Illustration 3.8 Chief Sitting Bull. *Timeline task. Low scorer*

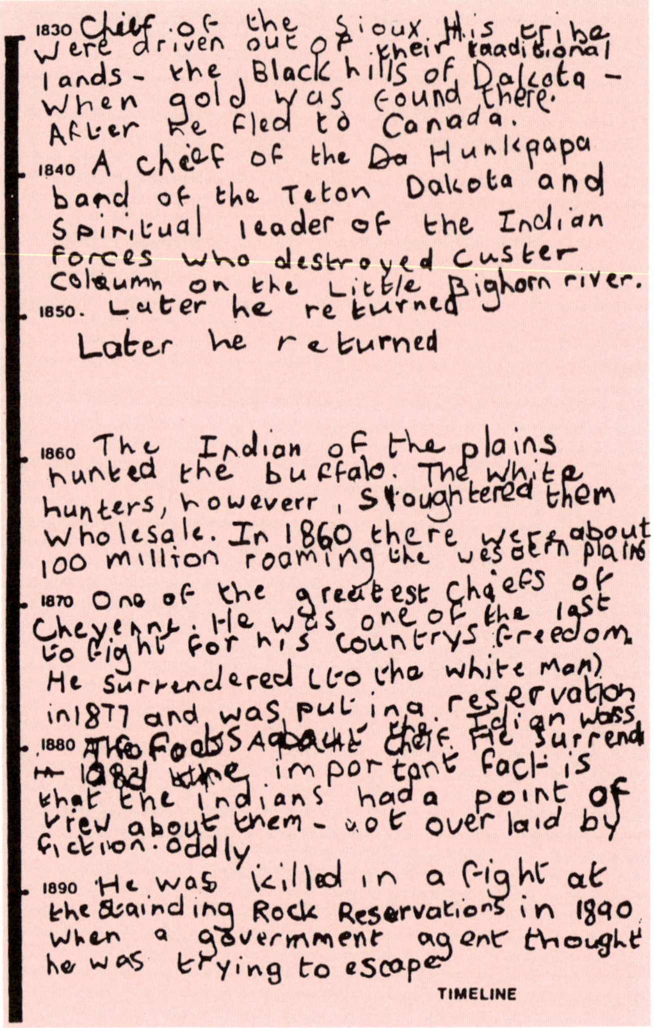

Having placed the events of Sitting Bull's life in chronological order, the next and final task involved writing a short biography, expanding upon the information presented on the timeline. As an introduction pupils were instructed to establish a context by providing a brief account of Indian history at the time of Chief Sitting Bull. The specimen below is a competent example of what was expected.

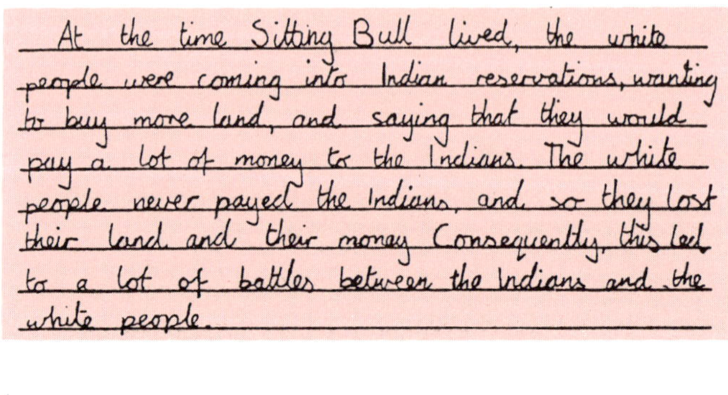

34

This introduction could only be written by direct reference to the text, whereas the material needed for the biographical account had already been worked upon in the previous exercises. This difference was reflected in the answers. 60 per cent to 70 per cent of low and high performers alike failed to provide the necessary contextual explanation or referred to the topic so cursorily that it did not fulfil the requirements of the task.

Perhaps the most notable difference between low and high performers, however, was the sequential arrangement of events recounted in the biography. 60 per cent of the high-scoring group composed an account that was acceptable in terms of this aspect of organisation. Of the remaining 40 per cent, 28 per cent had adhered to the unchronological text order while 12 per cent related the story in no apparent order at all. Amongst the low scorers 19 per cent presented the information in an accurate chronological fashion, 38 per cent copied the text, while in a further 43 per cent of their scripts no sequential ordering was discernible.

The following are examples of:

1. confused organisation

2. chronological order

Sitting bull was the chief of the Indians. [crossed out] His tribes were driven out of their traditional lands. He was killed in a fight at the Standing Rock Reservation in 1890. His 14 year old son was killed as well. Cavalry Regiment were killed by sioux Indian warriors led by sitting Bull and crazy Horse. The thenkpapa people were a subtribe of the sioux Indians. We indians are like an island in a sea of cwhites said chief sitting Bull. They wanted a war. He was killed in a battle. Sitting Bull was a warrior and a chief. Sitting Bull was taken prisoner. Sitting Bull was remember for his bravery.

The life of Sitting Bull
Sitting Bull was born in 1831.
In 1841 Sitting Bull was hunting with his father at the age of ten. At the age of fourteen he went on the war path against the crow Indians. when he grew up he became cheif. Sitting Bulls people won the battle of Little Big Horn and also destroyed Custom's column on the Little Bighorn river in 1876. In 1884 he was made live at Standing Rock Reservations and he took part in Buffalo Bill show. In 1890 a government agen't thought he was escaping his 17 year old son died with him.

Three possible deductions can be made about low performance on this task.

1. low scorers appeared to be unaware that biographies are traditionally recounted in time order.

2. they were confused about the order of events (as is also indicated by the fact that they generally performed poorly on the timeline exercise).

3. they accepted the order used in the text as a framework and did not venture to change it. This supposition is given some support by the fact that 48 per cent of low scorers and 24 per cent of the high-scoring group made no attempt to disguise the fact that they had copied verbatim those sections they had encircled.

This result seemed to indicate that almost half the low scorers did not process the information in their response to the task, nor did they take advantage of the work done in the previous exercise – but reverted to direct dependence on the text. Although such text duplication also occurs in the work of high attainers, most appear to have assimilated the data first and to have exercised some control over it in their selection and manipulation of the sections needed for the task.

The information included in the biography also differed substantially between low and high performers. Whereas high attainers tended to describe and focus attention on the more memorable incidents, low performers did not display this same ability to distinguish between the important and the trivial.

Low scorers revealed a tendency to omit significant events. 64 per cent of this group are recorded as failing to mention at least two of the four incidents for which Sitting Bull is renowned. The version below, for instance, omits all reference to Sitting Bull's flight to Canada, to his participation in Buffalo Bill films and to his death at the Battle of Standing Rock.

Sitting Bull's tribes were driven out of their traditional lands – the Black hills of Dakota – when gold was found there. In the last half of the nineteenth century there there had been a great amount of wars so they had to defend their last farming grounds. The Indians were hungry and desperate so the government tried to keep them on reservations – areas of land that were too small to live by farming or hunting.

Sitting Bull was a chief of the Hunkpapa band of the Teton Dakota and spiritual leader of the Indian forces who destroyed Custer's Column on the Little Bighorn River in 1876.

In contrast, 68 per cent of the high band, by fully relating all the highlights, displayed an ability to appreciate the importance of certain events. The significance of particular items can be weighed up by interpreting not only the import of the subject matter but also the time, space and attention given to each in the original text. The inability of low scorers to interpret these clues and to estimate the relative importance of the different elements of the story is also underlined by what in some cases appears to be an inordinate concentration on comparatively trivial issues. For example, the massacre of the buffalo, the education of children, the Indian philosophy of life or other secondary issues were featured in excess detail by 50 per cent of the low-scoring group. Although these may arguably deserve mention in a review of the background to Sitting Bull's life they are not of particular importance in the life of Sitting Bull himself. However, in deciding on the contents of the biography, most high performers correctly interpreted the relative importance of each item and attributed proportional attention to the key events. The example below illustrates the work of a lower performer.

> *Sitting bull was a wairior cheif he was brave and fought in many a battle White men tried to over his land sometimes winning sometimes losing.*
>
> *The life of an indian was hard and rough risking thier lifes for food, killing buffalo.*
>
> *The life of one indian boy was training to be a warior and that wasn't easy*
>
> *The indians hunted but however the white men slaughtered them wholesale The white men came and brought with them gun horses that changed the indians way of life.*
>
> *Diseases were brought by white men and indian terotory was taken from the indians.*
>
> *The white government put the Indians on poor wast land.*
>
> *Sitting Bull is a famous warior his people today are proud to know they once had a famous warior.*

Another point of difference between high and low performance is the relative incidence of mistakes in their work. While there is no evidence of high attainers reporting the facts inaccurately, 24 per cent of the low scorers misrepresented entire episodes of Sitting Bull's life.

This arose either from misinterpretation during reading or from the creation of erroneous associations between unrelated and disparate items in the text. The following is an example of such an inaccurate biography.

> Sitting bull was born in 1830, were he lived was at, a place called prairie, Sitting bull was an indian He wanted to died at home, but he'd have to Wait a little longer to die. Sitting bull must be about 14 years old if and only if he was, brave he Could go, and fight with all the other indians. So Sitting bull went to Fight. As years went by he got

> older and older. The bottles got stronger and stronger, But Sitting bull carried on Fighting. by Now sitting bull should have A horse and he did, so he called the horse crazy horse It was about now that there were; many tribes but now, sitting bull was, getting old so he diddent go and fight no more so, he started doing Flims by now he was good for doing Flims. Being he was getting old. He is very famos now for Films. But the desoter came. The very thing that he wanted was to die so sitting bull died and people remember him now. Because of all the good films that he has plaayed in. peek people liked him very munch because he was a chief

Transference of information

The tasks in the answer booklet were designed to follow a coherent and sequential order and to create the possibility of re-using the same information in all three parts of the test. This feature should have simplified the test since the first task delineates the body of information to be used in all subsequent sections. Nevertheless, there is evidence that not all pupils took advantage of this aid and carry-over of information between exercises did not take place automatically.

High performers

Errors are the most reliable indicators of transference. Therefore the observation of transference in high-scoring pupils is made difficult by the infrequent occurrence of errors in their work. However, the evidence available showed that 66 per cent of the errors committed by high scorers on the timeline were carried over and duplicated in the following exercise. Similarly, 60 per cent of the biographies appear to be derived from the timeline rather than based on the original text. Overleaf is a particularly representative example of a high performer whose biography was a direct expansion of the accompanying timeline.

Low performers

Although some errors were clearly carried from one exercise to the next, it is notable that many *correct* responses were not. For example, there was a 60 per cent failure to transfer facts from exercise 1 (circling exercise) to exercise 2 (timeline). The lack of order in the biography (exercise 3) and the prominence of copying from the printed text also indicate that little use had been made of the information assembled on the timeline. These tendencies

1831 — BORN

1840
841 — Hunting with his Father

1848 — Went to war against crow indians

1850.

1860

1870

1876 — Destroyed Custers Coloum with
crazy horse

1880

1881 — Returned from Canada
1884 — Joined Buffalo Bills show

1890 Death of sitting bull and his son
at the standing Rocks Reservation

Sitting Bull was born in 1838/1 At ten
he was hunting with his father. BAt the age
of 14 he went to war against the crow indians
In 1876 he he destroyed Custers coloum
killing Custer and most of his men. After doing
this he fled to Canada. He stayed
there for six years and then came
back in 1881. In 1884 he joined the Buffa
Bills Wild West Show Many people came
to see the indian chief who had killed
General Custer Sitting Bull was finally
killed in 1890 at the Standing Rock
Reservation along with his 17 year old
son. A government agent opened fire
on them when he thought
they were trying to escape from
the Reservation camp interior Sitting B
is remembered because he fought for
Freedom of the Indian people

suggest that low scorers generally tackled each section in isolation and that information was not profitably re-used nor carried from one exercise to the next. Likewise, most errors committed by this group were spontaneous rather than transferred from another exercise.

On the whole, high scorers seemed to recognise that all three tasks could be completed by recycling the same information. They took advantage of this to a greater degree than low performers and consequently high scorers' errors tended to re-appear from one exercise to the next. Since only a small proportion of low scorers' errors and accuracies were repeated across the booklet, it can be assumed that they did not re-use information or draw upon the work they had done in prior exercises. They appeared to start anew at the onset of each new exercise and to use the printed text as their only source of information.

3.6 Conclusion

In attempting to identify characteristics of low and high performers, it becomes apparent that features of low performance are considerably easier to determine and describe than those of high scorers. Errors are, in a sense, more informative than correct responses. An error may help to reveal the location and nature of a problem area and to provide insight into the processes that give rise to certain mistakes. A correct response, on the other hand, indicates the ability to execute a task but nothing about how the response was arrived at.

1. *Retrieval of information*

The high performers in this sample were versatile in the types of tasks they could accomplish. Low performers were most at ease in the retrieval of clearly stated information, whether verbal or pictorial, in which very little or no interpretation was necessary. Even on such tasks, this group usually responded with about 50 per cent accuracy. Greatest success tended to be achieved by the low-scoring group when the presence of a key-word in the question facilitated the location of the answer. Any task which required the extraction of implicitly stated information presented difficulties for low scorers. It was characteristic of this group to provide an inappropriate quotation from the text, rather than to infer the correct response, indicating a rather heavy reliance on a literal reading of the test. Evidence demonstrates that high performers encountered few difficulties with tasks of this nature, except when required to make hypothetical, speculative deductions (see **Accident**).

2. *Adherence to text*

When asked to express an opinion or draw a conclusion from a given text, low scorers frequently offered acceptable answers. However, from the reasons given it was clear that many responses were not derived from the passage but based upon personal knowledge and experience, external to the test with less reference to the text evident. High performers were more likely to extract their explanations from the given information or to justify their opinions and conclusions by reference to what they had read.

3. *Use of tabulated and diagrammatic information*

While low performers usually possessed the skills necessary to interpret charts, tables and maps, they were less able to manipulate the contents in anything other than the most straightforward ways or to explain the purpose of these tabulations. The high-scoring group was generally more flexible in its use of such tables and executed various related tasks competently. An exception is the formulation of definitions. Only 50–60 per cent of high attainers were normally able to deduce and describe the purpose of a table even after practical experience in its use.

4. *Reformulation of information*

High performers were generally successful at selecting and re-organising various facts from a text and reformulating them into an independent abstract of the original. This group met with fewer difficulties in re-ordering (and manoeuvring) evidence and appeared more able to explain the 'gist' of a passage than did the low scorers. The latter were rarely able to extract the essence of a text or to assimilate, re-arrange and synthesise a string of related facts with the success of high performers.

5. *Recycling of information*

Low scorers appeared to be less experienced at building upon their own work re-using information that they themselves had amassed from the text in previous exercises. High performers worked more economically and tended to exploit their own work as well as the text wherever feasible.

6. *Reassessment of interpretation*

High attainers were more likely to adapt their understanding of a text, making alterations to or reversing their limited opinions and interpretations in order to accommodate newly received information. While reading they appeared to check that the new message could be integrated into what they had read. The low-scoring group tended to be reluctant to revise its first perceptions. Their answers frequently indicate that their initial ideas about the contents of the text moulded their comprehension of subsequent reading areas to exclude any interpretation incompatible with their initial assumptions.

Annex 3.1

The performance of primary pupils on four tests

Pupils' performance on four reading tests at three levels of attainment (top 20 per cent, mid 60 per cent and bottom 20 per cent).

Test 25. Bicycles

1. Who is this report written for – children or their parents?

	MEAN	LOWER	MID	UPPER
BOYS	36	17	34	69
GIRLS	42	15	41	63

2. How can you tell?

	MEAN	LOWER	MID	UPPER
BOYS	6	0	3	23
GIRLS	15	0	8	42

3. 'The most difficult decision you'll need to make is what size of bicycle to buy – especially for an 11 or 12 year old'. Why is this decision difficult?

	MEAN	LOWER	MID	UPPER
BOYS	28	6	29	58
GIRLS	36	0	32	71

4. Write down one good reason for buying a secondhand bike.

	MEAN	LOWER	MID	UPPER
BOYS	69	53	72	81
GIRLS	68	41	67	90

5. What checks should you make on the:

Frame

	MEAN	LOWER	MID	UPPER
BOYS	75	39	82	100
GIRLS	80	33	86	100

6. Wheels

	MEAN	LOWER	MID	UPPER
BOYS	65	22	74	92
GIRLS	71	30	73	97

7. Brakes

	MEAN	LOWER	MID	UPPER
BOYS	46	8	50	81
GIRLS	58	15	55	95

8. Gears

	MEAN	LOWER	MID	UPPER
BOYS	41	8	43	77
GIRLS	64	22	66	90

In Annex 3.1, the mean scores of boys and girls in groups representing three levels of attainment are given in tables relating to questions pupils answered on the four tests reviewed in this chapter. The data relates to the performance of pupils in the top 20 per cent, mid 60 per cent and bottom 20 per cent of the sample.

9. What else should you check?

	MEAN	LOWER	MID	UPPER
BOYS	48	25	48	81
GIRLS	59	33	54	87

10. Look at the section 'Should you get a bike with gears?' What difference do gears make to a bicycle?

	MEAN	LOWER	MID	UPPER
BOYS	76	39	85	96
GIRLS	69	52	65	92

11. *Which type of bike?* If you were given a free choice which type of bike would you buy? Explain why.

	MEAN	LOWER	MID	UPPER
BOYS	86	69	93	85
GIRLS	81	56	83	95

12. Explain in your own words what the table is about.

	MEAN	LOWER	MID	UPPER
BOYS	15	3	13	39
GIRLS	30	7	26	55

13. How many 11-year-olds were killed from running into the road?

	MEAN	LOWER	MID	UPPER
BOYS	83	58	87	100
GIRLS	85	56	89	97

14. How many 10-year-olds were killed hanging on to moving vehicles?

	MEAN	LOWER	MID	UPPER
BOYS	79	50	84	100
GIRLS	87	63	90	97

15. How many children aged 8 to 13 were killed because they crossed the road without looking?

	MEAN	LOWER	MID	UPPER
BOYS	68	39	72	92
GIRLS	69	26	70	100

16. How many cyclists between the age of 8 and 13 were killed because they failed to stop at major roads?

	MEAN	LOWER	MID	UPPER
BOYS	73	33	83	89
GIRLS	69	26	73	92

17. How many 11-year-old cyclists were killed?

	MEAN	LOWER	MID	UPPER
BOYS	34	0	37	73
GIRLS	40	11	36	71

18. How many 10-year-old pedestrians were killed?

	MEAN	LOWER	MID	UPPER
BOYS	21	3	17	58
GIRLS	24	0	24	42

19. What was the way *most* cyclists were killed?

	MEAN	LOWER	MID	UPPER
BOYS	52	6	59	89
GIRLS	54	11	53	84

20. What was the way most *pedestrians* were killed?

	MEAN	LOWER	MID	UPPER
BOYS	54	17	60	81
GIRLS	66	11	70	95

21. In which age-group did the most children die?

	MEAN	LOWER	MID	UPPER
BOYS	56	33	59	77
GIRLS	59	19	63	79

22. How many children between the age of 8 and 13 – pedestrians and cyclists – were killed?

	MEAN	LOWER	MID	UPPER
BOYS	49	11	52	89
GIRLS	52	15	49	84

23. Read the letters through and make a list of the ones you think are: in favour of people riding cycles on the pavement.

	MEAN	LOWER	MID	UPPER
BOYS	21	8	19	46
GIRLS	39	7	37	66

24. against people riding on the pavement.

	MEAN	LOWER	MID	UPPER
BOYS	33	8	35	62
GIRLS	21	11	16	40

25. One letter suggests another way of solving the problem. Which letter? What does the writer suggest?

	MEAN	LOWER	MID	UPPER
BOYS	48	8	54	81
GIRLS	59	19	58	90

Test 13. Accident

Please write down the date and time the accident took place:
1.

	MEAN	LOWER	MID	UPPER
BOYS	76	56	78	91
GIRLS	74	45	77	93

2.

	MEAN	LOWER	MID	UPPER
BOYS	73	56	79	72
GIRLS	74	62	75	80

Where did the accident take place? (Give as much detail as possible.)

3.

	MEAN	LOWER	MID	UPPER
BOYS	72	53	75	84
GIRLS	73	69	71	83

4.

	MEAN	LOWER	MID	UPPER
BOYS	28	9	26	50
GIRLS	34	3	38	53

Who was involved in the accident?

5.

	MEAN	LOWER	MID	UPPER
BOYS	79	47	83	97
GIRLS	85	66	87	100

6.

	MEAN	LOWER	MID	UPPER
BOYS	76	56	79	88
GIRLS	85	72	84	100

Witness (who *saw* the accident take place)

7.

	MEAN	LOWER	MID	UPPER
BOYS	82	59	83	100
GIRLS	79	41	85	100

8.

	MEAN	LOWER	MID	UPPER
BOYS	45	34	54	31
GIRLS	46	38	51	40

The people involved in the accident remembered the things that happened differently.

(For example Mrs. Biggs says that David bought an ice cream, while Mr. Ford claims it was a lollipop.)

Can you complete the following table by writing in the other points of disagreement?

Mrs. Biggs

9. Time?

	MEAN	LOWER	MID	UPPER
BOYS	88	59	94	97
GIRLS	85	55	91	97

10. Colour of car?

	MEAN	LOWER	MID	UPPER
BOYS	68	44	67	94
GIRLS	68	45	67	93

11. Day?

	MEAN	LOWER	MID	UPPER
BOYS	87	63	91	100
GIRLS	92	72	97	100

12. Weather?

	MEAN	LOWER	MID	UPPER
BOYS	71	41	76	88
GIRLS	75	41	80	93

Mrs. Johnson

13. Time?

	MEAN	LOWER	MID	UPPER
BOYS	74	31	81	97
GIRLS	80	35	88	100

14. Colour of car?

	MEAN	LOWER	MID	UPPER
BOYS	64	25	72	81
GIRLS	61	28	64	87

15. Day?

	MEAN	LOWER	MID	UPPER
BOYS	71	34	74	100
GIRLS	81	35	89	100

16. Weather?

	MEAN	LOWER	MID	UPPER
BOYS	74	31	79	100
GIRLS	76	31	84	97

Mr. Ford

17. Time?

	MEAN	LOWER	MID	UPPER
BOYS	60	47	60	72
GIRLS	67	52	65	87

18. Colour of car?

	MEAN	LOWER	MID	UPPER
BOYS	75	41	79	97
GIRLS	73	31	81	90

19. Day?

	MEAN	LOWER	MID	UPPER
BOYS	74	34	79	97
GIRLS	80	38	88	97

20. Weather?

	MEAN	LOWER	MID	UPPER
BOYS	79	56	79	100
GIRLS	82	45	91	93

Good investigators don't believe everything they are told, or read. They have suspicious minds. They like to be able to check their facts.

Can you think of a good reason **not** to believe, or **not** to rely on the following people's accounts of the accident? You must say **why** you think so.

21. David

	MEAN	LOWER	MID	UPPER
BOYS	3	0	4	3
GIRLS	6	3	5	13

22. Michael

	MEAN	LOWER	MID	UPPER
BOYS	8	0	10	9
GIRLS	11	3	11	20

23. Mrs. Biggs

	MEAN	LOWER	MID	UPPER
BOYS	28	6	23	63
GIRLS	39	17	37	67

24. Mr. Ford (the man in the ice cream van)

	MEAN	LOWER	MID	UPPER
BOYS	29	6	28	56
GIRLS	40	10	37	77

25. Mrs. Johnson

	MEAN	LOWER	MID	UPPER
BOYS	18	3	15	41
GIRLS	22	0	21	40

Test 24.   Chief Sitting Bull

1. Look through the Red Indian booklet and find all the bits that mention the Indian Chief, Sitting Bull. Use a coloured pen or pencil (if you have one) and draw a line round these bits like this.

Sitting Bull 1831–1890

Chief of the Sioux. His tribe were driven out of their traditional lands – the Black Hills of Dakota – when gold was found there. After winning the Battle of Little Big Horn he fled to Canada. Later he returned. He was killed in a fight at the Standing Rock reservations in 1890 when a government agent thought he was trying to escape. His 17-year-old son was murdered with him.

	MEAN	LOWER	MID	UPPER
BOYS	89	83	88	99
GIRLS	87	75	86	100

2. Oddly enough, in 1884, while Sitting Bull was living on the reservation, after his return from Canada in 1881, he took part in a series of shows organised by Bill Cody – 'Buffalo Bill'. In these 'Wild West Shows' Sitting Bull dressed in traditional costume and showed off Indian riding tricks – but most people came to stare at the famous chief who was now reduced to riding in a circus.

	MEAN	LOWER	MID	UPPER
BOYS	93	83	95	99
GIRLS	95	88	96	100

3. Great war leaders like Dull Knife, and Red Cloud, Santana and Sitting Bull, led their people into rebellions and uprisings.

	MEAN	LOWER	MID	UPPER
BOYS	90	80	92	94
GIRLS	91	90	89	100

4. Sitting Bull (1831–90), a chief of the Hunkpapa band of the Teton Dakota and spiritual leader of the Indian forces who destroyed Custer's column on the Little Bighorn River in 1876.

	MEAN	LOWER	MID	UPPER
BOYS	98	94	99	100
GIRLS	97	93	99	98

5. The battle of Little Big Horn 1876

This was just one of the savage battles fought between the Indians and the US army towards the end of the last century. It was one of the last Indian victories. In the space of about half an hour 244 men from the Seventh Cavalry Regiment were killed by Sioux Indian warriors led by Sitting Bull and Crazy Horse.

Sitting Bull was a chief and a warrior, but he was a medicine man – a spiritual leader of his people – as well. A few days before the battle he had performed the Sun Dance (to bring divine guidance) and was still weak from the effects. He planned the battle and Crazy Horse led the warriors.

After the battle . . . it was a great victory for the Indians but the American government and people were furious. Sitting Bull and his people headed towards the Canadian border, chased by soldiers all the way. They stayed in Canada five years but at last they came back to the United States. Sitting Bull was taken prisoner, but eventually he and his people were sent to live on a reservation.

	MEAN	LOWER	MID	UPPER
BOYS	98	92	99	100
GIRLS	99	95	100	100

6. The famous chief, Sitting Bull, for example, was hunting with his father by the time he was 10 years old. At the age of 14 he went on the warpath against the Crow Indians. Late in his life he remembered how he first saw that the lands belonging to his people were being taken over by the white farmers.

	MEAN	LOWER	MID	UPPER
BOYS	77	56	77	97
GIRLS	78	67	78	89

On the next page is a timeline for the life of Sitting Bull. Mark in all the important things that happened to him.

7. 1831. Sitting Bull born

	MEAN	LOWER	MID	UPPER
BOYS	63	34	64	88
GIRLS	55	30	55	82

8. 1841. Hunting with father

	MEAN	LOWER	MID	UPPER
BOYS	26	2	22	59
GIRLS	18	0	11	59

9. 1845. Went on warpath against Crow

	MEAN	LOWER	MID	UPPER
BOYS	19	0	13	54
GIRLS	17	2	10	56

10.   Battle of Little Big Horn
11. 1876.   fled to Canada
10.

	MEAN	LOWER	MID	UPPER
BOYS	72	30	77	99
GIRLS	68	21	75	89

11.

	MEAN	LOWER	MID	UPPER
BOYS	10	0	7	27
GIRLS	9	0	4	37

12. 1881. Return from Canada. Sent to reservation.

	MEAN	LOWER	MID	UPPER
BOYS	45	17	44	74
GIRLS	54	23	56	82

13. 1884. Performed in Bill Cody's wild west shows.

	MEAN	LOWER	MID	UPPER
BOYS	46	17	49	65
GIRLS	59	39	58	82

14. 1890. Died in battle at Standing Rock Reservation.

	MEAN	LOWER	MID	UPPER
BOYS	77	44	83	96
GIRLS	82	58	85	98

The use the information you have assembled to write a short account of the life of Sitting Bull.

15. Birth

	MEAN	LOWER	MID	UPPER
BOYS	40	22	34	72
GIRLS	35	16	34	61

16. Hunting with father.

	MEAN	LOWER	MID	UPPER
BOYS	33	8	27	69
GIRLS	31	9	26	70

17. War with Crow.

	MEAN	LOWER	MID	UPPER
BOYS	26	6	19	65
GIRLS	29	4	23	76

18. Battle of Little Big Horn.

	MEAN	LOWER	MID	UPPER
BOYS	74	31	80	97
GIRLS	71	30	77	93

19. Fled to Canada.

	MEAN	LOWER	MID	UPPER
BOYS	47	14	48	78
GIRLS	48	18	49	76

20. Return to Reservation.

	MEAN	LOWER	MID	UPPER
BOYS	50	25	45	84
GIRLS	60	28	64	79

21. Acting.

	MEAN	LOWER	MID	UPPER
BOYS	39	13	41	59
GIRLS	48	18	50	74

22. Death.

	MEAN	LOWER	MID	UPPER
BOYS	61	27	62	90
GIRLS	58	25	58	93

Test 1A: Whales

Write down three ways in which whales are similar to man and other mammals and not like fish.

1.

	MEAN	LOWER	MID	UPPER
BOYS	68	44	72	81
GIRLS	74	48	77	91

2.

	MEAN	LOWER	MID	UPPER
BOYS	67	31	70	91
GIRLS	69	39	70	94

3.

	MEAN	LOWER	MID	UPPER
BOYS	49	22	48	81
GIRLS	48	19	52	66

4. How do whales find their way about?

	MEAN	LOWER	MID	UPPER
BOYS	65	19	70	97
GIRLS	58	29	59	84

5. Explain what is the difference between toothed whales and whalebone whales.

	MEAN	LOWER	MID	UPPER
BOYS	77	41	85	91
GIRLS	93	71	98	100

From Page 3 can you find out the name of 3 different toothed whales?

6.

	MEAN	LOWER	MID	UPPER
BOYS	60	38	62	75
GIRLS	64	29	68	84

7.

	MEAN	LOWER	MID	UPPER
BOYS	65	38	66	88
GIRLS	73	36	77	97

8.

	MEAN	LOWER	MID	UPPER
BOYS	44	19	41	78
GIRLS	49	26	50	69

9. Which of the whales mentioned on Page 3 are whalebone whales?

	MEAN	LOWER	MID	UPPER
BOYS	71	25	78	94
GIRLS	76	42	79	100

10. From your reading booklet find out the name of this whale.
(illustration)

	MEAN	LOWER	MID	UPPER
BOYS	72	44	77	84
GIRLS	72	45	75	88

11. Is it a toothed whale or a whalebone whale?

	MEAN	LOWER	MID	UPPER
BOYS	75	38	83	88
GIRLS	69	42	72	84

12. From your reading booklet find out the name of this whale.
(illustration)

	MEAN	LOWER	MID	UPPER
BOYS	90	56	97	100
GIRLS	85	65	88	97

13. Is it a toothed whale or a whalebone whale?

	MEAN	LOWER	MID	UPPER
BOYS	89	56	96	100
GIRLS	86	52	94	97

14. At the beginning of the 'Whales' booklet there is a CONTENTS PAGE. What does this page tell you?

	MEAN	LOWER	MID	UPPER
BOYS	32	19	31	59
GIRLS	29	0	28	59

15. Which page would you turn to if you wanted to know more about:
Whalebone whales

	MEAN	LOWER	MID	UPPER
BOYS	87	53	93	100
GIRLS	92	71	98	97

16. Toothed whales

	MEAN	LOWER	MID	UPPER
BOYS	92	59	99	100
GIRLS	94	71	100	97

17. How whales manage to live in water

	MEAN	LOWER	MID	UPPER
BOYS	78	47	82	97
GIRLS	81	52	84	100

18. Small whales like dolphins and porpoises

	MEAN	LOWER	MID	UPPER
BOYS	65	41	65	88
GIRLS	68	42	70	88

19. What does the index page tell you?

	MEAN	LOWER	MID	UPPER
BOYS	44	13	47	69
GIRLS	51	13	57	69

20. How is it arranged?

	MEAN	LOWER	MID	UPPER
BOYS	61	0	68	100
GIRLS	66	16	73	94

21. Which page would you turn to in order to find out:
About seals

	MEAN	LOWER	MID	UPPER
BOYS	75	13	87	100
GIRLS	78	23	89	100

22. About Killer whales

	MEAN	LOWER	MID	UPPER
BOYS	76	16	88	100
GIRLS	78	23	88	100

23. About toothed whales

	MEAN	LOWER	MID	UPPER
BOYS	84	41	93	97
GIRLS	87	45	96	100

24. What rorquals are

	MEAN	LOWER	MID	UPPER
BOYS	70	19	78	97
GIRLS	74	19	84	100

25. What krill is

	MEAN	LOWER	MID	UPPER
BOYS	79	19	92	100
GIRLS	78	19	90	100

26. What plankton is

	MEAN	LOWER	MID	UPPER
BOYS	76	22	86	100
GIRLS	76	19	87	100

27. How whales communicate

	MEAN	LOWER	MID	UPPER
BOYS	77	22	87	100
GIRLS	81	23	94	100

28. How big whales are

	MEAN	LOWER	MID	UPPER
BOYS	67	16	75	94
GIRLS	72	16	82	97

29. What do you think a glossary is?

	MEAN	LOWER	MID	UPPER
BOYS	32	0	32	66
GIRLS	28	3	25	63

30. When would you use it?

	MEAN	LOWER	MID	UPPER
BOYS	32	0	31	72
GIRLS	30	3	30	56

Look at the list on the opposite page and decide which of the books you would want to refer to if you were interested in:

31. Whales that live in the Arctic.

	MEAN	LOWER	MID	UPPER
BOYS	38	0	36	81
GIRLS	40	3	38	81

32. How the Eskimos catch whales.

	MEAN	LOWER	MID	UPPER
BOYS	61	13	66	94
GIRLS	62	10	68	97

33. Whales and other mammals.

	MEAN	LOWER	MID	UPPER
BOYS	37	3	37	69
GIRLS	42	7	42	75

34. Fish.

	MEAN	LOWER	MID	UPPER
BOYS	62	3	69	97
GIRLS	62	10	68	94

Synopsis

In each of the reading surveys at secondary level, pupils have been asked to read materials that are designed to reflect something of the range of reading that they need to undertake in and out of school. The materials generally include works of reference such as they would encounter in school, materials that they might make use of in daily life, and works of literature. None of the reports issued previously has contained detailed comment on the latter and it was thought appropriate to include such commentary in this final report on the first phase of monitoring.

In the following chapter, pupils' responses to five short stories are analysed. Their responses to one short story, *The Landlady* by Roald Dahl, showed the extent to which they could interpret aspects of plot and character on the basis of a gradual accumulation of verbal and situational evidence which gives rise to a mood of excitement or narrative tension. A second story portrayed an 'adventure' in which two pilots brutally and thoughtlessly killed an eagle hawk. The external action depicted is of less narrative interest, however, than the development and change in the attitudes of the pilots from elation to shame, as they consider the implications and effect of the 'duel'. A third story portrayed the emergence of a young boy into a stage of independence or maturity symbolised in a swim involving danger and great physical effort. In this case also, the external action of the story is of less narrative significance than the psychological change that is represented. *A Horse and Two Goats* by Narayan depicts an encounter between two characters, each supposedly representative of values embodied in their respective cultures. The prevailing narrative tone is one of restrained humour. In particular pupils were not always able to appreciate the humour implicit in the situation depicted and in the dialogue. Low performers tended to find the story lacking in interest and 'action'.

Finally, pupils were asked to read and interpret the opening section of *Brave New World*. Many failed to appreciate the ironic tone and satirical impact of the work, in part because they were not alert to the implications of the imagery used in the description of the Central London Hatchery.

On the basis of an analysis of pupils' responses, some generalisations about the approaches adopted by relatively good and poor readers are put forward. These include the suggestion that good readers tend to view the works they read as artifacts in which each element has relevance to the work as a whole. They also appear to hold in mind a number of possible lines of development in character and plot which they are willing to modify as they proceed. Good readers also attempt to discern the authorial viewpoint underlying a story, recognising that this will not necessarily be reflected in the views of any specific character in the story. We conclude the chapter by noting that an interpretation of the beliefs and intentions of the writer is a prerequisite to all intelligent reading, both of literary and non-literary materials.

4.1 Introduction

The response to literature: the short story

In each of the reading surveys at secondary level, pupils have been asked to read a wide variety of materials selected to reflect something of the range of reading that pupils have to undertake in and out of school. The materials included works of literature. For practical and methodological reasons the majority of the literary texts were short stories, though some included materials extracted from longer works of fiction or autobiography. This chapter contains a commentary on pupils' responses to a number of these works. It does not therefore contain references to the performance of pupils when reading for information or for study. *As in the previous chapter, the discussion focuses on the performance of pupils whose scores placed them in the top and bottom 20 per cent of the sample* (cf. Annex 4.1).

The stories selected for commentary reflect something of the variety of traditions in short story writing. In structure and content, *The Landlady* by Roald Dahl has many of the characteristics associated with thrillers or mystery stories; *The Wedge-tailed Eagle* by G. Dutton is an adventure story, though with somewhat more of an emphasis on the motivations and responses of the characters involved than is usual in many stories in this genre. *Through the Tunnel* by Doris Lessing is a story that depicts the personal development and psychological growth of a young boy, emerging from childhood; *A Horse and Two Goats* by Narayan depicts, with restrained humour, the situation in which the representatives of two cultures make contact without communication. The extract from *Brave New World* portrays, satirically, an imaginative world in which humans are manufactured to the convenience of the social and political order.

The assessment of the response to literature

It seems relevant to refer briefly to some of the reasons for including these and other works of literature in the monitoring programme. The first reason is that almost all pupils have had the experience of reading literature as part of a well-ordered curriculum, though older pupils are often deprived of an opportunity for contact with literary works if these have no place in the examination syllabus for which they are preparing. Secondly, we believe it to be the case, as did the contributors to the Bullock Report, that there is a sense in which literature brings a pupil 'into an encounter with language in its most complex and varied forms'. While all literate pupils are capable of responding to stories that are appropriately selected, they differ in their ability to respond thoughtfully *and* with feeling to what they read. Even the simplest of the short stories used in the surveys is capable of being interpreted at different levels of complexity. A sensitive interpretation of such works involves both an intellectual and emotive response to what is written. Readers have to be alert to meaning carried by nuances of style, particularly in language attributed to characters. They have, moreover, to be conscious of the work as an integrated whole in which each element contributes to the overall effect. James Britton has suggested that

> *in terms of developing response to literature, pupils' progress lies in perceiving gradually the complex patterns of events, in picking up clues more widely separated and diverse in character, and in finding satisfaction in patterns of effects less directly related to their expectations and more particularly, their desires; at the same time, it lies in also perceiving the form of varying relationships between elements in the story and reality, as they increasingly come to know that commodity.*[1]

Literacy and other uses of language

The interpretation of literature and in particular short stories may therefore impose demands on readers that are not imposed by some of the non-literary materials they encounter; but the capacities required to interpret language used for literary or aesthetic purposes do not differ in any fundamental way from those needed to interpret language used for other purposes. All intelligent reading involves the creative interpretation of the information given selectively by the writer. All reading, however factual the topic, requires the reader to make inferences and to construct meanings on the basis of the information provided. Intelligent reading also necessarily involves an attempt to understand the underlying intentions or purposes of an author as these are not always signalled overtly.

The types of questions asked

It should be emphasised that the questions the pupils were asked about the short stories did not assume prior knowledge of literature or of literary criticism. The questions

---
[1] Britton J., reported in J. Dixon, *Growth through English*, NATE, 1967, p. 57.

generally requested the interpretation of what was written, primarily with reference to the depiction of character and setting, action, and theme. Pupils were not asked to evaluate what they read in comparison with other works of the same character or genre. They were, however, generally asked to indicate whether they had enjoyed reading the story and to give reasons for their response.

4.2 An analysis of responses to five stories

The Landlady by Roald Dahl can be considered to be representative of a rather simple form of thriller or mystery story. A young man is depicted as visiting Bath for the first time to find accommodation before starting work. Late in the evening he finds lodgings at a guest house. The landlady has a number of endearing if slightly eccentric characteristics. Gradually, however, evidence is accumulated to indicate to the reader that she is a more sinister personage than the hero supposes. It appears to the reader that Billy is in danger firstly of being poisoned and secondly of being pickled. The hero remains unaware of these possibilities, though at the end of the story his suspicions have been aroused. The main source of narrative tension and interest in the story derives from the incongruity between the perceptions of the main character and the reader's own interpretation of what is described.

The landlady's intentions can be deduced by an alert reader from what she is represented as doing and saying. *There are no overt statements by the author or the character to indicate what these are; they have to be inferred from an accumulation of verbal and situational evidence.*

In general, pupils found it relatively easy to answer questions that dealt straightforwardly with the *sequence of events* and with Billy's actions and reactions. *They found it easy to understand the plot, in the course of which minor details of behaviour or of talk take on significance* in the context of the landlady's eccentric behaviour. For example, one question asked if the pupils had recognised the link between three incidents described by the author: the ways the landlady carried a teatray into the room, a strange smell, and the bitter taste of the tea. A little over one-third of the pupils had correctly established a plausible link between these incidents.

In *The Landlady*, the description of the setting and the development of characters are subordinate to the development of the plot. However, as suggested above, there are certain features of the description of the two characters and their ways of speaking that are meaningful. For example, the author depicts the hero's naive but self-confident outlook in the language he attributes to him in the initial stages of the story. It was suggested to the pupils that 'in several parts of the story the writer describes the situation in words that Billy might have used if he was giving the account'. They were asked to give an example of such description with reference to a phrase or sentence used on page 1 or 2 of the story. Only 24 per cent of the pupils were able to quote appropriate examples such as 'the big shots up at Head Office were absolutely fantastically brisk all the time'.

A related question focused on details of the landlady's behaviour. Pupils were asked to point to features of the landlady's hands, face or person that suggested something sinister about her. Just over half of the pupils (54 per cent) located a reference e.g. the description of her 'small, white, quickly moving hands and red fingernails' or of the landlady 'smiling down at him with her pale lips' or 'watching him over the rim of her teacup'.

In general, pupils found it easier to identify relevant aspects of behaviour than to interpret the implications of stylistic variations exploited by the author to provide information about the background and mentality of the main character.

Attitudes to the story

The large majority of pupils (approximately 80 per cent) said that they had enjoyed reading the story. 5 per cent gave replies that were non-committal. 8 per cent said they had not enjoyed reading it. In explaining their responses to the story, pupils were particularly appreciative of the narrative tension built up by the author:

The author is very good at holding the reader in suspense I was on the edge of my seat for over half the book and was willing Billy to get out . . .

I enjoyed it because it has mystery to it and although I knew that something strange was happening it kept you in suspense giving you clues to work out the story for yourself.

A substantial number of pupils (almost 30 per cent) commented favourably on the craftsmanship shown in the ending of the story (which concludes on a note of suggestion and of menace):

The ending was the best part of the story because it left a lot to the imagination and it didn't simply state what happened to Billy.

However, about 10 per cent of the pupils felt that the story was incomplete, vague or inconclusive. They would have preferred the ending to have been spelt out in much more detail.

It does not even have a proper ending, but leaves you feeling angry as you do not know what really happened. These kinds of stories annoy me as I am left to make up an ending for myself.

The Wedge-tailed Eagle – a story by the Australian writer G. Dutton – tells of the killing of an eagle by two fighter pilots who pit their skill against the 'inborn mastery' of an eagle. The pilots are depicted as viewing the action as a contest or a duel with a bird of great size and grace.

The author implies that there is something childish in this view.

A pilot in a small, aerobatic aeroplane is like a child. He longs for something to play with. He can be happy enough rolling and looping by himself in the sky, but happiness changes to a kind of ecstacy when there is something against whom to match his skill or someone to applaud him when he low-flies through the unforeseeable complications of tree and rock, hill and river. The contest becomes more wonderful the nearer it approaches death.

In both the plot and the style of the story there is something reminiscent of the adventure stories written some years ago for boys' annuals. However, Dutton is a skilful writer and he conveys effectively, *without direct authorial comment*, the shame and remorse felt by the pilots after the death of the eagle. Their naive exultation in the chase is replaced by shock at the sight of the 'blood-stained heap of bone and feathers' that results from the contest. The pilots are shown as realising, after the event, the futility of their destructive game; but this change of view has to be inferred from their actions in burying the bird and avoiding any contact with the farmer on whose land they were and who had earlier shown his contempt for the eagle.

The opening paragraphs of the story emphasise in a number of ways the size and nobility of the eagle and its extraordinary strength in flight. These qualities are contrasted indirectly and overtly with the appearance and flight of the little biplanes used at that time by the pilots in training for warfare.

When an Air Force station was established in their country in 1941, they were not alarmed by the noisy yellow aeroplanes. Occasionally they would even float in circles across the aerodrome itself, and then disappear again behind the hills; the pilots had little fear of colliding with one of these circling, watchful birds. The vast, brown-black shape of the eagle would appear before the little Tiger Moth biplane and then be gone. There was nothing more to it. No question of haste or flapping of wings, simply a flick over and down and then the eagle would resume its circling.

Pupils were asked to look carefully at the first five paragraphs and select words or phrases that gave an impression of the eagle's size, it unhurried way of moving, its ability to fly at a great height and its 'attitude' towards the aircraft. In each case, there were not less than four references in the text and as many as seven, which were considered to be appropriate answers by the assessors. Between 88 per cent and 98 per cent of the high performers identified specific references in relation to these qualities. Between 37 per cent and 67 per cent of the low-performing group were judged to have given an appropriate answer.

In response to a related question, only 16 per cent of the low-performing group as opposed to 98 per cent of the high-performing group were able to identify one of several references which appeared to imply that the eagles regarded the aeroplanes as being, in some sense, inferior. It can be inferred from these two exercises that *many of the pupils in the low-performing group were unfamiliar with the method of close examination of the text which was required to answer the question.*

In a subsequent question, students were asked to take note of certain images that help to build up the impression of an impending duel or fight to the death. There are a number of these, including three which made reference to the qualities of a gun or a gun barrel. Just under 74 per cent of the high performers wrote down one of the phrases as opposed to 15 per cent of the low performers. Again, one may infer from this that as a group *they were less alert to the fact that a skilful writer may exploit imagery in general and metaphor in particular to help establish a mood or atmosphere* to provide a context in which the action that takes place might be interpreted, or to reflect underlying themes in a story.

After the initial description of the setting and the eagle, the writer depicts the pilots in conversation with one of the farmers over whose land they flew. The farmer objects to the pilots' view of the bird 'as the most magnificent, majestic bird there is'. Together, they make arrangements for both pilots to seek out and kill an eagle. The 'chase' is later depicted as taking place over the farmer's land.

Virtually all the pupils who obtained high scores recognised that the pilots saw the action they envisaged as a contest between well-matched protagonists rather than as a hunt and, similarly, 97 per cent of them recognised that the author did not intend to portray the pilots as being cruel men. Just over half of the low performers (54 per cent) also drew this conclusion from what they read. An understanding of the pilots' viewpoint in this respect is essential for an understanding of the main narrative action.

In parallel with the portrayal of the 'duel' between the planes and the eagle hawk, the author depicts the change in the views and feelings of the pilots. This change comprises *the internal action* of the story. The feelings turn from emotions of elation to feelings of shame and regret as they realise the pointlessness of their action. The climax of the story and the change in the pilots' mood occurs when the eagle collides with one of the planes.

> *It flashed, wings still gloriously outstretched, straight into the right-hand end of the upper mainplane of the aircraft, exactly where the metal slot curves across the wood and fabric. Its right wing, at the point where the hard, long feathers give way to the soft, curved feathers of the body, snapped away and fluttered down to earth. The left wing folded into the body, stretched and folded again, as the heavy box of bone, beak and claw plunged and slewed to the ground. The pilot could not watch the last few feet of its descent. For the first time he was grateful to the roar of the motor that obscured the thud of the body striking earth.*

The pupils were asked to suggest why the pilot could not bear to watch the last few feet of the bird's descent. A substantial number of low performers simply copied out the sentence that indicated that the motor obscured the sound of the body hitting the earth. In effect, these pupils gave a physical or mechanical explanation for the fact that the pilots did not watch the fall of the eagle, ignoring, or not recognising, the fact that the action reflected the pilots' shame and remorse. The response is in keeping with a view of the pilots as being callous or cruel men: thus representing an alternative and inaccurate interpretation of the internal action. As was noted earlier, one characteristic of some less able readers is that, having formed an opinion or interpretation of a character, they are reluctant to modify or revise it.

The pilots are then depicted as burying the eagle, in silence.

> *The two of them stood in silence. The moment of skill and danger was past, and the dead body before them proclaimed their victory. Frowning with the glare of the sun and the misery of their achievement they both looked down at the piteous, one-winged eagle. Not a mark of blood was on it, the beak glistening and uncrushed, the ribbed feet and talons clenched together. It was not the fact of death that kept them in silence; the watcher could not always keep his station in the air. What both of them could still see was the one-winged heap of bone and feathers, slewing and jerking uncontrolled to earth.*

Despite the difficulty in interpreting the specific implications of such phrases, 97 per cent of the high performers and 60 per cent of the low performers appreciated why it was that the pilots buried the eagle silently, in a wish for concealment or respect for a dead enemy, or simply because they were ashamed of what they had done. While understanding for the most part why the writer referred to the 'misery of their achievement' a substantial number of the pupils in the lower-performing group found it difficult to explain clearly what their perceptions were. *The difficulty that pupils have in such circumstances does not necessarily stem from a lack of understanding but from the difficulty of responding lucidly in a way that clearly expresses their insights and feelings.*

Two questions were asked which drew attention to an element of craftsmanship in the structure of the story, which both begins and ends with reference to a black dot circling high above the planes. Again, virtually all the higher performers (96 per cent) and just under one-third of the lower performers (32 per cent) recognised that the author was attempting to indicate in this way the futility of the men's efforts to destroy the eagle; that is to say *they were able to appreciate the thematic significance of this pattern of events.*

Attitudes to the story

After completing the questions pupils were asked to say whether they found the story interesting. 92 per cent of the high performers and 58 per cent of the low performers expressed positive interest. Those that commented on the story, as many did, tended to refer to the sense of excitement that derived from the gradual development to the climax in the death of the bird. Many also commented on the interest that arose from the change of mood at the end of the story, as in the following examples.

Examples
Did you find this story interesting?
Explain why or why not.

> Yes, I think it is exciting the way the ~~it~~ builds up to the climax of the hunting ~~do~~ down and killing of the bird. I think it has an interesting ending: sad Because the bird is dead and the pilots are sad and ashamed of killing it.

> I found the story quite interesting, mainly because the descriptions were so good. The struggle between the men and the eagle, the desire to be the victor, these were very well described. The end was very good as well, the way in which it ended in the way it began. I think the best part of the story was ~~the~~ when the pilots saw their destruction and felt such guilt and sorrow.

> Yes, because it was unpredictable and it was exiting and well written.

Low performers who professed not to enjoy the story tended to point to the fact that it was long and therefore boring and also, in some cases, that it was somewhat sad. These attitudes are succintly expressed in the following quotation.

> The story is to boring and sad, and to long.

One pupil wrote:

> I didn't like this story. For a start I didn't understand it. I've read better storeys in comics.

Some pupils expressed distaste for the subject of the story; and a small number suggested that the type of story was one that would be more suitable for boys than girls, e.g.

> The story was boring. We girls like different story not about eagles and war.

A few objected not to the topic but to the narrative approach:

> This type of story does not appeal to me. I prefer to read fiction as if I want reality I can read a newspaper.

For others, what they interpreted to be the 'realistic' qualities of the story provided its main interest.

> Yes, there was a lot of excitement. It was something that could really happen. Very interesting.

In the sample as a whole, however, *just over 80 per cent of the pupils professed to finding the story enjoyable to read*, including some whose initial impressions were negative.

> On first reading, the story was not very interesting – but after having looked at it more deeply I found that I enjoyed it much more.

Through the Tunnel is a story written by Doris Lessing which portrays an incident in the life of a young English boy who is on holiday somewhere in Africa with his widowed mother. The boy, Jerry, who is approaching adolescence, demonstrates his independence, resourcefulness and courage by traversing a tunnel underneath the sea. He tells nobody about what he has done. However, the external action of the story, though it is vividly represented, is of less interest than the writer's representation of the boy's growth in self-awareness and maturity.

To understand the nature of the change that takes place in his conception of himself it is necessary to understand the change in the boy's relationship with his mother. Jerry is an only child and she is a widow determined 'to be neither possessive nor lacking in devotion'. The boy's attitude to his mother is complex. He is dependent on her for companionship and conscious of her vulnerability. He also feels in some sense responsible for her, having taken the place, as it were, of his father. He is anxious, therefore, not to offend her by asserting his independence, but is nevertheless driven to do so.

The natural setting in which the story takes place is an important element in the narrative. Initially, the boy is seen as having to choose between accompanying his mother, as he had in earlier years, to a 'safe' beach or leaving her to make his way to a wild and rocky bay. The symbolism in the contrast is obvious, the one representing the safety and security of his childhood and the other the dangers and the challenge of independence.

> Going to the shore on the first morning of the holiday, the young English boy stopped at a turning of the path and looked down at a wild and rocky bay, and then over to the crowded beach he knew so well from other years. His mother walked on in front of him, carrying a bright-striped bag in one hand. Her other arm, swinging loose, was very white in the sun. The boy watched that white, naked arm, and turned his eyes, which had a frown behind them, towards the bay and back again to his mother. When she felt he was not with her, she swung round, 'Oh, there you are, Jerry!' she said. She looked impatient, then smiled. 'Why darling, would you rather not come with me? Would you rather . . .' She frowned, conscientiously worrying over what

amusements he might secretly be longing for which she had been too busy or too careless to imagine. He was very familiar with that anxious, apologetic smile. Contrition sent him running after her. And yet, as he ran, he looked back over his shoulder at the wild bay; and all morning, as he played on the safe beach, he was thinking of it.

It was pointed out to pupils that the writer deliberately contrasted the beach and the bay in the story. They were asked to say what the two places represented to the boy. 87 per cent of the high performers were judged to have answered correctly, as in the following example.

The writer deliberately contrasts the beach and the bay in the story. What do they represent to the boy?

> ...The beach represents safety and his mother. The bay represents adventure danger, challenge and independence from his mother

However, 33 per cent of the lower-performing group (40 per cent of the boys and 26 per cent of the girls) omitted the question, the second part of which they may have had some difficulty interpreting. A simpler, related question asked pupils to note some of the differences between the beach and the bay. In this case 14 per cent of the lower-performing pupils were judged to have given an appropriate response. Clearly, *the majority of that group did not perceive the significance of the contrast between the two settings or the symbolic implications of the boy's choice between them.*

On the basis of what was written in the opening section of the story pupils were asked to say what impression they had formed about the relationship between the boy and his mother. *Over 70 per cent of the pupils showed that they had understood the complex nature of the relationship and many wrote perceptively about it.* Just under half of the pupils in the group of lower performers (45 per cent) were judged to have given an appropriate response to the question. Three examples follow:

From the first two pages what impression do you get of the relationship between Jerry and his mother?

> Jerry obviously loves his mother - he hates offending her and has a sense of 'chivalry' towards her - he feels it is his duty to protect her and do her will; even when he feels the need for excitement through old age.
> His mother loves her son; as he is an only child she is devoted to him - but she is always conscious that she expects him to do too much - she is unwilling to let him go yet recognises the same necessity to do so.

> Jerry's mother has protected and sheltered him from life but now he attempts to do something without her she is frightened but doesn't stop him. He is slightly rebellious but has a deep rooted love and dependance on her

> His mother loves him alot and she tries to be I do her best for him. He loves his mother but sometimes he wants to do what he likes. His mother is over protective.

The next stage of the narrative depicts the boy as having swum quickly away from the shore and into the 'real sea – a warm sea where irregular cold water from the deep currents shocked his limbs'. After swimming for a considerable distance he turns and looks for his mother in the distance. Having found her 'he swam back to shore, relieved at being sure she was there, but all at once very lonely'. 94 per cent of the high-performing group and 36 per cent of the low were able to suggest why Jerry looked for his mother at that stage.

The boy's loneliness is assuaged by his joining temporarily with a group of older local boys. After some time, the boys leave him to dive beneath a wall of rock that forms a barrier between the rocks and the open sea. He is unable to follow them and, embarrassed by his failure, he begins to clown in the water to attract attention to himself. *90 per cent of the high-performing group as opposed to 24 per cent of the low-performing group showed that they understood why he behaved in this way. The author indirectly relates the boy's clowning, in response to his failure to follow the boys through the tunnel, to earlier failures to secure his mother's attention.*

> *And now, in a panic of failure, he yelled up, in English: 'Look at me! Look!' and he began splashing and kicking in the water like a foolish dog.*

> *They looked on gravely, frowning. He knew the form. At moments of failure, when he clowned to claim his mother's attention, it was with this grave, embarrassed inspection that she rewarded him.*

His reaction when the boys leave him is equally childish. He cries openly 'fists in his eyes'.

In the second section of the story the boy is shown to be preparing systematically to swim through the barrier. He spends hours under water learning to hold his breath. The preparation continued for several days with 'a curious, most unchildlike persistence, a controlled impatience, . . .'

Two days before he was due to leave Jerry makes the attempt to swim through the tunnel in the rock. His imagination leaves him in no doubt about the seriousness of the undertaking.

> *. . . trembling with horror at that long, long tunnel under the rock, under the sea. Even in the open sunlight the barrier rock seemed very wide and very heavy; tons of rock pressed down on where he would go. If he died there he would lie until one day – perhaps not before*

next year – those big boys would swim into it and find it blocked.

The author graphically depicts the boy's progress through the tunnel and out into the open sea.

. . . he feebly clutched at rocks in the dark, pulling himself forward, leaving the brief space of sunlit water behind. He felt he was dying. He was no longer quite conscious. He struggled on in the darkness between lapses into unconsciousness. An immense, swelling pain filled his head, and then the darkness cracked with an explosion of green light. His hands, groping forward, met nothing, and his feet, kicking back, propelled him out into the open sea.

The boy returns to the hotel without telling his mother what he has done. She assumes her protective role, advising him not to swim any more. He accepts this without question as 'it was no longer of the least importance to go to the bay'.

The pupils were asked to say why they thought the author of the story ended it with the line quoted above. *92 per cent of the high performers and 24 per cent of the low performers understood and stated that it was because Jerry had succeeded in achieving his goal and that the tunnel therefore no longer had the importance it had had for him initially.*

Other questions attempted to probe the extent to which pupils had understood the implications of Jerry's swim in terms of his personal growth or development. This issue was touched on in one of the concluding questions which asked what the boy had achieved or learnt from his experience, apart from the achievement of swimming through the tunnel. Over 70 per cent of the high-performing group noted that he had achieved some independence from his mother, a degree of self-confidence, greater understanding of himself or that he had learnt perseverance in completing a difficult task. Only 6 per cent of the low-performing group were judged to have responded appropriately to the question. Pupils in that group were more likely to point to practical achievements that Jerry might be said to have made (e.g. he had learned how to hold his breath for long periods) and or to more general lessons (e.g. that water pressure causes nose bleeds) than were pupils in the higher-performing group, although pupils in both groups drew attention to such matters.

Attitudes to the story

When they were asked to say whether they found the story interesting, 92 per cent of the high-performing group and 73 per cent of the low-performing group responded positively (19 per cent of the lower group failed to react to the question).

Those pupils who responded negatively did so for a variety of reasons. Some viewed the story as being one more suitable for younger children than for their age group.

The following examples illustrate this viewpoint.

I found the booklet interesting but it is no longer the type of material I read as, like most people of my age, I have now grown out of the age of adventure stories.

This story was far below the level of books I am studying for 'O' level. It was more along the lines of an Enid Blyton story.

Another remarked that 'it seemed to be a book for younger children although some of the words were for older people'.

In this case as with the other stories discussed some pupils noted that they had enjoyed the reading task, despite the fact that they did not normally read stories of the type included.

Yes I have found out that if I have to read stories then I can enjoy them and now I will try to read more.

The booklet was interesting and well chosen for this type of test. I was pleased that it was not a straightforward story that you normally see in tests and exams. Although I personally do not take reading seriously out of school, it is an enjoyable, short story which I would like to read last thing at night.

I found the reading booklet very enjoyable, yet I felt a little sorry towards Jerry's ways of finding new friends. The detail was good. I do not usually read this kind of story, but this was good.

A Horse and Two Goats is a story by R. K. Narayan which depicts, with restrained humour, an encounter between an American tourist and an Indian peasant. The two characters, referred to throughout the story as 'the old man' and 'the red-faced man', can be regarded as representative figures embodying values and attitudes characteristic of their different cultures. The fact that they speak different languages accounts, ostensibly, for their total inability to communicate; but their lack of understanding of each other stems from something more than a difference in language.

The immediate reason for their contact is the tourist's wish to buy a horse made out of clay, which stood near the entrance to the village. The tourist, who views the statue as an attractive souvenir, wants to buy it from the old man whom he assumes to be the owner, or a partner in a business enterprise who is in a position to sell the statue. For the old man, however, the horse is an object of religious veneration, associated inseparably with the life of his family and his village. In local mythology the statue of the horse and its rider were assigned a role of cosmic significance, a fact to which the writer draws attention.

The village was so small that it found no mention in any atlas. On the local survey map it was indicated by a tiny dot. It was called Kiritam, which in the Tamil language means 'crown' (preferably diamond-studded) – a rather gorgeous conception readily explained by any other local enthusiast convinced beyond doubt that this part of India is the apex of the world. In proof thereof, he could, until quite recently, point in the direction of a massive guardian at the portals of the village, in the shape of a horse moulded out of clay, baked, burnt and brightly coloured.

As was the case with the other tests commented on here, the responses of pupils falling into the top 20 per cent and the bottom 20 per cent of the total sample were analysed. In this case, the top group (Group A) answered not fewer than 18 of the 20 items correctly. The pupils in the lower-performing group (Group B) answered not more than 12 of the 20 items correctly.

The introductory section of the story describes the statue and its place in the mythology of the village. The contrast between the 'gorgeous conception' that gave rise to the statue and its dilapidated appearance, brought on by the ravages of sun and rain and general neglect, is established in the opening section.

The story continues by depicting how on the day in question the old man was drowsing near the statue, watching a pair of goats graze. He was disturbed by a motorist who stops suddenly at the sight of the statue. The old man assumes, from the khaki dress of the tourist, that he is a police officer enquiring about a recent murder, from which the old man is at pains to dissociate himself. However, he subsequently deduces from the manner of the tourist, which is both perplexed and ingratiating, that he is searching for lost cattle. Neither of these assumptions is correct.

The American tourist explains details of his personal life as well as impressions he has gained of the country after travelling 5,000 miles in three weeks.

The old man made indistinct sounds in his throat and shook his head. Encouraged by this, the other went on to explain at length, uttering each syllable with care and deliberation, what brought him to this country, how much he liked it, what he did at home, how he had planned for years to visit India, the dream of his life and so forth – every now and then pausing to smile affably. The old man smiled back and said nothing, whereupon the red-faced man finally said, 'How old are you? You have such wonderful teeth. Are they real? What's your secret?'

The tourist then attempts to buy the statue from the old man, who takes the opportunity to explain, in detail, his conception of the successive visitations of the god Vishnu. At this stage, as the author notes, their mutual mystification was complete.

The tourist then offers a currency note to the old man, who is unaware of its precise value. He assumes that the money is being offered to purchase his goats. These he gladly sells, as he believes that the transaction will enable him to realise his dream of opening up a small shop on

that very spot. He departs, leaving the goats grazing peacefully and the tourist waiting for the assistance he needs to remove the statue.

The humour of the story derives in part from the fact that both of the main characters, being ignorant of each other's motivation and intentions, act in good faith. It is important to an understanding of the story that readers appreciate this. Virtually all pupils in the high-scoring group (96 per cent) understood that it was not the intention of the old man to cheat the tourist whereas *only 42 per cent of the low-scoring group reached that conclusion.*

Many pupils in the low-scoring group also misunderstood the motivation of the tourist, for example, in showing an interest in the old man's goats. All of the high-scoring group recognised that such an interest might please the old man and win his confidence (it would, in that respect, be 'sound policy'). However, only 25 per cent of the low-scoring group reached the same conclusion.

Practically all the pupils in group A (95 per cent) showed that they understood that the old man valued the statue as an object of religious veneration but only 14 per cent of the low performers indicated clearly that they had understood that point to a question directly relating to the issue, viz.

Why did the old man value it (the statue)?

Because the contrast in the viewpoints of the two characters is important to an interpretation of the story the same question was asked a second time in a different form, viz.

The old man's attention is drawn to the horse. What sort of meaning does the horse have for him?

94 per cent of the top-scoring group gave an appropriate answer and just over 30 per cent of the low-scoring group.

A small number of questions were intended to draw the pupils' attention to the craftsmanship exercised by the author in telling the story. For example, it was noted that the first and last paragraphs in the story had something in common. The pupils were asked to say what this was. 87 per cent of the high-scoring group noted that the author had depicted, in each case, a peaceful scene in which one man and two goats waited silently near the statue – the only change being that a different man is involved at the end of the story than at the beginning. *30 per cent of the pupils in the low-scoring group noted the similarities* between the two situations.

The author does not state at the end of the story whether or not the tourist removed the statue. There is, however, an indication in the opening paragraph that the statue was removed and pupils were advised to look closely at the first paragraph to see whether anything was said that would justify that inference. *Only 3 per cent of the low-scoring group detected the relevant reference as opposed to 53 per cent of the high-scoring group.*

Attitudes to the story

There was one other notable respect in which the perceptions of the low- and high-scoring groups tended to differ. At the end of the booklet the pupils were asked to say whether they had enjoyed the story. *84 per cent of the high-scoring group responded positively* (57 per cent) or by giving a balanced response (27 per cent). *Only 28 per cent of the low-scoring group gave either a positive response* (14 per cent) or a mixed or balanced response. Other pupils in the group either omitted the question (28 per cent) or responded negatively.

The general 'complaint' levelled at the story, primarily by the low scorers, was that it lacked action and excitement and was, for those reasons, boring. The following comments are typical of the comments of the minority who did not enjoy reading the story.

> really boring. I think they should have put a bit of excitement in it. It could have been better.

> It was only a story about 2 men having a conversation. Nothing much happened at all. It could have been better.

> really boring becaus it was all people talking and nothing ever happening.

> The story seemed to take hours to read whereas if there were a couple of pages telling abit of a horror stories or war books about people getting killed etc it would have seemed like five minutes of intresting reading

The following comments are characteristic of pupils who found the story to be of interest.

> I MOST STRONGLY DISAGREE WITH THE COMMENT "... really boring. No action or anything". To me THIS IS A CHARACTERISTIC OF THE MINDLESS KIND OF PERSON WHOSE ONLY AMUSEMENT IN LIFE ARE STORIES SUCH AS "THE RATS". DOES A STORY HAVE TO HAVE ACTION TO BE INTERESTING?

> Though the story was trivial I enjoyed it because it was simple and amusing and summed up peoples inability to comunicate to others, especially when they talk a different language.

Brave New World

The literary material considered up to this point has comprised complete short stories. For educational and methodological reasons it was judged to be important by those designing the reading tests that pupils would be presented with works that would give them the opportunity of judging a writer's craftsmanship in shaping a complete work. This strategy also allowed for more complex questions to be asked relating to the relationship of different parts of the stories and their integration into the work as a whole. However, in the booklet discussed below, a different procedure was used in selecting the materials to be read. Pupils were asked to read an extract from a longer work, *Brave New World*, by Aldous Huxley, after they had read a journalistic account of animal cloning and of the so-called 'test-tube baby' technique. *Brave New World* was selected so that we could investigate the effectiveness and insight with which the pupils interpreted satirical prose.

In style and approach the initial passage therefore contrasted with the pointed satire of the opening section of *Brave New World*. In both cases, however, the *authorial viewpoint and attitude* to what is being described is not immediately clear; in the first case, because the writer has no strongly held views, and, in the case of *Brave New World*, because these are *expressed ironically and indirectly*, primarily through the selection of words and images used to describe the setting and characters.

Before reading part of the opening chapter of the novel, pupils were told that:

> *The following passage is part of the first chapter of the late Aldous Huxley's book* Brave New World. *It was written in 1932 before cloning became possible. In the story, the author imagines what it would be like in a world where cloning was used to produce different types of human beings.*

The first set of questions asked focused on the opening description of the Central London Hatchery and on its Director.

BRAVE NEW WORLD

A squat grey building of only thirty-four storeys. Over the main entrance the words, CENTRAL LONDON HATCHERY AND CONDITIONING CENTRE, and, in a shield, the World State's motto, COMMUNITY, IDENTITY, STABILITY.

The enormous room on the ground floor faced towards the north. Cold for all the summer beyond the panes, for all the tropical heat of the room itself, a harsh thin light glared through the windows, hungrily seeking some draped lay figure, some pallid shape of academic goose-flesh, but finding only the glass and nickel and bleakly shining porcelain of a laboratory. Wintriness responded to wintriness. The overalls of the workers were white, their hands gloved with a pale corpse-coloured rubber. The light was frozen, dead, a ghost.

Only from the yellow barrels of the microscopes did it borrow a certain rich and living substance, lying along the polished tubes like butter, streak after luscious streak in long recession down the work tables.

'And this,' said the Director opening the door, 'is the Fertilizing Room.'

Bent over their instruments, three hundred Fertilizers were plunged, as the Director of Hatcheries and Conditioning entered the room, in the scarcely breathing silence, the absent-minded, soliloquizing hum or whistle, of absorbed concentration. A troop of newly arrived students, very young, pink and callow, followed nervously, rather abjectly, at the Director's heels. Each of them carried a notebook, in which, whenever the great man spoke, he desperately scribbled. Straight from the horse's mouth. It was a rare privilege. The D.H.C. for Central London always made a point of personally conducting his new students round the various departments.

'Just to give you a general idea,' he would explain to them. For of course some sort of general idea they must have, if they were to do their work intelligently – though as little of one, if they were to be good and happy members of society, as possible. For particulars, as everyone knows, make for virtue and happiness; generalities are intellectually necessary evils. Not philosophers but fretsawyers and stamp collectors compose the backbone of society.

'To-morrow,' he would add, smiling at them with a slightly menacing geniality, 'you'll be settling down to serious work. You won't have time for generalities. Meanwhile . . .'

The writer's view of the Director and of the fertilisation process is unstated. *The satirical purpose of the account can only be understood if the implications of the imagery used in the description are understood and if the element of recurrent irony is detected* in the representation of the views held by the Director. Several questions were asked which were designed to reveal whether the pupils had understood the satirical purpose of the description and whether they had perceived the 'real' view of the author about the conditioning process described.

At one point of the description, for example, the Director is referred to as 'a great man'. Pupils were asked to say whether this designation reflected the author's view:

Does the author really *think that the Director is 'a great man'? Give a reason for your answer.*

Just over 20 per cent of those responding said that the author did not in fact consider the Director to be 'great'. *In the low-performing group virtually none of the pupils answered correctly* and gave reasons to support their view. The question also proved to be difficult for the pupils in the high-performing group, 54 per cent of whom answered correctly.

In a subsequent question pupils were asked to say whose point of view was reflected in the Director's observations about the foolishness of focusing attention on generalities rather than on particular facts. The question was as follows:

Whose point of view is presented in the passage quoted above? The author? The Director? The students? Sensible people in general?

In the sample as a whole 40 per cent of pupils noted that it was the Director's view that was reflected in what was said. In the low-performing group approximately 27 per cent answered correctly. A slightly higher proportion incorrectly attributed the statement to the author. *A large proportion, approximately 30 per cent, omitted the question.*

The pupils' attention was then drawn to the Director's description of 'Bokanovsky's Process' in the following account.

'Bokanovsky's Process,'* repeated the Director, and the students underlined the words in their little notebooks.

One egg, one embryo, one adult-normality. But a bokanovskified egg will bud, will proliferate, will divide. From eight to ninety-six buds, and every bud will grow into a perfectly formed embryo, and every embryo into a full-sized adult. Making ninety-six human beings grow where only one grew before. Progress.

'Essentially,' the D.H.C. concluded, 'bokanovskification consists of a series of arrests of development. We check the normal growth and, paradoxically enough, the egg responds by budding.' Responds by budding. The pencils were busy.

He pointed. On a very slowly moving band a rackfull of test-tubes was entering a large metal box, another rackfull was emerging. Machinery faintly purred. It took eight minutes for the tubes to go through, he told them. Eight minutes of hard X-rays being about as much as an egg can stand. A few died; of the rest, the least susceptible divided into two; most put out four buds; some eight; all were returned to the incubators, where the buds began to develop; then, after two days, were suddenly chilled, chilled and checked. Two, four, eight, the buds in their turn budded; and having budded were dosed almost to death with alcohol; consequently burgeoned again and having budded – bud out of bud out of bud – were thereafter – further arrest being generally fatal – left to develop in peace. By which time the original egg was in a fair way to becoming anything from eight to ninety-six embryos – a prodigious improvement, you will agree, on nature. Identical twins – but not in piddling twos and threes as in the old viviparous* days, when an egg would sometimes accidentally divide; actually by dozens, by scores at a time.

'Scores,' the Director repeated and flung out his arms, as though he were distributing largesse. 'Scores.'

But one of the students was fool enough to ask where the advantage lay.

'My good boy!' The Director wheeled sharply round on him. 'Can't you see? Can't you see? He raised a

hand; his expression was solemn. 'Bokanovsky's Process is one of the major instruments of social stability!'

Major instruments of social stability. Standard men and women; in uniform batches. The whole of a small factory staffed with the products of a single bokanovskified egg.

'Ninety-six identical twins working ninety-six identical machines!' The voice was almost tremulous with enthusiasm. 'You really know where you are. For the first time in history.' He quoted the planetary motto. 'Community Identity Stability.' Grand words. 'If we could bokanovskify indefinitely the whole problem would be solved.'

Solved by standard Gammas, unvarying Deltas, uniform Epsilons.* Millions of identical twins. The principle of mass production at last applied to biology.

*Bokanovsky's Process: This is a process imagined by the author.

*Viviparous: A viviparous animal is one that bears live young.

*Gammas, Deltas, Epsilons: These are letters of the Greek alphabet (equivalent to C, D and E.)

The following question was put to the pupils:

Do you agree that making 96 human beings grow where only one grew before is 'a prodigious improvement' on nature?
('Prodigious' means 'great').

Just over 60 per cent of the pupils responded by giving what was judged to be a sensible response. Answers given by pupils in the high- and low-performing groups were analysed. It is of some interest that, among girls in the low-performing group, 25 per cent agreed that such a development could be considered to be a great improvement, whereas 55 per cent disagreed. In contrast, the proportion of boys agreeing and disagreeing was similar (approximately 35 per cent in each case).

The main point at issue, however, concerns the pupils' ability to distinguish between the author's viewpoint and those expressed by the Director, the spokesman for the regime. In the sample as a whole, 43 per cent of the pupils recognised that the author would not consider Bokanovsky's Process to be a great improvement on nature. In the low-performing group just over 10 per cent of the boys and just under 25 per cent of the girls answered correctly. Again, a substantial proportion of boys (58 per cent) in the group omitted the question as opposed to 35 per cent of the girls.

Finally, the pupils were asked the following question:

Now that you've read the passage, do you think that the writer (who wrote in 1932) was in favour of applying 'the principle of mass production' to the production of embryos? Was he strongly in favour of it, mildly in favour of it, not too concerned one way or the other, mildly opposed to it or strongly opposed to it?

In the sample as a whole just over 50 per cent of the pupils recognised that the writer was opposed to this principle. 89 per cent of the high-performing group recognised that the writer was opposed to it. Just over 20 per cent of the pupils in the low-performing group (15 per cent of the boys and 24 per cent of the girls) reached this conclusion.

Two further questions had the purpose of encouraging students to respond to what they understood to be the social implications of the process being described. One of these invited them to consider the nature of the 'problem' that the process was intended to solve. It was as follows:

The Director says 'If we could bokanovskify indefinitely the whole problem would be solved.' What problem do you think he is referring to?

The assessors were told to consider as correct any answer that referred to the application of these techniques for social control.

Approximately 22 per cent of the students were judged to have provided an appropriate answer to the question.

Another question referred back to a statement of the Director to the effect that good and happy members of society need to have as little exposure to or interest in general ideas as possible – 'Not philosophers but fretsawyers and stamp collectors compose the backbone of society'.

Why do you think that stamp collectors would be preferred to philosophers by those in control of the society described?

In analysing the pupils' responses, the assessors looked for some indication of an understanding that, in a totalitarian society, philosophical enquiry concerned with matters to do with change and possibility would be likely to be considered subversive. Again, 22 per cent of the pupils in the whole sample were judged to have given an appropriate answer. An even smaller proportion (12 per cent) were judged to have given an acceptable paraphrase or explanation of the Director's observation to the effect that '. . . particulars, as everyone knows, make for virtue and happiness; generalities are intellectually necessary evils'. Given the difficulty of the question, this response is not surprising.

To this point the questions discussed have focused on the pupils' interpretation of the satirical stance of the author and their understanding of the object of his criticism. To arrive at an appreciation of this stance, however, requires an imaginative interpretation of the words and images that the writer used to describe the fertilising room and those who worked there. The pupils' attention was drawn to this fact:

In describing the room, the writer also reveals the feelings the room arouses in him and his attitudes to the work being done.

They were asked to list three words or phrases used that helped to make clear the author's feelings about the work being done. Between 30 and 40 per cent (39 per cent, 36 per cent and 30 per cent) referred to phrases in the second paragraph that indicated the author's sense of the lifelessness and the lack of humanity exemplified in the technological replacement of the methods of reproduction used in 'the old viviparous days' (e.g. 'harsh thin light'/'pallid . . . academic gooseflesh'/'pale corpse-coloured rubber'/'frozen light', etc.) Some pupils referred to phrases used in other sections of the work; but *not more than 50 per cent were judged to have responded adequately to the question.* The failure to understand the author's viewpoint and to distinguish it from that of characters in the story appears to reflect both a lack of acquaintance with satirical modes of expression and, more generally, lack of sensitivity to connotations of significant words and images, particularly among lower performers.

4.3 Interpreting narratives: some differences between good and poor readers

Some of the differences in the approaches of good and poor readers in interpreting the short stories or extracts discussed can be highlighted at this point.

1. One difference is that good readers interpret the stories as integrated works in which the different elements have relevance to the work as a whole and in which each component is assumed to have been included for deliberate effect.

2. Good readers have a sense of form. They are able to perceive the overall structure of the story and elements within it which are deliberately patterned, such as the appearance of an eagle high in the sky at the beginning and ending of *The Wedge-tailed Eagle* or the situation depicted at the beginning and ending of the short story by Narayan, involving the statue, the goats and the waiting figure of a man.

3. A second difference has to do with the relative 'open-mindedness' of good and poor readers in interpreting character and action. Good readers appear to hold in mind a number of possible options or alternative scenarios as they read, being willing to modify their initial impression of the landlady as an endearing old lady; they would be prepared to modify this impression as more information about the character became available. Poor readers, on the other hand, having made a judgement about a character tend to maintain this, despite an accumulation of evidence that would support a different interpretation of that character or of the action being described.

Since they are prepared to envisage different options in terms of character and action good readers would have no objection to the open-endedness of a story, such as *The Landlady* where, in conclusion, different possibilities for action are suggested but not explored.

Indeed a substantial number took pleasure in being allowed to exercise their imagination in this case. Pupils who objected to such inconclusiveness, as they perceived it, tended to be in the low-performing group.

4. Good readers also have the qualities of mind needed to empathise with the characters portrayed and have an interest in the internal states of mind depicted. They recognised that 'action' can be embodied in changes of consciousness or ways of thinking as well as in action in the 'physical' sense. Poorer readers tend to find the depiction of states of mind of less interest. A number of the low performers castigated the author of *A Horse and Two Goats* on the grounds that the story lacked action (*it was 'all talk and no action'*). In doing so, some explicitly referred to the type of narrative action found in war books and horror stories in which human acts are portrayed with little or no reference to feelings and motivation.

5. In interpreting what is written good readers are more aware of the implications and effects of stylistic choices both in general terms and in terms of the language attributed to characters. They are aware of the connotations as well as the denotations of the words used. They appreciate the effect of metaphorical utterance in which writers associate ideas and the terms expressing these in new ways. The better readers are also sensitive to the implications of ironical statements. They are aware of the fact that what is *said* in such circumstances is not what is *meant,* whereas poorer readers tend to give a literal interpretation to what they read in such cases.

6. Good readers can also recognise and appreciate components of description or action that have symbolic implications. The contrast between the wild, rocky bay and the safe shore in *Through the Tunnel* has a clear symbolic meaning, but it requires an exercise of the imagination to appreciate this. Without such imaginative insight pupils would not, for example, be able to understand the value that the old peasant in *A Horse and Two Goats* places on the statue that stands outside his village.

7. The majority of the stories referred to in this chapter can be said to have an underlying theme, in the sense that the incidents or events described have some general significance. It is clear, for example, that, while the interests of the writer of *The Wedge-tailed Eagle* are centred on the development that takes place in the pilots' gradual realisation of the barbarity of their act of destruction, the story also reflects the writer's views about the beauty and enduring qualities of nature as these are symbolised by the eagle. Pupils varied in their ability to understand and to interpret the views of the writer and, consequently, to discern the underlying themes of this and other stories. A number of pupils, including some better readers, reacted with distaste, characterising the writer as 'cruel' or 'sadistic'. This type of response reflects the pupils' inability to distance themselves from the events portrayed in a story and to understand that the writer's perspective

is not necessarily to be identified with those of any of the characters portrayed.

8. The inability to discern an underlying theme and to recognise authorial viewpoint was shown most clearly in the pupils' responses to *Brave New World*. Fewer than half of the pupils understood that, far from endorsing the principle of mass production applied in Bokanovsky's Process, the author viewed it as abhorrent, reflecting as it does a total lack of respect for human life and individuality. However, in this case the lack of understanding was not restricted to those readers who did not succeed well in completing the test as a whole.

An inability to interpret an author's viewpoint often stems from the fact that pupils do not have the experience or awareness to enable them to appreciate the implications of stylistic choices deliberately made by an author in describing an event or character, to imply a judgement or convey a viewpoint about what is described. The perspective of the writer of *A Horse and Two Goats*, for example, is clearly established in the opening paragraphs of the story where the incongruity between the 'gorgeous conception' that the statue embodies and its dilapidated state established the detached, humorous perspective that the writer maintains throughout the story.

4.4 Conclusion: characteristics of responsive reading

In conclusion, it needs to be emphasised that an interpretation of the beliefs and intentions of the writer as these are expressed in the selection of words and phrases, and an understanding of what these presuppose and what they imply, is a prerequisite to intelligent reading. It is of much importance in the interpretation of newspapers and other documents in which an inexplicit point of view is presented or a view of life assumed, as is the case in the majority of the editorials that pupils would be exposed to. The skills required for the sensitive interpretation of literature are not therefore skills that are, in some sense, confined to such interpretation. As the authors of the Bullock Report remarked:

To read intelligently is to read responsively; it is to ask questions of the text and to use one's own framework of experience in interpreting it. In working his way through a book the reader imparts, projects, anticipates, speculates on alternative outcomes; and nowhere is this process more active than in a work of imaginative literature.[1]

In writing about the teaching of English in the secondary school, Holbrook[2] made a similar point more forcibly in

---

[1] DES, *A Language for Life*, HMSO, 1975.
[2] Holbrook D., *English for Maturity*, Cambridge University Press, 1961.

asserting that 'children have a hunger for information about human life' and that in response to the question 'What will adult life be like?' they must be given answers 'in felt terms, in fantasy, through the hands of a sensitive and responsive artist'. Not to do this, he suggested, would be to betray them into a habit of reading which will 'merely open them to those predators, in Fleet Street, the advertising world, and commercial publishers who have exploited the growth of literacy'. Whether or not one agrees with this passionate assertion, it is undeniable that intelligent reading involves *both* an *imaginative* and *thoughtful* response to the words on the page and the writer's intentions in assembling them.

Annex 4.1
The performance of secondary pupils on five reading tests

Pupils' performance on five reading tests at three levels of attainment (top 20 per cent, mid 60 per cent and bottom 20 per cent).

The Wedge-tailed Eagle

1. Where does the incident described take place?

	MEAN	LOWER	MID	UPPER
BOYS	90	79	91	100
GIRLS	87	74	88	94

2. From the first five paragraphs find and write down a word or phrase that shows:

(a) the great height of the eagle in the sky

	MEAN	LOWER	MID	UPPER
BOYS	67	40	71	88
GIRLS	70	39	71	94

3. (b) the eagle's unhurried movement

	MEAN	LOWER	MID	UPPER
BOYS	71	43	74	93
GIRLS	80	54	81	96

4. (c) the eagle's size

	MEAN	LOWER	MID	UPPER
BOYS	82	60	87	93
GIRLS	81	67	81	94

5. (d) that the eagle is noble or majestic

	MEAN	LOWER	MID	UPPER
BOYS	58	42	56	83
GIRLS	71	46	72	89

6. (e) that the eagle regards the aeroplane as inferior

	MEAN	LOWER	MID	UPPER
BOYS	54	17	56	95
GIRLS	63	21	62	100

7. Write down the way in which the eagle is compared to the aircraft.

	MEAN	LOWER	MID	UPPER
BOYS	49	30	50	68
GIRLS	55	26	54	83

8. After the opening paragraphs the pilots and the farmer are introduced. They have different views about the eagle.

(a) What is the farmer's attitude to the eagle?

	MEAN	LOWER	MID	UPPER
BOYS	63	36	64	93
GIRLS	59	28	56	96

9. (b) How do the pilots feel about the eagle?

	MEAN	LOWER	MID	UPPER
BOYS	61	23	67	93
GIRLS	68	44	67	92

10. The pilots develop a plan to kill the eagle (Page 2). Do they see this as a hunt or a contest?

	MEAN	LOWER	MID	UPPER
BOYS	82	59	87	98
GIRLS	90	80	90	98

11. Does the author give the impression that the pilots are cruel?

	MEAN	LOWER	MID	UPPER
BOYS	71	47	72	98
GIRLS	74	62	69	96

12. On Page 3 the pilots search for the eagle. The author uses certain images to help build up the impression of a duel or a fight to the death.

Write down one of these phrases:

	MEAN	LOWER	MID	UPPER
BOYS	44	17	44	76
GIRLS	37	13	33	72

13. At first in the 'duel' between the eagle and the planes the bird seems to be winning. What is the 'first sign of victory' (Page 6) that the pilots see?

	MEAN	LOWER	MID	UPPER
BOYS	63	38	65	86
GIRLS	73	41	75	94

14. As the bird falls from the sky, why can't the pilot bear to watch 'the last few feet of its descent'? (Page 6)

	MEAN	LOWER	MID	UPPER
BOYS	37	15	37	67
GIRLS	44	15	42	70

15. The pilots bury the eagle silently and avoid the farmer (Page 7). We have to guess their feelings from what they do. What do you think they are feeling at this point in the story?

	MEAN	LOWER	MID	UPPER
BOYS	78	49	83	98
GIRLS	82	72	79	100

16. In describing the way the pilots reacted, why does the writer refer to 'the misery of their achievement'? (Page 7).

	MEAN	LOWER	MID	UPPER
BOYS	67	26	75	93
GIRLS	83	44	88	100

17. What is similar about the beginning and end of the story?

	MEAN	LOWER	MID	UPPER
BOYS	60	23	64	98
GIRLS	80	54	81	100

18. Why do you think the author ended the story this way?

	MEAN	LOWER	MID	UPPER
BOYS	34	9	33	67
GIRLS	51	10	48	94

19. This story takes place in 1941, during the second world war. In what ways to some of the attitudes and events in the story reflect that period of time?

	MEAN	LOWER	MID	UPPER
BOYS	38	13	34	83
GIRLS	37	13	32	72

20. Did you find this story interesting? Explain why or why not.

	MEAN	LOWER	MID	UPPER
BOYS	70	43	71	98
GIRLS	77	67	74	96

The Landlady

1. Why is Billy alone in Bath?

	MEAN	LOWER	MID	UPPER
BOYS	57	29	59	87
GIRLS	67	26	71	91

2. What is Billy's impression of the room he sees through the window?

	MEAN	LOWER	MID	UPPER
BOYS	80	47	87	97
GIRLS	88	49	94	100

3. Billy's eye is caught and held by the 'Bed and Breakfast' notice. What does he do next?

	MEAN	LOWER	MID	UPPER
BOYS	88	78	89	97
GIRLS	91	63	95	100

4. In several parts of the story the writer described the situation in words that Billy might have used if he was giving the account.

Giving an example of such a description (a phrase or sentence) from page 1 or page 2 of the story.

	MEAN	LOWER	MID	UPPER
BOYS	40	12	37	82
GIRLS	46	14	44	81

5. Is there anything strange, up to the end of page 6, that the reader might notice, but that Billy doesn't?

	MEAN	LOWER	MID	UPPER
BOYS	51	12	56	82
GIRLS	69	26	70	100

6. What puzzles Billy about the former lodgers at the house?

	MEAN	LOWER	MID	UPPER
BOYS	76	33	87	100
GIRLS	89	51	95	100

7. On page 9, Billy says:
'Christopher Mulholland . . . wasn't that the name of the Eton schoolboy who was on a walking tour through the West Country, and then all of a sudden . . .'

How would Billy have finished this sentence if he had not been interrupted?

	MEAN	LOWER	MID	UPPER
BOYS	71	31	79	95
GIRLS	78	40	81	100

8. On page 8, the landlady came 'sailing into the room with a large silver tea tray in her hands. She was holding it well out in front of her, and rather high up, as though the tray were a pair of reins on a frisky horse.'

On page 10, Billy catches a whiff of a peculiar smell:

'pickled walnuts? New leather? Or was it the corridors of a hospital?'

On page 12, Billy found 'The tea tasted faintly of bitter almonds and he didn't much care for it.'

Can you suggest what might link these three incidents?

	MEAN	LOWER	MID	UPPER
BOYS	44	16	42	85
GIRLS	55	14	56	83

9. By pages 10 and 11, Billy seems to be getting a little uneasy. What things, in particular, are worrying him?

	MEAN	LOWER	MID	UPPER
BOYS	56	22	60	87
GIRLS	68	23	69	100

10. The landlady is described as having a 'warm, welcoming smile' and a round, pink face and very gentle blue eyes.

Can you find any description of her hands, face or way of moving, that implies something more sinister about her? If so, write it here.

	MEAN	LOWER	MID	UPPER
BOYS	55	8	62	92
GIRLS	71	34	72	98

11.

	AGREE	DISAGREE
'The author slowly builds up a sinister atmosphere.'	1	2

	MEAN	LOWER	MID	UPPER
BOYS	87	71	89	97
GIRLS	88	63	90	100

12. 'Billy doesn't interpret events in the same way that the reader does.'

	MEAN	LOWER	MID	UPPER
BOYS	67	37	73	87
GIRLS	69	23	73	95

13. 'The reader of the story can understand what is happening more clearly than Billy.'

	MEAN	LOWER	MID	UPPER
BOYS	73	49	75	97
GIRLS	81	57	84	93

14. 'Billy clearly has an overactive imagination.'

	MEAN	LOWER	MID	UPPER
BOYS	78	45	85	100
GIRLS	85	46	91	100

15. 'The landlady is a kind and generous soul.'

	MEAN	LOWER	MID	UPPER
BOYS	46	29	44	77
GIRLS	57	46	50	86

The Tunnel

1. Have Jerry and his mother stayed at that place before?

	MEAN	LOWER	MID	UPPER
BOYS	95	81	97	100
GIRLS	95	78	99	100

2. Which beach did they go to before?

	MEAN	LOWER	MID	UPPER
BOYS	40	14	42	65
GIRLS	46	14	48	70

3. Why are Jerry and his mother alone?

	MEAN	LOWER	MID	UPPER
BOYS	78	44	84	95
GIRLS	83	64	85	96

4. From the 'turning in the path' the beach and the bay can be seen. What are the differences between them?

	MEAN	LOWER	MID	UPPER
BOYS	47	14	48	81
GIRLS	45	16	45	70

5. The writer deliberately contrasts the beach and the bay in the story. What do they represent to the boy?

	MEAN	LOWER	MID	UPPER
BOYS	42	0	43	87
GIRLS	53	8	55	91

6. When Jerry says he would like to go and have a look at the rocks his mother says 'of course'. Does she really want him to go?

	MEAN	LOWER	MID	UPPER
BOYS	85	61	89	95
GIRLS	94	82	96	98

7. From the first two pages what impression do you get of the relationship between Jerry and his mother?

	MEAN	LOWER	MID	UPPER
BOYS	70	35	76	92
GIRLS	73	50	76	85

8. Swimming out in the bay Jerry floats for a while and looks for his mother. Why do you think he does this?

	MEAN	LOWER	MID	UPPER
BOYS	67	33	72	87
GIRLS	77	44	83	94

9. Jerry sees the boys swimming from the rocks. Why, do you think, does he 'crave to be with them'?

	MEAN	LOWER	MID	UPPER
BOYS	71	49	72	92
GIRLS	73	38	80	85

10. How do they react to him?

(a) at first

	MEAN	LOWER	MID	UPPER
BOYS	57	23	61	81
GIRLS	65	36	67	87

(b) later

	MEAN	LOWER	MID	UPPER
BOYS	48	16	49	81
GIRLS	52	24	52	80

11. Why does Jerry start splashing and kicking in the water?

	MEAN	LOWER	MID	UPPER
BOYS	41	19	42	65
GIRLS	36	24	37	46

12. In what way is the reaction of the boys to his clowning similar to the reaction of his mother?

	MEAN	LOWER	MID	UPPER
BOYS	61	21	67	87
GIRLS	67	26	71	93

13. Once Jerry has got his goggles and found the entrance to the tunnel, what does he have to practise?

	MEAN	LOWER	MID	UPPER
BOYS	83	37	92	100
GIRLS	78	44	82	100

14. What problems does he face?

	MEAN	LOWER	MID	UPPER
BOYS	81	44	87	100
GIRLS	79	42	85	100

15. Jerry is frightened of going through the tunnel but he decides to go. Why, do you think, does he feel 'if he did not do it now he never would'?

	MEAN	LOWER	MID	UPPER
BOYS	49	14	50	87
GIRLS	56	28	57	78

16. When he eventually emerges he goes back to the villa where he meets his mother. Why doesn't he tell her what he has done?

	MEAN	LOWER	MID	UPPER
BOYS	38	9	39	70
GIRLS	53	16	52	91

17. Why do you think the author of the story ends by saying 'it was no longer of the least importance to go to the bay'?

	MEAN	LOWER	MID	UPPER
BOYS	74	42	79	95
GIRLS	73	52	76	87

18. Jerry achieved what he set out to do – to swim through the underwater tunnel. What else has he achieved or learnt from the experience?

	MEAN	LOWER	MID	UPPER
BOYS	68	28	72	100
GIRLS	64	26	66	94

19. What did you think about this story? Did you find it interesting and/or enjoyable? Please explain why or why not.

	MEAN	LOWER	MID	UPPER
BOYS	36	9	37	65
GIRLS	41	8	38	78

A Horse and Two Goats

1. What is the name of the village where the story takes place?

	MEAN	LOWER	MID	UPPER
BOYS	98	94	98	100
GIRLS	99	95	100	100

2. The statues of the horse and rider have been changed by the 'ravages of sun and rain'. How have the beads worn by the warrior changed?

	MEAN	LOWER	MID	UPPER
BOYS	78	56	80	96
GIRLS	80	36	86	98

3. The statue of the horse now looks mottled. What was its original colour?

	MEAN	LOWER	MID	UPPER
BOYS	87	77	87	100
GIRLS	90	74	92	98

4. Some people who live in the village point to the statues as proof that the village is special. But do you think most people who live there would think this? Explain why or why not.

	MEAN	LOWER	MID	UPPER
BOYS	48	12	50	86
GIRLS	67	36	69	93

5. This story opens with a rather long passage of description; why do you think the author introduces the story in this way?

	MEAN	LOWER	MID	UPPER
BOYS	80	56	85	96
GIRLS	86	69	87	100

6. Why does the American tourist decide to stop at this tiny village?

	MEAN	LOWER	MID	UPPER
BOYS	82	44	93	96
GIRLS	82	51	87	95

7. What makes you think that the American tourist has learnt very little about the country he is visiting?

	MEAN	LOWER	MID	UPPER
BOYS	35	12	33	68
GIRLS	42	5	43	71

8. The two men in the story have difficulty in communicating with each other because they speak different languages. What other serious problems of communication do they seem to have?

	MEAN	LOWER	MID	UPPER
BOYS	57	21	58	98
GIRLS	67	33	67	95

9. On page 3 the old man's attention is drawn to the horse. What sort of meaning does the horse have for him?

	MEAN	LOWER	MID	UPPER
BOYS	69	29	76	96
GIRLS	73	39	75	95

10. On page 4 the old man tells the American about the religious importance of the horse and how it fits into the legends of the Hindu gods. What is the American talking about at this time?

	MEAN	LOWER	MID	UPPER
BOYS	83	52	91	98
GIRLS	85	44	92	100

11. Why does the old man decide that the American is a good man? (page 5)

	MEAN	LOWER	MID	UPPER
BOYS	68	27	76	93
GIRLS	75	44	79	93

12. Why does the old man laugh when the American first flourishes the hundred-rupee note? (page 6)

	MEAN	LOWER	MID	UPPER
BOYS	78	46	84	100
GIRLS	84	46	90	100

13. Why does the American show an interest in the old man's goats?

	MEAN	LOWER	MID	UPPER
BOYS	64	14	73	98
GIRLS	78	14	81	100

14. The old man needed 20 rupees to fulfil his dream of a lifetime. He managed to get 120. Did he deliberately cheat the tourist?

	MEAN	LOWER	MID	UPPER
BOYS	74	35	83	98
GIRLS	77	51	78	95

15. Is there any evidence that the old man was trying to cheat the red-faced tourist?

	MEAN	LOWER	MID	UPPER
BOYS	64	39	69	80
GIRLS	64	36	67	83

16. The horse had a different value for the tourist and the old man. How did the tourist value it?

	MEAN	LOWER	MID	UPPER
BOYS	52	17	55	82
GIRLS	52	7	55	85

17. Why did the old man value it?

	MEAN	LOWER	MID	UPPER
BOYS	62	17	68	98
GIRLS	69	10	77	93

18. Is there anything written in the story which tells whether or not the tourist removed the statue? (Look at the first paragraph closely).

	MEAN	LOWER	MID	UPPER
BOYS	19	4	13	55
GIRLS	28	3	25	66

19. The first and last paragraphs in the story have something in common. What is it?

	MEAN	LOWER	MID	UPPER
BOYS	52	21	51	89
GIRLS	60	33	57	98

20. This story says quite a lot about different ways of looking at the world and some of the resulting problems of communication. Does this aspect of the story relate to or remind you of anything in your own life or experience?

	MEAN	LOWER	MID	UPPER
BOYS	42	12	45	71
GIRLS	60	26	61	93

Clones

1. From what is written what did you learn about the properties of the nucleus of a living cell (human and non-human)?

	MEAN	LOWER	MID	UPPER
BOYS	25	0	23	69
GIRLS	24	2	23	44

2. What two techniques could be use to clone human beings?

A.

	MEAN	LOWER	MID	UPPER
BOYS	55	16	61	88
GIRLS	59	16	59	88

B.

	MEAN	LOWER	MID	UPPER
BOYS	82	64	85	95
GIRLS	79	52	83	91

3. Why do you think the phrase 'genetic engineering' is used to refer to the processes that are described?

	MEAN	LOWER	MID	UPPER
BOYS	43	9	45	83
GIRLS	38	4	30	82

4. From what is written do you think that the writer believes that scientists should be completely free to carry out experiments involving human cloning? Please give a reason for your answer.

	MEAN	LOWER	MID	UPPER
BOYS	39	3	41	83
GIRLS	47	10	42	90

5. Does the writer of the article you have just read think that cloning of the type shown in the cartoon will be possible in the future? Give reasons for your answer.

	MEAN	LOWER	MID	UPPER
BOYS	45	19	46	79
GIRLS	47	18	47	69

6. In what room and building, in what city, in what season and in what year was the tour taking place?

	MEAN	LOWER	MID	UPPER
BOYS	73	52	74	100
GIRLS	73	36	75	97

	MEAN	LOWER	MID	UPPER
BOYS	78	50	83	98
GIRLS	84	62	86	94

	MEAN	LOWER	MID	UPPER
BOYS	53	40	55	64
GIRLS	54	50	53	57

	MEAN	LOWER	MID	UPPER
BOYS	44	12	44	88
GIRLS	41	12	37	74

7. Who was leading the tour and who was being led?

	MEAN	LOWER	MID	UPPER
BOYS	88	64	93	100
GIRLS	94	74	97	99

	MEAN	LOWER	MID	UPPER
BOYS	84	52	93	98
GIRLS	91	68	95	99

8. Does the author *really* think that the Director is a 'great man'? Give a reason for your answer.

	MEAN	LOWER	MID	UPPER
BOYS	17	2	13	52
GIRLS	26	0	22	56

	MEAN	LOWER	MID	UPPER
BOYS	30	9	36	38
GIRLS	31	20	31	38

9. In the second paragraph of the passage there is a description of the fertilizing room. In describing the room, the writer also reveals the feelings the room arouses in him and his attitude to the work being done.

Do you get the impression that the writer approves of what is being done? (Give a reason for your answer.)

	MEAN	LOWER	MID	UPPER
BOYS	61	19	67	100
GIRLS	66	20	68	99

10. List three words or phrases used that help to make clear the author's feelings about the work being done.

	MEAN	LOWER	MID	UPPER
BOYS	35	2	37	74
GIRLS	40	4	35	78

	MEAN	LOWER	MID	UPPER
BOYS	31	3	31	71
GIRLS	38	4	32	79

	MEAN	LOWER	MID	UPPER
BOYS	28	0	25	76
GIRLS	32	4	25	69

11. The purpose of the tour is to give the students a general idea of the processes involved in cloning. 'For some sort of general idea they must have, if they were to do their work intelligently – though as little of one, if they were to be good and happy members of society, as possible. *For particulars, as everyone knows, make for virtue and happiness; generalities are intellectually necessary evils.* Not philosophers but fretsawyers and stamp collectors compose the backbone of society.'

	MEAN	LOWER	MID	UPPER
BOYS	11	2	4	48
GIRLS	12	2	8	31

12. Whose point of view is presented in the passage quoted above? The author? The Director? The students? Sensible people in general?

	MEAN	LOWER	MID	UPPER
BOYS	37	19	37	62
GIRLS	42	26	41	56

13. Why do you think that stamp collectors would be preferred to philosophers by those in control of the society described.

	MEAN	LOWER	MID	UPPER
BOYS	18	0	12	67
GIRLS	23	2	14	60

14. Do you agree that making ninety-six human beings grow where only one grew before is 'a prodigious improvement on nature'? ('prodigious' means 'great'.)

	MEAN	LOWER	MID	UPPER
BOYS	54	19	59	86
GIRLS	65	24	67	88

15. Do you think that this statement reflects the view of the Director or the author or both? (Give a reason for your answer.)

	MEAN	LOWER	MID	UPPER
BOYS	39	2	43	76
GIRLS	46	10	39	90

16. 'One of the students was fool enough to ask where the advantage lay' (of obtaining scores of embryos from the same egg). Does the writer think that the question asked was a foolish one? (Give a reason for your answer.)

	MEAN	LOWER	MID	UPPER
BOYS	35	10	33	79
GIRLS	47	24	37	88

17. The Director says 'if we could bokanovskify indefinitely, the whole problem would be solved'. What problem do you think he is referring to?

	MEAN	LOWER	MID	UPPER
BOYS	21	0	16	67
GIRLS	24	4	13	66

18. Now that you have read the passage, do you think that the writer (who wrote in 1932) was in favour of applying 'the principle of mass production' to the production of embryos? (Was he strongly in favour of it, mildly in favour of it, not too concerned one way of the other, mildly opposed to it or strongly opposed to it?)

	MEAN	LOWER	MID	UPPER
BOYS	47	16	46	93
GIRLS	54	24	49	88

5

Speaking and listening at age 11

Synopsis

The chapter opens by giving background information on the oracy surveys at both ages. Then the tasks used to assess speaking and listening at age 11 in 1983 are described.

The bulk of the chapter consists of detailed discussions of performance on four tasks, based on the results of analytic marking. In each case the discussion is illustrated by transcripts of three performances, one each from the lower, middle and upper parts of the range.

The final section of the chapter puts forward a number of conclusions drawn from the age 11 oracy surveys of both 1982 and 1983. The most important of these are:

- national monitoring of performance in speaking and listening at age 11 by the methods adopted is *feasible*

- satisfactory levels of *reliability* (inter-marker agreement) were achieved

- the instruments used in these surveys represent a significant advance in the testing of spoken language, particularly in terms of their communicative *validity*

- almost all 11-year-olds can modify their speaking strategies appropriately in accordance with the demands of different tasks and different audiences

- the level of performance varies according to the demands of different tasks: in particular, scores tended to be low on discursive tasks

- some of the features of successful performance are task-specific, especially those relating to content

- this implies that all those who assess children's language need substantial appropriate training.

5.1 Outline of Chapters 5 and 6

The structure of the two chapters on oracy is, briefly, as follows:

Chapter 5

- some background information relevant to the oracy surveys at both ages

- descriptions of the 1983 age 11 oracy tasks and of the general impression scores on them

- detailed discussions of performance on four age 11 oracy tasks, based on analytic marking results

- some conclusions about the age 11 oracy surveys.

Chapter 6

- descriptions of the 1983 age 15 oracy tasks and of the general impression scores on them

- detailed discussions of performance on three age 15 oracy tasks, based on analytic marking results

- comparisons of performance on oracy tasks

  (a) between boys and girls
  (b) between 1982 and 1983
  (c) between ages 11 and 15

- some conclusions about the age 15 oracy surveys.

5.2 Administration of the surveys

Oracy was monitored for the first time, at both age levels, in 1982. Details of those surveys are given in the two previous reports.[1] Small administrative changes were made between the 1982 and 1983 surveys.

Firstly, the proportion of pupils tested was increased from 10 per cent to 15 per cent of the main sample, i.e. from about 900 to about 1,200 pupils.

Secondly, the 1983 oracy surveys took place before the main surveys of reading and writing so that all the pupils in the oracy sample could be included in the main surveys.

Thirdly, more data were collected by increasing the number of tasks administered to each pair of pupils and by increasing the number of pairs tested each day from four to five.

The overall effect of these changes was that, in the 1983 surveys, a larger corpus of oracy data was gathered, and that, for *all* the pupils in the oracy samples, data were

---

[1] *Language Performance in Schools: 1982 Primary Survey Report.* London: DES, 1984.
Language Performance in Schools: 1982 Secondary Survey Report. London: DES, 1984.

available not just on oracy but also on their performance in reading and writing.

Despite these changes in the administration of the surveys, the stages and forms of assessment remained unaltered. These may be summarised as in Figure 5.1.

Figure 5.1 *Stages and forms of assessment used in 1983 oracy surveys*

On-the spot assessment Stage 1	Holistic scoring Stage 2
Overall impression (Scale 1–7)	Overall impression marking (Scale 1–7)
Orientation to listener (Scale 1–5)	Panels of 12–20 teachers
	All taped records
	Double-marking of taped records

Analytic scoring
Stage 3
(a) Propositional/semantic content
(b) Sequential structure
(c) Lexico-grammatical features (syntax, lexis)
(d) Performance features (self-correction/hesitation, tempo, etc.)
Scale 1–5, 1–3
Panels of 8–10 teachers
Random sub-samples of taped records
Double-marking of taped records

5.3 Description and categorisation of the 1983 primary oracy tasks

For purposes of comparison across years, it is usual in our surveys for a number of tasks from one year to be used again in subsequent years. Accordingly, of the seven primary oracy tasks used in 1982, two (**Pictures** and **Spiders**) were used again in 1983. In addition, there were six new tasks. The eight tasks used in 1983 will now be described with an indication of their communicative purpose and a suggested categorisation.

A. Task involving description of an object for identification

The **Bridges** task had been devised for the 1982 secondary oracy survey, was used in the 1983 primary survey to allow cross-age comparison, and was used again in the 1983 secondary survey (see Chapter 6).

The task required one pupil to describe pictured objects for the other pupil in the pair to identify. The second pupil had black-and-white pictures of six single-span metal bridges (see illustration 5.1): the other pupil had only pictures 5 and 2, unnumbered, and the pair faced each other across a small screen so that neither could see the other's pictures. The pupil with two pictures described each of them in turn, and the other pupil was then asked to identify both bridges from the full set. The describer was assessed separately on each bridge. The identifications made by the listeners were noted, but only for statistical purposes: the listeners were not assessed.

B. Task involving relaying of information

The task known as **Spiders** had also been used in the 1982 primary survey and it had formed the second part of a task with the same name used in the 1982 secondary survey.

Two pupils listened to a tape recording of how a garden spider builds her web, and were asked to arrange six diagrams (see Illustration 5.2) to correspond to the order of the six stages of the process. They then listened to the recording again. Then, using the diagrams, one pupil explained the process to two other pupils, who had not heard the tape. This pupil's description of the process was assessed.

C. Tasks involving narrative

Three tasks (**Book Club, Transition** and **Pictures**) fell into this category.

The **Book Club** task was in two parts. First, each pupil in a pair was given a sheet depicting book covers (see Illustration 5.3) and asked to choose the books they would and would not like to read, and to give reasons for their choices. (The same selection of book covers was used in the survey of attitudes to reading.)

Then, the pupils were asked to recall a story they had just read, or one that had been read to them, and to re-tell the story to the assessor. The pupils were assessed on their recounting of the story.

Transition had three stages. In the first, two pupils listened to a tape recording of three children's recollections of their first day at school. They were asked a few questions about what they had heard.

Then each pupil was asked to recall his/her own first experience of school, and was assessed on this.

Finally, each pupil was asked to predict the changes they might expect to encounter on transferring to their next school, and to describe their feelings about the transition: again, each pupil was assessed.

The **Pictures** task had also been used in the 1982 primary survey. The two pupils sat facing each other across the same kind of low screen as that used in **Bridges**. In front of each pupil were two pictures from the four shown in Illustration 5.4. Each pupil then described his/her two pictures to the other, in this order: first pupil – Pit, Apple; second pupil – Bottle, Dog.

The pictures were then removed from the stand, and the pupils were asked to collaborate to put the pictures into a sequence and to make up a story based on this sequence. One pupil was asked to relate this story to the assessor.

The pupils then chose a new sequence for the pictures, and the second pupil related the new story to two other pupils.

Both pupils were assessed on their description of the pictures and on their story narration.

D. Tasks involving discussion between pupils

The **Sleuth** task had two parts and involved two pairs of pupils, who had the task of solving a crime. In the first part, each pair was asked to choose a suspect to investigate, from a set of four.

Each pair was asked to create a scenario to fit their suspect, and given several headings as guidelines (for the materials see Illustration 5.5). On completing these notes, one pupil from each pair was asked to tell the others what information they had discovered about their suspect.

Then the two pairs were asked to compare and discuss the information on the two suspects in order to decide which was most likely to have committed the crime. The pupils were assessed individually on their contributions to each part of the task.

The **Island** task also had two parts. In the description component, each of two pupils was given pictorial and written information about one of two fictitious plants, the Kava and the Bulo (see Illustration 5.6). They were asked to read the information, to make simple notes, and then to tell each other what they had learned about the plants and their suitability for growing as crops on an imaginary island, given certain climatic and other conditions. Each pupil was assessed on conveying the appropriate information.

In a further discussion stage, the pupils were asked to discuss the merits of both plants, and to decide which would be better to cultivate. Again the pupils were assessed, separately, on their contribution to the discussion.

E. Task involving collaborative speculation

This form of talk was tapped in one of the four components of the **Tracks** task. First, the assessor explained to one pupil how to perform a simple experiment (see Illustration 5.7 for the materials). This pupil then instructed his/her partner in performing the experiment, and was assessed on the relaying of these instructions. These instructions, represented in the diagrams in Illustration 5.7, consisted of six steps:

1. putting four green marbles in the track
2. dropping one glass marble down the track
3. dropping one steel ball down the track
4. positioning two glass marbles at the top of the track
5. dropping two glass marbles down the track
6. dropping two steel balls down the track

The second pupil was then asked to describe to the assessor what had been observed during the experiment and was assessed on the description.

In part 3 of the task both pupils were asked to discuss possible reasons for the effects they had observed. At the

Illustration 5.1 Bridges *pictures*

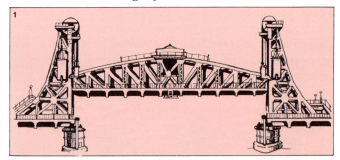
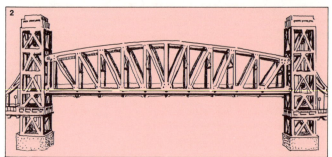
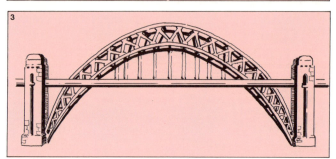

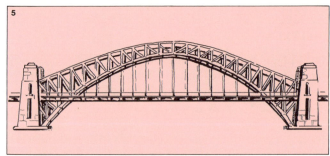

end of the discussion one pupil was asked to tell the assessor the reasons they had thought of to explain what had happened, and this report was assessed.

Finally (part 4), the other pupil was asked to relate all the details of the experiment to two other pupils and was assessed on the account.

Illustration 5.2 Spiders *diagrams*

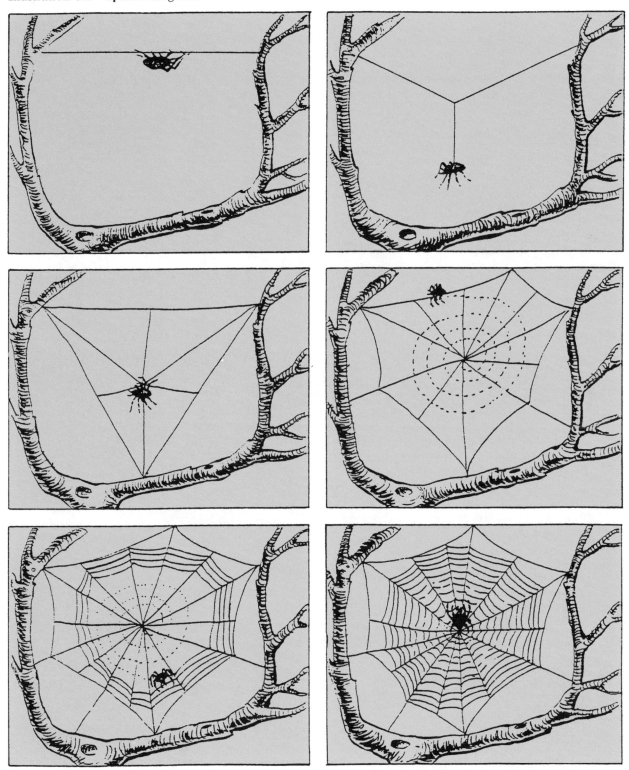

Illustration 5.3 Book Club *pictures*
(N.B. these materials were originally produced in colour.)

Illustration 5.4 *Pictures used in the **Pictures** task*
(N.B. these materials were originally produced in colour.)

Pit   Apple

Bottle   Dog

Illustration 5.5 Sleuth *materials*

Pupil No: _____   Suspect: _____   Assessor No: _____

SKILL ; _____

_____

MOTIVE _____
(Why)

TIME _____
(When)

METHOD _____
(How)

ACCOMPLICES _____
(Who)

MISTAKES _____

_____

ALIBI _____
(Excuse)

_____

_____

Illustration 5.6 Island *materials*
(These materials were originally produced in colour.)

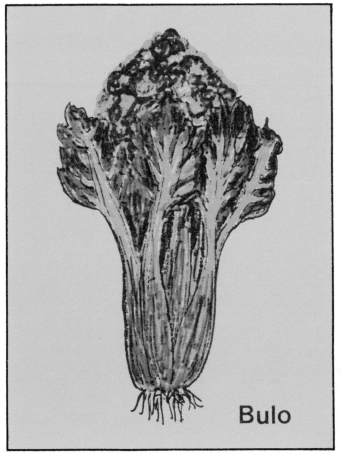

Bulo

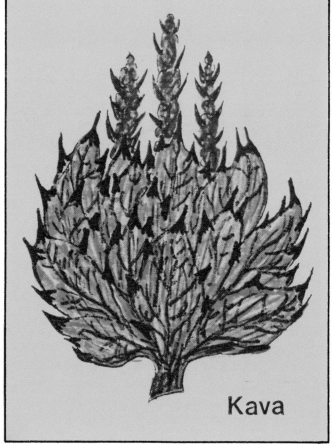

Kava

Illustration 5.6   Island *materials* (cont.) – (originally produced in colour)

The soil has to be dug well, to grow the Kava plant.

A lot of compost has to be added to the soil to feed the plants.

Once the plants have started to grow, they need very little water.

The plants grow stronger if the weeds are not allowed to flourish.

The Kavas are resistant to disease and pests.

the kava

When ripe the Kavas are difficult to harvest, as the leaves are very prickly.

They need a lot of preparation to cook them.

They are extremely tasty vegetables.

The seeds are very cheap.

The seeds have to be planted every year.

PLANTING
1980 KAVA BULO
1981 KAVA
1982 KAVA BULO
1983 KAVA
1984 KAVA BULO
1985 KAVA
1986 KAVA BULO

KAVA SEED ON SPECIAL OFFER

To grow the Bulo no digging is needed.

The seedlings thrive on poor soil and do not need any compost.

The plants need to be watered at least twice every day.

The growth of the plants is not affected by weeds.

The plants are not very strong and are often attacked by pests.

the bulo

Ripe Bulos are easy to harvest.

They need very little preparation for cooking.

When cooked they are rather tasteless.

The seeds are expensive.

The plants are biennial and only have to be planted every other year.

PLANTING
1980 KAVA BULO
1981 KAVA
1982 KAVA BULO
1983 KAVA
1984 KAVO BULO
1985 KAVA
1986 KAVA BULO

BULO SEED NEW INCREASE IN PRICE

Illustration 5.7   Tracks *experiment*

Step 1

Step 2

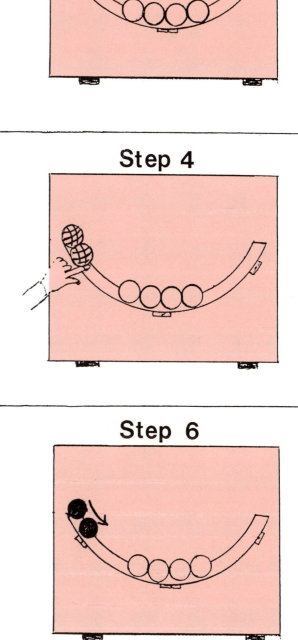

Step 3

Step 4

Step 5

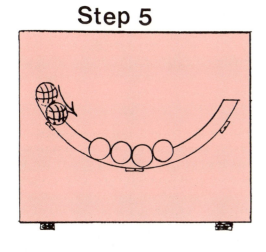

Step 6

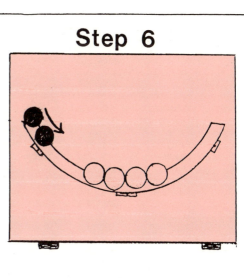

5.4 Results from impression-marking

A summary of the results for all eight of the primary oracy tasks is given in Table 5.1. The following data are reported for each task:

1. The number of pupils who attempted it.

2. The mean overall impression mark on the rising 1–7 scale used. This mean score is based on the two sets of impression marks given for each task by the second markers.

3. The mean scores, derived in the same way, for boys and girls, with an indication of any differences that were found to be statistically significant.

4. The mean score for orientation to listener, on the rising 1–5 scale used for this category. These scores are based on the marks given by the on-the-spot assessors.

In addition, for **Bridges** only, the percentage of correct identifications is shown.

The lowest overall mean scores were those for **Bridges** and the discussion component of **Sleuth**. The result for **Bridges** matches the finding at age 15 – see Chapter 6.

Table 5.1 *Summary of impression-marking results for 1983 primary oracy tasks*

Task		N	Impression marks (1–7 scale)			Orientation to listener (1–5 scale)
			Overall	Boys	Girls	
Bridges†	1	615	3.8	3.9*	3.7*	3.5
	2	615	3.8	4.0*	3.7*	3.4
Spiders	Relaying	228	4.3	4.2	4.3	3.4
Book Club	Story	942	4.4	4.4	4.4	4.0
Transition	Anecdote	1,332	4.3	4.2*	4.4*	3.9
	Prediction	1,332	4.1	4.0	4.1	4.0
Pictures	Description	470	4.3	4.3	4.3	3.9
	Story	461	4.5	4.4	4.6	3.8
Sleuth	Relaying	518	4.6	4.5	4.8	3.5
	Discussion	446	3.8	3.9	3.8	3.5
Island	Description	455	4.4	4.5	4.4	3.6
	Discussion	449	4.4	4.5*	4.3*	3.8
Tracks	Instructions	260	4.8	4.9	4.7	4.2
	Observation	221	4.1	4.2*	3.7	4.0
	Hypothesis	234	4.4	4.6*	3.9*	4.1
	Retelling	228	4.7	4.9*	4.5*	4.1

Key * Statistically significant difference in performance between boys and girls: these differences will be discussed towards the end of Chapter 6.

† the correct identification rates for **Bridges** were:
first bridge (no. 5) – 52%
second bridge (no. 2) – 69%

Note: Where the numbers of pupils differ between different components of the same task, the reason is that some recordings were not available for second-marking.

5.5 Detailed commentary on selected tasks

The four following sections analyse in greater depth pupils' performances on parts of three of the 1983 tasks (**Pictures**, stories, **Island** – both relaying and discussion, and **Tracks**, hypothesis), plus one 1982 task (**Jobs**). In each case the commentary will draw on the results of analytic marking, and will be illustrated by three transcripts: these will represent low, average and high performance.

A general note on the analytic assessment categories

The analytic assessment framework is designed to give a more detailed understanding of variations in spoken language performance than can be obtained from general impression marking. The categories used in the analytic marking scheme include:

– overall organisation (sequential structure)

– lexico-grammatical features

– performance features

– various task-specific categories covering meaning or propositional features.

Several of these categories contain further sub-categories, which will be discussed in detail below with respect to particular tasks.

In the surveys, a sub-sample of tapes of each task was double-marked by a panel of 6–8 markers, using a rising 1–5 scale for each category and sub-category, with the exception of 'performance features', where a rising 1–3 scale was employed at age 11.

Extended treatments of the analytic framework can be found in the short report on the Assessment Framework,[1] and in the 1982 Primary Survey Report.[2]

5.6 Task 1: Pictures – stories

Objectives of the task

This task, which was used in both 1982 and 1983, was designed to assess pupils' use of narrative forms, and their ability to imaginatively construct a story line out of a series of discrete events. In this latter respect the task contrasts with another narrative task (**King Lion**) administered in the 1982 survey, where pupils were asked to re-tell a story they had listened to on tape, and with the two other tasks involving narrative (**Transition, Book Club**) in the 1983 survey.

---

[1] Gorman, T. P. *Framework for the Assessment of Language.* London: DES, 1986.

[2] *Language Performance in Schools: 1982 Primary Survey Report.* London: DES, 1984.

Comments on performance: analytic assessment

The analytic categories applied in this task were:

Category	Sub-categories
1. STORY SEMANTICS	(i) Complexity of episodes
	(ii) Characterisation and story elaboration
	} Task-specific
2. OVERALL ORGANISATION (SEQUENTIAL STRUCTURE)	
3. LEXICO-GRAMMATICAL FEATURES	{ (i) Lexical selection
	(ii) Syntax
4. PERFORMANCE FEATURES	{ (i) Hesitation/self-correction
	(ii) Tempo and pacing
	(iii) Verbal assertiveness

In terms of performance on this particular task, these categories indicate that, in order to perform well, pupils must be able to:

transform the material shown in each picture into a series of 'episodes' ('Complexity of episodes');

link these together to form elements of a 'plot', in accordance with traditional principles of narrative organisation ('Overall organisation');

incorporate narrative features such as characterisation, motivation, and feelings ('Characterisation and story elaboration');

select words which appropriately convey atmosphere, action and detail ('Lexical selection');

use well-formed grammatical structures appropriate for conveying the relationships of time, cause and consequence associated with story telling ('Syntax');

speak in a fluent and confident manner, at an appropriate tempo, avoiding undue hesitation or self-correction ('Performance features').

However, as we shall see overleaf, where examples of performance on this task are discussed in more detail, pupils' stories need not necessarily show a high degree of competence with respect to every analytic category, in order to be judged highly successful in overall terms. For instance a story which contains many imaginative features relating to Characterisation and story elaboration, and ingenious construction of individual episodes (Complexity of episodes), may be judged very successful (attaining a general impression mark of 7), even if the plot transitions from one picture to the next (Overall organisation) are rather pedestrian and unimaginative.

The qualities of a 'highly successful performance', therefore, are not homogeneous: different examples may be judged successful on the basis of different strengths or qualities. However, it does appear that markers' overall judgements of success are influenced more strongly by aspects of performance relating to the *task-specific* and *overall organisation* categories than to the other analytic categories, considered independently. This perhaps is not surprising, since listeners tend to focus on the meaning and the message of talk, rather than on the 'nuts and bolts' of its construction, as conveyed through grammatical and lexical features.

Examples of performance

Three examples of performance on this task are discussed and compared below, in terms of the analytic categories outlined above, to show how the more successful attempts differ from the less successful ones. The first example represents a fairly poor attempt, the second exemplifies a performance typical of the mid-range, and the third represents a very successful attempt. The general impression mark assigned to each example, on a rising 1–7 scale, indicates in general terms the degree of success attained:

7 = a very good performance
4 = an average performance
2/1 = a fairly poor performance

Performance at the lower end of the range

Performance receiving a general impression mark of 1 or 2 would be considered fairly poor attempts. Relatively few pupils achieve such low ratings on this task: in the 1983 survey, for instance, only 3.5 per cent of the sample received ratings of 1 or 2.

Performances at this level are clearly inadequate with respect to many, if not all, of the analytic categories used. They often display inadequate overall structuring, for instance, and each episode is presented in a very brief and cursory way. Features relating to story elaboration are miminal or absent, and this is reflected in the words selected. Such performances are also frequently hesitant and tentative, with a high frequency of pauses or 'false-starts'. Overall therefore, it is clear that the pupil is having difficulties with most or all aspects of the task.

Example 1. Impression mark: 2

1. there's a little dog, and there's- and- they see the little-
2. um- little pup- a little (pause) and then when the- pup has gone-
3. they um- see an apple and they start eating (pause), an' -they
4. see a- um- (pause) bottle um- one of the um- snails go into it-
5. and- all the hedgehogs look around, and then they start making (um)
6. a- hole- (pause) to live in. And one go- and they start looking
7. around, and one goes in- in- um- in there to see if it's all right.

Comments

Comments

This attempt is poorly organised: the *opening* phase, for instance, fails to introduce the hedgehogs and snails adequately – referring to them on first mention as 'they' (1). There is no explicit *closing* phase, and the structure of the middle section is rudimentary: the animals simply 'see' (1,3,4,) the next event, or else 'look around' (5).

Each episode is outlined very briefly, in comparison with the elaborated episodes found in examples (3) (overleaf) and, to a lesser extent, (2).

Characterisation and story elaboration are almost entirely absent from the account. There is, for example, no detail about the animals' thoughts or reactions, and no attempt to create a sense of excitement, suspense or action. And, as the original recording of this example shows more clearly than the transcript, the pupil's speech is hesitant and tentative, with many false starts, pauses and self-corrections.

Performance at the mid-point of the range

An average performance would receive a general impression mark of 4 or 5. In terms of the detailed analytic assessment procedures, we would expect such a performance to be recognisably a 'story' – comprising a series of episodes related sequentially over time, and some attempt at characterisation and story elaboration. Typically, however, performances at this level are less accomplished in terms of the narrative features deployed, and they tend to provide a less elaborated account of individual episodes than the more successful attempts. Lexical choices are correspondingly less imaginative and evocative than those of the more accomplished stories.

Example 2. Impression mark: 4

1. there was three hedgehogs and three snails, walking along, and they
2. found- an apple which somebody- had chucked down so they all crowded
3. round- it and started smelling it (laughs). (pause) So they went away
4. 'cause they thought it didn't smell very nice. So they walked along
5. (pause) and saw this dog. So they all curled up so the dog couldn't
6. get them. (pause) And then (pause) they all walked off, and the
7. hedgehog fell down the hole. So they all crowded round, and they got
8. the hedgehog out. And then one snail- went off while the other one-
9. while the others were going- another way. An' he was playing around-
10. and he got stuck in a milk bottle so they all came round, and got him
11. out of the milk bottle.

This story provides an opening statement (1) which introduces the six characters, and provides some context for the action to follow. This, however, is fairly minimal (i.e. the animals are walking along). There is no explicit *closing* phase: the action simply comes to a halt with the termination of the last episode (11). The plot transitions in the middle section are fairly basic, consisting mainly of variations of the 'walking along' theme (e.g. 4,6), although the last link (between the 'pit' and 'bottle' pictures) is slightly more elaborate: i.e. one snail went off while the others were going another way (8–9).

The account of each individual episode is only slightly less 'skeletal' than in the previous example: this pupil does not explain, for example, how the hedgehog came to fall down the hole, nor how the other animals subsequently got it out. Similarly, there is no attempt to explain how the snail got out of the bottle. However, an account is given of how the apple came to be on the ground (2), there is a brief explanation of why the animals curled up (5–6), and a minimal account of how the snail ended up in the bottle (i.e. he was playing around (9)).

It is in relation to this category of characterisation and story elaboration that this story is most noticeably less successful than the following one. There is little attempt, for instance, to invest the animals with credible characters, so that we get very little idea of what they think and feel. The action is also fairly badly described, with little elaboration or sense of immediacy. As a result, this example appears less 'story-like' in its overall character. Also, the relative lack of characterisation and development of episodes is reflected in the words selected by this pupil. For example he uses few adjectives to inject descriptive detail or atmosphere into his rather sketchy account of events.

On the whole this pupil's use of syntax is appropriate to the nature of the task. However, his repetitive use of clauses beginning with 'so . . .' especially where a relationship of consequence does not seem to be indicated (e.g. 'so they walked along and saw this dog' (4–5)), strike the listener as stylistically inelegant. It should not be assumed, however, that repetitiveness of grammatical structures is *necessarily* associated with an inadequate command of stylistic features of talk. In contrast with certain kinds of writing task, where repetitiveness often indicates an immature command of stylistic conventions, spoken language characteristically contains more 'redundancy' in information content, and more repetition of items and structures.

Performance at the upper end of the range

Highly successful stories would receive a general impression mark in relation to the top two points of the scale: i.e. 6 or 7. When performance is further 'broken down' in terms of the analytic assessment categories, we would expect a highly successful attempt to be well-structured in terms of the organisation required of narratives, to include a series of well-constructed episodes relating to the individual pictures, and to contain narrative features which create a 'story-like' atmosphere – features which invest the animal protagonists with character or personality, provide 'atmospheric' detail, and give a sense of immediacy, excitement or action to the series of events related. We would expect that lexical and grammatical choices would be appropriate to these objectives, and that the 'delivery' of the story would be reasonably fluent and confident.

Example 3. Impression mark: 7.

1. Well, these hedgehogs and snails decide to have a day out together, an'
2. so- they all go into the fields, and then suddenly they see this snail,
3. um- cooped up in this little bottle and he looks very- unhappy and he's
4. crying, and so the hedgehog(s) goes round the back- and- hits the back
5. of the bottle and the- snail comes flying out. Anyway after all this
6. ordeal they all come- and get over this shock and they all go- into the
7. o- next field, and this little hedgehog is so- excited and happy that-
8. he doesn't look *where* he's going and he tips up into this- um- ditch.
9. Anyway the other- he- manage to scrambles up, and gets out, then they
10. forget about *that* and come into the *next* field, and they see this
11. gigantic apple- so they think oh after all this and- any- and anyway
12. it's um dinnertime and they're hungry- they start nibbling away at
13. this- um- apple. Um- after they've had all the apple they come- into
14. the next field and the owner's there walking his dog. Anyway these-
15. -this dog sees them all- and- um- they-re so scared they roll up into
16. a ball and keep still. And the little dog's looking *every*where for
17. them, and then he decides that it wasn't worth chasing them anyway, so-
18. er- he goes back to his *owner*. And then they all scramble out before
19. the dog can see them again and go back home.

Comments

This story is well organised in terms of the overall structure required of stories: it starts with an *opening* phase (lines 1–2) introducing the 'characters' and providing a context for the action to follow (i.e. having a day out together), and ends with a *closing* phase which brings the story to an end in a plausible way (16–19). The middle section consists of series of related events forming the 'plot'.

In order to construct a plot, pupils must find some means of making a credible transition between the events shown in the different pictures. This pupil achieves this mainly in a *linear* manner: the animals proceed after each encounter into the next field (7, 13–15), where a new event takes place.

This fairly simple linking device contrasts with more sophisticated techniques used by other pupils. For instance some pupils *combine* the events shown in two or more separate pictures into a single episode:

> . . . *and then the dog came out to see what was happening, and brought an apple core with him ('dog' and 'apple' pictures).*

However, although this pupil's plot transitions are not among the most sophisticated found in the surveys, they are well-constructed, and this aspect of his performance does not detract from the overall success of his story.

In contrast to less successful attempts (see pp. 75, 76), where pupils give only an outline description of the events shown in each picture, this pupil provides expanded episodes which explain how the situation depicted came about (7–8, 14), the animals' motivations for their actions (11–12, 15) and the strategies they use to resolve the 'dilemma' shown in the picture (4–5, 9, 16–17).

Also, in terms of characterisation and story elaboration, this story contains many of the additional features which transform an account of a series of events into a narrative proper. When these are absent (see above), pupils' accounts sound less 'story-like', and more like an unmotivated series of actions which happen to take place one after another in time. Characterisation, for instance, is built up here through references to the animals' thoughts and feelings, so that we get some idea of them as 'personalities': e.g. the snail in the bottle looks very unhappy and is crying; the animals get over this shock; the little hedgehog is excited and happy. The reported speech at 11–12 lends immediacy to the narrative and further invests the animals with characterisation. The sense of action is heightened by the use of phrases such as 'flying out' (5), 'tips up' (8), 'scrambles up' (9).

Although performance features cannot be accurately conveyed from a transcript, this pupil's speech is well-constructed in this respect. He speaks at a fairly even tempo, and segments his utterances into manageable 'chunks' (as indicated by the punctuation marks in the transcript). His speech is not noticeably hesitant or faltering, and he seldom needs to correct himself, thus adding an impression of fluency to the other good qualities of his performance.

5.7 Task 2: Jobs

Part 1: Description

This task was the first component of a combined activity, administered in the 1982 survey, in which pupils were first asked to describe a particular job, and then to discuss the jobs they had chosen, in order to decide which should receive a pay rise (see below). A similar activity was carried out in the 1982 and 1983 surveys of performance at age 15, to allow comparison of performance between the two age groups. This topic is pursued in the next chapter.

Each pair of pupils was given an illustrated sheet showing people carrying out ten different jobs, selected to cover a range of occupations with which pupils might be expected to be familiar. These were:

shop assistant	hairdresser
ambulance driver	librarian
teacher	vet
secretary	police constable
doctor	pilot.

Each pupil was asked to choose one job to talk about, and it was emphasised that they should try to pick a job that they knew something about, as they would be asked to tell one another as much as possible about what was involved in carrying out the job each had chosen. At age 11 in 1982, it was found in both parts of the task that pupils who chose professional jobs gained higher mean scores than those who chose non-professional occupations (see 1982 Primary Report, p. 65).

Comments on performance: analytic assessment

The analytic categories applicable to this task were:

1. MAJOR EMPHASES[1]   (i) Specification of skills/activities

    (ii) Preparation and professional aspects

} Task-specific[1]

2. OVERALL ORGANISATION

3. LEXICO-GRAMMATICAL FEATURES   (i) Lexical selection

    (ii) Syntax

4. PERFORMANCE FEATURES   (i) Hesitation/self-correction

    (ii) Tempo and pacing

    (iii) Verbal assertiveness

---

[1] The analytic framework at secondary level includes the additional task-specific category of 'Evaluation'. This is not applied separately at primary level as examples seldom appear in the accounts of 11-year-olds. Where evaluative comments do occur, these would be taken account of under 'Preparation and professional aspects'.

Considering these categories in relation to this particular task, in order to do well pupils must:

give a reasonably clear idea of what the job involves on a day-to-day basis – although minute detail is not necessary, and may be inappropriate ('Specification of skills/activities');

refer to qualifications, training or particular aptitudes/qualities required of the job-holder, and give an indication of her/his function vis-à-vis those with whom he/she works ('Preparation and professional aspects');

provide a well-structured account which begins with a general statement of some main function or aspect of the job, followed by additional detail ('Overall organisation');

select words which appropriately describe the skills and activities involved, including technical terms where relevant ('Lexical selection').

(Syntax: as for other tasks)

(Performance features: as for other tasks)

In relation to the task-specific categories, by far the majority of pupils focus on the day-to-day skills and activities involved in carrying out the job, with varying degrees of accuracy and competence. Relatively few pupils mention the more general and abstract aspects of the job implicit in the category of 'Preparation and professional aspects', such as training or qualifications, or the status of the job in relation to others within the occupational structure (i.e. who the job holder is responsible to, or for). More general matters such as those relating to salaries, promotion, job satisfaction or social usefulness are seldom mentioned, even though some pupils do refer to these in the subsequent component of the task (see pp. 81–83).

In general therefore most pupils of this age – as might be expected – confine their accounts to the everyday activities and visible aspects of the job selected, and without considering the job in a wider social or professional context.

Comparison of performance across different jobs is problematic, as different jobs appear to predispose pupils to focus on different aspects of the work involved. Occupations such as hairdresser, librarian, shop assistant and police constable are most often described in terms of a detailed breakdown of the various activities involved (weighing goods, taking money, stamping books, cutting and drying hair, etc.), with fewer references to more general aspects. Other jobs – such as secretary, doctor and pilot – are more often described in more general terms. It is possible – though we may only speculate – that jobs in the former group are selected because pupils have had practical opportunities, as clients, customers or observers, to see these jobs being carried out, and are therefore drawing on their own, necessarily limited, perceptions. The second group of jobs, on the other hand, may tend to be chosen on the basis that pupils have been told about them (by a parent, for instance), and have therefore acquired a more general perspective on the nature of the job. In any event, it is possible that the amount and type of knowledge which pupils are able to bring to this task is associated with the particular job chosen.

Because of the difficulties of comparing performance across different types of jobs selected, we shall consider three examples of performance in relation to one particular job: that of librarian.

Performance at the lower end of the range

Example 1. Impression mark: 2

1. Er (pause) A lot of people come, to get books out (pause). People
2. bring us (more) (laughs). There's a lot of – books that you choose,
3. – about history, geography – radio and things (long pause).

(Assessor: Anything else now about the librarian's job – what the librarian does?)

(pause)

4. I stamp the books (laughs) (long pause) em – (long pause)

(Assessor: Anything else?)

5. No.

Comments

This pupil is clearly having difficulty in thinking of anything to say: each utterance is preceded and followed by long pauses, and she manages to give only a few items of information about the job even after prompting by the assessor. It may be that, despite being advised in the assessor's instructions to 'choose a job you know quite a bit about', she has chosen one that is largely unknown to her.

Performance at the mid-point of the range

Example 2. Impression mark: 4

1. They have to – um – when people's – taking the books back they have to
2. put them – back on the right shelves in the right order. (pause) That
3. the numbers go in (pause). They have to – um – stamp all the books –
4. and they have – if people ask them – where you can get the books from
5. they have to know which shelves they go on, so that they can tell
6. them (pause). They have to know what kind of books they've got, and
7. what they haven't (long pause). And if people want books that
8. aren't in the library they – have to – order them for them.

Comments

This account is typical of those attaining a general impression mark of 4. The pupil gives an accurate description of some of the routine activities carried out by a librarian (e.g. putting books on shelves (2), stamping books (3), ordering books (8)), but does not refer to more general aspects of the job. There is no opening statement: instead the pupil launches straight into the list of activities involved. Again, there are several fairly long pauses in the course of the account.

Performance at the upper end of the range

Very few pupils received a rating of 7 at each of the three stages of general impression marking (i.e. on-the-spot, first- and second-marking from the cassette tapes).

A successful account (i.e. receiving a general impression mark of 6 or 7) would characteristically present an accurate and clear description of what the job involves on a day-to-day basis, together with some reference to the more general aspects such as training, working conditions, position in the occupational hierarchy, etc.

Example 3. Impression mark: 6

1. Well usually a librarian is – a part-timer and they
2. don't work all the time, in the library. Um – and
3. they – (say and) they only do, um – say – one –
4. one and a half days out of every – week. And . . .
5. they have to know – they have to have read lots of
6. books and everything, and, know where everything is –
7. in the – on the shelves, about every kind of – (pause) um subject
8. like nature, aircraft and ships and everything – and . . .
9. er, you've got . . . he's . . . hm . . . he's got he's got to –
10. know where to put the books, and what references they are,
11. and what kind of book they are and, – have – and
12. know, quite a bit about the alphabetical – order 'cause
13. they've got all – masses of tickets and everything, and . . . the . . .
14. sometimes on Saturdays they're very very busy, and – er,
15. they've got to make sure young children do it in the right
16. way and not go to the wrong – place, not – have their –
17. ticket – their books stamped (out) without . . . having – changed their
18. book.

Comments

This account gives a fairly good idea of what skills and activities a (public) librarian's job involves on a day-to-day basis, and also refers more generally to the skills and knowledge required of a librarian. The pupil not only mentions, for instance, the visible and practical aspects of the job such as putting books on shelves (7) and issuing tickets (13), but also knowledge of subject matter (7) and the reference system (10–11).

In contrast to less complete accounts, this pupil refers also to the working practices of a librarian – i.e. a 'part-timer' (1) – even though this may not be strictly accurate in terms of the usual working pattern of librarians. His comments about the kinds of knowledge required of the librarian, referred to above, and his general remark that 'they have to have read lots of books' (5–6) can also be seen as referring to the background or professional skills required for the job, as can his closing comments about interaction with young children (15–18).

Pupils are not required to follow strict principles of organisation for this task: the main requirement is simply to list attributes or activities associated with the job chosen. However, more successful accounts also include an opening statement which refers to the job in general terms, or gives a broad characterisation of the main function of the job holder. This pupil's initial remark – 'well usually a librarian is – a part-timer' – can be understood as an opening remark of this kind.

In terms of performance features, although this is a fairly successful attempt, there is some hesitation, particularly at (7–9). This was not uncommon on this task – a fact which suggests that pupils did indeed find it fairly difficult, as they often appeared to be searching for something to say next.

Jobs. Part 2: Discussion

After each pupil of the pair had described the job he or she had chosen, they were asked to imagine a situation in which only one of them would be eligible for a pay rise, and instructed to discuss the merits of the job each had chosen, in order to decide which one should receive the rise.

As it was found during the description component of the activity that 11-year-olds varied widely in their substantive knowledge of the jobs they had chosen, each pupil was read by the assessor a short written description of the job he or she had selected, after completing the first, descriptive component. By providing such information, we attempted to provide all pupils with some substantive knowledge of the job involved, as a resource to be drawn upon in this second, discussion component.

Objectives of the task

This part of the task was designed to encourage a form of discussion in which each participant would have a personal 'stake', and which would therefore require participants to adopt an oppositional stance. In this respect the task contrasts with the **Island** discussion task described later, where a more collaborative type of interaction is

appropriate. The **Jobs** discussion task clearly relies on the willingness of both pupils to participate and to score points off each other. Fears that able pupils with less able partners might not have the chance to give of their best proved unfounded: on the whole, pupils chose for their partners friends of similar ability, and this task in particular provoked some of the liveliest performances.

Comments on performance: analytic assessment

Analytic categories:

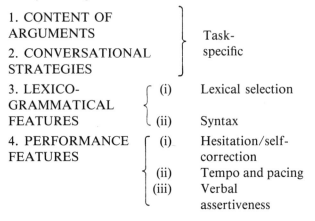

1. CONTENT OF ARGUMENTS		Task-specific
2. CONVERSATIONAL STRATEGIES		
3. LEXICO-GRAMMATICAL FEATURES	(i)	Lexical selection
	(ii)	Syntax
4. PERFORMANCE FEATURES	(i)	Hesitation/self-correction
	(ii)	Tempo and pacing
	(iii)	Verbal assertiveness

Description of task-specific categories

Content of arguments

This category relates to the substantive points pupils raise with respect to their own and their partners' jobs, their ability to justify or challenge these points, and the 'levels' at which they pitch their arguments.

Some pupils, for instance, emphasised the effort or the boredom associated with the job, using these as grounds for claiming the wage increase. Others claimed that the professional preparation (studying, getting qualifications) or the responsibilities and status involved in their job merited the increase. Most pupils interpreted the task as one requiring role-play, and accordingly projected themselves into the role of the job holder. Some however took their role identification much further than others, and invented fictional autobiographies and personal circumstances as ground for their arguments – e.g. stating that they had a wife and four (or, on occasion, ten!) children to support. It is interesting to note, in passing, that such fictionalised domestic scenarios tended to reflect highly stereotyped and at least partly outmoded views of gender roles and family lives, with 'husbands' in jobs 'supporting' their 'wives', and working wives citing (perhaps with greater sociological accuracy) additional domestic duties such as cooking and cleaning as grounds for more money.

The most successful discussions in relation to this category were those in which pupils made (realistic) reference to 'professional' and 'practical' aspects of the job in support of their claims – for example to the dimensions of professional preparation, effort, boredom, or job responsibility mentioned above. Pupils who argued predominantly in the 'personalised' role-play mode, inventing elaborate personal circumstances to back up their arguments, tended to receive lower general impression marks – possibly because such arguments tend to be less well-grounded in a knowledge of the job itself, and because they often lead to an inflationary spiral of implausibly dramatic descriptions of domestic trauma, with each pupil attempting to 'trump' the other's claims for special consideration.

The more successful attempts also showed an ability to *shift* the level of argumentation from one to another of these dimensions or levels, in the light of challenges or counter-claims from opponents. Thus for example pupils who moved from arguments based on the inherent boredom of their job, to the hard work involved, or the unsocial hours, or the lengthy training, were judged more successful than those who simply reiterated one particular line of argument.

The least successful attempts in relation to this category were those in which pupils relied mainly on asserting their own claim and rejecting their partner's with almost no reference to the demands/experience of the job itself. These attempts tended to take the form of arguments consisting of a series of minimal oppositional statements – e.g. A: 'I think it (the pay rise) should be mine!' B: 'No, it should be mine' . . .

Conversational strategies

This category relates to the strategies or devices used by pupils in order to convince, persuade or coerce their partners into conceding the pay rise.

The most successful attempts were those in which pupils attempted to engage directly with the substance of their partner's arguments, diagnosing flaws in these, or suggesting that aspects of their own job were equally or more relevant to the issue, or arguing that an equivalent or similar claim could be made on their own part.

Pupils who took conversational initiatives, in proposing new arguments, and in insisting that opponents justify their own claim, were judged more successful than those who simply 'mirrored' the claims of their opponent, finding equal or equivalent points for each of those introduced by the other.

It should be noted that for this interactive task the analytical category of 'overall organisation' was not applied. This decision was originally made in connection with the argument part of the **Jobs** task when it was used with 15-year-olds (see the 1982 Secondary Report, p. 68). It was based on the fluctuating nature of argument, which produces a structure, if any, which is quite unlike that of one-way talk which the speaker can to a much greater extent plan in advance.

The other categories imply that, in order to do well on this task, pupils must be able to:

construct arguments in support of their own claim to the rise, mostly on a 'professional' basis ('Content of arguments');

overcome their opponent's points by reasoned argument ('Conversational strategies');

(Lexico-grammatical and Performance features: as for other tasks).

Examples of performance

Performance of the lower end of the range

Example 1. Impression marks: 2 (both pupils)
(Pupil A = Librarian. Pupil B = Shop Assistant.)
1. A: em – (pause) 'cause I work – work a long hours. (long pause) I have
2.   to do a lot of stamping. (long pause)
  (Assessor: indistinct)
3. A: and if people, er – don't put the books in the r – the right – places,
4.   I have to put them in the right places. (pause)
5. B: well you don't have to do – sort of – () (laughs)
6.   I have to (hang up) (pause) I have to keep the place clean an' tidy
7.   an' fill up the shelves (pause)
8. A: if any books are torn I have to repair them (long pause)
9. (Assessor: Right. Think what more you could say) (pause)
10. B: I have to weigh things out (long pause)
11. A: I have to put them away – the – books away (long pause)
12. (Assessor: What about you Denise?)
13. B: um – (pause) You have to dress well (very long pause)
14.   I have to put a uniform on (long pause)
15. B: I have to keep everything clean (pause)
16. A: I have to keep my hands clean in case I dirty the books. (pause)
17. B: So have I (pause)
18. B: I have to be kind – I have to be kind to my customers (pause)
19. A: I get a lot of people an' I have to keep them – to make them
20.   be quiet (pause)
21. (Assessor: Is that it girls?)
22. A/B: Yes

81

Comment

This performance would attract low marks on almost every analytic category, with the possible exception of Content of arguments, and even here the marks could not be very high.

Performance at the mid-point of the range

Example 2. Impression marks: 4 (Pupil A)
                                    2 (Pupil B)

(Pupil A = Hairdresser. Pupil B = Librarian.)

1. A: Pay rise should be mine, 'cause – peop – 'cause my job's harder than
2.   yours. You have to style hairs and cut it – so the pay rise should be
3.   mine not yours. All you do is sit around telling people to be
4.   quiet, and stamping books.
    (both laugh)
5.   no – (pause)
6. (Assessor: Not going to agree with her yet are you?)
7. B: no! (laughs)
8.   the pay rise should be mine, because – I have to work long hours,
9.   before you. I've got to get up earlier, before you. (pause)
10. A: So do *I* have to get u – up early every morning. The pay rise should be
11.   mine 'cause I – cause I have to tidy up, *you* don't have to. All you
12.   have to do is sit around stamping books, an' uh – telling people to be
13.   quiet an' gettin' them out, putting books back. I have to cut
14.   people's hair, wash people's hair, and sweep the floor. *You* don't
15.   have to do that. My job's harder than yours.
16. B: but sometimes you've gotta wash up
    (pause)
17. A: so do we
    (laughs)
18. B: we gotta show people – around where the books are, and – sometimes you
19.   have to sweep the floor
20. A: we sweep the floor more often than you do. 'N when we get home we
21.   have to do the dinner
    (pause)
22. B: so do we
    (laughs)
23. A: I still say the pay rise should be mine
    (pause)
24. (Assessor: Going to give it to her?)
25. B: yeah (laughs)

Comments

This discussion is clearly better than the preceding example, but still somewhat limited in the range of arguments, as the pupils confine their arguments to variations on the theme of the hard work involved in their respective jobs. Thus A begins by claiming that her job is 'harder' than B's, and then denigrating B's job by characterising it as 'sit(ting) around telling people to be quiet, and stamping books' (1–4). B counters with an opposing claim based on the 'long hours', which A matches before going on to enumerate the chores involved in her job, and reiterates her characterisation of B's job as less demanding (8–15). The discussion continues rather half-heartedly in this vein for a few more utterances, before B concedes the point. Throughout, A shows rather more ingenuity in constructing her arguments, even though these are confined to one particular aspect of the job, while B tends merely to follow her lead and try to come up with a comparable argument on her own side.

A is also rather more adept than B in terms of the conversational strategies she uses. For instance, like pupil B in Example 1 above, she attempts to deflate the status of B's job by caricaturing its worth (e.g. 3–4), and she takes the initiative in pointing out aspects of her own job and comparing these with aspects of B's. B on the other hand takes a more passive role; she follows A's lead by pointing out some of the more arduous duties of a librarian (e.g. 8–9, 18–19), but does not explicitly challenge or comment on A's arguments.

Neither pupil, however, shows the versatility displayed in the following example: there is much less engagement with, and logical rebuttal of one another's arguments, and very little development of the points raised. Towards the end of the extract the contributions of each become minimal, with little effort to persuade or convince one another.

At the syntactic level, it is noticeable that comparatives are used several times by both pupils, as the task might seem to demand.

Performance at the upper end of the range

Example 3. Impression marks: 6 (Pupil A)
                                      7 (Pupil B)

(Pupil A = Vet. Pupil B = Librarian.)

1. A: Well I think the pay rise should be mine because – well, I had to –
2.   study harder – and – my job's more – more important than yours.
3. B: aye but you enjoy your job. But yours isn't boring, there's people
4.   in all the time for *your* job with – and if you're playing on with all
5.   the nice cuddly animals an' that, but – *I* just have to stand there
6.   behind a desk, fiddling on with tickets, an' putting books back.
7. A: but you always – you said that they're always cuddly they're not
8.   cuddly, sometimes – they can be horrible. Sometimes you might have to

9.   put animals *down* an' that. And then that's not
10. B: I know but then –
11. A: – very nice is it?
12. B: I know but them – going to sleep – like – as if they're just going to
13.   sleep at the night *don't* they?
14. A: yeah but they never wake up again
15. B: aye, but – *you'll* never wake up again one day
16. A: an' that's a nice thing to say isn't it?
17. B: well it's true
18. A: well – an' I think I – I've *studied* harder than you I've studied
19.   longer than you.
20. B: so? It doesn't matter. It doesn't matter how long – you study
21. A: yeah it does
22. B: you're not studying now are you?
23. A: no, but I – but I've studied five s – or more years, an' I've been
24.   – an' *I* should have a better job than – I should have more pay
25.   than you.
26. B: I know but, your job – your n' – job's not boring an' that
27.   is it?
28. A: it is sometimes
29. B: aye but – em – there's lots of us doing it, there's only one of you,
30.   so you can get a pay rise some other time.
31. A: but there *isn't* some – only one of us – me, there's – there's all me –
32.   helpers, who help me, me secretaries an' everything.
33. B: just – I know but you're the top of them aren't you? *I'm* not I'm just
34.   low down ()
35. A: yeah
36.   but I have to pay them as well don't I
37. B: oh but listen I have to do a lot of things, I have to put books
38.   back, tidy them, stamp them, put them under the desk, tell people
39.   where the toilets an' things are, where they can get – certain books
40.   from, I have to get the tapes out the drawer I have to file books
41.   when they come in, you – I have to do *much* more than you.
42. A: I don't, I have to clean the surgery an'
43. B: that could be very boring
                                  'n you have all the *other*
44.   people to do it – with you – for you, there's a – when you've
45.   finished – when you've just seen a – an a – em – animal – you don't clear
46.   the desk yourself, another person does it for you. But *I* clean the
47.   desk meself at night.
48. A: how do you know? because I could of –
49. B: because I –

50. A: sometimes I do that, to
51. B: make sure it's thoroughly done
                                  because when I –
52.   oh, sometimes, sometimes. I do it every night
53. A: well, I think you're – I th – don't think that you should get the
54.   pay rise, because –
55. B: well I don't think you should have it

                    •
                    •
                    •

(continues for several minutes)

Comments

These pupils are fairly skilled in constructing arguments in support of their claim, and in challenging or criticising those of their opponents. For instance at the start of the extract A makes a claim on the grounds of the studying involved (1–2) and – perhaps more dubiously – the importance of her job. B counters this claim by raising the issue of boredom, and arguing that A's job is more enjoyable (and therefore less worthy of the pay rise) than her own (3). This claim is backed up with 'evidence' in the form of details concerning the work done by each (3–6). A in turn counters this by picking up a point in B's argument concerning 'cuddly animals', and in challenging this assertion puts forward an argument about the unpleasantness of her own job (i.e. that it's 'not very nice' (7–9)). After a rather personalised digression at lines 14 to 17, A raises again the issue of study and preparation, which B again challenges, this time dismissing it as irrelevant to the question, and again raises the matter of the boredom of her job (26). Slightly further on, they discuss the issue of status – B pointing out that she is 'just low down', and A countering with the argument that she has to pay all her 'helpers' and 'secretaries' (29–36). B then turns to the question of the effort and hard work involved in her job (37–42), which A attempts to counter by claiming equivalent burdens in her job. Her case is less well argued than B's at this point; and throughout, A provides rather less evidence for her arguments than does B.

In terms of content, therefore, these pupils are able to construct fairly sophisticated arguments in support of their cases, ranging across professional preparation, the unrewarding nature of the job, the hard work involved, status and responsibility.

In terms of conversational strategies, each pupil in general puts across her arguments in a challenging but logical manner. Each makes her arguments relevant to those of the other – either denying the validity of her opponent's argument and providing justification (e.g. 7–9), or by proposing alternative arguments and claiming greater importance for these (e.g. 37–46). In general these challenges and counter-arguments are based on some plausible aspect of the job concerned, although one minor exception to this occurs at (15–17), where B makes the rather irrelevant rejoinder that A, like some of her animal patients, will 'never wake up again one day'.

B in particular is very skilful at undermining her partner's arguments by setting up a characterisation of the work which her partner does, and then belittling it or denying its validity. Note for instance how she focuses on 'cuddly animals' to depict the 'soft option' of the vet's job, and counterposes this to the tedium of her own job, which she sums up as having to 'stand behind a desk, fiddling on with tickets . . .' (4–6). This facility would also be reflected in the rating for 'lexical selection'.

Although the tone is adversarial and fairly assertive, the discussion does not descend into personal invective, as happens with some pupils. Nor, on the other hand, does it consist only of a bland series of opposing statements. Each pupil therefore appears, on the one hand, to be genuinely involved in trying to convince the other of the merits of her claim, while on the other avoiding overstepping the bounds of reasonable conflict and resorting to bullying or aggressive tactics.

Both pupils are adept at using comparisons, but actual comparatives, in the syntactic sense, occur only in the first few lines (2–24).

5.8 Task 3: Island

Part 1: Relaying

Objectives of the task

This task was designed to assess pupils' ability to assimilate and convey to others information acquired through reading (with supplementary information presented in the form of pictures).

Comments on performance: analytic assessment

The analytic categories applied in this task were:

1. INFORMATION CONTENT
2. ORGANISATION OF INFORMATION } Task-specific

3. LEXICO-GRAMMATICAL FEATURES { (i) Lexical selection (ii) Syntax

4. PERFORMANCE FEATURES { (i) Hesitation/self-correction (ii) Tempo and pacing (iii) Verbal assertiveness

In terms of performance on this task, these categories indicate that, in order to do well, pupils must:

accurately convey the information given on their picture sheets and check lists ('Information content');

present this information in a clear and comprehensible way, relating the information to the island situation which has been described to them ('Organisation of information');

paraphrase the information appropriately in their own words, or, if reading aloud, do this in a naturalistic and fluent manner ('Lexical selection');

use grammatical constructions which are appropriate for conveying several items of information in succession, and for expressing hypothetical and evaluative concepts ('Syntax');

if reading aloud, observe the requirements for conveying, in speech, material which has been read ('Performance features').

Examples of performance

The three examples discussed below relate to the Kava plant (see Illustration 5.6).

Performance at the lower end of the range

As we find in relation to all tasks, those attempts which receive a general impression mark of 1 or 2 are clearly identifiable as ones in which a pupil is having serious difficulties at almost all levels of the construction of the message. Pupils often experience additional difficulties on this task, as a result of poor reading skills.

Example 1. Impression mark: 2

1. A: Well you didn't really – you didn't have to go down to the river to
2. get lots of water and (pause) um – (long pause)
3. (Assessor: What else did you find out?)
4. A: That – they're not – *dear* –
5. and – um – (pause) you – don't have to plant them every year.
6. B: C2: You do!
7. A: C1: don't
8. B: C2: you do, it's got it there. Seeds have to be planted every year.
9. B: C2: That's *mine* – not to have to be planted every year.
10. A: C1: Mine's a bad point.
11. B: C2: Mmm
12. (Assessor: Mm hm)
13. A: Um – they're cheap, the seeds are very cheap, and –
14. (long pause)
15. (Assessor: d'you (remember) anything else about it?)
16. A: The vegetables are very nice an' – um – (long pause)
17. (Assessor: Anything else you've found out about it?)
18. A: No.

Comments

This pupil clearly has trouble in reading, and this has prevented her from assimilating and conveying most of the information presented. However, she has made some attempt to convey information, probably on the basis of the pictures accompanying the text on the information sheet. (It should perhaps be noted that this was the only task in the oracy survey with a significant reading element. Having said that, it would be unreasonable to ban all reading or writing elements, because in practice language tasks rarely exhibit such rigid separation.)

Performance at the mid-point of the range

An average performance (receiving a general impression mark of 4) would characteristically convey each item of information accurately - usually by reading aloud from the information sheet, in a reasonably fluent manner. Evaluative comments relating each item to the island context would, however, be largely absent.

Example 2. Impression mark: 4

1. The soil - the soil has to be - dug well - to grow the Kavia plant.
2. A lot of com - compost has to be added to the soil to feed the plants.
3. Once the plants have started to grow, they need very little water.
4. The plants grow stronger if the weeds are not allowed to flourish.
5. The Kavia - Kvas are res - res -
6. (Assessor: Resistant)
7. - istant to di - to disease and pests.
8. When ripe, the Kavias are - difficult to harvest at the - as the
9. leaves are very prickly. They need a lot of preparation to cook
10. them. They are extremely tasty - tasty vegetables. The seeds are
11. very cheap. The seeds have to be planted every year.

Comments

This attempt is typical of those at the mid-point of the range. The information is accurately conveyed ('Information content'), but no evaluative comments are given and the manner of reading aloud is more 'literal' and less fluent than that of the following example ('Organisation of information'). For instance this pupil reads out each item as a self-contained unit, with little attempt to smooth the transition from one item to the next. She also has a slight problem in reading one or two words - e.g. 'Kavia/ Kvas' for Kava (1,5,8), and hesitates over the word *resistant* (5). In terms of 'Performance features', therefore, her attempt is less accomplished than the next example, bearing several signs of a literal reading aloud, in contrast to the fluent, naturalistic character of the speech in example 3. Since this pupil sticks to the vocabulary and sentence constructions of the original information sheet, her choice of words and grammatical structures is appropriate, but not innovative ('Lexico-grammatical features').

Performance at the upper end of the range

This task requires pupils to assimilate and accurately convey all or most of the items of information they have acquired, bearing in mind the context in which the task is embedded: i.e. that of evaluating the suitability of the plant for growing on the imaginary island. Although each item of information can be accurately conveyed by reading aloud the relevant caption from the information sheet, the most successful attempts are those which also provide evaluative or speculative comments which relate each item to the hypothetical island.

Example 3. Impression mark: 7

1. Well I found out, first of all, that - it's a bad point in a way,
2. because the soil has to be dug - well - to grow the Kava - the Kava plant,
3. and that involves a lot of work, and . . . you can't - do - it'd be - easier -
4. to have one, where it doesn't involve so much digging and work. And -
5. on number two - a lot of compost has to be added to the soil to feed
6. the plants, and that - that's a bad point because - compost can be
7. expensive - and - um - it's (too) - it's - work putting it on as well. And -
8. a good point is, once the plants have *started* to grow, they need very
9. little water and as the - river's quite a long way away from - the - where
10. the - the - plants would be growing, it's - a - good idea because - they
11. don't have to travel all that way to - collect - to collect water . . . And -
12. the plants grow stronger (so that) weeds are not allowed to flourish,
13. and that means that a lot of hard work - picking out their - *weeds*, with
14. the sun on the back and everything which can give you backache, so I
15. thought that was a bad - point - and - the good point is the Kavas are
16. resistant to disease and pests, so they won't be - ruined - and (pause)
17. go bad. (pause) It's a bad point that - um - Kavas are - ever so
18. difficult to harvest, because er - rea - their leaves are so prickly, and
19. it's also a bad point that they need such a lot of preparation to cook
20. them. But they're extremely tasty - tasty vegetables . . . and the seeds
21. are very cheap so - that could make - all the hard work - altogether -
22. worthwhile in the *end*. And the seeds have to be planted every year.
23. And even if they're cheap, if you have to plant them every year, the
24. money mounts up.

Comments

This is a highly successful attempt, showing that the pupil has not only digested all the information presented, but that she has carefully considered each item in relation to the island context. Each item of information given on the sheet is accurately conveyed, the pupil gives helpful evaluative comments in relation to each item of information. She usually reads each item from the information sheet, often prefacing it with a comment as to whether it is a 'good' or 'bad' point, before going on to remark on its implications with respect to the island conditions. The reading is so fluent and well-embedded in her own commentary, however, that it would not be apparent to a listener who had not seen the information sheet that certain utterances were read rather than spontaneously delivered.

The vocabulary chosen is entirely appropriate to the task. The colloquial tone of the comments – e.g. 'so that could make all the hard work – altogether – worthwhile in the *end*' (21–22); 'the money mounts up' (23–24), indicates that the pupil is making every attempt to present the information, and her own opinions, in a way which will be helpful and accessible to her partner. Moreover, complex constructions containing one or more subordinate clauses are used competently to express conditions, reasons, consequences and implications in the commentary.

Island. Part 2: Discussion

This task, administered in the 1983 survey, followed on from the one described above, involving crops to be planted on an imaginary island. After each pupil had conveyed the relevant information about her or his plant (i.e. the Kava or Bulo), they were then asked to discuss the relative merits of each plant, and to decide which one should be planted on their island.

Objectives of the task

The task was designed to assess pupils' ability to take part in a discussion which involved pooling information acquired individually, and evaluating arguments leading to a decision based on this information.

Comments on performance: analytic assessment

Analytic categories:

1. CONTENT OF ARGUMENTS ⎫
2. CONVERSATIONAL STRATEGIES ⎬ Task-specific
3. CONVERSATIONAL STYLE ⎭

4. LEXICO-GRAMMATICAL FEATURES
   - (i) Lexical selection
   - (ii) Syntax

5. PERFORMANCE FEATURES
   - (i) Hesitation/self-correction
   - (ii) Tempo and pacing
   - (iii) Verbal assertiveness

Description of task-specific categories

The analytic assessment procedures for this task differ in some respects from those in which the focus is on individual pupils.

Content of arguments

This category relates to the ways in which pupils incorporate the given information into their arguments for or against choosing one of the plants. Pupils must not only extract the various items of information given in the information sheets, but must also evaluate and explore the implications of each item with respect to the island situation. They must also be able to provide counter-arguments to those of their partners, or to propose solutions to challenges or problems posed. For instance a pupil may accept that the Kava is difficult to harvest, but point out that gloves could be worn.

Conversational strategies

This category relates to the strategies or techniques used by each pupil in order to get her/his own point of view across, and to acknowledge and incorporate those of the partner. Pupils must be able both to take conversational initiatives (by offering new points for discussion) and to show a recognition of their partner's contributions (by making their own turns relevant to what has gone before, and developing or challenging points made by their partner).

Conversational style

Pupils' discussions often fall into one of two main styles of argumentation: consultative and adversarial, though many discussions contain features of both styles. In consultative discussions the pupils adopt a style which is predominantly collaborative, involving an attempt to reach agreement, based on pooling the information each has acquired. In adversarial discussion pupils are more combative: they tend to challenge, oppose or disagree with one another, and each is concerned to 'win' the argument over the other. For this particular kind of discussion task, a style which is predominantly consultative is the more appropriate since pupils are being required to weigh up alternative items of information with respect to a hypothetical situation in which both are equally involved, and neither is therefore expected to 'win' or 'triumph' over the other.

In terms of performance on this particular task therefore, the analytic categories indicate that, in order to perform well, each pupil must be able to:

put forward well-constructed arguments based on the information they have been given, e.g. by commenting on the relevance of the various items of information to the island scenario, justifying the points raised, and developing or criticising those made by her/his partner;

take initiatives in proposing points for discussion and developing topics, and attempt to persuade or convince her/his partner, while acknowledging the relevance of the partner's contributions.

Examples of performance

Performance at the lower end of the range

Attempts receiving general impression marks of 1 or 2 would be considered fairly poor attempts. In the 1983 survey 10 per cent of pupils taking part were awarded marks with respect to these two points on the scale, a proportion which is relatively high in comparison with the other tasks administered in that year.

As is found across all tasks, attempts at this level are clearly inadequate in many respects, and this suggests that – for whatever reasons – the pupils involved were at a loss in undertaking the task. In the case of this particular task, reading difficulties during the preceding component of the activity (see above) may have prevented some pupils from assimilating much of the information on which arguments must be based. It is also possible that a small proportion of pupils found the nature of the task – i.e. discussion – particularly difficult or stressful, despite the attempts to overcome such feelings which are built into the design of the oracy tasks.

Example 1. Impression marks: 2 (Pupil B), 1 (Pupil A)

(Pupils are identified by 'A' and 'B'. Pupil A was originally given information about the Kava and pupil B about the Bulo. The symbol [indicates a point at which the speakers overlap in their conversational turns.)

1. A: No not that one
2. B: mm? Yes, that's it. 'cause you've got one two three, three and
3.   I've got one two three f – four fi – five good points. Yes that's it.
4.   (pause) (That's good) –
5. B: they – they're not very nice when – (pause) they're not very *nice* –
6.   [an –
7. A: [mm
8. B: they – they're expensive. (pause) They're – dear (quietly)
9.   (pause) an' they have to be – planted every other year (pause)
10. A: they're easy like – to harvest (pause)
11. B: (indecipherable)
12. A: mm?
13. B: we can pick that as well
14. A: mm
15. B: pick (indecipherable)
16. (Assessor: you've decided have you? Well now, which one have you decided – ?)
17. A: The Kava

Comment

This performance is noticeably hesitant and tentative, with long pauses between turns. There is little genuine attempt by either pupil to engage with the arguments of the other, and very few points are raised for discussion. Neither pupil makes much attempt to develop or refute the points of the other. The pupils mainly confine themselves to counting up (inaccurately) the number of 'good' and 'bad' points about each plant, in a very tentative manner, before reaching what appears to be a fairly arbitrary decision. Pupil B takes rather more conversational initiatives than A, and this may explain B's slightly better mark.

Performance at the mid-point of the range

In an average performance, receiving general impression marks of 4 or 5, we find many of the characteristic features of a collaborative discussion. Pupils are able to raise points for discussion based on the information given, and to challenge those made by the partners.

However, their arguments are typically less sophisticated and well constructed than those characteristic of a highly successful performance, containing fewer evaluative comments and a few attempts to overcome the problems associated with each plant. In terms of conversational strategies, attempts within this range of performance are again rather less sophisticated – often consisting mainly of a reiteration of points for or against one or other of the plants, with only minimal acknowledgement of the force of the partner's arguments. Persuasive techniques therefore consist mainly of a dogged insistence on the merits of the pupil's own plant, in opposition to the claims of the opponent.

Example 2. Impression mark: 4 (both pupils)

(Pupil A was originally given information about the Bulo, and B about the Kava.)

1. A: yours needs a lot of – um – digging.
2. B: mm. an' yours needs a lot water
        [and –
3. A: [yours a lot of compost though (both laugh)
4. B: an' the water is – quite far away
5. A: yeah but it needs a lot of compost
6. B: yeah
7. A: an' a lot of digging (pause)
8. A: an' mine don't mind *weeds*, but yours do
9. B: mm
10. A: and mine doesn't like disease
11. B: um – the Kava; foods are cheap
            [
12. A: [an' mine – mine (both laugh) (pause)
13. A: seeds and compost are more than ( ) see? (laughs) (pause)
14. A: (where) yours are – em –

87

15. B: mine are prickly, and . . . they need a bit of –
they're
16.   hard to harvest
17. A: mine are easy to harvest
(pause)
18. B: an' – mine are tasty
19. A: mine aren't (laughs)
(pause)
20. B: they taste . . . (pause)
21. A: mine – mine don't need a lot of preparation to
cook . . .
22. B: um . . . mine needs a lot. (pause) and –
23. A: yours needs compost mine doesn't, mine ( )
24. B: mine doesn't need to go – have water very often
so – if they've –
25.   a lot of energy goes in the river
26. A: yeah but you gotta dig ain't you? (laughs)
(pause)
27.   so it doesn't make much difference (laughs)
(pause)
28. A: yeah well yours only – yours – planted – every
year (pause)
29. B: I don't know though (both laugh)
(pause)
30. A: yours are on special offer so they might go up
soon (both laugh)
31. (Assessor: Sorry I didn't hear that. What was that?)
32. A: hers are on special offer so they might go up soon
33. B: um . . . well, you do save money on them
34. A: yeah but you have to buy the compost. *I* don't
have to.
(pause)
35. B: they're both . . . oh I don't know
36. A: (well then)
(pause)
37. B: what do you think?
38. A: I don't now (laughs)
(long pause)
39. B: I think yours is – a bit better. Uh – the seeds are
expensive . . .
40. A: yeah yours needs compost
41. B: and . . . I think yours. What do you think?
42. A: don't know (laughs)
43. B: 'cause you don't have to do so much work on
yours.
44. A: yeah but you have to get two lots of um – water
twice a day
45. B: mm. (laughs)
46. A: you can do it if you want to
(pause)
47. B: mm. I still think yours (i.e. Bulo)
48. A: all right then

Comments

Each pupil covers most of the items of information given
in the information sheet. However, there is relatively little
evaluation of these items, and neither makes much attempt
to explore their implications in relation to the island
context. Instead, each pupil tends mainly to state, in turn,
one point for or against the plant in question. However,

there are exceptions to this, particularly towards the end
of the excerpt. For instance at (24–26) A and B consider
the implications of the effort involved in watering as
opposed to digging, while at (30) A counters B's point
about cheapness by pointing out that, as the seeds are on
special offer, they might go up soon.

In terms of conversational strategies, and in comparison
with example 3 below, the pupils here strike the listener
as continuing along separate tracks for much of the
discussion, rather than confronting or negotiating points
of difference. Each tends to 'mirror' the arguments of the
other, rather than extending or developing these. The
series of arguments at (8–23), for instance, are constructed
as a sequence of 'mine are . . .' or 'mine aren't . . .'
statements, with little explicit acknowledgement of the
preceding point, and no attempt to convey the argument
in a persuasive or challenging form.

Towards the end of the discussion (39–45), the pupils do
begin, however, to try to put themselves in one another's
position, and B twice solicits A's opinion as to a solution
(37,41).

Performance at the upper end of the range

Example 3. Impression mark: 7 (both pupils)
(Pupil A was originally given information about the Kava,
and B about the Bulo.)
1. A: These are tastier than those.
2. B: Yes, and yours needs lots of digging and mind
doesn't.
3. A: Yeah, but if you're on the island then you have
to do a lot of carrying . . . of water, to f . . .
water them twice a day.
5. B: Ye – es, but . . .
6. A: And they get the bugs once you *have* watered
them.
7. B: Yeah but yours get . . . yours are hard to harvest.
(pause)
8. B: ⌈And . . .
9. A: ⌊Mm . . . (pause) Well they're very *cheap*, and
they're not expensive even though you
10.   have to plant them . . . every year.
11. B: But yours take a lot . . . a lot of hard work to
cook.
12. A: Yeah (quietly)
13. B: – if you wanted to eat them
(pause)
14. A: It wouldn't say . . . be . . . so bad, really, if you
got used to it, don't
15.   suppose. (pause) There's . . . you have to carry
. . . water, twice a day,
16.   an' the bugs get at them an' you . . . pay a lot
of money, and then
17.   they taste . . . they're tasteless.
18. B: Yeah, but you have to buy yours every *year*.
Mine is not every *year*.
19. A: W' you could always get a big stock of them.
20. B: M-mm (pause)

21. A: But there again I have to buy compost as well.
22. B: Yeah an' I don't.
23. A: An' I have to do a lot of digging (laughs) . . . *and* pulling up weeds.
24. B: M'yep.
25. A: But if disease got them, or . . . the bugs did anything to them . . .
26. B: Mine's get . . .
27. A: You could be ill.
28. B: Yeah. (pause) Yeah, but you could always . . . make sure they . . .
29.   didn't have anything in 'em, before you ate them . . . ⌐when you were cookin' 'em
30. A: └yeah but if you, say put
31. A: 'em in a bowl of Dettol or something . . . (laughs)
32. B: No – o! Not Dettol! (both laugh) Wash, or summ'at!
33.   Or cut . . .
34. A: That might not get them – out
         ⌐though –
35. B: └Yeah but he's . . . he's
36.   chopping them up isn't he? (referring to pictures of man preparing
37.   'Bulo' plant for cooking). When you chop them up if there was
38.   something in 'em *you'd* be able to get it out.
39. A: Not necessarily, because you might not *see* it (pause). It might
40.   just *taste* . . . bad.
41. B: You'd spit it *out* wouldn't you? (both laugh)
42. A: Yeah, but . . . at least if you'd *done* all that hard work you'd have a
43.   nice . . . meal, and you'd be healthy for next year's hard work.
44. B: Yeah, but . . . mine's easy to cook, and although it's not . . . very nice,
45.   it's better than nothing (laughs).
46. A: Yeah, I wouldn't *enjoy* it though (laughs) (pause)
47. A: Could you have half of each? (to Assessor)

Comments

Both pupils make good use of the information given in constructing the content of their arguments for or against each plant. For instance they mention the taste of the plants, whether or not they need watering, digging and compost, resistance to disease, harvesting and cooking requirements, and consideration of cost and planting. Equally importantly, they also try to evaluate these various points in relation to one another, and to the island situation: for example taste versus effort in digging (1–2) and watering (3–4); cost versus disease, cost and taste (14–17). As far as conversational strategies are concerned, each pupil shows an awareness of her partner's arguments, and takes account of these in developing further arguments. For instance A accepts B's arguments against the Kava at line 14, before pointing out comparable disadvantages associated with the Bulo. And similarly, at (28), B accepts the point that the Bulo is susceptible to 'bugs', but offers a solution that might overcome this problem.

At the same time, each pupil takes conversational initiatives in raising new points for consideration.

Their discussion also shows features of both conversational styles – consultative and adversarial. Consultative features include the 'yes, but . . .' strategy adopted by each pupil when countering points raised by her partner (e.g. 3, 5, 7, etc.), and the fact that each acknowledges criticisms and proposes solutions to overcome these, rather than simply disagreeing, or attacking one another's arguments directly. Note also that at (21) and (23), A raises a point *against* her own plant ('But there again I have to buy compost as well'), while at (26), B too begins to make a point against her plant. At this point (i.e. 25–27) A and B in fact *jointly* construct an argument relating to one of the plants.

On the other hand, the discussion also shows adversarial features: each pupil tries, in the main, to defend her own plant against the claims of her partner; and towards the end of the discussion they become noticeably more combative, although this is done in a humorous manner (cf. the discussion about 'Dettol', 25–32).

Nevertheless, the overall impression of the discussion is one of a genuinely collaborative effort in which, though each is concerned to defend her own position, due respect is paid to the contributions of the other. This consultative approach is reflected in the final solution proposed – i.e. that they might plant *half of each*.

5.9 Task 4: Tracks – hypothesising

This was the third component of the **Tracks** task. In the earlier stages, the pupils were expected to observe and report what happened to the four green marbles at the bottom of the track.

On each occasion of impact, either one or two of the green marbles furthest from the point of impact moved up the track. Pupils were expected to mention each of the conditions under which the green marbles were struck, and the effect observed in each case; i.e.

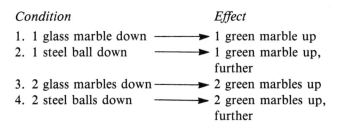

Condition	*Effect*
1. 1 glass marble down	1 green marble up
2. 1 steel ball down	1 green marble up, further
3. 2 glass marbles down	2 green marbles up
4. 2 steel balls down	2 green marbles up, further

In the third component of the task, which we shall focus on below, one pupil of the pair was asked to give reasons to explain what had happened (i.e. to hypothesise), after discussing possible reasons with her/his partner.

Comments on performance: analytic assessment

Analytic categories:

1. EXPLANATION OF EFFECTS
2. OVERALL ORGANISATION

} Task-specific

3. LEXICO-GRAMMATICAL FEATURES
4. PERFORMANCE FEATURES

} sub-categorised as for other tasks

Description of categories

Explanation of effects

Adequate hypotheses should attempt to explain the three principal phenomena highlighted by the experiment, i.e.:

1. displacement of green marbles: when green marbles are hit, one or two are dislodged at the opposite end from the impact, while the others remain stationary.

2. steel vs glass: steel ball(s) moved green marble(s) further than glass marble(s) did.

3. two balls vs one: one ball dislodged one green marble, while two balls dislodged two green marbles.

Pupils were given credit for *attempting* to explain these three phenomena, even if their explanations were not scientifically accurate, as this would require a degree of scientific knowledge beyond the resources of many 11-year-olds.

Overall organisation

Pupils were expected to observe the principles of scientific discourse: e.g. to avoid descriptive and irrelevant detail and to focus on the major conditions, effects and reasons.

In terms of the analytic categories employed, successful performance on this task would include the following:

pupils must attempt to explain all three phenomena ('Explanation of effects');

pupils' explanations must be conveyed in a form appropriate to scientific discourse ('Overall organisation);

grammatical features must be adequate for conveying relationships of time, reason, cause and effect, and comparison ('Syntax');

pupils must accurately refer to, and distinguish between, objects, distances, etc., and use terminology appropriate to explanations of scientific processes ('Lexical selection');

(Performance features: as for other tasks).

Some pupils found the task fairly difficult, perhaps because pupils of this age are not accustomed to explaining events in scientific terms, especially in the spoken mode. The task also made greater conceptual demands on pupils than some of the others included in the surveys.

Pupils were required firstly to note the salient *effects* occurring in the experiment, then to identify the relevant *contrasts* between these different effects, and finally to come up with an *explanation* which would account for these contrasts. In order to do this they were required to refer accurately to past events (i.e. the conditions and associated effects) and to use causal and consequential arguments to construct possible explanations.

Performance at the lower end of the range

Example 1. Impression mark: 2

1. when the two iron . . . iron . . . balls, hit 'em, the two went like
2. that because it was heavier than the . . . the . . . striped ones.
3. (Assessor: Yes.) 'N the same thing happened when you did it
4. with two . . . They were heavier . . . than the . . . striped ones. Is
5. that what you think? (to partner, who whispers 'Don't know').
6. (Assessor: And what happened when there was just the *one* ball?)
7. (pause)
8. Gave less power it only moved up one.

Comments

This account is quite poorly structured, and the explanations are not very clearly expressed. The pupil does not attempt to explain the *displacement of the marbles* as a process in itself. He explains the difference in effects caused by steel and striped balls in terms of weight (2) but does not attempt a clear explanation of the differences caused by one as opposed to two balls until prompted by the assessor.

The account does, however, attempt to observe the requirements for scientific language which have already been mentioned, focusing on the main events and attempting to use scientific concepts (weight and power). But he fails to distinguish clearly between the various objects referred to, and the number of these. In this case the lack of specificity makes it very difficult for the listener to grasp which conditions and effects are being explained at each point. For instance there is confusion over what is being referred to by 'it' in (2) and (8), 'they' in (4), and 'one' in (8).

Performance at the mid-point of the range

Example 2. Impression mark: 4

1. Well, we thought . . . if – f one, 'squirly' went down there, it only had
2. the power to knock one up. (Assessor: mm hm.) An' it w'only went
3. up to there. An' if one 'Steelsey' went down there, it only . . . had
4. the power to knock one up but it went further. (Assessor: mm hm). An'

90

5. if there's two . . . marbles, knocked two up, an' it would just have
6. enough power to go up. But if with two steelies, it would ha - knock
7. power up, go up here with two marbles.

Comments

Explanation of the effects is attempted less successfully than in the following example. This pupil does not, for example, attempt to explain the *displacement of the marbles* as a process in itself. He uses the concept of 'power' to explain *both* of the remaining phenomena, namely the *relative distances* travelled by the green marbles and the *number* of marbles dislodged (i.e. one ball only has the power to knock one green marble up but a steel ball has the power to move this further (1–4); and two balls have the power to move two green marbles, but the steel balls have the power to move these further). However, although the explanation is less sophisticated than in the next example, in that it does not consider *why* two balls should dislodge two marbles, it is nevertheless a reasonable attempt to explain the phenomena observed.

The overall organisation of the performance is in general appropriate for the nature of the task, although the comments that one green marble 'only went up to there' (2–3) and that 'it' would 'go up here with two marbles' (7) are perhaps more appropriate to the observational phase.

This account is rather poorly structured in terms of grammar: the utterances at (5–7) are rather loosely constructed, and constructions such as 'if with two steelies', and 'knock power up' are not well-formed in terms of the rules of grammar. This should not be taken to suggest that this pupil has not mastered grammatical rules such as these, but rather that the conceptual demands of the task are influencing his management of the grammatical aspects of communication. Similarly, in terms of vocabulary the listener has some difficulty in identifying which, and how many, balls are being referred to, as the use of pronouns and quantifiers is rather vague: for example 'one' and 'it' (2), 'it' (6–7).

Performance at the upper end of the range

One of the major characteristics of the most successful hypotheses was an attempt to identify and explain all three of the main phenomena listed above. In this respect these hypotheses contrast with many of the less successful attempts, where pupils often failed to mention at least one of the three phenomena, or else 'collapsed' their accounts of two of the phenomena into a single explanation: for example accounting for both the relative distance travelled by the green marbles and the number of marbles dislodged in terms of the steel balls having more 'force' than the striped marbles (see above).

The more successful attempts also showed a good grasp of the selection and editing processes required of scientific accounts: pupils were able to identify the (scientifically) relevant events, and to discount incidental or irrelevant occurrences (e.g. the fact that one of the green marbles might have fallen out of the track at the top of its trajectory).

Accurate use of scientific vocabulary, and the ability to convey clearly the complex relationships involved in the task, were also characteristic of the most successful attempts.

Example 3. Impression mark: 7

1. Well . . . when the . . . you put the f - four green marbles there, if a
2. striped, em . . . you put the . . . when the striped one *falls*, it . . .
3. gathers up speed . . . and em . . . *hits* the green marbles. The mo - the
4. momentum, is passed through the green marbles, and makes the end
5. one . . . go up. (partner whispers). Because em . . . there's em . . . a lot
6. of . . . force still left *in* an' it's being pushed by all the green –
7. rest of the green *marbles*. When you place the *steel* ball there,
8. it . . . it was - went faster, because there is m - it's *heavier,* and
9. *therefore* the *green* one had more fo . . . had been *pushed,* with more
10. force, an' it went further up . . . And . . . when you put *two* marbles
11. . . . at the top of the chute, because the end one, couldn't take all
12. the force . . . the secon . . . what happened I think was, the . . . the other
13. one went shooting up . . . and then . . . go . . . very, very, sh - shortly
14. afterwards, em . . . th - the next marble hit it . . . an' the momentum,
15. went on to the *third* marble (Assessor: mm hm). 'Cause . . . and so . . .
16. they wo . . . both went . . . up. And they both went up further because
17. they . . . the steel balls gathered up more force . . . than the . . . striped
18. ones.

Comments

This pupil attempts to explain each of the three main phenomena, using scientific concepts quite well in his explanation.

1. The displacement of the marble(s) is explained in terms of speed, momentum and force (lines 1–7 and 14–15).
2. The contrast between the conditions involving *steel and glass* marbles is explained in terms of weight and force, in relation to the distance moved by the green marbles (lines 7–10 and 16–18).

3. The contrast between the conditions involving *one ball and two* is explained, though not entirely clearly, in terms of force and momentum causing the third green marble in the row to be dislodged shortly after the fourth one had gone 'shooting up': resulting in two green marbles being dislodged.

The account also observes the principles of scientific discourse, avoiding descriptive and irrelevant detail and focusing on the major conditions, effects and reasons. The attempted explanations draw upon scientific concepts.

The complex conceptual relationships involved in this task require pupils to use quite complex grammatical structures such as comparative constructions (e.g. 'heavier than . . .'; 'more force . . .'; 'further . . .') and subordinate adverbial clauses of time ('when . . .'; 'shortly afterwards . . .') and reason ('because it's heavier . . .'; 'because they gathered up more force . . .'). Adjectival phrases are needed to distinguish between the various objects (steel, striped and glass marbles) and the number of these being referred to. This pupil's use of grammatical constructions is quite complex, and appropriate in these respects. The use of scientific terminology, and of words to identify clearly the objects and processes being referred to, is also appropriate to the requirements of the task.

Because this task makes complex conceptual demands on pupils, hesitations, false starts, pauses, etc., occur with greater frequency, as this account indicates. The use of contrastive stress to distinguish between items is effective.

5.10 Conclusions

At the most general level, the successful running of the 1982 and 1983 surveys of oracy at age 11 demonstrated the feasibility of the national monitoring of performance in speaking and listening by the methods adopted.

Satisfactory levels of reliability, in the statistical sense of inter-marker agreement, were achieved. The levels were at least as high as those typically reached in the double-marking of written scripts.

More important than reliability, however, in all forms of assessment is the validity of the measures employed. This is especially important in considering the contribution the APU assessment model can make to the development of an explicit oracy curriculum in schools. It seems reasonable to claim that the instruments used in these surveys represent a significant advance in the testing of spoken language, both in their attempt at communicative realism, and in the range of types of talk assessed.

In connection with the latter point, it should be noted that in the 1983 age 11 oracy survey a conscious effort was made to increase the number of tasks which required interaction between the pupils in the pairs being tested. The new tasks that were developed for this purpose were **Island, Sleuth** and **Tracks.**

Given this pressure to broaden the range of oral work, another finding assumes some importance. Almost all 11-year-olds are capable of modifying their speaking and listening strategies appropriately in accordance with the communicative demands of different tasks. The great majority show some sensitivity to the different purposes for which speaking and listening are used, to the different types of language appropriate to each, and to the needs of their partner(s) in communication.

Performance does vary, however, according to the communicative purpose of different tasks. Eleven-year-olds are able to handle some communicative purposes more successfully than others, as already indicated in section 2.5.

On the **Spiders** task, which involved the relaying of information, for instance, it was noticeable that very few pupils achieved the top raw score of 7, despite the fact that the content appeared relatively easy and that relaying or repeating back of information seems to be a frequent classroom activity.

It was also noticeable that average scores tended to be low on discursive tasks, i.e. those involving joint evaluation of evidence to reach a conclusion. It may be that pupils need greater experience of this form of talk and that performance would improve rapidly with practice and appropriate teaching.

From these examples and others it follows that some of the features of successful performance are task-specific. In devising the schemes for analytic marking, it was found that some categories could be applied to all tasks: this was true of the categories relevant to surface linguistic characteristics such as Syntax, Vocabulary and Performance features. The 'Organisation' category, however, was only relevant to one-way talk. Most strikingly, the categories which related to the content of what was said were different for every task. Though this might be expected, it has two strong implications.

First, criteria for this aspect of what constitutes successful performance cannot be determined in advance: they have to be developed on the basis of close knowledge of what pupils actually say in response to the particular tasks they are set.

Secondly, those who carry out assessments of children's oral language need appropriate training in devising suitable tasks, in achieving agreement in marking, and in working out appropriate criteria to suit the tasks they devise. This applies to both initial and in-service courses, and to all primary-phase teachers, not just to those with a special responsibility for language.

Speaking and listening at age 15

Synopsis

The chapter begins with a description of the tasks used to assess speaking and listening at age 15 in 1983.

As at age 11, the bulk of the chapter consists of detailed discussions of performance on a small number of tasks, based on the results of analytic marking and illustrated in each case by three transcripts, one each from the lower, middle and upper parts of the range.

Two of the tasks analysed were of a scientific nature, having been adapted for use in the oracy survey from practical experiments previously used in the monitoring of performance in science. A novel feature of the analytic commentaries in these two tasks is that they were written collaboratively by a member of the Language Monitoring team and two members of the age 15 Science Monitoring team. The results are tentative because of the small sub-samples of performances involved, but seem to indicate enhanced performance on the 'oracy' versions of the tasks compared to analogous 'science' versions.

The penultimate section of the chapter investigates whether there were any significant differences in oracy performance between boys and girls, and between pupils aged 11 and 15:

1. There were no overall differences in performance between boys and girls, and the instruments therefore seem largely free of sex bias. Differences in perform-ance were statistically significant on a few individual tasks, however. On all but one of these tasks the difference was in favour of boys. The nature of the tasks on which sex differences occurred defied generalis-ation, except that girls did less well on two tasks where the content was, broadly speaking, technological.

2. Fifteen-year-olds performed more competently than 11-year-olds, as would be expected, across the whole range of tasks. However, on the few tasks which were used at both ages, two opposed trends were noted. The superiority of 15-year-olds' performances on most of these tasks in terms of content was greater than would be expected simply on the basis of the age difference. But the best 11-year-olds displayed a fresh-ness and liveliness that was largely missing from other-wise highly competent performances by 15-year-olds.

The final section of the chapter points out that all the general conclusions reached about oracy at age 11 (con-cerning feasibility, reliability, validity, etc.) also apply at age 15. It is also suggested that the age 15 testing pro-gramme has profound implications for oral components of examinations at 16+; in particular there is a need to assess a broad range of talk, and to do so on a continuous basis. To support this, there is a substantial need for training in this area.

6.1 Description and categorisation of the 1983 age 15 oracy tasks

For purposes of comparison across years, it is usual in our surveys for a number of tasks from one year to be used again in subsequent years. Accordingly, of the seven age 15 oracy tasks used in 1982, three (**Bridges, Descrip-tion of a Place** and **Jobs**) were used again in 1983. In addition, there were seven new tasks. The ten tasks used in 1983 will now be described with an indication of their communicative purpose and a suggested categorisation. The results are given and discussed in the next section.

A. Tasks involving description for identification

The four tasks in this category in 1983 were **Bridges, Ships, Beetles** and **Gulls**. In all of these, one pupil described pictured objects for the other pupil in the pair to identify.

In **Bridges**, one pupil had black-and-white pictures of six single-span metal bridges (see Illustration 5.1 – this task was also used in the 1983 primary survey): the other pupil had only pictures 5 and 2, unnumbered, and the pair faced each other across a small screen so that neither could see the other's pictures. The pupil with two pictures described each of them in turn, and the other pupil was then asked to identify both bridges from the full set. The describer was assessed separately on each bridge. The identifications made by the listeners were noted, but only for statistical comparison with the marks awarded for the descriptions: the listener was not assessed.

For the 1983 secondary survey, one slight change was made in the format of the task: the listener was allowed to ask one question about each bridge. This was intended to increase the game-like quality of the task, and to keep up the listeners' interest. Not all listeners availed themselves of this opportunity, because many of them were already fully confident about the identity of the bridges before they were asked if they wished to put a question. These listeners, as just implied, were those who felt that they had to wait until the assessor indicated they could ask a question before doing so. Others interpolated their questions when they felt they needed to. It seems that this change made very little difference to the listeners' success in identification: the proportions of correct identifications of the two bridges were 64 per cent and 79 per cent in 1982, 62 per cent and 80 per cent in 1983.

Ships, Beetles and **Gulls** were identical in format to the 1983 secondary version of **Bridges**. The pictures, however, were of (respectively) six sailing ships, six beetles and five gulls. The ships and beetles were in black and white (see Illustrations 6.1 and 6.2), the gulls in colour (see Illustration 6.3). The sailing ships were drawn, as the bridges had been in 1982, in imitation of real examples. The beetles were all black beetles that occur in Britain, and their common and scientific names are shown in Illustration 6.2. The gulls were also all real species: their common names are shown in Illustration 6.3. The identification rates for these tasks, which were all very high, are shown in Table 6.1 in the following section.

The reason for having four such similar tasks was this. In 1982 **Bridges** was found to be a good initial task. It

Illustration 6.1 Ships *pictures*

Illustration 6.2 Beetles *pictures*

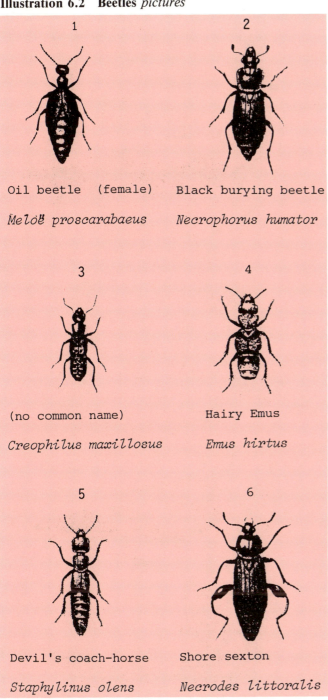

1 Oil beetle (female)
Meloë proscarabaeus

2 Black burying beetle
Necrophorus humator

3 (no common name)
Creophilus maxillosus

4 Hairy Emus
Emus hirtus

5 Devil's coach-horse
Staphylinus olens

6 Shore sexton
Necrodes littoralis

Like all the tasks in this survey, these four were marked impressionistically at two stages, that is by the on-the-spot assessors and by the second-markers. (For details of the assessment procedures, see the 1982 Secondary Report, pp.17–23 and 199–201.)

B. Task involving description to the assessor of information provided by the pupils

In 1982, two tasks were used in this category, **Recent Learning** and **Description of a Place**. One of these, **Place**, was used again in 1983 and in that year was the only task in this category.

In this task, each pupil of a pair first described a place which she/he knew well but which was unknown to the assessor. The on-the-spot assessors were told to allow each pupil to say what she/he wanted to say uninterrupted, and then by appropriate questioning to develop the task into a conversation. The fact that they would be given the opportunity to speak at first without interruption, and that then the assessors would ask questions, was made clear to the pupils at the outset.

The reason for the stipulation that the place be unknown to the assessor was that it is unnatural, communicatively, for speakers to be required to tell people facts they already know.

Each pupil was assessed separately on the initial description and on contribution to the subsequent conversation with the assessor. In 1982, pupils who did this task had been assessed only on the initial description, while pupils who did the **Recent Learning** task (where the assessor was instructed to develop the task into a conversation as early as possible) were given one assessment on their performance throughout the task. The separate assessments on the two parts of the 1983 version of **Place** were designed to provide extra information.

C. Tasks involving discussion between pupils

The two tasks in this category which were used in 1983 were **Jobs** and **Clones**, which contrasted sharply because the first required competitive argument, the second collaborative exploration of a moral issue.

In **Jobs**, each pupil of a pair was first asked to describe a job she/he knew about. Then, without prior warning, the two of them were asked to imagine that they were in the jobs they had just described, and to discuss which of them should get a pay rise, given that only one of them could have the rise. They were assessed separately on both description and discussion.

This task had been used in the 1982 secondary survey and, in a rather different format, in the 1982 primary survey. The 1983 secondary version was identical to the 1982 secondary version. The 1982 results for this task, including those from analytic marking, were given in full in the 1982 Secondary Report (pp. 62–73). Comparisons

was the on-the-spot assessors' impression that when a pair of pupils were presented with **Bridges** as their first task, they were encouraged to find that it was well within their capacity, as shown by the high proportion of correct identifications (though this was not reflected in the mean overall impression mark). The pupils then seemed to settle better to the other two tasks they had to do. However, if faced with any of the other, more complex tasks first, pupils seemed to take longer to overcome any initial nervousness. In 1983, therefore, it was decided that all pupils would be given a **Bridges**-type task. Each pair of pupils would do two such tasks. In the first, pupil A would be the describer and pupil B the listener, and vice versa in the second.

Illustration 6.3   Gulls *pictures*
(originally produced in colour.)

1 Ring-billed gull

2 California gull

3 Common or mew gull

4 Herring gull

5 Thayer's gull

of performance at the two ages, and in the two secondary surveys, are given towards the end of this chapter.

In the **Clones** task, two pupils listened to a three-minute tape-recording about human cloning. Another pair of pupils were then brought in, and the first pair relayed to them the information from the tape. In a further stage of the task, all four pupils had a discussion on the topic, based on a list of questions provided. One of the pupils who had not heard the tape acted as chairperson. The first two pupils were assessed on their relaying of the information, and all four on their contributions to the discussion.

D. Tasks involving collaborative problem-solving

The varieties of talk tested in the 1982 secondary survey by no means exhausted the range of purposes for which spoken communication can be used. In particular, none of the 1982 tasks tapped what we feel to be one of the most educationally relevant and generally useful forms of talk, collaborative problem-solving. For this reason, three of the ten tasks used in 1983 (**Woodlice**, **Tin** and **Map**) were designed to sample this area.

The **Woodlice** task required two pupils to discuss how they would go about a scientific experiment to discover which of four environments woodlice prefer, namely dry and dark, dry and light, damp and dark, or damp and light. They were given a list of the equipment they would have (see Illustration 6.4), and told that the experiment, if carried out, would have a time limit of 30 minutes. Both pupils were assessed on the quality of their discussion, which the assessor drew to a close after ten minutes if the pupils had not already finished.

Illustration 6.4 *List of equipment for* **Woodlice** *task*
20–30 woodlice
1 grey plastic tray, 30 cm × 20 cm × 5 cm deep
1 sheet foam rubber, 30 cm × 20 cm
1 sheet black card, 30 cm × 20 cm
1 sheet white card, 30 cm × 20 cm
1 black plastic dustbin bag
1 paintbrush, 5 cm wide
jug of water
roll of sellotape
stopclock
pair of scissors
perspex frame 30 cm × 20 cm × 8 cm deep
paper, pencil and ruler

In the task called **Tin**, two pupils were asked to find out as much as they could about the contents of a sealed tin. Only one pupil was allowed to handle the tin; the other had to draw and write their conclusions on a diagram (see Illustration 6.5). The only pieces of equipment they had were a 30-cm ruler and a magnet, and they could not open or damage the tin, though they were allowed to shake it, roll it, etc. All this was made clear to them before they started. Both pupils were assessed on the quality of their discussion. Again, there was a ten-minute time limit.

Illustration 6.5 **Tin** *diagram*

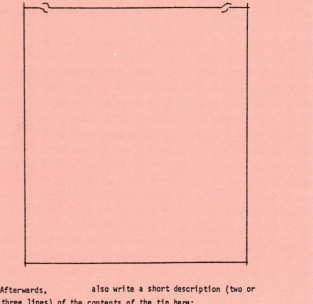

Draw what you think the contents of the tin are like in the outline below. Show in your drawing as much information as you can about what is in the tin. (You can use labels.)

Afterwards,   also write a short description (two or three lines) of the contents of the tin here:

In **Map**, one pupil of a pair B was asked to wait outside the room for a few moments. The other member of the pair A was then given a map and asked to imagine that he or she was on a country walk between the two villages shown, but that the intended route was barred by a motorway that was not shown on the (evidently out-of-date) map. A was then told to phone B for directions when B had been brought back into the room. On returning, B was given an up-to-date map, but no explanation beyond the idea of expecting a phone call from A who was on a country walk. To add a little verisimilitude to the task by preventing eye-contact, the pupils were made to sit back-to-back. Copies of both maps are shown in Illustration 6.6.

Woodlice and **Tin** were adaptations of tasks that had originally been devised and used by the APU Science Monitoring Project at the University of Leeds. Details of their versions of the two tasks, and of pupils' performance on them, are given in the Science team's reports. (For references see sections 6.3 and 6.4 below.) For language monitoring purposes, the tasks were modified in various ways.

1. In the science surveys, the tasks were tackled by one pupil at a time: in this survey, by pairs.

2. In the practical science version of **Woodlice**, a pupil was actually presented with live woodlice and asked to carry out the experiment. Planning of a sort came into this, but was done in silence. The actual carrying out of the experiment by pairs of pupils would not have fitted well into a language survey, and in any case we judged that discussion of how to go about the experiment would produce the desired kind of collaborative

Illustration 6.6
Map no. 1

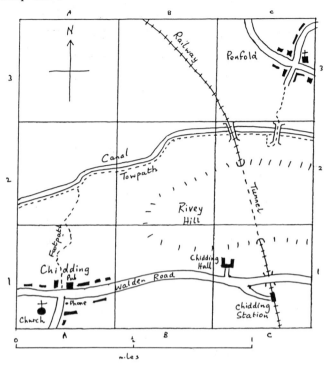

Map no. 2

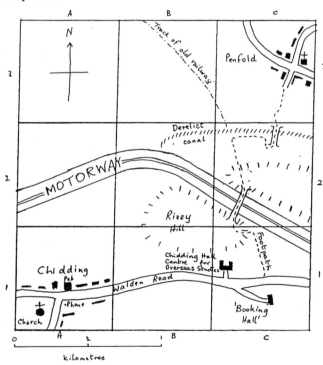

rather than both pupils handling the tin and making inferences about it silently.

4. In the 1982 age 15 science survey, the sealed tin contained a brass weight suspended on a spring from the inside of the lid. This was a noisy object, so noisy in fact that pilot tests proved impossible to decipher on tape. For the language survey therefore, the item inside the tin was changed to a cylindrical rubber bung or doorstop sliding up and down a metal rod, the ends of which were screwed to the middle of the lid and base of the tin. In addition, the top of the doorstop and the inside of the tin lid were padded with felt, so that when the doorstop slid along the rod it made a distinctly duller noise when striking the lid than when striking the base. The outside of the tin was painted a uniform gunmetal black. (See Illustration 6.7.)

Illustration 6.7 *Contents of the tin*

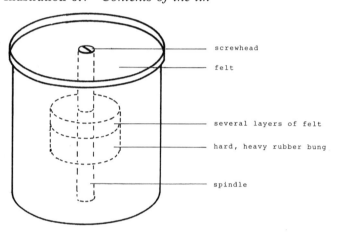

Even with these modifications, both **Woodlice** and **Tin** remained genuine scientific as well as linguistic tasks. Advantage was taken of this in assessing them. In addition to the usual impression-marking carried out on the spot and after the event by teachers of English, detailed analyses and commentaries were written jointly for these two tasks by a member of the Science team and a member of the Language team. Both commentaries will be found in a later section of this chapter.

The **Map** task was marked both impressionistically and analytically. This task also presented an opportunity for collaboration with another APU team, since the geographical nature of the task called upon spatial aspects of mathematical ability. Comments on this task by a member of the Mathematics Monitoring Project at NFER have been incorporated into the commentary on **Map** in this chapter.

The three tasks in this group were designed to tap three rather different sub-varieties of collaborative problem-solving talk: proposing and evaluating different approaches in **Woodlice**, speculating and forming hypotheses in **Tin**, and negotiating the contradictions between two sets of information in **Map**.

problem-solving talk. The language version of **Woodlice** therefore consisted only of planning the experiment.

3. When **Tin** was tackled by one pupil, she/he had both to investigate the object and to write and draw the conclusions. In the language version, these roles were separated, the purpose being to ensure that the two pupils discussed the problem, in particular by the pupil doing the drawing needing to ask the partner questions,

Table 6.1 *Inter-marker agreement on 1983 secondary oracy tasks*

Task		On-spot assessor vs. second-marker A			On-spot assessor vs. second-marker B			Second-marker A vs. second-marker B		
		= %	± 1%	rho	= %	± 1%	rho	= %	± 1%	rho
Bridges	1	37	83	0.70	31	76	0.59	33	75	0.62
	2	29	77	0.66	29	72	0.62	31	78	0.67
Ships	1	36	80	0.68	35	79	0.65	32	78	0.62
	2	33	79	0.72	30	82	0.70	39	82	0.69
Beetles	1	31	74	0.59	26	72	0.53	32	78	0.59
	2	31	74	0.58	24	72	0.54	33	81	0.63
Gulls	1	31	82	0.59	30	73	0.49	26	80	0.56
	2	30	76	0.58	30	76	0.55	38	80	0.58
Place	Description	33	80	0.67	34	81	0.65	36	78	0.64
	Conversation	35	76	0.61	34	75	0.59	30	75	0.62
Jobs	Description	32	79	0.64	34	79	0.65	35	78	0.62
	Discussion	31	72	0.54	34	73	0.61	31	70	0.52
Clones	Relaying	27	72	0.61	32	74	0.64	32	74	0.64
	Discussion	27	68	0.51	25	64	0.49	34	83	0.53
Woodlice		29	73	0.55	31	72	0.57	27	67	0.50
Tin		32	73	0.63	30	72	0.59	28	70	0.58
Map		27	68	0.47	24	64	0.51	31	69	0.56

Key: = %   percentage of exact agreement
± 1%   percentage of agreement within ± 1 mark
rho   Spearman rank correlation coefficient

6.2   Results from impression-marking

In this section the results of impression-marking are reported under the headings of inter-marker agreement and general impression marks. Differences in performance between boys and girls are considered towards the end of the chapter.

Inter-marker agreement

Measures of inter-marker agreement were given and discussed on pp. 81–85 of the 1982 Secondary Report. Table 6.1 shows the corresponding data for 1983. As in 1982, for each task the two sets of second-impression marks are compared with each other, and each of these is compared with the on-the-spot assessments. And three measures of comparison are again given:

– the percentage of cases in which markers agreed exactly

– the percentage of cases in which markers agreed either exactly or within one mark either way

– the rank correlation coefficient.

For present purposes, the most important of these measures is the second, and here the figures are high, ranging from 63–83 per cent. It might be objected that this still leaves 17–37 per cent of cases in which the markers disagreed by 2 marks or more: but it must be remembered that our statistical procedures are designed to cope with this. For one thing, all oracy performances in our surveys are triple-marked, which is in itself a more reliable procedure than single-marking. For another, these measures of agreement are based only on the raw scores. In order to calculate scaled scores for reporting against background variables, the raw scores are put through a rigorous procedure which estimates:

(a)   the relative leniency or severity of each marker, and

(b)   the relative ease or difficulty of each task compared to the other tasks.

Only when stable estimates of these factors have been obtained are the raw scores for each pupil converted into scaled form on the 0–200 scale used for reporting against background variables.

An example may help to clarify the implications of this procedure. Suppose that a pupil, on a particular task, has been awarded scores of 2 by one second-marker and 5 by the other. If these raw scores were simply averaged, this pupil would receive a mark of 3.5, i.e. somewhat below the mid-point (4) of the 1–7 scale. This might translate into, say, 95 on the 0–200 scale. But raw scores are not simply averaged, as might be the case in forms of testing where two examiners are required to produce an agreed mark. Instead, allowances are made for task and marker characteristics.

In the fictitious example being considered, therefore, suppose further that the task has been estimated by the statistical procedure to be of exactly average difficulty, within the range of tasks used in that year: this will mean that no adjustment need be made to the raw scores on this count.

However, suppose that marker A has been found to be definitely one of the more severe markers who took part that year, whereas B is known to be only slightly on the lenient side of the average of all markers. When allowance is made for this, the pupil's mark might turn out to be, say, 4.5 on the 1–7 scale, which might in turn translate into 110.5 on the 0–200 scale. In fact, a pupil might end up with an averaged mark that was *higher* than that given

Table 6.2 *Summary of impression-marking results for 1983 secondary oracy tasks*

| Task | | N | Mean scores | | | | |
| | | | Impression marks (1–7 scale) | | | Orientation to listener (1–5 scale) | Correct identification (%) |
			Overall	Boys	Girls		
Bridges	1	304	3.4	3.8*	3.1*	3.0	62
	2	304	3.4	3.8*	3.1*	3.1	80
Ships	1	305	3.7	4.0*	3.4*	3.2	78
	2	305	3.8	4.1*	3.6*	3.3	82
Beetles	1	304	3.5	3.4	3.6	3.2	84
	2	304	3.6	3.5	3.7	3.2	77
Gulls	1	300	4.0	4.1	3.9	3.3	97
	2	300	4.1	4.2	3.9	3.4	89
Place	Description	402	4.3	4.4	4.2	3.6	
	Conversation	402	4.4	4.4	4.4	3.9	
Jobs	Description	394	3.8	3.8	3.7	3.4	
	Discussion	394	3.7	3.7	3.7	3.6	
Clones	Relaying	350	3.8	3.9	3.7	3.4	
	Discussion	700 (175 groups)	3.7	3.8	3.6	3.4	
Woodlice		388	3.9	4.0	3.8	3.5	
Tin		400	3.7	3.9	3.6	3.7	
Map		376	4.1	4.3	4.0	3.6	

Key: * Statistically significant difference in performance between boys and girls (see the discussion towards end of Chapter 6).

Note: The impression marks for **Clones** discussion are based on group marking (see the discussion in the 1982 Secondary Report, pp. 58–60 and 83–85)

by either marker, if both were found to be severe. Similar arguments apply to the estimation of task difficulty.

This procedure therefore results in greater fairness for the individual pupil and may hold an implication for the conduct of the oral element in public examinations. For this, the fairest procedure might be double on-the-spot marking by examiners who not only do not attempt to produce agreed marks, but do not even make known to each other their separate marks and leave it to a subsequent statistical process to cope with discrepancies.

Such a model of assessment would be most immediately relevant to oral examining which is done on a single occasion towards the end of a course, but it could be adapted for continuous assessment. It also relies implicitly on individual markers, however lenient or severe relative to others, being consistent.

General impression marks

A summary of the results for the ten tasks is given in Table 6.2. In the Table, as in the 1982 Secondary Report, the following data are reported for each task:

1. The number of pupils who attempted it.

2. The mean overall impression mark on the rising 1–7 scale used. This mean score is based on the two sets of impression marks given for each task by the second-markers.

3. The mean scores, derived in the same way, for boys and girls, with an indication of those differences which were found to be statistically significant.

4. The mean score for orientation to listener, on the rising 1–5 scale used for this category. This score is based on the marks given by the on-the-spot assessors.

In addition, for the description-for-identification tasks **(Bridges, Ships, Beetles, Gulls)** the percentage of correct identifications is shown.

Among the overall mean scores, the two lowest were for **Bridges** and **Beetles**. The first task attempted by any pair of pupils was always one of these, and performance on them may therefore have been slightly depressed for this reason. **Bridges** also had the lowest mean score in 1982, when it was also always done first.

The highest mean scores, in descending order, were achieved on **Place**, **Map** and **Gulls**. No single explanation seems capable of handling three such different tasks as a group. **Place** seems to have evoked lively and engaged performances and to have been highly rated by both the on-the-spot assessors and the second-markers because of that. In the case of **Map**, it may be that the role-play aspect and practicality of the task influenced both pupils and markers. Where **Gulls** is concerned, the explanation seems to be simply that this was the easiest of the four identification tasks.

In fact the identification rates rank the four identification tasks in ascending order, as follows: **Bridges, Ships, Beetles, Gulls**. A small proportion of the high success rate on **Gulls** might be due to guessing, because in this task these were only five pictures to choose amongst instead of six: but this could only explain a very small part of the difference. (This effect can be estimated mathematically as a *maximum* of 3.3 per cent on the first gull and 5 per cent on the second.) Rather, the rank order of identification rates seems to correspond very well with the perceived order of difficulty of the pictures as objects for description.

Detailed commentary on selected tasks

The following sections analyse in much greater depth the pupils' performances on three of the 1983 tasks (**Woodlice, Tin, Map**).

6.3 Woodlice

(Commentary written in collaboration with R. Gott, formerly of the APU age 15 Science Monitoring team, University of Leeds)

Since this task has already been used in the science programme at ages 13 and 15 in both practical and written form it is worthwhile to set the scene by summarising the data already available.

Practical version of **Woodlice**[1]

In this task, pupils were presented with the problem of finding out which of four kinds of environments woodlice prefer.

Illustration 6.8 *Question for science practical* **Woodlice** *task*

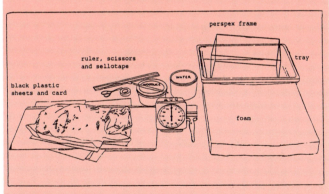

In this experiment you are to find out about the kind of place that woodlice prefer.

You cannot ask woodlice what kind of place they like to be in. You have to find out by watching where they go.
If you look for woodlice they are often under rotten wood.

This is what you have to find out:

What combination of conditions,
damp and dark,
dry and dark,
damp and light
or
dry and light
do woodlice prefer?

perspex frame

ruler, scissors and sellotape

tray

WATER

black plastic sheets and card

foam

You can use any of the things in front of you. Choose whatever you need to answer the question.
Make a clear record of your results so that another person can understand what you have found out.

---

[1] This commentary on the practical version of **Woodlice** is drawn from *Science in Schools. Age 15 Report No. 2.* DES: London, 1984, pp. 108–110.

Apparatus

Individual pupils were provided with a perspex frame and mats of plastic foam to set up the four environments. Each pupil was given black plastic sheets, card, water and a paint brush to provide the different conditions required. They also had a supply of woodlice, a brush with which to transfer them, a ruler, scissors, Sellotape and a stopclock.

The task, as set, asks:

> *If woodlice are given the choice of the four places below, which one do they choose to be in:*
>
> *damp and dark*
> *dry and dark*
> *damp and light*
> *or*
> *dry and light?*

The apparatus that was provided was designed to give pupils considerable flexibility in the ways they could perform the task. It was anticipated that the frame would be used as a choice chamber, but whereas a conventional choice chamber has defined areas in which different environments can be created, this apparatus gave pupils less guidance as to the way to proceed – the number, position and relative areas of different environments had to be planned by the pupil.

Apart from demonstrating how the woodlice could be handled with a brush and checking that each pupil could start and stop the stopclock, the administrator gave no information about the use of the apparatus.

There are a number of aspects of this problem which it may be pertinent to review before describing pupils' performances. 'Woodlice preference' needs to be defined in some measurable way. It might be expected that pupils would obtain information on this variable either from the amount of time woodlice spend in the different environments or from the number of woodlice which settle in the different environments.

In carrying out the task reliably it is also important to take account of the fact that living organisms are likely to vary in their behaviour, and information from a number of woodlice should therefore be obtained. In carrying out any trials other factors such as where to place the woodlice initially and for how long to leave them are points which may need consideration.

The results are summarised in Table 6.3.

Only a third of the pupils used quantitative criteria – i.e. counting or timing woodlice in each of the environments – with only a fifth presenting all four environments simultaneously.

The qualitative criteria used by pupils included various judgements about the state of woodlice contentment derived from such statements as – 'see which place the woodlice like best'.

Table 6.3 *Approaches to the* **Woodlice** *task*

Environments	% pupils using (n = 201)		
	quantitative criteria	qualitative criteria	total
All 4 environments presented together	13	8	21
All 4 environments presented in pairs allowing choice on both variables	8	14	22
All 4 environments presented in pairs allowing choice on one variable or both uncontrolled	12	18	30
Environments presented separately	0	26	26
Other	0	1	1
Total	33	67	100

Source: *Science in Schools. Age 15 Report No. 2*, pp. 114–115.

Other versions of **Woodlice**

We turn now to the results from the same task presented as a paper-and-pencil planning question. For pupils at both ages 13 and 15 and across a number of investigation tasks, differences in performance have been found between performing investigations in a practical situation and writing a plan of the same investigation. In most cases performance on the practical task is better than when the question is presented in written form with a diagram of the apparatus, which in turn is better than the written question without the diagram.

A summary of the data comparing the practical performance of 15-year-old pupils with that on the pictorial version of the question is given in Table 6.4 below.

Table 6.4 *Comparison of pupil performance (age 15) on practical and pictorial versions of* **Woodlice**

Approach	% pupils	
	practical (n = 201)	pictorial (n = 298)
All 4 environments presented together	21	23
Combinations of 2 or 3 environments	52	16
4 separate environments presented	26	25
No discernible approach/non response	1	36

Source: *Science in Schools. Age 15 Report No. 2* and *Age 13 and 15 Report No. 3*.

About a fifth of pupils proposed an experiment in which all four conditions were offered simultaneously, with the woodlice effecting the choice as to where to take up residence. The percentage suggesting two pairs of consecutive experiments (to test each variable separately) is, however, quite different between practical and written versions, with some two-thirds of pupils allowing some choice in the practical version and less than half in the written version.

Examples of pupils' discussions of **Woodlice**

Three transcripts of pairs of pupils planning their approach to the **Woodlice** investigation in the oracy survey are given below. They are accompanied in each case by the impression mark for language, a language commentary on the performance, a science commentary and a science score.

Scoring of responses: the transcripts were given an overall impression mark for language on a 1–7 scale, applying the criteria described in *Language Performance in Schools – Secondary Survey Report No. 2* (DES, 1984).

Science scoring was on a 0–7 scale judged by the effectiveness of the pupils' approach to setting up an effective investigation. The analysis of the scientific content of this task has been based on the problem-solving model first outlined in the reports of the 1981 science survey and further amplified in *Science Assessment Framework, age 13 and 15* (DES, 1984). The model is reproduced as Figure 6.1.

Figure 6.1 *Problem-solving model*

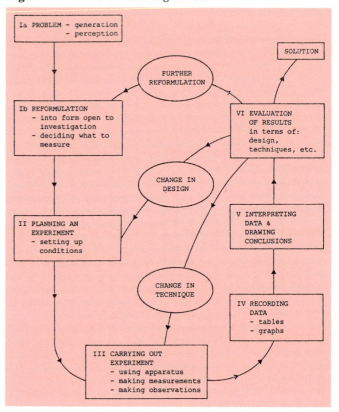

Performance at the lower end of the range

Example 1. Overall oracy impression mark: 1 (pupil A)
2 (pupil B)

Total time of complete performance: 6 min. 20 sec.

1. A: we could have the foam rubber and the jug of water
2. B: pour the water on that until till it's damp, put in the
3. plastic bag (long pause) have a (undecipherable) how about
4. that? how about then, pour the water on it, then put it on
5. top, then put a, not put anything in it, then put the perspex
6. on top, see if they settle in there (long pause)
7. A: would we need them for definite?
8. B: we would need the jug of water (long pause)
9. A: then how would we do it?

102

10. B: donno (pause) put the, water in it then (pause) put the foam
11.   rubber on it right? pour the water on it
12. A: um
13. B: um then um carry on with that black sheet, card all on top and
14.   er, put er the woodlice in
15: A: (inaudible)
16. B: put a, put a plastice bag on it
17. A: perspex frame? see if they settle in it? (long pause)
18. (Assessor: um thank you. You haven't any more ideas, no?)
19. B: um
20. (Assessor: Right can you tell me what you decided so far?)
21. B: we would have the grey plastic tray, er have the rubber foam
22.   pour the water on it, until it gets damp, then er put the
23.   woodlice in it, put er the plastic sheet on top there and put
24.   the perspex on top (long pause)
25. A: that's all, isn't it?

Language commentary

This transcript represents all that was said in over six minutes: the talk actually occupied less than a quarter of that time. Pupil A contributes very little. B shows traces of grappling with the problem (3–6, 10–14), but the outcome is less than adequate. Many of the poorer performances were brief when transcribed, though marked by long pauses. The pauses possibly indicate time spent searching for ideas to bring to bear on the problem.

Science commentary

Science score – 0

In this example, the pupils never came to grips with the problem. The first stage in the diagram, that of reformulating the problem into one that can be tested, has not been even discussed; the whole of the six minutes was spent in a consideration of what could be done with the equipment with no idea of the aim of the experiment.

Performance at the mid-point of the range

Example 2. Overall oracy impression mark: 4 (both pupils)

Total time of complete performance: 4 min. 35 secs.

1. A: um well, it gives, damp dark dry dark so, what we would try
2.   and do is, take the woodlice and divide them into sections,
3.   shall we have them in five groups?
4. B: yeh
5. A: and try and create these conditions and see what happens
6.   see if the woodlice wander off in favour of something else
7. B: yeh
8. A: then we could study them
9. B: yeh we'd want four, groups because we have got the
10.   four
11. A: so we've got the four groups so, let's
12. B: do the damp and dark first
13. A: right
14. B: (inaudible)
15. A: well, we want some water, we could use the plastic tray
16.   and fill it with a bit of water
17. B: we could use this black bag it's dark isn't it?
18. A: and then cover the water with the plastic bag and put
19.   the woodlice in it
20. B: (laughs)
21. A: (laughs) for dry and dark, well you could use a
22.   sheet of black card
23. B: yeh that's true
24. A: 'cos that's dry
25. B: leave it on its own
26. A: I think we would have to cover it
27. B: yeh
28. A: er
29. B: er
30. A: and the sheet of rubber and then you put the woodlice
31.   on the sheet of rubber and cover it with the em black
32.   card, so the woodlice got something nice
33.   dry and dark
34. B: dry and dark yes let's see damp and light
35. A: damp and light
36. B:
37. A: (indecipherable whispering)
38. B: put the frame round the white cardboard and put the
39.   water in (laughs) if we wanted it, if we wanted
40.   it light (pause) the paintbrush (pause)
41. A: em well we could make th- the white card damp, by you know
42.   just submerging it in water
43. B: uh huh
44. A: and then put the woodlice on that and see what
45.   happens. For dry and light, well, em (pause)
46. ? (whispering)
47. A: we could use the em frame just put it on em a
48.   table top and put the lice in there 'cos that would
49.   be dry and light
50. B: light yes
51. A: in where there's sunlight, put the
52. B: and then we need
53.   the w- we want something for dampness tho so
54.   perhaps the em
55. A: dry and light tho
56. B: dry and light oh sorry I thought we'd done that
57. A: (inaudible)
58. B: and then just see what
59. A: study each day what happens, you know, have a list

103

60. of headings and, see, how many of them have
    stayed
61. where
62. B: and how long
63. A: and how they are getting along yeh how well
64. they look (pause)
65. B: (to assessor) that's it

    •

    •

(Report to assessor continues for 1 min. 35 sec.)

Language commentary

Two noticeable features of this performance are the way
in which pupil A takes the lead throughout most of the
discussion, and the fact that the two pupils never deviate
from A's first plan. The first feature is not necessarily
representative of performances at this level, but helps in
this case to accentuate the second feature, which is fairly
typical.

A's leadership is shown clearly in the early exchanges
(1–8), where B merely interjects 'yeh' (4, 7), and at (11),
where A usurps B's point (9–10). A does consult B over
a detail of the plan at (3), and accept a suggestion from
her at (12–13), but then continues to act as if she had
had ideas which B had put forward (18, 41–42), and even
contradicts B, though gently (25–26, 55, 63).

That all this may reflect these pupils' usual working
relationship is suggested by the naturalness with which B
completes a sentence A had begun (11–12), and by the
occasions on which they whisper together (36–37, 46 and
others not transcribed).

None of this is meant to suggest, however, that these
pupils are *linguistically* less competent than others. On
the contrary, within the limits set by A's first idea they
work together very confidently and without discord to
plan the investigation of the four experimental conditions
as four separate, successive experiments:

	(lines of transcript)
general plan	1–11
damp and dark	12–19
dry and dark	21–34
damp and light	35–45
dry and light	45–56
recording outcome	58–65

This analysis of the structure of the discussion reveals,
however, that it is too closely tied both to A's first idea,
and to the order in which the four environments were
listed on the sheet which was handed to pupils during the
assessor's introductory instructions. It might be that if
these pupils had engaged in more exploratory give-and-
take discussions, they might have modified their ideas in
constructive ways and come closer to a worthwhile experimental design.

Science commentary

Science score – 1

In this example the pupils reformulated the problem but
made no attempt to evaluate their experimental design.
Their plan was based on an assumption that it is possible
in some way to measure the happiness of a single wood-
louse – by the size of their grin perhaps. There is an early
mention of 'wandering off in favour of . . .' (6) but this
is not followed up by a design incorporating a choice.
The score on science was 1, but this is an example of a
case where the practical application of their plan may
possibly have resulted in their modifying their design away
from this 'four igloo' approach.

*Further language commentary on middle-range
performances*

Other features which seemed to be characteristic of at
least a proportion of performances in the middle of the
range were the following. Some pupils had memories, not
alway recent or accurate, of having carried out such an
experiment, and were prone to rely too heavily on them.
This tendency overlapped with, but was not identical to,
a tendency to be dominated by 'knowing' the 'right'
answer. A rather more linguistic facet of some middling
performances, noticeable also in some of the (much
briefer) ones at the lower end of the range, was the use
of exophoric reference. This term denotes the use of
pronouns to refer to objects, events, etc., which are not
specified in the immediate *linguistic* context, i.e. which
are not named in the sentences currently being uttered
but typically are present in the immediate non-linguistic
surroundings. The following extract is the opening few
seconds of another performance on which both pupils
were awarded a 4:

1. A: um I thought we could use *that for em putting
   all the stuff
2. in couldn't you?
3. B: um (pause) *that – we would have to section *it
   off
4. A: um
5. B: you'd have to, and you wouldn't be able to get
   *them all
6. together would you? *some would have to be dry
   and *some
7. would have to be damp *some would have to be
   dark and
8. *some of them light
9. A: what is *that for?
10. B: (laughs) (pause) what is *it? I don't know. I
    suppose you
11. put the black card over one, part of *it for the
    dark, or . . .

Here the referents of the asterisked words are not entirely
clear from listening to the recording or reading the transcript. It must be emphasised that this is not a linguistic
deficiency: situated pronominal reference of this sort is
perfectly reasonable and efficient in a situation where, as

here, both participants can see and read the same information and, presumably, point to it for each other's benefit. However, it does seem to be the case that exophoric reference was largely absent from performances at the higher end of the range.

Performance at the upper end of the range

Example 3: Overall oracy impression mark: 6 (both pupils)
Total time of complete performance: 9 mins. 00 sec.

1. A: um to find out whether they liked damp and dark, I'd use the
2.   black card because it'd absorb the light.
3. B: well would you start with the ⌈tray
4. A: ⌊tray
5. B: the see-through tray (inaudible) because it has four compartments
6. A: right would you divide it up divide it up into, em,
7.   compartments?
8. B: right
9. A: with with, the two ones which are dark, you could use black
10.   card for those
11. B: well first of all you'd have to put em em well you'd have to
12.   you'd have to hope it was in quarters, 'cos if it wasn't in
13.   quarters (pause)
14. A: if you soaked the foam rubber in the water to get it wet, and
15. B: no I don't think you would need the foam
16. A: you do, to make it damp
17. B: you don't when you just
18. A: and em, em, you put, the tray, and put that in this you
19.   drop it this black (pause) if you divide the tray up into
20.   sections
21. B: into four you mean we have four things
22. A: yeh, you ma- you make, the first one damp and dark by using
23.   black card, sort of a roll of black card
24. B: well if you took the foam rubber when you put
25. A: no you would, put the roll and you would put the foam rubber
26.   inside the, roll of black card
27. B: why have you got the grey plastic tray?
28. A: it goes inside the grey plastic tray because it's wet, isn't
29.   it and it, would just run all over the table and then, you
30.   would do another one with em dark dry and dark one when you
31.   wouldn't use the, em you couldn't use the, water, you'd just
32.   use, em the black card the roll of black and then
33. B: so you'd have two with the foam rubber

34. A: and two ⌈and the one
35. B: ⌊and the one in the foam rubber would be black
36.   ⌈one wouldn't
37. A: ⌊one wouldn't
38. B: and one would ⌈be white
39. A: ⌊would be white using the white card
40. B: and then you'd have two which hadn't got any water in and one
41.   would be black and one would ⌈just like that
42. A: ⌊you you
43.   you could use like little rolls of them and
44. B: yes
45. A: you'd release all the, wood all the woodlice to, into the
46. B: f- first of all first of all, you put the you'd sort the
47.   ⌈parts out
48. A: ⌊we've already done that, and em (pause) then
49. B: then
50. A: you'd put the woodlice in and you'd see which conditions they
51.   went to
52. B: you must put them in the middle
53. A: yes
54. B: ⌈we'd need the stopclock
55. A: ⌊you would put put them in at one side and then you'd time them
56. B: no in the middle you wouldn't you'd put
57. A: no you'd put them in in the in the middle of the thing and
58.   you'd have an equal distance to each of the four corners of
59.   the tray.
60. B: and you'd have to hope it had airholes
61. A: well it would because it wouldn't have a lid would it?
62. B: oh that's, yes, I suppose not. You wouldn't need the perspex
63.   frame
64. A: and then you'd time, we'd er we'd give them a time limit so
65.   that'd be about enough time for, the woodlice to go from,
66.   place to place
67. B: about twenty minutes . . . (inaudible)
68. A: yeh and then after that time you'd take the the take the
69.   count the amount of woodlice in each of the things and the one
70.   with the most in, would probably be the condition they
71.   preferred most
72. B: and then we'd draw up the table if we had to draw up a table
73.   with the paper and that

       •
       •

(continues for a further 5 min. 45 sec.)

Language commentary

This was a highly co-operative performance. There is no question here of a dominant partner, nor of either pupil sticking to an idea in disregard of the other. Pupil A starts by considering how to tackle only one of the environments (1–2), but B immediately suggests that all four could be set up simultaneously (3–5), and A instantly accepts this procedure as being superior (6–7) and begins to elaborate it (9–10). Soon afterwards it is B who drops an objection to an idea of A's (14–16), as indicated by the uncompleted tailing off of B's remark at (18). The extent to which the two pupils are thinking along similar lines is particularly shown by the substantial amount of overlap in their talk at (34–42), where they even spontaneously use the same words simultaneously. All the while the tentativeness of their language indicates how they are searching both for the best way to carry out the experiment and for the clearest and most appropriate way to express their plan: see especially (11–12, 18–19, 22, 31–32, 46) and, for later examples (56, 68–69).

By (44) or (48) they have arrived at what to them is a satisfactory design for the experiment, though some of the details are not fully spelt out in what they say but rely on shared understandings. For instance, it seems as though they mean to put the foam rubber into the grey plastic tray and dampen half the rubber, and roll the sheets of white and black card (into small balls, or into tubes?) to produce the dark areas. But it is not entirely clear whether this would be dark enough, or in which fashion the four sectors of the tray would be arranged.

About the need to start the woodlice off in the most neutral position, the middle of the tray, however, they very soon reach agreement. B proposes this (52) and A seems to agree (53) but then states a different approach (55). When B insists, gently, that the middle is the best place (56), A falls in with this and even gives a fairly scientific reason for it (57–59). Indeed throughout this utterance A seems to be convincing herself rather than B, and her 'no' at the beginning of (57) seems to mean 'Cancel my previous remark' rather than 'I disagree'. The remainder of the transcribed part of the performance consists of a co-operative thinking out of the timing of the experiment and the recording of the results.

In all of the respects discussed, this performance is fully representative of the higher end of the range. The reason this particular pair did not receive 7s seems to be connected with the remaining 5 min. 45 sec. of talk (which included reporting the plan to the assessor): during all this time the two pupils added nothing of significance to their discussion, and seem therefore to have been marked down slightly for verbosity.

Science commentary

Science score – 7

It will have been apparent from the above discussion that many cycles of problem-solving activity are evident in this extended discussion. Their solution begins with the igloo solution, moves to a four choice chamber, considers the area of the four sections of the choice chamber, positioning the woodlice in the centre, and finally decides on a numerical strategy for determining preference. The remainder of the transcript consists of a series of amendments to plans for putting this plan into effect.

Overall science commentary on the oracy version of **Woodlice**

Each of the 33 transcripts of the discussions of the pairs of pupils taking part in the oracy survey was analysed along similar lines to those adopted for the practical science version. The results are shown in Table 6.5 below. It is important to note that the sample is very much smaller than for the practical investigation and so the figures in the body of the table are the numbers of pupils rather than percentages.

Table 6.5 *Pupil approaches to the oracy* **Woodlice** *task*

Environments	number of pupils using (n = 33)		
	quantitative criteria	qualitative criteria	total
All 4 environments presented together	3	7	10
All 4 environments presented in pairs allowing choice on both variables	3	1	4
All 4 environments presented in pairs allowing choice on one variable or both uncontrolled	0	2	2
Environments presented separately	0	7	7
Other	0	5	5
Unclear	0	0	5
Total	6	22	33

With the proviso that comparisons must be tentative with such a small sample being analysed in this oracy task, the figures here seem to be more in keeping with the results for the practical investigation than with those for the pictorial version of the question. Qualitative measurements are, however, slightly more in evidence in the oracy sample, although it is often difficult to interpret the intended meaning of 'and see where the woodlice go'. In practice this apparently qualitative approach may or may not be turned into a quantitative measurement of 'how many'.

It has been suggested that improved performance in the practical task over the written version is a result of pupils' 'thinking on their feet' in interaction with the apparatus. The results obtained when pupils talk about the experiment may well also be better than in the written **Woodlice** for similar reasons, the 'thinking on their feet' being replaced by a 'thinking aloud' stimulated by the interaction between the pupils.

The correlation coefficient between the science and language scores for **Woodlice** was 0.62 (t = 3.87; p < 0.001; 28 df). It is not surprising that performance is highly correlated. Inspection of the transcripts suggests that the high correlation is due at least in part to the fact that the ability to enter into the science of the problem governs the subsequent discussion. If pupils do not know what the problem is about and have no idea how to proceed, they do not really have a great deal to talk about, the weather and the miner's strike being ruled out by the context in which the pupils find themselves. Equally, if they cannot discuss or describe even with limited fluency then there is unlikely to be much science worthy of the name in what is said.

The degree to which language influences performance in science is unresolved. Obviously a lack of vocabulary and other language structures must limit expression in the descriptive aspects of science. Similarly, concise and accurate use of language is important in the formulation of the problems in investigations and logical operations in science. Language is the medium through which we carry out science, and the medium through which science is assessed. Clearly there is a need to develop the language skills alongside the processes of science.

6.4 Tin

(Commentary written in collaboration with G. Welford of the APU age 15 Science Monitoring team, University of Leeds)

The recordings of pupil conversations in response to **Tin** were scored in a similar way to **Woodlice** – an impression mark for language on a 1–7 scale, and a science score between 0 and 7. (Again, this task was not marked analytically for language.) Scientifically, the task as a whole depends upon the collection of data by observations, on the selection of which to investigate, how to carry out the investigations, etc., and then which hypotheses to reject and which to use in formulating the final conclusions. The effect of pupil confidence on their findings is hard to quantify, but it must be significant in that some findings are not built into final statements. The knowledge background of pupils is also a variable affecting performance. For example, the pupil who says 'it is not metal because it is not magnetic' concludes correctly that the contents are non-metallic, but for incorrect reasons.

The approach whereby each aspect of the contents, viz. materials, size, shape, presence or absence of spindle and so on, are systematically explored, reasonable tests employed, selective observation applied and findings evaluated, matches the scientific criteria most closely and so scores 7. Scores of less than 7 signify approaches where aspects of this ideal approach are missing, and usually show a failure to investigate thoroughly, or a failure to make (or recognise the significance of) the necessary observations to allow progress in establishing the nature of the contents of the tin.

Performance at the lower end of the range

Poorer performances on this task seemed to be mainly distinguished, linguistically, by an apparent reluctance to discuss the problem. At its most extreme, this tendency could result in a performance such as Example 1.

(In this and following examples of this task, pupil A has the tin, magnet and ruler and is the only one allowed to handle them; pupil B has the diagram and pencil and has to draw and write the conclusions. Also, the pauses marked in the transcripts, which are much more frequent and extensive in this task than in others, do not indicate, as they might on other tasks, periods when the pupils were not actively engaged in doing it. During the pauses on the tapes there can frequently be heard the sounds of the tin being shaken or rolled, or investigated with the magnet or ruler, and of tentative diagrams being erased.)

Example 1. Overall oracy impression mark: 2 (pupil A)
                                    not scored (pupil B)

Total time of complete performance: 3 min. 00 sec.

1. A: heavy (pause) it's not made of metal (long pause) it's not very
2.   noisy, it's fat (?) (long pause) it's quite a large object
3.   (long pause) I can't think of anything else to describe it

Language commentary

There was far more silence than talk in this performance, and pupil B did not contribute. Pupil A was clearly testing the tin with the magnet (1) and by shaking, and did attempt to make deductions about the contents (2). That pupil B, though silent, was also attempting to make some sense of the object is shown by his diagram (Illustration 6.9), and by the brief description below it:

Illustration 6.9   Tin *diagram of pupil B in example 1*

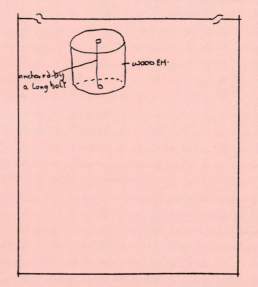

Draw what you think the contents of the tin are like in the outline below. Show in your drawing as much information as you can about what is in the tin. (You can use labels.)

Afterwards,   also write a short description (two or three lines) of the contents of the tin here: A wooden cylindrical block with a slightly smaller size than the tins volume. Held in the centre by a long bolt.

Science commentary

Science score – 0

Naturally, there are many different approaches to solving this problem, but the effectiveness of any approach must be judged by whether the pupil making the drawing has enough information to be able to do so.

All approaches, irrespective of the final usefulness of the investigation, start in a similar fashion. The pupil picks up the tin, shakes it and presumably examines its exterior surface. This exploratory phase is often followed by a fairly extensive initial statement or series of hypotheses.

In the case of the first example this marked the end of experimentation and the task was seen as completed.

In the light of the marked lack of vocal communication between the pupils, the quality of B's drawing is surprising. The conclusion – written and drawn – is very close to the truth. However, only the dialogue has been scored for science, and since so little was said it is not so surprising that the scientific content is almost non-existent.

Example 2. Overall oracy impression mark: 1 (pupil A)
2 (pupil B)

Total time of complete performance: 9 min. 00 sec.

1. (Assessor: (long pause) You talk about this to some extent because we're interested in how you work it out)
2. A: it's round (long pause)
3. B: put it down (long pause) hold it, does it roll up?
4. A: no (pause) it's rubber
5. B: it's a ball? (long pause) is it a ball? a ball? (long pause)
6. A: is it magnet? is that-
7. A: no (long pause)
8. B: is it moving while you're doing that?
9. A: yeah
10. B: it is (pause) is it as big as the tin do you think?
11. A: no (pause) it's heavy
12. B: it's heavy
13. A: yeah (long pause)
14. B: is it moving when you shake it up and down?
15. A: yeah (long pause) it's a ball (pause)
16. B: do you think it's rubber?
17. A: yeah (long pause)
 •
 •

(continues for 4 minutes: 13 lines of transcript omitted)

Language commentary

This example again illustrates the taciturnity of pupils whose performances received low scores, though in a slightly less extreme form. After more than a minute's silence, the assessor intervened to prompt the first statement by pupil A. In the full nine-minute performance, pupil A made 19 utterances, of which eight were monosyllabic replies to questions from B, while B made 18

utterances, mainly questions, the two longest being ten words each (10, 14).

This example is typical of poorer performances in another respect, namely the tendency to jump to a conclusion almost at once and stick to it thereafter. Here A's statements that the object is round (2) and rubber (4) naturally lead B to conclude that it is a ball (5), and this was shown in his diagram, with a few supporting details in the description. The diagram consisted simply of a circle drawn within the tin outline and labelled BALL. The description read:

It is a round object, because it rolls in the tin. It's not magnetic, it's heavy, because it makes the tin Ping when it hits it.

This tendency to jump to a conclusion also means that in poorer performances the pupils typically do not make all the observations required to come close to divining the nature of the tin's contents.

Science commentary

Science score – 3

In this example, there was a limited attempt to collect and review the data. However, the evidence was given scant attention and no further propositions were attempted or explored. In some cases at this lower end of the range one of the two pupils overrode the opinion of the other, and in some neither of the two had the confidence to change their mind from the first initial hypothesis – this even though the conflicting information was strong. In most cases either the pupils did not recognise the significance of their observations or chose to ignore conflicting data. They certainly never discussed the issues, although from the sounds of their experimentation and the long pauses in the dialogue, such data would seem to have been available to them.

Some pairs of pupils appear to fail to reach a complete picture of the contents because of failure in one of two ways. *Either* they fail to make all the observations necessary to describe all the attributes of the contents, *or* they do not test adequately their hypotheses regarding these contents. A third group do not make their observations or their tests in a systematic manner and so fail to collect and review all the necessary data. Some pupils do all this, but do not press their findings on into definite conclusions, presumably either lacking confidence or perhaps not recognising the relevance of their observations to the task in hand.

Performance at the mid-point of the range

In average performances the pupils usually did make a substantial number of relevant observations about the tin, but usually did not analyse them sufficiently. This is well illustrated in the next example.

Example 3. Overall oracy impression mark: 4 (pupil A)
                                         5 (pupil B)

1. A: (pause) it's heavy, solid
2. B: solid?
3. A: yeah and there's, it's, attached to like a rod that goes
4.   straight down the middle, cos it won't move any other way,
5.   well, er (pause)
6. B: can you try the magnet on it? (pause) try it underneath
7.   (long pause) so it's not metal
8. A: it's just, the tin can't be (pause) well it is slightly,
9.   cos there's a bit of, there's a bit there, but the thing
10.   inside can't be
11. B: well where is it now, is it ⌈is it at the bottom?
12. A: ⌊it's at the bottom it's, heavy
13.   so that i- if you put it to the top it will fall back to the
14.   bottom, um
15. B: does it roll?
16. A: no because it is on a, like a rod that goes from the top to
17.   the bottom seems to be, um (pause) when you're holding it it
18.   seems to be about, that big, I don't know (pause) it seems
19.   like one of those, those you know those hard solid balls that
20.   you bounce and that keep bouncing and don't stop well, it
21.   seems like one of those, I think
22. B: so you think it, is round?
23. A: yeh, I think it's round (long pause) wait wait wait, wait,
24.   listen, now listen to it fall this way, now listen to it fall
25.   that way it's as though, it's got a flat bottom when it runs
26.   that way and a curved,
27. B: top
28. A: does it sound like it?
29. B: yeah
30. A: it's got more surface on the bottom part when it runs (pause)
31.   it's kind of, like that (pause)
32. B: when you roll it does it, feel like it's round or square?
33.   (long pause) how big do you think it'd be how, tall? (pause)
34.   could it come up more than half of it?
35. A: yeh but what can we use these for? we're suppo-sed to (long
36.   pause) whatever it is it's something solid, the object it's
37.   got a flat bottom (pause) I don't know whether it is on a
38.   thing in the middle I can't, see if it w- (long pause)

39. B: would you s- swinging it from side to side? it could it could
40.   be ⌈not all that big
41. A: ⌊about that big, or it could be bigger that, than what the,
42.   that goes, through the, thing, couldn't it, that's what makes
43.   the noise
44. B: yes it could it not be big then? like, fill up most of the
45.   tin, so it can't move freely, could be as wide
46. A: oh yeah it could just be a bit smaller than the tin
47. B: yeah
48. A: to make it (pause) yeah
49. B: you think it is
50. A: it is, yeah (pause) let's use this here (pause)
51. B: try it at the side (pause)
52. A: no it's not at the side
53. B: so it could be quite high then, let's try the middle (pause)
54. A: yeah but there's like a post (?)
55. B: at the end?
56. A: um but not down there (tapping) I think, it's smaller than the
57.   actual, ⌈tin
58. B: ⌊tin
59. A: because I can feel it knocking on each side
60.   but it could be, just small enough to get it in
61. A: yeah, so it will just fit in and allow room for it to
62.   ⌈(inaudible)
63. B: ⌊so you don't think it's on nothing?
64. A: no (pause)
       •
       •

(continues for 3 min. 10 sec.)

Language commentary

Ironically, if these pupils had stuck to A's initial idea, their result would have been closer to the truth. Pupil A immediately observes that the object is heavy and solid (1). Then apparently from the screwheads on the top and bottom of the tin, and the fact that the object moves up and down but not sideways (3-4), and won't roll (16) she correctly deduces that it is on a rod (3-4, cf.16). Pupil B's questions and instructions at (6), (11) and (15) are all intended to gain clarification of the initial insights, but seem to have the net effect of confusing A, to judge from the tentativeness of her replies at (8-10) and (12-14), both of which contain hesitations. Then A suddenly comes up with the new idea that the object is a ball (19), which does not quite fit with the idea that it is on a rod.

This in turn is immediately superseded by a new and wholly accurate observation by A, namely that the object makes a softer sound when it hits the lid of the tin than when it hits the base (24-25). Her excitement at this point is shown by her repeated 'wait' (23). She follows this observation up with a hypothesis to explain it (25-26, 30) and B's questions at (32-34) seem to be intended to define

109

the shape of the object: this may well be because B will eventually have to draw it. A almost ignores the questions, however, and continues puzzling over the object, repeating two of her observations or inferences (36–37), but then half-withdrawing her insight about the rod (37–38). B's request at (39) seems to be intended to test the rod idea, and both pupils then explore an alternative explanation of the fact that the object does not seem to roll inside the tin (39–46), namely that it almost fills it, sideways. At (41–42) A's talk is particularly hesitant, which may indicate that she is grappling with the implications of the alternative explanation.

Quite what is going in at (50–56) is not entirely clear, but from the tapping at (56) it seems that A has been trying to establish by knocking the tin (and listening for hollow or dull sounds?) whether the object is close to the sides, and, if so, how much of the tin it fills. At (59) she makes what seems to be an incorrect observation, since the object was so constructed inside that it could not touch the sides. At (60–61) the pupils affirm the new explanation. When B invites A to reject the rod idea (63), A assents (64). The rest of the discussion (not transcribed) consisted of inconclusive attempts to decide whether the object and/or the tin was magnetic, and re-affirmations of the conclusions stated in the diagram (Illustration 6.10):

Illustration 6.10 **Tin** *diagram of pupil B in example 3*

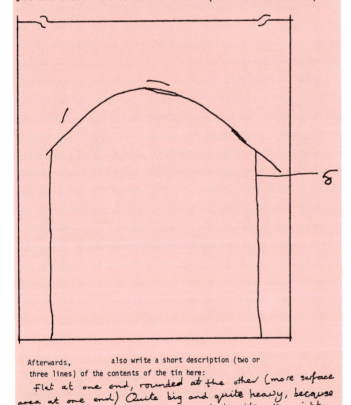

Draw what you think the contents of the tin are like in the outline below. Show in your drawing as much information as you can about what is in the tin. (You can use labels.)

Afterwards, also write a short description (two or three lines) of the contents of the tin here:
Flat at one end, rounded at the other (more surface area at one end) Quite big and quite heavy, because it doesn't move much. From side to side. It might just have been a bit narrower than the tin. Could have been magnetic.

In this case, therefore, the pupils made several correct observations, but did not integrate them. In particular, the outcome would have been much more accurate if the two pupils had held on to both the rod idea, and the observation of the two different noises. Somehow they seemed to argue each other away from A's correct initial insight, towards a hypothesis that is certainly easier to draw, though this may not have been the cause of their change of view. In changing their minds, however, they began to make the evidence fit the new theory: at least, this seems to be a possible explanation for A's erroneous observation at (59).

Science commentary
Science score – 5
Many of the points of significance from a scientific point of view have been described in the language commentary. Most of the necessary observations were made, but the significance of these was not realised and redundant data were not actively rejected. In the end the conclusions were weak because much of relevance was not recognised. This transcript is typical of several where observations are not explored, hypotheses not tested and so conclusions appear very halfhearted and lacking in conviction – as though the inadequacy is obvious to both pupils but the relative safety of being half right (and half wrong) is preferred to any probability of being entirely wrong!

Performance at the upper end of the range

From what has been said about lower and average performances, it will already be clear that better performances were distinguished by the ability to talk through the problem, to make all or most of the pertinent observations about the tin and to integrate them. All of these facets are illustrated by the following example.

Example 4. Overall impression mark: 7 (both pupils)
Total time of complete performance: 5 min. 10 sec.

1. A: it er (pause)
2. B: is it moving around?
3. A: yeh it, seems to be er, fill the sides of the tin
4. B: is it heavy?
5. A: er no not really, I don't think. It's fairly heavy it's er
6. (pause) I think it's er, s-seems cylindrical, it
7. sort of it rolls up and down
8. B: is it sort of like a ball shape?
9. A: no it's no- it's not, definitely not a ball, you see it
10. doesn't it only moves (pause) it doesn't move when you,

110

11. turn it that way (pause) it's I think it seems to be, in the
12. tin, don't think don't think the magnet will help (pause) it's
13. er (pause) I'd say that it is, cylindrical, it's about roughly
14. (pause) (to Assessor) can you use like, clues from the outside
15. ⌐when you
16. (Assessor: yes⌐certainly)
17. A: say there's a, there's a, pole, through there with it sliding
18. up and down with it because, you can feel it when you er shake
19. it from side to side it's got a hole in the middle, well I
20. think, you can feel it, er (pause)
21. B: ⌐the magnet, yeh
22. A: ⌐it seems sort of er, dead you know it's not it's not metal or
23. B: is it quite he-
24. A: wood or anything
25. B: is it, bulky, heavy?
26. A: yeh I think it it feels pretty dense but er
27. B: could be padded on the end, look
28. A: only that end, it's in that end (pause) can we er er could be
29. er er plasticine or a rubber a rubber, cylinder (pause)
30. because that end makes more noise than the other (pause) yeah
31. I'd say there's a rubber cylinder, on a, on a pole up the
32. middle
33. B: so what makes it, noisier one end?
34. A: I think it's just the, tin really, cos that would be that
35. wouldn't make very much noise anyway cos it's (pause) that
36. the er like thinner end of it, and the shape of the tin there
37. ⌐wouldn't make that much noise
38. B: ⌐could that absorb some of the sound there?
39. B: yeah must do (pause) although it could be harder at one end,
40. could be made of two different, things two halves (pause) I'd
41. say it was rub- er rubber or something li- er and a cylinder,
42. with a hole in the middle like that, hole hole in the middle
43. there, moves up and down on a, a bar, think that's it I
44. wouldn't worry about it. Do you want my rubber?
45. B: yeah, you think it's like it's on an axis
46. A: yeah that's it (long pause)

    •

    •

(continues for 1 min. 50 sec.)

Language commentary

The opening exchanges here are notable for their tentativeness. Ideas about the size (3), weight (4–5) and shape (6) of the tin's contents are floated but not yet made definite enough to rule out alternatives. It is not until (9) that pupil A makes any definite statement about the object, and even that is negative, leaving all other possibilities open. In fact A might not yet have made even a negative statement but for B's attempts to define the object's shape as 'like a ball' (8). This idea was a reasonable interpretation of A's statement 'it sort of rolls up and down', but A seems to realise that B's inference is a misapprehension because 'roll' was the wrong word to describe what he could feel about the object's movements. He immediately moves to correct it, both by denying that the object is a ball and by providing evidence, namely that it 'doesn't move when you turn it that way' (presumably barrel-fashion, about its axis).

Soon afterwards, A begins to put his observations together into several correct deductions, about the object being cylindrical (13), the presence of a 'pole' (17), and the fact that the object slides along the 'pole' (17–18), because there is a hole through it (19). Then comes another set of exchanges in which B's question (25) and suggestion (27) help A concentrate on the weight of the object and the dullness of the sound it makes, so that A makes explicit the difference in the sounds the object makes when it hits the lid and the base of the tin (28). Such is the degree of understanding and co-operation that this last point is made in three words. At (29–32) A breaks off the investigation to re-affirm the conclusions he had stated at (13–20), but B immediately returns to the pursuit of an explanation of the two sounds (33). A offers an hypothesis (34–37), but tentatively, so that B is able to ask, in effect, whether that hypothesis will do (38). A then offers an alternative view (39–40) which is nearer to B's suggestion at (27).

A now re-states the conclusions they have reached (41–43), and the rest of the discussion (not transcribed) was occupied by B producing a diagram and A's comments on it. This part of the discussion included the acceptance by A of the idea that the object was of two materials, and his making it clear to B that the top end was softer. All of this is well shown in B's diagram (Illustration 6.11).

The description reads:

The object inside the tin appears to be cylindrical, made of two materials. One material is soft and is joined to the second material which is harder than the first. The axis is a smooth material, and causes no friction on the cylinder.

This sticks closely to the observed facts, and does not try to go beyond them, e.g. into stating exactly what the object is or deciding whether or not it is magnetic. A few pairs of pupils guessed accurately that the object was a doorstop (one pupil called it a 'roller skate stopper'), and that it was padded at the top. None suspected the fact

Illustration 6.11 **Tin** *diagram of pupil B in example 4*

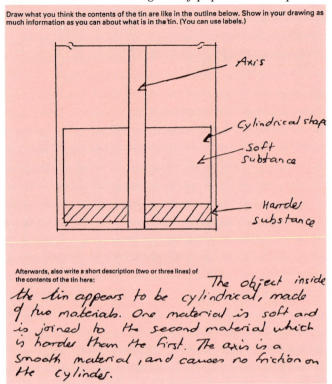

Draw what you think the contents of the tin are like in the outline below. Show in your drawing as much information as you can about what is in the tin. (You can use labels.)

Axis

Cylindrical shape

Soft substance

Harder substance

Afterwards, also write a short description (two or three lines) of the contents of the tin here: The object inside the tin appears to be cylindrical, made of two materials. One material is soft and is joined to the second material which is harder than the first. The axis is a smooth material, and causes no friction on the cylinder.

that the inside of the lid was also padded, and it would have been surprising, given the few observable facts about the tin, if any had inferred this.

These pupils exhibited, as already said, the ability to talk the problem through, to make accurate observations and to integrate them. All of this, however, also required co-operativeness in talk, and a willingness on both pupils' part to let ideas begin vague and become clearer. This is shown by the tentative, even sometimes hesitant, way in which suggestions are made, and contrasts with the approach of less good performances, where pupils typically seemed to want to get the answer quickly. Yet despite their willingness to explore ideas, and if necessary amend them, these pupils arrived at a more accurate solution much more quickly than those in either Example 2 or Example 3.

Science score – 7

In this example the pupils showed both the recognition of the relevance of their observations, and a systematic exploration of the hypotheses which were advanced. Their discussion was marked by a periodic review of the findings to recapitulate on the data, before moving on to test the next hypothesis. It was also marked by the exploration of some irrelevances but these were recognised as such and were not used in the final summary of contents.

Performance on other science versions of **Tin**

For both the oracy and science surveys essential features of this task were the same. Pupils had to make a series of observations to determine the unseen contents of a tin and use these observations to make a drawing of the contents.

A very similar question, based on a similar tin with different contents (a lump of plasticine firmly fixed to one side inside the tin), was reported in detail in *Science in Schools: Age 15 Report no. 1*, p. 76. The 1982 age 15 science survey included a question in which the tin's contents were almost the same as that used for the oracy project.

It is worth presenting a brief review of the 1982 pupil performance data on this question set in a science context in order to make a broad comparison with performance on the oracy task. Such comparison is fraught with the interpretational difficulties which derive from attempting any (however limited) generalisation based on the sample of only 30 from the oracy project analysed for science content.

Table 6.6 *Pupil performance on science version of* **Tin**

	% pupils (N = 753)
Drawings containing all features of contents	9
Drawings containing two features of contents	19
Drawings containing one feature of contents	33
Drawings containing only speculative elements	36
No drawing attempted	4

Table 6.7 *Pupil performance on oracy version of* **Tin**

	Number of pupil pairs* (N = 30)
Drawings containing all features of contents	5
Drawings containing two features of contents	11
Drawings containing one feature of contents	10
Drawings containing only speculative elements	4
No drawing attempted	0

*Results presented as raw numbers of pairs rather than as percentage of sample due to the small sample size.

In the science test with individual pupils working on their own and given six minutes to complete the task, although 60 per cent of the drawings contained at least one correct feature of the tin, fully 36 per cent of the drawings contained only speculative elements. Furthermore, although not depicted in Table 6.6, while 39 per cent of pupils' drawings were entirely consistent with their written observations all the remainder contained speculative elements which had not been included in their written observations.

By way of contrast only four (of 30) drawings from the oracy test were entirely speculative, and only four of the remainder contained elements which were not consistent with the observations made during their discussions. All the others, although not featuring *all* the contents of the tin, were free of previously unrecorded components.

The correlation coefficient between the science and language scores for **Tin** was 0.84 (t = 79.92; p < 0.001; 28 df) and the comments made in the previous section

(Woodlice) about the close relationship between language and science apply here also. Those pupils working on their own in the science surveys produced *less* successful hypotheses as to the contents of the tin than did the oracy pairs working co-operatively. The drawings of the former group were less comprehensive, and there was far lower correspondence between stated observation and resultant drawings.

The science data were based on a large sample of pupils, and those in the science/oracy exercise came from only 30 pairs of pupils. This notwithstanding, the preliminary conclusions must be that the opportunity for discussion and co-operative effort whilst using apparatus has resulted in enhanced scientific performance.

6.5 Map

(Commentary incorporating suggestions from G. Ruddock of the APU Mathematics Monitoring team, NFER)

Comments on performance: analytic assessment

The analytic categories applied in marking this task were:

Category	Sub-categories	
1. PROBLEM-SOLVING	(i) Statement of problem	
	(ii) Statement of solution	Task-specific
	(iii) Negotiation	
	(iv) Use of map aids	
2. LEXICO-GRAMMATICAL FEATURES	(i) Lexical selection	
	(ii) Syntax	
3. PERFORMANCE FEATURES	(i) Hesitation/self-correction	
	(ii) Tempo and pacing	
	(iii) Verbal assertiveness	

In the terms of performance on this task, these categories indicate that, in order to do well, pupils must be able to:

give a clear opening statement of the problem – pupil A ('Statement of problem');

begin a clear explanation of the solution to the problem – pupil B ('Statement of solution');

work out collaboratively strategies for dealing with the differences between the two maps ('Negotiation');

in doing so, make effective use of the cartographic symbols, etc. ('Use of map aids');

select words which appropriately name the features of the maps, directions, distances, etc. ('Lexical selection');

use well-formed grammatical structures appropriate to conveying instructions, problems, queries, etc. ('Syntax');

speak in a fluent and confident manner, at an appropriate tempo, avoiding undue hesitation or self-correction ('Performance features').

In theory, this task could be accomplished very efficiently by a minimal exchange such as the following:

A: 'Hi Fran, it's Viv. You know I was going on a country walk? Well, I'm at Chidding, trying to get to Penfold, but my map must be out of date because when I went north out of Chidding on the footpath past the pub I found a motorway in the way and I can't see how to get across it. I know you've got a new map, so can you give me directions? I'm at the phone box in Chidding.'

B: 'O.K. Viv. Come out of the phone box, face the pub and turn right along Walden Road, O.K.? Walk for about a kilometre until you pass Chidding Hall on your left. Then about another 400 metres along on the left you'll find a footpath going north. If you stay on that it'll take you over the motorway and the canal and direct to Penfold. Got that?'

A: 'Yes, thanks, Fran. Bye.'

B: 'Bye.'

However, this ideally efficient solution is obvious only to those who can see both maps, and in practice no pair came very close to it. Moreover, the requirement to *draw* the new route means that pupil A must ask for more detailed information, e.g. about distances and directions. Also As varied greatly in the clarity with which they stated the problem, and virtually all Bs gave or tried to give much more detailed explanations of the new route. In doing so, they inevitably referred to features of the area which had altered since Map 1 had been printed, and As therefore raised queries about details they could not immediately understand. Variation in performance was then largely determined by the skill with which both parties handled the discrepancies between their descriptions of the maps, and with which they used the various map aids (grid, compass, etc.).

There were several discrepancies between the two maps, besides the central one of the appearance of a motorway across A's intended route. The changes were all designed to be plausible in the context of a rural area which had once had both a branch railway and a canal and was now crossed by a motorway. The railway had been torn up, and part of its old course used as the basis of the route of the new footpath. The railway bridge over the canal had been demolished. The railway tunnel under Rivey Hill had not only gone out of use when the railway was closed but had been obliterated when a cutting for the new motorway was made through that part of the hill. The canal had become derelict, and part of its course had then disappeared beneath the motorway. Chidding Station had been sold off as a private house and punningly renamed 'Booking Hall'. Chidding Hall, apparently no longer in private hands, had become a Centre for Overseas Studies. The final change from Map 1 to Map 2 was that the units of the distance scale had been altered from miles to kilometres.

(The area depicted is of course fictitious, and both village names are imaginary though plausible. Several of the feature names, however, derive from real places on the South Cambridgeshire–N.W. Essex border.)

Three map aids were provided: a scale, the principal compass bearings, and a set of grid squares with alpha-numeric references in the margin. The grid did not, and was not intended to, correspond to that used on Ordnance Survey maps. The compass shown was not a full Cardinal compass but was a North-only compass: but it is known from results of APU Mathematics monitoring that only about 2 per cent of 15-year-olds confuse East and West, at least in *written* items.

In several other ways the maps were much simpler than recognised cartographic practice: for example, the use of monochrome rather than colour, the use of shading instead of contour lines for hillsides, and the labelling of the tunnel, canal, footpath, motorway and so on directly on the map rather than on a key. All this was done to reduce the complexity of the maps to a manageable level, and also to reduce the dependence of the ability to perform the task on previous experience.

Not all map features were labelled, however: it was assumed that pupils of this age would know or infer the meaning of the conventional representations of bridges, houses, etc.

The change of scale posed difficulties only for those pupils who chose to try to estimate the 'real' distance from Chidding Hall to the beginning of the new footpath. When it became apparent that the two maps had different scales, most pupils avoided the problem by saying, for example, 'two centimetres (along the map)', or 'halfway to the edge of the map', or by assuming that over such a short distance the difference between yards and metres would be negligible.

Performance at the lower end of the range

Example 1. Overall impression mark: 1 (both pupils)

Total time of complete performance: 2 min. 50 sec.

(In this and following examples of this task, pupil A has the out-of-date map.)

1. A: hello G –
2. B: hello M –
3. A: this is this is I am as you know I was going to Penfold on a
4. walk but now I'm s – I'm stuck as I was coming out from

5. Chiddington I realised that there was a, a path here a, a
6. thing which I could not get past now I have no directions on
7. how to get to Penfold Penfold as there is a path in front of
8. me that I can't get past it to go along to towpath and I
9. wonder can you give me some directions?
10. B: oh so you want me to give you some directions
11. A: yes.

.

(10 sec. digression)

.

12. B: right then. the first thing you would do is – the foo – you see
13. where the footpath is?
14. A: yes
15. B: well you would go u – up the footpath and turn left, O.K.?
16. A: uh huh
17. B: then you would go straight on, you walk straight on
18. until the end of the road, and then you'd, you would um go on
19. ahead there until you would turn right, and then you would er
20. come back a bit there you would turn right and then you would
21. come back and then you would turn right again, and here
22. there's a road here before you turn right there's a road, and
23. you go up that road, and then you go straight on and it's a
24. kind of a, made like a roundabout you go round there, and you
25. go on ahead on it to a road. And here the road is a,
26. crossroads, d'you know, right?
27. A: I see the crossroads.
28. B: and then you go you turn left then and that's the way to
29. Penfold.
30. A: so would you explain that again from Chidding-ton again?

•

•

(continues for a further 40 sec.)

Comments

In this example pupil A states the basic problem, that she cannot get to Penfold, adequately (3–4), but then begins to confuse her partner. A minor point is that she misnames Chidding. More systematically misleading is her failure or reluctance to use the word 'motorway' – which in fact neither pupil used throughout the task, even though it was marked on B's map and had been used in the assessor's explanation to A. Also A does not state her current location, and appears to call the motorway a 'path' (5). All this probably explains why B assumes that A is somewhere near the beginning of the new footpath in square C1 (12–13). Even so, the incompleteness of A's statement of the problem does not fully account for the vagueness of B's explanation of the solution. She specifies too many right turns (19, 20, 21, 22), and instead of 'turn left' appears to use the phrase 'come back (a bit)' (20, 21). Also throughout, she seems to describe the footpath as a road, and it is unclear what she intends by 'round-about' (24). It is therefore not surprising that A asks for a repetition of the explanation (30): but the second version (not transcribed) was no clearer than the first.

It is noticeable that neither of these pupils makes any use of the grid, the scale or the compass, and that differences between the two maps are also scarcely mentioned. In the conversation, the latter point is reflected in the fact that pupil A does not interrupt B's explanations at all to seek clarification. But at least these pupils did not display left/right confusion, which was a feature of many poor performances and even of some average ones.

In general, performances at the lower end of the range seemed to display two main characteristics, both of which are present in Example 1. The first of these was a tendency, especially marked in the pupils with the up-to-date map, to take too much for granted. One pupil, for example, after telling his partner to walk along Walden Road, said 'Don't turn to Booking Hall and carry on along the footpath'. The second characteristic was a reluctance, usually on the part of A, to seek clarification of unclear directions or information. This was not compensated for by an ability to infer what was meant, since the routes drawn on Map 1 by low-scoring As were in general wildly inaccurate. This tendency was not restricted to As, however, as can be seen from this extract from another performance:

1. A: have you got the new map handy?
2. B: yeah I got it
3. A: right look at Chidlington
4. B: yeah
5. A: you s – is there a footpath leading up f – from Chidlington
6.   past the pub, up to the canal?
7. B: yeah
8. A: yeah? is th – there's a motorway um, going across there now
9.   isn't there?
10. B: yeah

In this example pupil A takes the lead throughout, and scarcely any of his misleading assumptions are challenged by B, who fails to correct A's information even when directly asked about features of the old map that are no longer present.

Performance at the mid-point of the range

Example 2. Overall impression mark: 4 (both pupils)

Total time of complete performance: 7 min. 30 sec.
  1. A: A –
  2. B: yeh

3. A: er I've got a road map here and I wanted to go from Chidding
4.   to Penfold, and I can't go cos, when I was just going out of
5.   Chidding I found out there was a motorway there and no foot-
6.   bridge to go over, so – I was wondering if you could give me
7.   directions to get from Chidding to Penfold.
8. B: (pause) oh dear (sighs, coughs, long pause) well if you go
9.   down, Welden Road, should be a footpath down there
10. A: how far down?
11. B: you go past er, it's opposite, Booking Hall, if you go down
12.   there it's opposite there. There's a footpath across there,
13.   go across there and you come to (pause)
14. A: wait a minute where's where's Booking Hall? wait a mo
15. ⌈is that Chidding Hall?
16. ⌊It's at the bottom of. what?
17. A: you mean Chidding Hall?
18. B: Booking Hall, it's at the bottom of, Welden Road, just going
19.   off there
20. A: then which way?
21. B: well if you don't turn round that corner just go straight down
22.   just past there, there's a footpath there, foo – foo – footpitch
23.   if you go across that
24. A: no I don't get this (pause) you're sure it's not Chidding
25.   Hall?
26. B: it's Booking Hall
27. A: it's Chidding Hall on here
28. B: (pause) it's Booking Hall down here (pause)
29. A: which way from there?
30. B: when you get to a foo – , a footpath, must go straight across
31.   there, till you get to a, Rivey Hall (pause) then you come to
32.   motorway (pause) there's a cro – footpath
33. A: ⌈there
                              ⌊do you pass
                              the railway?
34. B: (pause) no (pause) do you know where it says footpath?
35. A: (pause) no
36. B: do you know where Booking Hall is?
37. A: (pause) no
38. B: (pause) you know where Walden Road is?
39. A: yeh
40. B: well the road you go straight down there to the right
41. A: yeh
42. B: just keep coming down there at the bottom of there there's
43.   Booking Hall isn't there?

44. A: no
45. B: yes there is (pause) can't you see it? do you know where
46. Walden Road is?
47. A: yeah
48. B: well if you go down there on your right
49. A: do you go past Chidding Hall?
50. B: yeah
51. A: yeah
52. B: well at the bottom of that it says Booking Hall dunnit?
53. A: no
54. B: it does (pause) do you know where Chidding Hall is?
55. A: yeah
56. B: just a (unclear) is Booking Hall (pause) in't there?
57. A: no
58. B: (pause) there is on my map
59. A: that's cos yours is newer than mine
60. B: well if you, go to Booking Hall down Walden Road and near
61. enough to the bottom on your right, it says
62. A: [footpath
do you know where
63. the, Chidding Station is? (pause) it's near Chidding Hall.
64. B: (pause) no
65. A: can't you see that?
66. B: (pause) it's not on my map
67. A: (pause) I don't think they'd have
68. B: [ripped the station up
do you know where.
69. right start again. you know Walden Road?
70. A: yeh.
71. B: go straight acr – straight down there, there's a footpath in't
72. there?
73. A: no not on mine. Your map's newer than mine though
74. B: (pause) well just straight down Walden Road you come to
75. Chiddington Hall opposite there there's a footpath, if you
76. come to that footpath, you keep going you turn round
77. A: it leads me to a train station
78. B: it leads you to the motorway
79. A: it leads me to the train station
80. B: (pause) it doesn't on my map, it leads you to a motorway on my
81. map
82. A: I won't be – I don't want to be at the motorway, I want to be
83. at Penfold
84. B: I'm getting you to Penfold
85. A: where did you start from?
86. B: Walden Road
87. A: yeah I know that but where? Where from Walden Road?
88. B: straight down

89. A: did you start from Chidding pub?
90. B: (pause) yeah. do you know where Chidding pub is?
91. A: yeah
92. B: well if you go down there there's Walden Road isn't
93. there?
94. A: yeah
95. B: well if you go straight down to the bottom of Walden Road
96. A: yeah
97. B: not, near enough to the bottom, there's a footpath
98. A: no
99. B: (pause) there *is*
100. A: no, your map's newer than mine so there won't be on mine
101. B: well just follow my map (pause) you go down Walden Road
102. A: yeh
103. B: from Chidding pub go down Walden Road go straight down until
104. you come to Chidding Hall (pause) it's a bit further than
105. Chidding Hall, there's a footpath if you go up that footpath,
106. and round, you come to a motorway, you go straight across the
107. motorway, and you come straight up until you come to the
108. (pause) there, go straight up, from the motorway straight up
109. there's a footpath, you turn right, you follow this footpath,
110. you go straight up through the (pause) darelict (sic) channel, have
111. you got that on your map?
112. A: the what?
113. B: the darelict channel
114. A: do you mean the canal?
115. B: canal yeah that's it (pause) you go straight across that over
116. a bridge
117. A: yeah
118. B: have you got it?
119. A: yeah
120. B: (pause) well you follow that, still following the footpath
121. A: yeah
122. B: (pause) there's, you go into the little (pause) er village I
123. think er it's called Penfold
124. A: right
125. B: know where it is?
126. A: yeah

Comments

The most notable feature of this performance is the amount of time the two pupils spent arguing over the discrepancies between the two maps and only slowly coming to grips with them. A states the problem quite fully (3–6), and despite his not stating his exact position B assumes correctly that he is in Chidding (8–9). B begins a promising explanation (8–9), which might have short-circuited much of the subsequent confusion, but then difficulties arise. B has to try to indicate, in answer to A's question (10), how far it is to the new footpath, but he chooses not to use the scale but named features of the map. Then it seems that he intends to use Chidding Hall as a reference point – 'You go past, er . . .' (11) – but faced, on map 2, with its new and fuller name 'Chidding Hall Centre for Overseas Studies', turns instead to the much less useful Booking Hall (11). This is one of several apparent hints that B is a not fully competent reader ('Welden Road', 9, 18; 'footpitch', 22; 'Rivey Hall' 31; 'Chiddington Hall', 75, the hesitation after 'Chidding Hall' 104; 'darelict channel', 110, 113; cf. the hesitation in 108). Having picked on Booking Hall, B rejects inquiries from A about Chidding Hall at (15–17) and (24–25) and it is not until (50) that B is brought to recognise it.

This insistence on the details of the two maps as they stand is a characteristic of these boys' performance (26–28, 42–45, 52, 56–58, 64–66, 71–73, 77–81, 97–99), and entails several breakdowns in their attempt to sort out the new route, and therefore several re-starts (34, 45–46, 60, 69, 74, 85, 101), mostly initiated by B. However, B persists in referring to features that are not on A's map despite A's complaints. On a few occasions A attempts to obtain information that might have led to a quicker solution (33, 62–63, 85–89): in particular, his remarks about whether the station had been ripped up (67) might have led B to infer its new identity, if B had not been speaking at the same time. More fruitful in the end is A's gradually increasing insistence on the fact that B's map is newer and contains information that is not on his, A's, map (59, 73, 100): this eventually prompts B into giving an explanation (101–123) that starts from a point that they have clearly established is on both maps, does not assume knowledge on A's part that he does not have, and with only a minor need for clarification (112–115) provides a satisfactory guide to the new route.

This example illustrates, in an extreme form, a tendency common to many of the average performances on this task. That is, the pupils were not content, as those at the lower end of the range were, to let obscurities in the explanation go by without query. Instead, they wisely insisted on clarifying these difficulties. On the whole, this strategy was positive and effective, in the sense that As generally ended up knowing enough about the new route to have found it if the problem had been real: the evidence for this is the adequacy of the lines drawn on their copies of Map 1. However, what pupils in the middle of the range typically could not do was surmount easily the confusion caused by the differences between the maps: this generally required considerable time and re-explanation.

Performance at the upper end of the range

Example 3: Overall impression mark 7: (both pupils)

Total time of complete performance: 7 min. 30 sec.

1. A: hello D – ?
2. B: hello
3. A: erm I've got a problem
4. B: what's that?
5. A: well I've a map and I wanted to get from Chidding to Penfold
6.   but the map's out of date so I wondered if you could direct me
7.   to Penfold because I found a new motorway and I haven't got it
8.   on my map
9. B: er all right
10. A: if I tell you where I am do you think you could direct me
11.   please?
12. B: yes O.K. (pause)
13. A: the telephone
14. B: yes
15. A: in Chidding
16. B: yes
17. A: can you see that?
18. B: yes
19. A: that's on the (pause) right-hand side of the road as you look
20.   at it
21. B: yes
22. A: and there's a church on the other side of the road
23. B: yes
24. A: (pause) where (pause) huh – there's a, there used to be a foot-
25.   path, that comes from the pub on opposite the telephone
26. B: yes
27. A: used to be a footpath that goes (pause) to the canal (pause)
28.   have you got a footpath that goes to the canal?
29. B: (pause) O.K.
30. A: if you haven't that means the motorway's gone through it
31. B: oh yes right
32. A: whereabouts does the motorway start?
33. B: erm, well, it starts a bit just past the telephone box. Do
34.   you know Walden Road?
35. A: yes
36. B: well you have to walk down there until you come near Chidding
37.   Hall Centre for Overseas Studies
38. A: ⌐yes
39. B: ˡhave you got that?
40. A: yes
41. B: and now there's a footpath so you walk, ⌐down
42. A: ˡwhereabouts is this
43.   footpath?

44. B: its about (pause) er about quarter of a kilometre away from
45. Chidding Hall, Centre, and em this footpath it leads you to,
46. Rivey Hill
47. A: Rivey Hill. does the footpath, is it in between can you see a
48. railway?
49. B: (pause) yes
50. A: is the footpath between Chidding Hall and the railway?
51. B: oh it's – it's not near the, railway it's,
52. just
53. A: ⌈(inaudible)
54. B: railway erm it's em it's gone now because of the motorway
55. A: ah I see so the footpath leads to (pause)
56. ⌈Rivey Hill
57. B: ⌊it's Rivey Hill and then you'll have to go over a
58. footbridge over the motorway
59. A: right whereabouts?
60. B: so you, go up to the, is it, sort of, looks
61. like the top of Rivey Hill, it sort of, sort of, like is Rivey
62. Hill sort of erm, an ovalish shape?
63. A: yes
64. B: well it's on erm the right-hand side of the oval that you come
65. into it
66. A: yes
67. B: (pause) erm then you have to go over a, a foot – erm a
68. footbridge, over this motorway and the motor-way sort of comes
69. by the side of Rivey Hill it goes near very near one side sort
70. of the top n – , the top, right-hand s – we – not corner but the
71. top right-hand side of Rivey Hill
72. A: does it go over the top of the hill or does the motorway go
73. underneath?
74. B: erm it just misses the, Rivey Hill the motorway just passes
75. very nearby
76. A: so is it n – , near the, the sort of more pointed end?
77. B: well it's along one side of it it's one side of it's very,
78. sort of straight the other one's very rounded.
79. A: ⌈yeah
80. B: ⌊its on that straight side the motorway is so what you'll do
81. is you'll, go, n – very n – , I think you'll go on Rivey Hill
82. A: ⌈yes
83. B: ⌊to to get to this bridge
84. A: (pause) does the m – motorway go near the canal?
85. B: (pause) erm yes it's derelict now because of that and, it

86. stops very near
87. A: there used to be a tunnel (pause) have you got a tunnel
88. written on your (pause) under Rivey Hill?
89. B: no I haven't no
90. A: oh so they must have got rid of the tunnel erm
91. B: you know where it says Booking Hall?
92. A: Booking Hall I haven't got th – one of those
93. B: erm erm erm (pause) so there's a footpath that leads to the
94. motorway
95. A: yes
96. B: but which crosses the motorway and I think it goes to another
97. hill, in, have you got, numbers up the side?
98. A: yes
99. B: well the f – foot the footbridge is sort of, in box two this
100. footbridge it goes from, in the m – , from, one, 1C ⌈to
101. A: ⌊from 1C yes
102. B: yes i – sort of in the middle
103. A: ⌈yes
104. B: ⌊that's where the footpath is
105. A: right
106. B: and the, and Rivey Hill's sort of on the line of, between
107. one and two
108. A: yeah
109. B: and well it's very it's on the line of 2, 2C it's,
110. ⌈it's a it's
111. A: ⌊yeah yeah whereabouts is the motorway on these numbers and
112. letters?
113. B: it's erm from 2A
114. A: from 2A yes
115. B: and it goes all the way through 2A and just into the corner of
116. 1C
117. A: right (pause)
118. B: it sort of curves and then goes straight again
119. A: (pause) so there's a footpath that goes over the motorway
120. B: yes (pause) through another sort of section of, in number
121. two of high land
122. A: ⌈right
123. B: ⌊in 2C then it it goes sort of straight on and when you come
124. to the derelict canal
125. A: there's a bridge that used to have the em, the railway over it
126. B: y – yes but that's probably been knocked down and you turn
127. right
128. A: well th – th – have you got two bridges or one?
129. B: I've got, I haven't got a bridge erm from the, from the old
130. railway, now cos it's an old railway cos of the motorway

131. A: yeh so you've just got one bridge that just goes
    over the
132. canal that didn't have a railway over it.
133. B: yes that that's right
134. A: I've got that
135. B: ⌐so
136. A: ⌐so, so you go over a footpath
137. B: over the motorway
138. A: yeh and there used to be a towpath that went
    all along the
139. canal
140. B: I think you follow that towpath
141. A: ⌐yeh
142. B: ⌐until you come to that bridge
143. A: you go over the bridge
144. B: yes
145. A: and then, do you carry on, on a footpath to
    Penfold?
146. B: yes and have you got a erm I think its a church
    with a
147. (pause)
148. A: yes
149. B: a tower
150. A: yeah there's a (pause)⌐yeah
151. B: ⌐is a cross a crossroads
152. A: yeah
153. B: well that's where you're into Penfold
154. A: right can I go over that again?

    •

    •

(continues for 50 sec.)

Comments

This exemplifies almost all the attributes that could be expected of an excellent performance. The opening statement is clear (5–8), and is followed by a precise specification of A's position (13–22). Almost at once A begins to explore where the new route begins to diverge from the old one (27–28). Her question about the footpath leading north from Chidding to the canal is not directly answered by B (29), but B's noncommittal response is immediately interpreted by A as implying not only that the footpath no longer leads to Penfold but that it has been obliterated by the motorway (30).

A then begins to ask about the course of the motorway (32), but this approach is shelved (and not resumed until 107) because B wisely takes the initiative and begins instead to explain the new route (33–34). Her explanation starts unhesitatingly from where A is and takes nothing for granted: at (39), for example, she pauses to check that A has Chidding Hall on her map. At (44) B makes accurate use of the scale, and it seems that A has the knowledge needed to translate 'about quarter of a kilometre' into an imperial equivalent, or at least knows that a quarter of a kilometre and a quarter of a mile are almost equal.

At (47–48) A raises the potentially very confusing question of the railway. This is natural, since it is the next salient feature on her map after Chidding Hall, and she appears to have deduced correctly that the requisite distance beyond the Hall would, on her map, bring her to the railway. B's hesitant replies (49, 51, 54) seem to show that she is working out, first, whether there is any trace of a railway and then how best to deal with it. Very few pupils worked out the relationship between the old railway and the new footpath, and in less good performances the disappearance of the railway was a cause of difficulty. This pair, however, tacitly agree to ignore it and concentrate on the new footpath (55ff.).

The next feature tackled is the relationship of the motorway to Rivey Hill. This again is potentially problematic, since the hill has been cut in two by the motorway and on the new map only the western half is named. B's speech in this section (60–83) is again marked by repeated pauses, ums and self-corrections, which seem to indicate a (reasonably successful) search for a clear way to explain the relationship between the hill, the footbridge and the motorway. A's understanding of this is perhaps assisted by the fact that B's description of the shape of Rivey Hill could equally apply to the feature so named on Map 1. The change in the hill's topography is not (yet) explicitly mentioned.

This successful progress along the new footpath is briefly interrupted by a digression on the canal, the railway tunnel and Booking Hall (84–92). In picking up the route of the footpath beyond the footbridge, B at length feels the need (perhaps remotely prompted by A's question at 59) to specify fairly precisely the location of the bridge, and makes accurate use of the grid to do so (97–109). Again her hesitations seem to indicate the exploratory nature of her handling of the problem.

At (111–112) A brings the discussion back to the question of the route taken across this piece of countryside by the motorway, and this is handled quickly and efficiently, again by use of the grid (113–118).

The strategy of detailing the course of the new footpath is resumed at A's suggestion at (119), and now B does mention the fact that there are two areas of 'high land' (120–121). A's 'right' (122) seems to show either that she has inferred the splitting of Rivey Hill, or at best that she realises that only confusion will result if she pursues the matter at this point. The collaboration between the two pupils is by now working exceptionally well: at (123–127) they are both making correct inferences about the other's map, and A even adds a syntactically correct completion to a sentence that B begins. Having reached the canal at the point where the railway used to cross it, A now seems to deduce, correctly, that the rest of the new route is identical to the old one and takes back the initiative in the conversation (136ff.). B confines herself to confirming A's description and adding supporting detail (see especially 140 and 146–149). Finally, A, for reassurance, requests a recapitulation (not transcribed) of the route (154): in this she described her understanding of the new route and B was again limited to confirming it.

This example has been transcribed almost completely and annotated in some detail to show how the pupils' performance exhibited virtually all of the features of excellent performance on this task. The only missing feature, perhaps, is succinctness. Other pairs completed the task with great efficiency in a shorter time: an example of that sort would show that not *all* of the strategies which could contribute to good performance needed to be used in order to tackle the task with great success. But by the same token such an example would not have exemplified so many of those strategies.

A few details from other high-scoring performances will round out the picture. Two girls whose mother tongue, to judge from their accents, was German showed a high degree of skill in overcoming slight problems with the idiomatic vocabulary needed. Pupil B in that pair, not knowing the English-speaking motorist's metaphorical usage of the word 'fork', described the fork near Booking Hall as a 'diversified road'. In another pair, B merely said 'Bad luck' to her partner when they discovered the change of scale, but gave a highly efficient description of the course of the motorway: 'it runs through all the squares numbered two'. In one of the few cases where the relationship between the new footpath and the railway was tackled, the entire reference to it was this:

A. *is the footpath parallel to the railway?*

B. *yes*

B's laconic answer seems to conceal a very rapid, accurate and detailed process of inference, coupled with a decision that his partner would be better served by a clear, even though oversimplified, reply than by a roundabout statement of the qualifications to it that would be necessary for a full answer.

The crucial features of excellent performances on this task can perhaps be summed up as follows. The ability to make inferences from conflicting evidence is obviously involved, and may well rely heavily on prior knowledge of maps and of the effect on the countryside of changes in modes of transport. In addition, effective performances were marked by a willingness to refrain from interrupting the partner when a difference between the maps became evident, but might not be critical, coupled with an ability to distinguish such cases from those where clarification was essential.

6.6 Comparisons between sexes, years and ages

In this section, data from all four oracy surveys are treated comparatively, in order to investigate factors that may not be obvious from any one survey.

Differences in performance between boys and girls

In all ten surveys, girls achieved significantly higher mean scores than boys in *writing* and the difference was consistent across all tasks. Similar overall results occurred in

several surveys in *reading*, and where the difference was non-significant it still tended to be in favour of girls.

In *oracy*, the picture is quite different. The *overall* differences in performance were not significant in any one of the four relevant surveys (1982 and 1983, age 11 and age 15). There were, however, differences on particular tasks, and these are all listed in Table 6.8. Except where stated, all the differences were in favour of boys.

Table 6.8 *Significant differences in oracy performance between boys and girls on particular tasks, by age and year*

Age	Year	Task
11	1982	**Jobs**, description
11	1983	**Island**, discussion
		Tracks, observation
		Tracks, hypothesising
		Tracks, retelling
		Transition, anecdote N.B. Girls' mean score higher than boys'
		Bridges
15	1982	**Bridges**
		[**Spiders**, note-taking N.B. this was a writing task, and the girls' mean score was higher than the boys.]
		Jobs, description
		Jobs, argument
15	1983	**Bridges**
		Ships

The result on the note-taking component of **Spiders** was entirely consistent with all the evidence on writing tasks mentioned above.

The most consistent oral task was **Bridges**, on which boys' performance was significantly better than girls' on all three occasions when it was used. Together with the **Ships** result, it suggests a slight but distinct advantage for boys on tasks with what might be termed technological content.

The least consistent task was **Jobs**. In addition to the three occasions when parts of this task produced a difference in performance, there were another three occasions when they did not. That is, in the 1982 age 11 survey the argument part of the task did not show a difference, and in the 1983 age 15 survey neither part did. On the basis of the significant 1982 results at both ages it was suggested in the 1982 Secondary Report that the explanation might lie in sex-role stereotyping, but this is now difficult to uphold. If such a factor in the wider social context were responsible, its influence would not be expected to disappear between one school year and the next; and no alternative explanation of this pattern of results, or of the **Island** argument result, suggests itself.

The only oral task in any of the four surveys on which the difference was both significant and in favour of girls was the anecdote component of **Transition.** Considered in isolation, this result might suggest a preference on the part of the girls for an 'expressive' task, or one that seems to be more in the 'affective' domain. But this would not explain the absence of a significant difference on the 'prediction' component of **Transition**, or on other tasks which seem equally expressive or affective, e.g. **Description of a Place** (1982 and 1983, age 15) or **Recent Learning** (1982, age 15).

Similarly the results on the observation, hypothesising and relaying components of **Tracks** might suggest an advantage for boys in a task with scientific content. But there were several other tasks with such content (1983, age 11: **Tracks**, instructions; 1983, age 15: **Beetles, Gulls, Tin, Map**), none of which produced a significant difference.

Thus the differences in performance between boys and girls (except on the 'technological' tasks **Bridges** and **Ships**) do not fit into any discernibly consistent pattern. It can therefore be claimed that the oracy surveys are largely free of sex bias.

Differences in performance between 1982 and 1983

It is necessary to exercise great caution in comparing results across the two years of oracy surveys. For one thing, in the oracy surveys there are only two years' data to work with, unlike the five-year data base in reading, writing and attitudes. For another, any change in performance between the two years might be due to any one of (at least) three factors, or to any of their possible combinations. An example will make this clearer.

The overall mean score for general impression for the **Bridges** task at age 15 was 3.7 in 1982 and 3.4 in 1983. The format of the task was (with one small exception concerning the *listener's* role) identical in the two years. It is therefore almost certain that the change in mean score was not due to changes in the task. It might be the case that the pupils in the 1983 sample as a group produced less good performances than those in the 1982 sample, i.e. that the drop in the mean score actually reflected a real or absolute drop in average performance. Or it might be that the 1983 markers were slightly more severe than the 1982 markers: if this were the case then there might have been no 'absolute' fall in performance at all. Or again, there is a third and more complicated possibility. It might be that the pupils who attempted **Bridges** in 1982 and 1983 were performing at the same 'absolute' standard, and that the 1983 markers were marking the full battery of tasks to the same perceived standard as the 1982 markers had marked the 1982 tasks, but that the markers perceived **Bridges** as being in some sense 'easier' in the context of the full 1983 battery than in the context of the full 1982 battery, and therefore expected a slightly higher level of performance on the task in 1983, and, not finding it, produced a somewhat lower mean score. Or the truth, if it can be discerned, might be a mixture of any two or all three of these possibilities.

In this connection, it is worth noting the range of mean scores across all the tasks for both general impression

Table 6.9 *Range of mean scores, oracy tasks, 1982 and 1983*

		1982	1983	average difference*
age 11	general impression	3.6–4.5	3.8–4.7	+ 0.20
	orientation to listener	3.3–4.0	3.4–4.2	+ 0.15
age 15	general impression	3.7–4.7	3.4–4.4	− 0.30
	orientation to listener	2.8–3.8	3.0–3.9	+ 0.15

*Caution: see text before interpreting these data.

and orientation to listener for both ages and for both years. This information is set out in Table 6.9. In interpreting this information it is important to remember that the four rows represent the judgements of four completely separate groups of markers, because the general impression marks are derived from the after-the-event marking from tape (second-marking), whereas the orientation-to-listener scores were given by the on-the-spot assessors, and there was no overlap in the markers of the two age levels. Hence there is not necessarily either any mutual support in the two upward 'trends' at age 11 or any contradiction at age 15 between the 'fall' in general impression means and the 'rise' in orientation-to-listener means. However, it should also be recalled that within any one row there was substantial continuity in the teams of markers. For example, of the 11 second-markers at age 15 in 1982 ten were also members of the team of 20 who did the second-marking in 1983.

As shown in Table 6.9, that team of 20 markers in 1983 produced a spread of mean scores that was 0.30 of a point (on the 7-point scale) lower than had been given by the team of 11 in 1982. Despite the continuity in membership, it is the present writer's judgement, from working closely with the markers, that the 'fall' in the range of scores is entirely attributable to the slightly greater severity of the 1983 panel as a whole compared to the 1982 panel.

If justified, this judgement has three implications. First, the fall in the range of general impression mean scores at age 15 is more apparent than real. It need not imply any change at all in the level of pupils' performances. Secondly, equally little weight should be placed on the apparent rises in the other three rows of Table 6.9: they may also be due to changes in the markers rather than to change in the pupils' performance. Thirdly, if any reliable information is to be obtained on changes in levels of performance between 1982 and 1983, it will have to be found in *relative* changes, and not in the apparently absolute values of the mean scores.

Relative changes can only be validly investigated, in the oracy data at least, for the few tasks which were used in both years. At age 11, the repeated tasks were **Pictures** and **Spiders**, and at age 15 **Bridges, Place** (description only) and **Jobs**. Relative changes on these tasks might be looked at in two ways.

First, an attempt might be made to judge the apparent change in the mean score on a particular task against the general change in the mean scores for all tasks. Thus, to revert to the example of **Bridges**, it has already been mentioned that the raw mean score on this task fell from 3.7 in 1982 to 3.4 in 1983. But this is exactly the amount by which the range of mean scores fell, and that fall has already been attributed to slightly greater severity on the part of the 1983 markers. Apparently, therefore, the pupils' performance on **Bridges** was approximately the same in both years.

The mean score on **Place** (description component) was 4.3 in both years. The mean scores on **Jobs** (description) fell by 0.5 from 4.2 in 1982 to 3.7 in 1983, and on the argument component also 0.5 from 4.3 in 1982 to 3.8 in 1983. If 0.3 is the 'neutral' amount, i.e. the fall that can be attributed to the markers, then it might seem that performance on **Place** improved by 0.3, and performance on **Jobs** really did fall by 0.2 between the two years. However, a difference of 0.2 would almost certainly not be statistically significant, even if it were legitimate to test the two sets of data against each other. And the interpretation of a zero change which might conceal a real rise of 0.3 is also problematic. At age 11 it is not clear what the general shift of mean scores by +0.2 should be attributed to. This approach therefore does not seem very fruitful.

The second approach to relative changes is to look at the positions of the repeated tasks in the rank order of all tasks in the two years. Because the tasks were re-used in virtually the same form, differences in relative performance cannot be ascribed to the tasks themselves. Then looking at the rank order, i.e. in effect comparing each task to the overall mean for the tasks in each year, should rule out marker effects as the explanation for any changes in position. This should make it easier to attribute changes in position to changes in the level of pupils' performance.

The data for these comparisons are shown in Table 6.10. The mean scores for the tasks at each age level in both years were divided into high, mid and low groups, since to use exact numerical ranks would be to put an unreasonably strong interpretation on small differences in mean scores. Moreover, the number of tasks differed in each survey. Using this form of banding produced only two apparent 'shifts' in performance out of seven comparisons for general impression, and no differences at all for orientation to listener.

In so far as either of these methods of comparing oracy performance across the two years can be relied upon, therefore, there would seem to have been no detectable systematic change in levels of performance. Looked at more positively, this is actually a heartening result. It would be disturbing if tasks moved erratically up and down the rank order from one year to another. What these analyses seem to show is a measure of stability in the results and, by implication, in the tasks used as instruments.

Table 6.10 *Rank order positions of repeated oracy tasks in 1982 and 1983*

Task	age	1982 position	1983 position	direction of change
Pictures, description	11			
– gen. imp.		mid	mid	0
– or. to lis.		mid	mid	0
Pictures, story	11			
– gen. imp.		high	mid	–
– or. to lis.		mid	mid	0
Spiders	11			
– gen. imp.		mid	mid	0
– or. to lis.		low	low	0
Bridges	15			
– gen. imp.		low	low	0
– or. to lis.		low	low	0
Place, description	15			
– gen. imp.		mid	high	+
– or. to lis.		high	high	0
Jobs, description	15			
– gen. imp.		mid	mid	0
– or. to lis.		mid	mid	0
Jobs, argument	15			
– gen. imp.		mid	mid	0
– or. to lis.		high	high	0

Key: gen. imp. general impression
    or. to lis. orientation to listener

Differences in performance between pupils aged 11 and 15

Much of the argument in the previous section against reliance on 'absolute' differences between years also applies to reliance on 'absolute' differences between ages. Moreover, it is clear that markers expect more of 15-year-olds than of 11-year-olds and adjust their marking accordingly. If the data in Table 6.9 are reconsidered from the point of view of cross-age comparisons, it can be seen that at both ages the markers produced a similar range of mean scores for general impression, operating with an overall mean of about 4.1 (on the 7-point scale). For orientation to listener there is an apparent slight difference. At age 11 the range is slightly higher, with an overall mean of about 3.7 (on the 5-point scale): the overall mean at age 15 is about 3.4. But it is impossible to tell whether this numerical difference represents a 'real' difference in (this aspect of) performance or a difference in the on-the-spot assessors' expectations.

Again, therefore, relative differences have to be inspected, and only on the rank order of repeated tasks. 'Repeated' tasks here means those which were used on at least one occasion at each age level. The data for these comparisons are shown in Table 6.11. Data for the two years of surveys are not shown separately because where these four tasks were concerned there were no differences in rank order between the two years.

In interpreting Table 6.11 it must be remembered that on all the tasks performance at age 15 was undoubtedly better than at age 11 in absolute terms. That is, if the same panel of markers had been asked to assess tapes from both ages there would have been large and significant differences. However, this is not what happened. There

Table 6.11 *Rank order positions of oracy tasks used at both ages*

Task	age 11	age 15	direction of difference*
Bridges			
– gen. imp.	low	low	0
– or. to lis.	low	low	0
Spiders, web			
– gen. imp.	mid	high	+
– or. to lis.	low	high	+
Jobs, description			
– gen. imp.	low	mid	+
– or. to lis.	low	mid	+
Jobs, argument			
– gen. imp.	low	mid	+
– or. to lis.	high	high	0

Notes:* 0 indicates no difference
+ indicates higher rank order position at age 15
– Caution: see text for interpretation.

were separate panels of markers, using their experience to judge performances against what they felt it was reasonable to expect of 11- and 15-year-olds respectively.

However, Table 6.11 does seem to show that there were some differences in performance that were greater than would be expected solely on the basis of the difference in age. This applies especially to **Spiders**, which was very easy for 15-year-olds but which might for that reason have evoked casual performance but seems not to, and to **Jobs** (description). On **Jobs** (argument), the similar rank order position for orientation to listener demonstrates yet again the finding that this task brought out some of the liveliest performances at both ages: however, the content and deployment of 15-year-olds' arguments was of course superior. The equivalent rank order positions on **Bridges** again reinforce the impression that this was a relatively difficult task at both ages and that it was not distinguished by involved performance: moreover, 15-year-olds' performance seems to exceed that of 11-year-olds only to the extent that would be expected from the difference in age.

Thus there is a small amount of evidence suggesting that on the whole 15-year-olds are more *competent* than 11-year-olds at performing the tasks used in the oracy surveys. However, the general impression of the members of the team who have worked with pupils of both ages is that the very best performances of 11-year-olds display a freshness and liveliness that is missing from otherwise highly competent performances by 15-year-olds. This may of course merely reflect greater self-consciousness.

6.7 Conclusions

Most of the conclusions drawn about oracy at age 11 at the end of Chapter 5 apply also to oracy at age 15, and can be summarised as follows:

– Monitoring performance in speaking and listening at age 15 is *feasible*.

– Satisfactory levels of *reliability* were achieved.

– It can be claimed that the tasks used in the oracy surveys represented a significant advance in *validity*. As at age 11 in 1983, so at age 15 a definite attempt was made to increase the number of interactive tasks. The new tasks that were developed for that purpose at age 15 were **Woodlice, Tin** and **Map.**

– Almost all 15-year-olds can *modify* their speaking and listening *strategies appropriately* to suit the communicative demands of different tasks.

– This also implies that *performance varies* according to those differing *communicative demands*: see section 2.4.

– The main reason for this is that *some* of the *features* of successful performance are *task-specific*. As at age 11, the 'lexico-grammatical' and 'performance features' categories of analytic marking could be applied to all tasks, but the 'organisation' category only to one-way talk; and the content categories were different for every task.

– It follows that *criteria* for task-specific aspects of successful performance *cannot be determined in advance*, except on an empirical basis, e.g. from systematic pilot testing or from wide experience of very similar tasks.

– There is a substantial need for *training* of teachers and examiners in the oracy field.

It may be appropriate to close this chapter, and this whole section on oracy, by drawing out a few further implications of some of these points, particularly the ways in which they may relate to the oral component of GCSE English (Language) examinations. First, the range of types of talk that it is possible to assess in school should be somewhat broader than those tested in APU surveys: tasks that require preparation or which last more than a few minutes, and those which require an established relationship between pupil and tester, for instance, are impossible to include in one-off surveys.

Secondly, it follows immediately from the previous point that, even in schools and for public examination purposes, oracy assessment should not be carried out on a single occasion: it would be more natural if it occurred throughout the fourth and fifth years of secondary school, and in the context of a formulated approach to oracy coordinated with the rest of the curriculum.

Finally, the previous point in turn implies that the need for training in this area is very substantial. This is probably the part of the English curriculum which is least developed at present, and about which teachers feel least informed. The in-service courses that are to be mounted in preparation for the introduction of GCSE are a welcome opportunity for the diffusion of knowledge and skill in this area: but there will still be a great need for initial training courses for teachers of English to incorporate an oracy component. And beyond that it would be wrong to reinforce the notion that oracy is the sole responsibility of teachers of English, and thereby to neglect its cross-curricular importance.

7 The assessment of writing: writing based on pictures

Synopsis

This chapter discusses the results of two different writing tasks set in relation to coloured picture postcards. The first of the tasks to be discussed (**Rainbow**) used the picture as the starting point for an imaginative piece of writing, while the second required the comparative description of two insects.

The **Rainbow** task proved to be a very easy one for able writers, and for secondary girls in particular. Several approaches were possible here, but meditative and narrative writing prevailed; a minority of pupils chose to respond by writing poetry or epigrammatic captions. An element of task reluctance was evident in the minimalistic statements written by some of the lowest-scoring pupils, especially boys. Although varieties of free/creative/imaginative writing are universally practised from the earliest school days, some children are ill-equipped to meet the imaginative challenges such writing may present. It is equally true that a proportion of the most fluent writing in this context was marred by over-elaborate recounting of impressions with too little analytic scrutiny of their relevance. Low performances at age 11 and 15 merged with one another, but between high-scoring 11- and 15-year-olds clear distinctions were evident especially in the older age groups' sophistication in narrative techniques and sustained reflective writing.

The discussion of the comparative descriptive task draws upon the findings of previous reports concerning pupils' reluctance to vary the format of their writing to include tabular, summary information even where this would make for more efficient communication than continuous prose. Relatively few pupils of either age group can successfully write descriptions which contain all, and only, the required information. Questions are raised in the discussion as to whether it is pupils' linguistic resources which are insufficient to enable them easily to discriminate in writing between different phenomena, or whether it is their practical experience of the 'science' of observation which is insufficiently developed, thus making it difficult for them not only to test the relevance of their observations but also to find ways of presenting these.

A basic point to emerge in the course of Chapters 7 and 8 is that no one written genre, of the type discussed here, can be said to have a monopoly on high-order imaginative, conceptual or linguistic skills: successful writing involves the integration of these qualities all the time.

7.1 Introductory remarks

Earlier in this report the framework used for the assessment of writing was described, both in terms of the rationale for choosing certain kinds of writing tasks and in terms of the methods used for assessment. Familiarity with these descriptions is therefore assumed as background to this chapter. It will be recalled that in the writing component, as in the APU language surveys generally, care has been taken to devise tasks which relate to the range of language uses across the curriculum, not just those functions of language which may be more traditionally associated with the English lesson. The commentary sections of previous reports have emphasised these cross-curricular intentions: pupils' performance on a diversity of written activities has been illustrated; where possible, links have also been made between performance in written language and performance in reading and oracy.

In these chapters (7 and 8) we look in some detail at characteristics of pupils' performance on three writing tasks, reporting findings from previous years where applicable. Two of the tasks involve writing based on given pictures, while the third involves persuasive writing based on a strongly held personal opinion. Apart from their interest in illustrating different functions of writing, these tasks also afford the possibility of making some comparisons between the two age groups surveyed, since they were set for both 11- and 15-year-olds. Additionally, the tasks have been chosen for commentary because they represent three major functions of writing practised in schools and assessed in various ways by successive APU surveys, namely writing whose purpose is: a) argumentative, b) imaginative, c) descriptive. The commentary in these chapters focuses on specific tasks, but general points arise which may be linked with the summary remarks about writing performance over the first phase of surveying in Chapter 2 of this report, and which are also to be linked with the discussion of written work in schools (Chapter 10) and its pedagogical implications (Chapter 13).

The picture-based tasks made for very different kinds of writing: one was a free response task, the other was a written comparison of pictured insects. Writing of the first kind occurs mainly, if not exclusively, in the context of language classes, whereas the written description of specimens is most usually a feature of work in biological sciences. The two writing tasks based on pictures will be dealt with in this chapter, while the persuasive writing task forms the subject of Chapter 8. The comparisons which it is possible to make between high and low performance at age 11 and 15 raise developmental questions of particular interest to the teaching and practice of writing. Above all, from a consideration of the types of writing elicited by the three tasks discussed in this report, it should be apparent that no one task has a unique status as the focus of high-order imaginative conceptual or linguistic skills, contrary to what is sometimes assumed by some models of literacy teaching, which tend to polarise 'informative' and 'creative' writing on purely intuitive grounds.

7.2 Writing in response to a picture, pupils aged 11 and 15

At primary level, pictures and realia may be used for language development in a variety of ways. Especially in the early stages of learning to write, pupils' writing and drawing are deliberately inter-related; by contrast, evidence we have from work sampling at age 11 indicates that drawing has taken a decidedly inferior role to writing, being used as a decorative embellishment rather than a substantial component of the text. Writing about given pictures, although not done very frequently, is mainly the occasion of loosely descriptive/narrative writing. By the end of secondary schooling, writing about pictures appears to be even less frequently attempted, and then only perhaps as practice for the English language CSE/ 'O' Level essay option, for which a picture may be a starting point.

The writing task used in the survey was based on a coloured picture postcard, depicting rainbows emerging from – or descending into – a dustbin, against a plain black/blue background. The postcard was accompanied by a double page spread in the pupils' booklet illustrating by sketches and captions some of the functions writing might serve (e.g. writing to express feelings, make jokes, write a story, create poetry, sell something, give directions), as a way of indicating to pupils that they were free to choose their own form of written response. The topic was set as follows:

Look at the coloured picture in this booklet; what does it suggest to you? Create a piece of writing to go with the picture.

The task was an amalgam of constraint (the starting point provided) and liberty (there were no specifications regarding genre or readership). The combination of these factors made the task a difficult one for less able writers in the sample.

The table below shows the distribution of impression marks for boys and girls in each age group. Impression marks are awarded on a rising scale of 1–7. From these tables it can be seen that the task is slightly harder for boys than girls in both age groups.

Table 7.1 *Distribution of impression marks for the Rainbow task, 11- and 15-year-old pupils*

Per cent marks	Primary pupils (n = 310)						
	1	2	3	4	5	6	7
Girls	2.1	7.0	22.0	20.6	24.1	16.4	6.3
Boys	5.4	13.5	23.4	28.1	18.6	6.9	3.6
Total	3.9	10.5	22.7	24.7	21.1	11.3	4.8
All tasks boys and girls	2.6	10.1	26.4	32.2	19.9	8.2	2.5

Per cent marks	Secondary pupils (n = 464)						
	1	2	3	4	5	6	7
Girls	1.3	4.3	16.6	25.0	25.6	18.1	8.8
Boys	4.8	9.2	25.5	23.0	18.4	10.5	5.1
Total	2.8	6.4	20.4	24.1	22.5	14.9	4.5
All tasks boys and girls	1.9	6.7	19.6	27.0	23.9	14.6	5.8

Reference to the analytic mark distribution for this task showed primary boys' relative weakness to girls on all dimensions of this task, with the anomalous exception of *knowledge of grammatical conventions*. An explanation for this perhaps lay in the fact that one option for writing was the creation of brief, epigrammatic responses in the form of jokes or advertising slogans. Boys who chose this approach avoided the grammatical pitfalls of extended composition. At secondary level, differences between the sexes were likewise marked, with 70 to 80 per cent of girls appearing to find this a very easy task, whereas boys' analytic marks suggested that more problems were encountered across all categories.

Since approaches to the task showed considerable diversity the commentary on performance will illustrate some of this variety in terms of broadly defined low- and high-scoring bands. Scripts from both age groups will be discussed together.

Characteristics of low performance, 11- and 15-year-olds, Rainbow task

(i) Minimal responses: low performance

Despite their frequent exposure to and practice in modes of writing that are loosely called 'imaginative/creative' it is clear from results on this task that there are forms of writing which challenge imagination and creativity in ways that pupils are unprepared for. Amongst 11-year-olds, the reading and writing of 'imaginative' fiction emerges as a clearly preferred activity, presumably because it is perceived as an early and enjoyable pastime. However, by age 15, the still sizeable group of pupils who state preferences in this area includes more girls than boys. Boys' greater interest in what they perceive to be 'non-imaginative' (i.e. factual) modes of language may indicate the pragmatic withdrawal from language activity in which they do not shine. On the other hand a reason for doing less well may be attributable to a lack of incentive to use language for exploratory, reflective purposes: without the continual experience of reading in this genre, the lack of models is likely to become an increasing problem.

On the **Rainbow** task, those who stated baldly that they had *no* idea as to what the picture suggested, and wrote no more than that, tended to be boys. The following two examples, one from each age group, illustrate this kind of task reluctance:

> It reminds me of someone
> having a birthday and that is the ripping
> paper or at Christmas but it does not
> really suggest anything to me.

11-year-old

> This picture suggests to me rainbows leading
> out of the bin and at the end of it a pot of
> Gold. This is my suggestion about it as I can
> think of nothing else.

15-year-old

Low performance in general was associated with minimal response often amounting to no more than a brief observation on the picture:

> In the Picture is a dustBin
> With a Brocen rainbow in it

11-year-old

> I see a bin with a lot of
> brittle colord paper in it

15-year-old

At the lower levels too were found embryonic reflections or stories which seem to lack any principle for further development. Understandably, poorer writers relied in a literal way on suggestions provided in the booklet, transcribing or adapting several of the suggested options. Examples of these approaches are reproduced below.

> The END OF the RAINBOWS
> ther are six Rainbows pts in a dustbin the
> rainbows makes the Dustbin like a pot of Gold at
> the botam of the bustbin the bin is sivear and
> if you put the rainbows two youre agen
> you will get a ound bustbin.

11-year-old

> At the end of the rainbow
> there will be a bot of gold
> On the other side there will
> be a deusty bin

15-year-old

> This picture is like a broken rainbow in a dustbin.
> as if a man did not Wont to see a rainbow in his life.
> Theats Wot The pictur lookt like.

11-year-old

> we can make jokes
> We can draw pictures
> We can write stories
> We can write poetry
> We can give directions
> We can express feelings
> We can sell things
> We can buy things
> We can give signals
> We can show something
> We can give people bad/good expressions
> We can be funny people, we can be sad people.
> We could say and do things to hurt people's feelings

15-year-old

(ii)   Stories and reflections: low performance

At all levels of performance, the most common approaches to the task were either to write a story or to meditate reflectively on the significance of the picture. The narratives and reflections written by the lower-scoring pupils were often more substantial when they were drawing on the incidents in their own lives, rather than when they were borrowing scenarios from established fictional genres (such as fairy tales, nurseryland tales, science fiction), or 'meditating' in the abstract.

Two examples are quoted which interpret the picture similarly as an image of party decorations in a bin. The writers are four years apart in age but the chronological advantage is really only evident in terms of a more settled style of handwriting and greater confidence in the management of written language conventions.

> It was chrismas in the year
> 1975 all the decorations had
> been put up the week before
> that chrismas the time went
> very qeiuk before you could
> say A, BC we were begening
> to take all the decoration doun
> again a frowing at all the
> broken ones and puting away
> all the good ones (an) when
> the ashbin men came the
> next day the dustbin lok
> like a rainbow. This is what
> this picture suggest to me.

11-year-old

The only that this picture of the rubbish disappearing into a dustbin reminds me of is when you have a big celebration like a birthday party, wedding receptions, and all of your friends being ahead of long pieces of brightly coloured pieces of paper for when the party lifens up they usually short these brightly coloured pieces of paper all over. Then after the party has finished just shot all these bits of paper into the bin and thats what the picture reminds me of.

15-year-old

where in the country. And if you spend all your money you can have your summer house to look forward to Every year And possible rent it out in the winter And you will be making A very big profit Every year And be making your self richer Every year. And then buying more house And rent them out in the summer charging double money. then be richer than you Ever though of being

15-year-old

The amount of imaginative displacement shown in such scripts was slight, although it could be said that the writing shared an implicit understanding of the role of metaphor in interpreting and shaping experience. In other respects, lower-scoring scripts were more likely to be characterised by a literal-minded approach; for example, the relaying of jokes transcribed from a common stock of school humour rather than a new creation in response to the picture or the linking of the Pot of Gold legend with straight consumerism. Weaker writers also relied on the TV series 'Rainbow' to form the staple of their compositions, not necessarily in close association with the picture.

Examples of low performance, **Rainbow** task

The picture of the rainbow reminds me of the television programme called rainbow for the kids it has lots of rainbow colours in the programmes thats why they call it rainbow they always Draw a pitcure and then it brakes. they drew a pitcure before of a rainbow and then braking then fell in the bin. the programe is wally on every day.

11-year-old

AT The end of every rainbow you may not find what you want you may find A pot of gold or may find an old dustbin full of unwanted rubbish waiting to be took Away. And if you do find your pot of gold you will be rich And have big house And couple of cars And buy A summer house some

(iii) Versification: low performance

We conclude this brief exemplification of low-scoring scripts with reference to two instances of poetry writing, both from 15-year-olds. Surveys of reading have consistently revealed that reading poetry is enjoyed by a number of pupils who do not score highly in reading (see Chapter 10 of this report for example), the poetry preferred being short, humorous rhyming verses, which obviously are not the most demanding type of reading material. The poems quoted below may well have been inspired by reading of this genre, and show a conscious attempt to 'create a piece of writing' to go with the picture of rainbows within the limits of the writers' resources.

Poem

There was a multi coloured Dustbin which thu boy with up held he thought of thu Dustbin a palot, and made it his Rainbow Dream word

It was Guy Fawkes night and the Bonfire was alight and next to it stood a Dustbin a firework was lighted and the boy go excited and the Dustbin Blue up in flames

Poetry.

THE Rainbow in THE Bin.

"Look THERE's Something in THE BIN,"
ITS a RainBow in the Bin
Some
THE Colours were BRight and
some WHERE dim.
But still my EYES STARTED TO
Spin.
Each RainBow did ITS own
THing,
and THat BRought my FACE a
grin.
BEcause I Had NEVER seen a
RainBow in a Bin.

Characteristics of high performance: Rainbow task, 11- and 15-year-olds

Most of the high-scoring pupils wrote long and fluent pieces, original and imaginative in subject matter. Very few high-scoring pupils limited themselves to an epigrammatic response or wrote a collection of discrete impressions. The favourite options were again story and reflection, with poems occurring on their own or in conjunction with a general comment in fewer than ten scripts. The category of story was overwhelmingly represented by girls' scripts, especially in the form of children's fiction and romantic/autobiographical narrative; other forms of story were allegorical/science fiction.

Typical of all the good writing in this category was the way in which the episode of the rainbow-filled dustbin was embedded in a plot structured in such a way that its appearance fitted the cause-and-effect sequence generated. For example, these stories developed a plot explaining how the rainbow and the bin came to be associated or used an interpretation of the theme of the picture as the setting for a more fantastic narrative, such as a mythological tale concerning the invention of rainbows, the futurist vision of emerging from a nuclear bunker after the destruction of contemporary civilisation, or an invasion of rainbow-coloured aliens. The melancholic interpretation of broken rainbow/broken dreams provided the idea for stories about tragic loss or injury, as well as fictions about sad love affairs. The 'children's' stories were entirely optimistic in outlook, bringing a trail of events occasioned by the rainbow fragments to a happy ending. As on the children's story task set elsewhere in the survey, both 11- and 15-year-olds showed themselves able to create a narrative suited to the interests of a much younger age group.

(i) Narrative writing: high performance

At lower levels of performance, writing by 11- and 15-year-olds was often indistinguishable; however, between the top-scoring groups of pupils at each age there was a striking difference, despite the similarities of approach. We quote two top-scoring stories, one from each age group, both constructed round the search–warning–disaster motif which was used by many other writers in the survey.

Jim was very interested in rainbows. Every wet day he would sit at the window and watch for the rainbow to appear. He had heard a story about if you found the end of a rainbow their would be a pot of gold buried underneath. It. One day he set out to find the end of a rainbow. He noticed that as he walked closer to the rainbow it got farther away. He was about to turn back when it suddenly stopped. Running forward he noticed something bright and red sitting on the grass. He was amazed to find a little leprechaun leaning up against the rainbow snoring his head off. Jim accidently fell heavily on the grass wakening the little man. Looking up the little man retorted "Who in the world are you?". Jim struggling to get up replied "I'm Jim and I'm after the pot of gold at the end of the rainbow?" The leprechaun explained to him that if he takes the pot of gold the rainbow will crack up and

fall to the ground. Jim did not listen to the little man and dug on. He thought of how rich he would be with all that gold. When he reached to pick up the pot the rainbow cracked up and fell to the ground with a thundering crash. Jim now regretted ever following the rainbow. He began picking up the pieces and when he got home threw them in the dustbin.

11-year-old

Example of high performance, **Rainbow** story

One day, the evil Wizard — Narsus stared out through the window of his tower. Up in the sky he saw a strange sight. It was a curved thing of many colours that stretched in an arc above the countryside. Either end vanished behind the hills. "What is this strange devilry?", he thought to himself. He decided to look up in his books of ancient wisdom to find out. After flicking through several dusty, leather bound volumes, he came across a picture of the many-coloured curve. It was called a Rainbow and usually appeared after a storm or rain. Then, Narsus saw something that appealed to his nasty side (the only side he had). At the end of a rainbow there was supposed to be a pot of gold. He suddenly thought of a mighty hoard of gold coins, jewels and gems .... and they'd all be his!

At once he ran down stairs to the gate of his tower. His servant fetched his horse. "Where are you going master? Shall I come with you?"

"No!", replied the wizard not wanting any one else to share in his money. "I shall go alone. I only want to collect a few ingredients for a new spell."

With that he spurred his horse and galloped into the valley. Already the Rainbow had begun to fade. He'd better hurry or the treasure would be gone.

It did not take too long to find the end of the Rainbow which lay behind some hills, but as he got nearer he saw an old man with a long white beard and cloak.

Narsus dismounted and walked towards the man hiding his wand beneath his long black cloak. He suddenly noticed a large metal pot full of gold coins. He dashed over to it ignoring the old man.

"Gold!", he yelled, "Gold! I'm rich!"

For the first time the old man spoke:
"Yes. There's a lot of gold. But I found it first so it's mine. I'll let you have half though."

Narsus looked up. "Half! I'm going to have it all!"

A bolt of light shot from his wand, and hit the old man who vanished in a puff of smoke. As he did so, the rainbow suddenly flickered and vanished. Narsus looked round only to see that the pot was now a large metal container — a bin. He peered inside and saw broken pieces of a small rainbow. The gold had gone! Narsus felt bad. If only he'd shared the gold! He'd still have much more than he now had. And so from that day, he changed his ways, and became known as Narsus the good. He never saw another rainbow though, ever.

15-year-old

Differences between the two stories are not simply a matter of length, paragraph organisation and other conventional features, nor the fact that one story is set entirely within a mythological framework while in the other elements of magic intrude into everyday life. Although each story is written in the third person, thereby allowing for the possibility of authorial comment on the events, only in the work of the older pupil is this possibility developed. The younger writer devotes little time to a depiction of the hero's attitude and motives: these are conveyed only in a few adjectives, 'very interested', 'amazed', 'regretted', while the impulse which leads to his pursuit of the rainbow is summarised into statements. By contrast, the process by which the evil wizard Narsus plans to secure the promised gold is traced through his first wonderings about the rainbow phenomenon, through his spoken questions ('What is this strange devilry?'), to his eventual discovery of the rainbow entry in 'his books of ancient wisdom'. Like Narsus, the reader too is invited to linger over the contemplation of a 'mighty hoard of gold'.

In structural terms we note that the implications of evil in the first description of Narsus are picked up in the aside about his nastiness, and moved forward with the story, making his destructive greed at the end of the tale more convincing. There is no comparable use of recursive elements in the 11-year-old's story which, after the scene-setting opening, unfolds in straightforward linear time and ends abruptly with the last action – 'he threw them in the dustbin', leaving the reader to speculate on the significance of the story as a whole.

(ii) Reflective writing: high performance

After stories, the second largest group of scripts from both age groups comprised reflective meditations on the nature of the postcard, what it suggested and what the intentions of the artist had been in devising it. At secondary level, these tended to be melancholic in tone, melodramatic even, and the few pupils who stressed the cheering qualities of rainbows generally did so against a gloomy background of their own forebodings. Again, reflective compositions from the high-scoring 11- and 15-year-olds showed the greater ease which older pupils have in writing in this mode. At the same time, it should be apparent that, although awarded high marks vis-a-vis their peers, many 15-year-olds in this category might be thought to be capable of further development especially as regards the precision with which their reflections were described and analysed.

Comparisons between 11- and 15-year-olds show that older pupils were better able to extend their perceptions and to measure these against assumptions about other people's beliefs and feelings; they were less likely to explain the inspiration for the picture in terms of specific crisis in the life of the artist; they were generally aware of the formal requirements to set their meditations in context. Some of these differences can be seen in the following extracts:

THE END OF THE RAINBOWS

This painting of "The End of the Rainbows" by Patrick Hughes is very cleverly done. When you first look at it, it does not appear to mean very much. It does, however, make people look at the painting for a while, to see what they understand by it. The beautiful colours of the rainbow are contrasted very well with the drabness of the dustbin and the darkness of the background. In this case I think one of the most important things about the painting is its title - "The End of The Rainbows". This is an essential part in making people think about it. When people talk about the end of the rainbow they usually mean the place where the end of it lies. I would feel that, as the rainbow is such a beautiful phenomenon, the place where it ends must be some sort of paradise - a beautiful area with many colourful flowers and animals. The painting would therefore shock some people when they saw it. They might say scornfully that the artist thinks that there are dustbins at each end of the rainbow!

15-year-old

Okay, so a dustbin is a boring old piece of equipment! But wait - is it really? When you see a dustbin, what do you immediately think of? Rubbish? Don't be so dooty. Taking a good look at the dustbin in the photograph, it immediately makes dustbins seem much more exciting. Lively colourful rainbows coming out of a dingy dustbin in a dark, dreary background.

15-year-old

Wordiness was however a problem that 15-year-olds especially succumbed to. Where 11-year-olds' scripts became too long this seemed to be because more and more separate thoughts about the significance of broken rainbows were generated in the course of writing; more typical of over-long secondary scripts was the elaboration of discrete impressions as can be seen in the following extract.

The harsh, ugly thought of growing up breaks into the world of fairy tales and dream-land fantasies and steals their value and meaning away to a place where they are not able to operate, when they have left the mind, they are useless.

The adolescent's mind soon fills up with adult dreams which may someday be shattered by realities in life too, and another broken-dream will be thrown away and made useless, like the blueness of a sky without a rainbow. The colours have faded, there is no colour left, but a desolate emptiness filled with tranquility, and reality, no fluffy cloud, just space for another hope or dream to grow and the colours will be renewed once again.

15-year-old

The idea of a broken rainbow in a dustbin was a very good idea. It shows that someones dreams have just ended. Like it is the end of the world for someone because the rainbow is broken up. The lid is not on the dustbin so the rainbow could piece together again and make someone else happy. Because people always say that their dreams lie at the end of a rainbow. The rainbow even though it is broken up is still giving light so it may still brighten someone up and give them new hopes about things. I think the artist had a fire or an accident that made him down-hearted. So he drew this picture to show that he had given up hopes of having dreams that come true.

11-year-old

Impressionistic writing of this kind, attempting to realise the stream of consciousness engendered by the picture, was rarely attempted by younger pupils. It is arguable whether it is well-suited to discursive prose at all or whether the attempt to pack together so many conflicting images might not be better tackled in the form of poetry.

130

In the event, few pupils wrote poetry and of those who did most chose a narrative line and quasi rhyming stanzas. An exception was provided by one 15-year-old who attempted in blank verse to create a sense of an opiate vision of rainbows:

A myriad of blazing colour
blasted out from a bin.
The fiery projectory cut sudden
by dark space.
Forced through some tight slot
is pulled and forced
is gone
engulfed
by space

Again a sudden spurt
false colours fly up
and out.
Leaving a buzzing image
— on the retina – 'down damned spot'
sudden thought spins through
the opened mind.
Cackling witches create
new light, mesmerizing
hypnotic phases thrusted up
from crinkled finger-tips.....
No from a bin.

The blackness from behind blurs
the woven tapestry comes undone
Reality floods a flying mind
It drops lower.
The opium wears off
a dull dustbins stares
me in the eye.

This may be contrasted with an 11-year-old's poem, more typical of the conception of poetry evident throughout the sample. For all its ingenuity, there is really no reason for the choice of verse against prose in this composition.

Poetry   The Sorrowful Rainbow

The rain-bow gleams all
day long
The birds start singing
their happy song.
'Tis a beautiful day
If I may say.

Then all of a sudden
the sun went in
And all the sky went dim
What is happening?
I said aloud.
What is happening?

I hurried back home
And found out a strange
man had come.
He was all different colours
And full of multicoloured
flowers.

He was the rainbow man
Who was called Rainbow Sam
He looked very sad
Like an orphan without
a mum or dad.

Then at last he told me
why
And said that he could
no longer fly.

Rapidly I made him two
wings
Out of feathers and things
Now the man went away
And made the rainbow
come out the next day

131

7.3 A written comparison of pictured insects, pupils aged 15

In contrast with the free-response type of writing task discussed above, we turn now to an analysis of results obtained from a task in which the writing to be done was much more directly shaped. The task involving a written comparison of pictured insects was one of several tasks which assessed the use of writing for specific purposes of learning; others were concerned with planning activities or experiments, giving an account of things learnt, organising in note form selected information from written and spoken texts, and so on.

From the evidence provided by pupils' performance on written tasks such as these, together with that provided by work sampled from classrooms, there are indications that pupils are given less exposure to or instruction in writing for this range of purposes than they are in the writing of narrative fiction. If the English teacher has neither the time nor the training to cover the writing curriculum for all subject areas, it is also a fair assumption that subject specialists are equally at a loss to communicate the explicitly linguistic demands which certain genres of writing entail. Learning how to write well in all areas of the curriculum becomes a matter of osmosis rather than a response to explicit instruction over time. The process is exacerbated by the hiatus between primary and secondary school assumptions about what constitutes appropriacy in written work: typically, in primary school, children are encouraged to write 'expressively', with little emphasis on the structure of written genres apart from that loosely associated with 'stories'. In the secondary years, the formal writing of essays or accounts of experimental work is often 'taught' through work sheets, dictation or notes on the board: in the case of science lessons in particular, it is rare for pupils to continue to experiment with forms of written expression, or to use writing as a means of planning for themselves how a problem or experiment might be worked out. (These observations are based on work reported in the 1982 Secondary Survey Report.)

In the report of the fourth primary survey, we analysed 11-year-olds' performance on a comparative-descriptive task. This was a description of two tropical moths. Pupils were each given coloured picture postcards of the moths and asked to write a description which highlighted the significant differences between the two. This task proved to be difficult for pupils in ways which emphasised features of an expository, factual genre:

1. Problems in the selection and organisation of content. Only 11 per cent of pupils gained full marks in this category as compared with *c.* 17 per cent over all tasks used in the survey and 37 per cent on a task inviting a free imaginative response. Pupils proceeded to write their descriptions in an additive way rather than by logical selection, producing an unfocused listing of similarities and differences without benefit of an overview; descriptions were often vague and lacking in accuracy. Almost 25 per cent of pupils received the lowest marks for content and organisation on this task (i.e. marks of 1 and 2), compared with the figure of *c.* 16 per cent over all tasks.

2. Pupils' preferred method of organising their description was in terms of paragraphing; in practice, a single paragraph. Judging from the evidence of redrafting in some pupils' booklets, it seemed that the use of numbered points was exploited for pre-writing use but not thought suitable for finished text, although the use of numbers or tabular form could have given clarity to these descriptions.

3. Stylistic problems were encountered in pupils' writing which simply started where the topic left off. Whereas pupils writing stories or letters are accustomed to use standard ways of creating a context for the reader (Once upon a time/Dear —) their ways of writing descriptions suggested that it was rare for them to think that 'style' was an aspect of their work that needed attention here, whether in terms of the overall orientation of their writing or at the level of lexical variation. Thus many scripts began and ended in mid air, and contained repetition of items of immediate reference. Marks for appropriateness and style on this task showed that 11 per cent of pupils achieved grades of 5 contrasted with 20 per cent on a free response task, and 19 per cent on an informal letter.

4. Generally speaking, the writing of descriptions based on discrete points of observed contrast facilitated the use of grammatical punctuation to mark sentence boundaries. However, there were specific problems encountered on this task with respect to the management of comparative structures. The proportion of pupils receiving grade 5 was 14 per cent compared with 16 per cent over all tasks.

5. Minor but specific problems were noted in orthographic conventions: errors in the use of capital letters for naming and labelling specimens. The proportion of pupils receiving grade 5 was 12 per cent; over all tasks 14 per cent.

With these broadly defined characteristics of younger pupils' performance in mind, we turn to an analysis of secondary pupils' performance on a similar task, involving the comparative description of two damsel flies. As with the 11-year-olds, pupils were each given a pair of picture postcards in association with the following writing topic:

Illustration 7.1 *Writing topic, age 15*

Insects

Included in your writing booklet are two pictures of demoiselle flies.

Study the pictures carefully to find at least four differences between these flies.

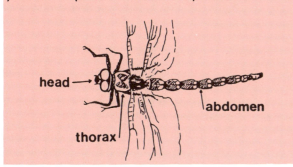

> Now write a description comparing the two flies. Your aim should be to emphasise the differences most important for telling them apart.
>
> The cards have been labelled 'A' and 'B' for ease of reference.
>
> The following diagram of a demoiselle fly is given to help you refer to parts of this insect by name.
>
> head →   abdomen
>
> thorax

Results from impression marking indicated a pattern that was close to the average across all tasks.

Table 7.2 *Impression marks: raw score distribution, 15-year-olds*

(i) Comparative description (mean = 4.2)(n = 464)						
Per cent or marks	1 & 2	3	4	5	6	7
	7.1	21.3	28.2	24.1	12.2	4.9
Girls	5.4	19.5	26.6	26.1	16.2	5.8
Boys	14.9	24.0	30.8	20.8	2.1	3.6
(ii) All tasks (mean = 4.3)						
	8.6	19.6	27.0	23.9	14.6	5.8

There was a difference between boys' and girls' scores as had been found at primary level. Girls' mean score was 4.4, boys' 3.8.

Discussion of findings from analytic marking

The analytic marks were referred to for more information as to the particular problems which this task might have posed. It appeared that the writing of a descriptive comparison raised problems for secondary pupils similar to those noted for the younger age group, and that these were mainly encountered in the areas of content and organisation. Approximately 11 per cent of pupils gained full marks for content on this task compared with the average of 27 per cent across all tasks, while 8 per cent received full marks for organisation, compared with over 14 per cent across all tasks. Once again, it proved to be the case that on a task requiring specific items of content in a logical framework, pupils performed less well. When the scores for boys and girls in each of the analytic categories were separated, it appeared that 'task difficulty' was more associated with boys' performance. Although analysis of girls' scores showed that they did experience some difficulties with this task, to the extent that fewer of them gained full marks for content and organisation, in other categories their scores were closer to the average. For boys however, the task seemed to present more problems in all categories.

Scripts in the top and bottom score bands were extracted for closer analysis, and the general characteristics of each group are discussed below with reference to the analytic assessment categories.

Content

Pupils were asked to identify four salient differences and using these observations to write a description of the insects highlighting the characteristics most important for telling them apart. The task was thus not a literal record of observations in the manner of a spot-the-difference puzzle, but a selective account of observed contrasts. Many of the difficulties experienced on various aspects of the task derived from this initial conceptual difficulty which entailed making a decision about what to select and why, and then finding a way to present this analysis in writing.

Lowest scores for content went to those pupils who announced differences without any descriptive element, as in the following example:

> A is Different from B Because the heads are different. The Thorax are Different the wings are different and the abdomins are Different.

This kind of writing makes sense only in relation to the given pictures and would have some function as a spoken introduction to them. As a text to accompany the given pictures it is superfluous, since any observer can see contrasts at this level of generality.

Average to low scores were typically associated with writing in which the level of generality was not well judged: either the scripts contained too little detail, or they focused over-elaborately on some features (or on one insect) to the point where the comparison was confused.

Certain features such as those of colour, shape and size provided more substantive differences between the insects than merely fortuitous, transient ones (position of legs, antennae, wings or whether the insect was positioned on a flower or a leaf). On one picture, only four legs of the fly were visible: many pupils asserted that the insect *had* only four legs without remarking the anomaly of their observation. In judging the relevance of content, markers took account of these aspects of selection. Similarly, to make clear distinction between the insects, more precise statements of difference were needed than that one was bigger/smaller, fatter/thinner, lighter/darker than the other:

> *A has a much wider and darker wing span than B though B looks longer*

> *B's head is rounder than A's head, and A's abdomen is straight while B is pointed going downwards.*

The thorax on fly A is fatter than that of fly B. The abdomen on fly B is longer than that of A. The heads are different.

Observed differences needed to be anatomised more closely by reference to a particular feature or dimension, and to be described so as to be visually identifiable, as in this description:

The wings of the banded demoiselle are brown in colour and look quite strong and are not easily torn. The diameter of the wings are about two centimeters. In the white-legged damsel fly's case the wings are very fragile. The wing veins are a pale shade of green and the wing is transparent. At the tip of the wings are three tiny patches of brown. The wings are about the same lengths as fly (A) but their diameter is about one and a half centimeters long.

As stated above, the converse of minimalist descriptions were over-detailed ones which made visualisation of the insects difficult. Lower marks were also given to scripts which were written with an unbalanced focus on one or two aspects, resulting in a failure to create an impression of either insect. As the following quotation shows, writing of this type could proceed from perceptive attention to the evidence but was generated by an attempt to write down *all* that could be seen rather than only what was relevant and crucial:

The two flies are different colours and look much the same. Fly A's colours are legs black, wing light, dark and medium brown, its thorax is purple and green with little shades of brown. Its abdomen is grey with some touches of light blue. Fly B's legs are grey with a few bits of black. Its thorax is black with lines of blue and shades of brown. Its wing has a green outline and is fragile looking. Its abdomen is the same colour as its thorax, and its head is blue.

'Good writers' were especially prone to over-interpret the requirements of the task, and sought to maximise their impressions at length, showing in this the influence of instruction in essay writing where word length and personalised impressions are emphasised:

Demoiselle A has the colour of autumn leaves, browns, blues, greens, mauves and yellows, whereas Demoiselle B has very light colours, he is a very light one with a spot of pink and green, his back and tail has the colour black mixed in as well. Demoiselle B has a very long back, if he was a man he would be very tall and slim.

Fly 'B' is found on a bright flower. It is also a bright colour so may be camouflaged. Fly 'B' could be a male fly. It is brightly coloured to attract female flies. Usually, female animals are less attractive than males.

From looking at the backgrounds in both pictures it is obvious that the two flies live in different environments. B is resting on a flower, whilst A is surrounded by reeds. 'A' obviously lives around ponds.

In fact, it was not necessary for these scripts to be long: 'bonus' marks were not given to pupils who piled up differences, since one purpose of the task was to assess pupils' abilities to select and organise significant details. Writing about life-style, habitat, reproduction and so on was not part of the requirements of the task, and though such speculation could serve to create some context for the discussion of distinctive characteristics, as subject matter this could not substitute for the precise comparison of the pictured insects.

Pupils' speculative impressionistic writing about the presented evidence revealed certain preconceptions which ran counter to biological knowledge, or applied it without foundation. Such preconceptions were as likely to appear in the scripts of good writers as in poorer ones, and related to the association between speed, size and weight, as well as to the connection between colouration and habitat. The darker colours of fly A led to its being described as 'bulkier', 'heavier', 'sturdier' than fly B; pupils thought that all these features combined to make for slower flight but better endurance over long distances; the darkness of A's wings was assumed to make them stronger, and less fragile with the alternative hypothesis associating delicacy with strength unexplored. Others elaborated their characterisation further, suggesting that there might be seasonal differences in the life cycles of the insects, fly B appearing in summer, fly A in winter. As illustrated in the quotations above, the presence of different background 'scenery' led pupils to remark on quite different habitats, going so far as to locate fly B 'on the barks of trees and greenery . . . (his) six sturdy legs to help him balance and support himself while in the trees'.

Of course, this writing task was not conceived as a test of biological knowledge. (A labelled diagram of a damsel fly was given for reference so as to minimise unevenness of biological knowledge amongst pupils.) It would perhaps have been more 'realistic' to have provided 900 specimens for pupils to observe at first hand, but just as a great deal of 'science' can be carried out away from the laboratory, so too can written descriptions be generated from a variety of source material. Observing the ways in which pupils tackle a more abstract version of comparing specimens can afford clues as to how they might best benefit from 'hands-on' experience. When pupils meet material which may resemble that from another subject area, in the context of an assessment of language, it may well be the case that they interpret the task in different ways, and write more for the expected audience of the English teacher than the science teacher. This factor may account for the proliferation of erroneous assumptions about scientific and mathematical relations in pupils' descriptions. On the other hand, the less formal and less constrained context in which the writing was set may have served to reveal these assumptions with greater clarity. For teachers of both science and language there are questions to be explored: do pupils lack the resources of language that would enable them to make the fine discriminations necessary to distinguish specimens relative to one another? Is it for this reason that fairly subtle differences are grossly exaggerated in order to fill out the comparison? Or are many of the problems in writing this kind of description to be traced to the fact that pupils have little real practice in testing the relevance of such observations, or indeed working out for themselves how such observations might most helpfully be presented to a reader?

Organisation

A well organised description was accounted to have its distinct points clearly evident, beginning with a general statement or brief title. The use of numbering or separate paragraphs was a sign of systematic organisation in which, for example, points relating to colour or to the structure of the insects were grouped together, and gross differences distinguished from finer ones. Lower marks were given to scripts in which it was not apparent that any order was imposed on the description and which hence jumped from one feature to another, resulting in an inventory of unconnected items.

Examples of well-organised descriptions are reproduced in full below. The first two examples show the successful use of tabular and point form layout, chosen by a minority of pupils who interpreted this task in 'scientific' terms. Example three is more typical of the organisational methods adopted, or attempted, by the majority of pupils; as shown here the framework of paragraphing could make for a reasonably well-organised description. Nevertheless, we note that in the example reproduced, despite the clear, methodical discussion of colour differences in each part of the insects' anatomy, there is really *too much* writing. Part of the reason for the unnecessary length of this script can be traced to the writer's impulse to maintain a coherent flow of prose within and between paragraphs, even though the repetition of reminders about 'distinct . . . differences', 'coloured differently', 'aids (to) recognition' are superfluous comments given the clarity of much of what is observed and recorded.

Example 1: comparative description, point form.

Example 2: comparative description, tabular form.

Example 3: comparative description, paragraph form organisation (typeset because of its length)

The proportions of each part of these two demoiselle flies are very similar. However, many parts of the body of the fly in A are coloured differently to the same parts of the fly in B.

The abdomen of A is a dark browny blue colour which does not attract the eye towards it. Where the blue colour fades the abdomen is seen to be a white colour. In contrast to this the abdomen of B has a bright florescent blue colour. This colour stands out against a background of leaves or plant stems and this aids recognition. Where there is no blue colour the abdomen is black in colour.

The wing of fly A is dull brown in colour with branching veins. However, this is in direct contrast to the wing

135

of fly B which is transparent with veins which have a touch of green colour in them. This great difference in the appearance of the wings of the two flies also aids the process of differentiating between them.

The thorax of Fly A has a different colour to its abdomen. The bottom half is a bright green colour which immediately attracts ones eye while the top part is a dull mauve colour. The thorax of fly A is the most brightly coloured part of the whole fly. The thorax of fly B is quite different. It is a florescent blue colour all over. This colour is the same as that of fly A's abdomen. This is another colour difference which allows one to distinguish between the two flies.

The legs of both fly A and B have hair on them but there is a distinct colour difference between them. The legs of fly A are dark black in colour which seems to match the general dullness of the fly. However the legs of fly B are the same blue as the majority of its body.

The colour of the head of the two flies is also different. The head of fly A is a light brown colour which is only broken by one black line running horizontally through it. The head (or more strictly speaking the eyes) of fly B is the same colour as the rest of its body; a florescent blue which stands out amongst the flowers and leaves in which it lives.

Fly A's colouring is much duller that of fly B. This makes it reasonably easy to distinguish between the two. Fly A having dark colours while fly B has one bright blue colour.

Two recurrent features of poor organisation showed themselves in all but the top-scoring group, and both of these had been noted at primary level among pupils tackling the same kind of task. There were pupils who began by noting down in numbered points the four differences which first caught their eye, then proceeded to write a longish paragraph (or several paragraphs) either repeating what they had already jotted down, or adding to it with other less relevant information or speculation. We quote two typical low-scoring instances of this approach:

> a) 1) fly A has six legs.
>   fly B has only got four legs.
> 2) fly A has a bigger smaller wing spam
>   fly B has a big wing spam
> 3) The abdomen of fly A is abroder
>   than fly B
> 4) fly A has bigger eyes than fly
>   B.
>
> b)   fly B is much bigger than
>   fly A Because fly B is the female
>   and fly A is the male. The female
>   lays 200-600 eggs.
>   fly A lives on grass but fly
>   B lives on flowers fly B is
>   collecting or eating the pollen that
>   can be founded in the of flowers

> fly A has a thicker tummy
> than fly B some of these flys
> have four wings two on each
> side. one under each other
>   The two fly's are of different
> colour A Blue, green and black
> B blue and Black. The wings of
> The flys are very thin this enables
> them to fly easily The fly's dont
> weigh that much either.
>   The wing pattern of fly B has
> got square shaped lines in the
> wing, But in fly A the lines are
> single and straight

Secondly, there were pupils who wrote two paragraphs, one for each insect, more or less covering the same features of each specimen in roughly the same order. Some of these paragraphs contained reasonably full and accurate descriptions, but in so far as the business of comparison was left to the reader, both this approach and the one described above suggested a failure to fully conceptualise the comparison as central and explicit. The lack of any comparative framework, together with a minimal record of observed detail, combined to produce some of the lowest performances on this topic:

> A
> A has nine sections to it abdomen. it has
> got a small head it has six legs it had
> a gray abdomen and a green thorax. it wings
> are shorter and longer than a
>
> B
> B has an eight section blue abdomen. it has
> a blueish-black thorax. it has only for legs.

Appropriateness and style

Pupils were asked to provide a text to accompany the pictures so as to direct and focus the reader's attention. While the pictures were assumed to be in front of the reader, reference to them needed to be made fairly explicitly. A clear, concise style was looked for; this could be achieved by the correct use of biological terms (apart from those given, this meant reference to mandibles, segments, forelegs, hind legs), although it was also the case that effective descriptive phrases of a non-technical kind could be achieved by figurative language.

For example,

The head of A looks like a helmet. It looks tough and strong.

It has two plates as eyes . . .

B has a wing like a web

A has . . . longer, more fan-shaped wings.

. . . a small needle-like end, like the top of a fountain pen.

Less appropriate for describing insects were anthropomorphic terms such as knee-caps, face, pupils, feet, mouth and neck, especially where these intruded into a more technical lexical field (thorax, feelers, *face*, abdomen). Nor was it appropriate to refer to 'the colour scheme' of the insect. Various difficulties of a related kind occurred in giving descriptions of dimensions:

The thorax is small in height

It has a taller thorax

A's eyes are averagely large but nowhere near the size of B's.

The better writers were able to refer precisely to shades of colour on the insects: 'flourescent', 'pearly', 'jet black', rather than noting the presence of blue, grey or dark toned areas. By contrast, a reduced lexical range was evident in weaker writing on this task, in common with many others. This was shown at both individual-word level, and in the repetitive use of linking phrases:

B has got a bigger . . . A has got a bigger . . ., It has got . . .

Another difference that shows up . . ., Another difference seems to be, the difference is . . .

For an eye B has only a dot with half of a white thing on top. Fly A also has two things coming out of the top of his head, where B has only one.

Weaker writers commonly misused *like* as the all purpose comparative signal ('You can't see through the wings *like* B'), in contexts where written style calls for more precise phrasing: such usage is of course commonplace in speech. In lieu of specific comparison, vague expressions, also of a colloquial type, were used repetitively: 'rather', 'quite', 'kind of'.

Matters of style and organisation were closely connected on this task; and pupils' ways of tackling both showed considerable variation, again perhaps because the context in which the task was set did not appear to privilege or to preclude one approach more than another. The adoption of a succinct, formal style (rather in the register of a biology text book) has been illustrated above in the examples shown for organisation. Other pupils seemed to be drawing upon different models, perhaps influenced by the style of television documentaries, and stressed the text/picture connection by means of specific pointers: 'you will notice . . .', 'we can see that . . .'. The result was something quite close to a spoken commentary:

Notice the legs. The white legged damselfly legs are white, this is a main difference to tell them apart, while the other's legs are deep black.

Most pupils however chose to write in continuous paragraphs. At best this stylistic choice meant that the paragraph division could serve as a spatial convenience for the bracketing of a succession of linked points; at worst, it was the occasion of 'overwriting' in an exaggerated allegiance to notions of prose continuity. The latter phenomenon made for dull reading, and such scripts would have been improved by a more radical revision into point or tabular form.

The banded demoseille's body is more heavily built than the damselfly's and its wing is large and a greyish brown colour. The demoseille's wing is slightly mauve and is opaque. The damselfly's abdomen is a mixture of bright colours of blue and black with a little brown whereas the demoseille's abdomen is a dullish grey blue.

The demoseille's thorax is more shorter and more compact than the damselfly's and is slightly more raised. The damselfly's thorax is turquoise blue, while the damsel's is a mixture of brown, pale blue and dull purple.

Knowledge of grammatical conventions

Pupils' ability to use the grammatical conventions of written English successfully, to ensure that their texts are clear and unambiguous, is often enhanced when they are not required to write in a way that entails a complex structuring of points of view or to wrestle with divergent time/tense sequences.[1] This task, requiring a descriptive record of observations, eliminated some problems in the management of grammatical conventions. Pupils were writing in the present tense, presenting information which could be sequenced as separate units; forward and backward reference over lengthy stretches could be avoided. However, the aspect of comparison between the observed pictures seems to have accounted for the slightly depressed score for grammaticality overall, and for the markedly depressed score for boys in particular. We list below some of the grammatical problems specific to this task. It seems likely that were pupils asked to read back over their writing, some of these would have been easily picked up.

1. Errors in the use of comparative adjectives and structures:
   Very black in colour and much more bigger.
   A's body is more heavy than B's.
   The body of B is more sturdier looking.
   The legs of fly A are a lot hairy than fly B.
   The fly in A is not such a good flyer than in B.
   Generally speaking, A looks a heavier creature than that of B.
   There are certain differences between the body structure.

---

[1] This point has been illustrated in the context of previous reports on pupils' writing performance, and applies especially to the writing of letters of request.

2. Errors in marking agreement of number in singular and plural forms:

There is something like three rectangles.
The colour on its wings are brown, black, purple.
The wings on fly A are wider but shorter than that of insect B.
The abdomen on each flies are similar in size.
The first difference I have found are the wingspans.
The both thorax of the both insects are very different and so shows up a lot.

3. Errors arising from the confusion of like/alike:

A has a sting much alike the mosquito.

4. Errors arising from confusion of the use of pronouns, with *its* alternating with *his*:

Its eyes appear to be on the side of his head.

5. Errors in forming the negative, as in instances such as:

B looks with no sting.
Fly B has a not so nasty point.

Knowledge of orthographic conventions

It might have been thought that on this task, with certain 'technical' words printed in the pupils' booklet, relatively few orthographic errors would have occurred. For girls, this seems to have been true, since their scores closely replicate the average overall tasks. However, since boys' scores were lower on this task, we detail some of the sources of problems.

(i) Misuse of possessive apostrophe: uncertainty as to whether or not *'its'* has an apostrophe or not led pupils to insert one erroneously. (This was not a problem confined to lower-scoring pupils.)

(ii) Specific spelling errors: certain of the comparative adjectives provided pitfalls of confusion for the uncertain speller because of the doubling of consonants and the changing of -y to -ier ('biger', 'thiner', 'fater', 'heavyer' etc.).

(iii) The convention of capitalising letters used in reference to specimens were difficult for some pupils to apply consistently, especially in conjunction with the use of apostrophes (A's, B's).

We conclude this section by quoting two highly rated scripts (7s in impression-marking), which between them illustrate two contrasting approaches to the task. On the one hand, the objective scientific mode, on the other, the fictional narrative. In quoting the scripts in full, we seek to underline the points made earlier in this discussion concerning the limitations of a view of excellence in writing which promotes fictional narrative above all other genres.

Comparative description: age 15. Impression mark 7 (exact transcription)

The Demoiselle Fly

The demoiselle fly in general has a short thorax long abdomen and bulbous compound eyes.

Type A has all the aforementioned qualities but differs from type B in the following ways:

1. It has six long black legs with long hairs on top and lower parts of its leg's. Type B only has four leg's and has hair's on the bottom of its forelegs and top of its hindlegs only.

2. Type A has opaque wing's which are short and wide. Type B has transparent wings which are noteably longer and thinner than type A's.

3. Type A has it's abdomen segmented into fairly small parts, the end section tapering to a point. Type B has it's abdomen made up of fairly small parts the end part tapering downwards to make it triangular.

4. The most notable difference between the two is their markings. Type A is Brown and green on it's thorax, having brown wing's which get lighter towards the edges and a brown abdomen. Type B is light blue and light brown on its thorax having colourless wing's apart from 3 brown spots on the end of it's wings and a blue brown and black abdomen with just a tinge of pink all over it.

5. Type A's eyes are brown, and bisected latterally with a jagged line. Type B's are blue (pale) with a black spot in the centre.

6. Type A has pointed mandibles but type B's is box shaped.

Comparative description: age 15. Impression mark 7 (exact transcription)

It is one of those lazy hot days in summer when everything is warm and very quiet. The trees surrounding the lake at the bottom of the hill are swaying silently and the ripples on the lake give the impression of peace and tranquillity.

At the end of the lake are reeds and lilies. Flies buzz dozily among the tall grasses, look for food. Bees laze among the pollen filled lilies, drinking their sweet nectar and the demoiselle flies perch motionless on the tall green fronds of the reids.

There are two in particular, one male, one female, that catch my eye as I lie against the sturdy trunk of an ancient oak. They are the most beautiful creatures I have ever seen, but they are both different.

One has lacy wings, so clear I can see the water's edge through them. Its colouring is of brilliant pinks and blues, and it stands out amongst the yellow buttercups that surround it. Its abdomen is long, like a finger, and incredibly thin. It looks so fragile, as though any sudden movement may snap it, like a twig. Its lacy wings stretch back, almost to the full length of the abdomen, like delicate fans, cooling its body. Its head is small but bold. It is completely blue with piercing black eyes on either side of its head. The legs of this magnificent creature are long and black, with what look like hairs of the finest thread, placed at even spaces down each side.

The thorax, the part next to its head, is large. It is not as slender as the abdomen, but it is very sleek, with patches of blue and black reflecting the brilliant sunlight.

As I watch, its head rotates and then suddenly it has disappeared, hovering over the lake.

The other demoiselle fly still remains. This is not such a beautiful creature as the first, but it has striking markings. The wings are a dull brown in colour. They are much wider and not as long. They appear to be much more powerful than the lacy, delicate wings of the other fly. The abdomen of this creature is much thicker. It is dull brown, like the wings, but has flecks of mauve and grey. It appears, just as with the wings, to be much stronger, more substantial, and more useful.

The legs are very thick, although they still have that same appearance of delicacy about them, with the thin hairs vibrating rhythmically. The thorax is not as long as that of the other fly, but is much thicker and more developed. It is green in colour with touches of brown, and gives the impression of strong armour plating.

The head is noble and bold. It is held high and the eyes are much larger and more powerful looking. It appears that this creature would be the male, as he appears stronger and more masculine in his appearance.

He waits, motionless for a few seconds, then hovers over the lake, searching for the other fly, then disappears.

I am now left alone by the waters edge, the sun beating down, the flies once again busy in their search for food.

The example of fictional narrative we have here is unquestionably a tour-de-force, and demonstrates many of the desired features of literacy as defined by traditions of English teaching. Thus, the writer shows evidence of a strong personal response to the task, an ability to empathise with the subject matter, and an imaginative power to create and animate a context for the writing; the range of vocabulary is wide, often precise, and sentence structures throughout are interestingly varied. In schematic terms the episode is well planned: a scene is set for the focus on first one, then the second of the insects; the description of each is neatly paralleled, beginning with wings then proceeding to abdomen, legs and head. Each description is brought to an end not with the sense that observation is exhausted, but because the damselflies leave the scene in turn.

Writing in this form however is not the most appropriate way of fulfilling the task requirements. The script demonstrates some of the ways in which commitment to a first person narrative mode actually obscures some of the clarity of observed detail which the 'story' contains, despite itself. For example, the opening paragraphs are an excursion into pure fantasy, which, however original in conception as a starting point for the description, is redolent with fairly well-worn clichés ('lazy hot days', 'ripples on the lake', 'pollen filled lilies', 'tall green fronds', 'sturdy trunk of an ancient oak'). From this conventional evocation of summer it is not surprising that the general adjective for describing the damselflies turns out to be the minimally informative 'beautiful'. In the same lexical range are other descriptors, 'magnificent', 'powerful', 'noble' and 'bold'. The progressive humanising of fly A leads to inaccurate description of what is visible; 'wings are much wider and not as long' (in fact, A's wings are a quarter as wide again as B's but the same length), 'abdomen much thicker' (the abdomens are the same size), 'legs very thick' (infinitesimally different), 'eyes much larger' (same size).

The optical illusion of darker colours creating an appearance of larger size confused many pupils, none of whom adopted the simple checking strategy of *measuring* the two specimens illustrated. The point to be stressed is that once committed to the narrating of impressions and personal fantasies, the possibility of introducing anything so bald as figures or measurements recedes even further. In this respect the narrative is a restrictive mode for a task in which precise descriptions are required.

The more scientifically ordered writing in the first script is not totally free from errors either; the wings of B are also described as 'notably longer than type A', and despite the fact that this pupil seems familiar with the biological characteristics of damselflies, he also states without qualification or surprise that 'type B has only four legs'. By adopting a framework of scientific description (general classificatory comment on the observed specimen followed by a numbered list of salient features), the writer has imposed a structural order on the writing. There is a sense in which this order is superficial: six points are given, with 'the most notable' appearing fourth on the list, while item three contains a trivial observation which would not serve to distinguish the two flies. We might guess that this writer proceeded to list all the visible differences, without pausing to consider, from the point of view of style, the overall impact of the commentary. Stylistic considerations appear to have gone unattended at a more local level too, as shown in the generally uniform sentence patterns, and repetition of 'fairly small parts' (point three). Yet it is almost certainly the case that had this piece been produced in the context of a science lesson, none of these criticisms would have been offered as language matters. On the other hand, given the findings reported in Chapter 9 of this report concerning the way schools organise writing about investigations in science and other areas of practical work, it is also perhaps unlikely that pupils of this age would have been given the opportunity to structure their work unaided, let alone to use the occasion of a description of insects as the inspiration for a fictitious scenario.

Concluding note

The writers of these two scripts could learn much from each other, and so, we might suggest, could their subject teachers. Beyond the hope of pupil collaboration, there is a need for a more integrated view of the challenges posed by all tasks involving extended writing. For teachers seeking to establish such a viewpoint, the creative imagination is not confused with fantasising (a propensity we earlier noted among some of the abler writers on the **Rainbow** task). At the same time, notions about the constraints of plain style and objectivity are not such as to preclude attention to the linguistic decisions that have to be taken in order to perfect it.

Argumentative writing: a comparison of primary and secondary pupils' performance

Synopsis

Eleven- and 15-year-olds were set the same writing task: they were asked to select a strongly-held personal opinion and to persuade another person to share it. This chapter analyses the performance of each age group so as to highlight similarities and differences in their approach to the task.

The context in which argumentative writing is typically set in schools, as far as this can be deduced from GCE/CSE examination papers in English, is briefly discussed and related to evidence collected in the work sampling component of the APU surveys. Such explicit practice in argumentative/persuasive writing as primary pupils receive appears to be conditioned by reference to practice at secondary level, especially in the area of topic choice. The practice of setting arguments in the English lesson, rather than encouraging this genre across the range of subject areas, imposes a restriction on the nature and scope of subject matter pupils may freely draw upon.

On the basis of the results presented here it is possible to challenge the assumption that argumentative writing is an especially difficult or intractable genre. The distribution of impression scores shows a spread of marks close to the average across all tasks for 11- and 15-year-olds. The analytic criteria serve to define areas of difficulty specific to the task, as, for example, those to do with the schemes used to stage the argument effectively, and the control of style needed to monitor a reader's response and secure conviction. However, an analysis of the lowest-scoring scripts at age 11 shows that, even at this level, pupils have a productive, if embryonic, concept of the argumentative function of writing, and would benefit from a greater exposure to the variety of ways in which language can be used for persuasive purposes.

A major difference between the two age groups, especially noticeable amongst high-scoring pupils in each, was in their methods of argumentation. Fifteen-year-olds exploited many more of the conventions of written prose than did 11-year-olds, whose written arguments drew more obviously upon spoken language conventions, and also upon typographic experimentation, often to good effect.

8.1   Introduction

Argumentative writing is a genre that attracts commentary from different points of view, both because of its accustomed place in the range of competencies required to be demonstrated in written English examinations and because of its interest to linguists as a discourse type against which theories of cognitive development are often tested. Amongst other things, successful argumentative writing has been associated with the ability to co-ordinate ideas and the transcendence of a wholly egocentric point of view (two notions of growth derived from Piagetian psychology). It is hard to imagine how any independent piece of writing could succeed without at least these two components; for example, writing instructions for someone else to follow or writing in dramatic form are just two genres which draw upon the writer's ability to accommodate other points of view, as well as entailing considerable complexity of ideas. It is perhaps the association of argumentative writing with traditional forms of logical thinking, proofs and refutations which has served so often to make it a testing ground for theories of cognitive growth and development.

In schools, it is perhaps not surprising that the writing of argumentative, discursive prose comes to be seen as a necessary, if difficult, skill to be acquired, given that 'argumentative' writing is identified as more uniquely associated with 'cognitive' complexities and demands than are other, also taxing, modes of written expression. This view seems implicitly contained in remarks made by Primary HMI, when they commented both on the infrequent practice of argumentative writing and on its suitability for 'older and able pupils':

> *It was rare to find children presented with a writing task which involved presenting coherent argument, exploring alternative possibilities, or drawing conclusions and making judgements. While it is recognised that this is a difficult form of writing for young children, it could have been more regularly encouraged among the older and able pupils.*[1]

In the older age group, there is ample evidence both from surveys and collections of written work that in the upper

---

1 DES, *Primary Education in England: A Survey by HMI Inspectors of Schools.* London: HMSO, 1978.

secondary years, time and effort is put into the teaching of argumentative writing. Instances of the type of writing which is expected by examination boards are illustrated by reference to published papers and course guidelines for CSE/GCE work in English. For example:

Topics in Section B will allow for...controversial treatment of topics of general interest...

South East Regional Examination Board 1981/2

... candidates have to write about a controversial subject from their own viewpoint, arguing their case as strongly as they are able and showing that they are capable of using evidence to back up their assertions wherever possible. Better candidates ought to demonstrate, in their writing, a consciousness of the arguments likely to be used against them by opponents of their perspective.

South London Consortium, CSE Mode 3 English 1984.

...To use language as an instrument of persuasion and reasoned argument.

Associated Lancashire Schools Examining Board, CSE, 1981.

An extended essay in the examination will test to what extent candidates have acquired the ability to communicate; convey information; analyse statements; state a case; express attitudes, opinions and critical judgements. They must be able to make value judgements in a persuasive and reasonable manner.

Certificate of Extended Education, Proposed Syllabus, English, 1979.

The topics set to test pupils' abilities in these ways include statements and questions such as:

'The British Police Force should be armed.' What are your views on this statement?

Fox hunters were once described as 'The unspeakable in full pursuit of the uneatable.' What are your views on fox hunting?

'There is too much competition in sport.' Do you agree?

'Smoking in public places ought to be forbidden by law.'

Sometimes the task of developing a point of view is set in the context of a given text, already exploited for the business of comprehension. After reading newspaper articles on vandalism and the rag-end trade, pupils were in each case asked:

Select one part of the article with which you agree or disagree.

Say why you agree or disagree with it.

and,

Do you think that rag dealers and tatters do an important job for society? Give reasons for your opinion.

In an attempt to provide some subject matter for the essay, rather than offering a bald statement whose controversial element may not be immediately apparent (e.g. 'There must always be one to command and one to obey'), some questions are set in relation to diagrammatic or note-type outlines, which aim to display a collection of possibly relevant issues. Such a topic is this one:

The diagram represents sketch notes on the subject of vivisection, or experimenting using live animals, in preparation for an essay entitled, 'Should live animals be used for scientific research?' Write a composition giving your views on vivisection. You may use any or all of the points made in the sketch, and you are free to add any further points of your own.

Current practice in the teaching and writing of the argumentative essay in secondary schools has been investigated recently by Dixon and Stratta, whose useful publications on the subject go a long way towards clarifying the issues that arise from questions about the place and purpose of argument in classroom contexts (specifically, in the context of English lessons). We will not rehearse here their generally critical appraisal of the selection of topics for debate under examination conditions, and the stereotyped, shallow responses these call forth. Our own reports have touched on similar issues both in discussion of pupils' 'choice' and handling of subject matter on questions which gave scope for the expression of strongly held opinions, and also as regards the nature of work collected from schools in response to requests for argumentative writing. It is this latter collection of work which provides us with some useful background information about the practice of argumentative writing at both primary and secondary level. As part of the 1983 primary survey, a sub-sample of schools was asked to provide examples of previously completed writing in relation to three categories. The categories were: writing based on practical work, argumentative writing and pupils' own choice of 'best work'. A total of 73 schools supplied 1545 pieces of written work, from 645 pupils. The largest number represented the pupils' own choice (60 per cent of samples), followed by writing based on practical work (550). Argumentative writing comprised the smallest collection, but nevertheless amounted to a total of 393 pieces and came from 47 schools. It may be that in the years since the 1978 HMI survey, more emphasis has in fact been placed on this form of writing in primary schools. How was this form of writing conceptualised?

Few primary pupils are being prepared for public examinations which require a set-piece essay of the GCE/CSE type. We might therefore anticipate that without the fatal magnetism of a predictable argumentative essay topic looming at the end of the school year, 11-year-olds might be discovering a more diverse application of argumentative skills than pupils four years further on in the system. A catalogue of topics used for written argument at primary level proved, however, to replicate those most frequently encountered in secondary school. Thus pupils' work centred mainly on these topics: animals (issues of cruelty, experimentation, hunting), school (uniform, rules, structure), sport, nuclear weapons, television, smoking.

So, the long apprenticeship had clearly begun. These topics replicated the major ones nominated by 15-year-olds when asked to write about a strongly held opinion in the context of the 1979 secondary survey: the only new arrival was the topic of nuclear weapons. Apart from that topic, there was little encroachment on political themes, apart from a handful of arguments connected with the general election (announced just prior to the 1983 survey).

Because our survey populations are drawn from both primary and secondary age groups it is of interest to compare the performance of pupils, separated by four years of schooling, on a common task used in the 1983 surveys. Before looking at high and low performance in each age group on that task, we summarise some of the findings from previous surveys in relation to argumentative writing.

8.2 Summary of previous findings

In previous reports we have looked at argumentative and persuasive writing in various forms, at both primary and secondary level. For example, in the first secondary survey report we discussed the results of a writing task which invited pupils to develop a strong opinion in writing so as to persuade someone else to share their point of view. In the third secondary report pupils' responses to the question of whether or not there should be one legal age or several were analysed from two components of the survey: writing and oracy.

We have so far analysed 11-year-olds' performance on an argumentative task comparable to those discussed at secondary level, although in the process of reporting on their performance in a written version of **The Balloon Game** (second Primary Report), it became apparent that there was some overlap between pupils' approach to this form of dramatised argument and to more 'essayist' versions of persuasive writing.

Each time we have looked at pupils' ways of handling types of written argument, we have seen that they encounter certain difficulties which we can focus in terms of main areas of writing assessment. These are summarised in broad outline below:

Content
– the subject matter chosen to support an allegedly strongly-held personal opinion is often less original than when pupils are asked to write about other matters of equally personal concern, such as newly learnt interests or particular skills which they possess. The standard topics provided in school for debate and discussion may not be a fair reflection of children's immediate social and political concerns.

– primary pupils, although keen to tackle large questions of morality and social organisation, often reveal a lack of the most basic facts of public and political life which makes it difficult for them to develop a point of view in other than domestic and familiar terms. The general practice of writing arguments in English lessons poses some restrictions on the amount and scope of subject matter pupils may freely draw upon.

Organisation
– good organisation is crucial to an effective argument. Pupils who are accustomed to relying on chronological ordering, typical of narrative and many reporting styles, are less assured in making an emphatic selection among competing elements of strongly held opinions.

Appropriateness and style
– two main problems are encountered here. Firstly, the need to keep a reader in mind so as to influence a presupposed point of view presents writers with an especially acute version of a condition of all writing; in so far as younger writers are often in the process of changing their own opinions as they write, it is all the more difficult for them to monitor the text from an outsider's standpoint simultaneously. Secondly, ways of connecting together elements of the argument have to be found: replacing the ubiquitious *then* and *and* of stories we find the phrases *another thing*, and *also* used to a monotonous extent. The work of 11-year-olds also illustrates a searching for a greater stylistic range by means of graphic experimentation. Many of them resort to underlining, capitals, and exclamation marks in an effort to capture and direct the reader's interest.

Knowledge of grammatical and orthographic conventions
– when the overall direction or form of a piece of written work is uncertain, as can be the case with many an argument, grammatical clarity and coherence suffers. Whereas a common failure in the writing of narrative prose is the omission of punctuation to define sentence boundaries, pupils' written arguments appear to suffer from the contrasting problem of too many sentence breaks (for example, full stops before conjunctions). A possible cause of this is the writers' adherence to a system of meaningful pauses in speech which do not correspond to full stops in written language.

– as regards orthographic conventions, it appears that in all writing tasks which take issue with matters of public, political life, pupils are using a vocabulary which is less practised. Especially in the case of 11-year-olds, spelling errors in content words are more notable in this type of writing task than in others which draw upon the more familiar areas of the school curriculum.

Pupils in the 1983 primary and secondary surveys were set the following task:

(The illustration was omitted in the secondary booklets.)

Illustration 8.1: *What can we do with writing?*

There are many uses for writing apart from describing things, telling stories, writing letters, plays, songs, notes... and so on.

Writing is also a very useful way of saying what you think about something, and persuading your reader to agree with you. It's a way of making your case heard, and getting your viewpoint across.

We would like you to think of a subject about which you have a strong opinion. The choice of subject is up to you. Write about it in some detail so as to persuade somebody who does not share your opinion to change their mind, and see things your way.

For each age group, the distribution of impression marks is shown below, with separate tables for girls' and boys' scores. Impression marks are awarded on a rising scale of 1–7.

Table 8.1 *Distribution of impression marks for persuasive/argumentative task, 11- and 15-year-old pupils*

Per cent marks	1+2	3	4	5	6	7
	Primary pupils (n = 388)					
Girls	5.4	20.1	39.7	27.8	9.2	2.7
Boys	13.2	26.2	29.7	18.4	7.5	3.9
Total	9.6	23.3	34.4	20.5	8.9	3.4
All tasks boys and girls	12.7	26.5	32.1	18.0	8.2	2.5
	Secondary pupils (n = 429)					
Girls	5.6	13.4	23.1	31.3	17.5	8.8
Boys	8.2	19.3	26.6	22.6	16.5	6.3
Total	6.8	16.1	24.7	27.3	17.0	7.7
All tasks boys and girls	8.6	19.6	27.0	23.9	14.6	5.8

For both age groups, the marks for this task correspond fairly closely with the spread across all tasks; for neither age group was this the most difficult task, nor the easiest. This kind of evidence raises a question mark over the idea of a unique association between argumentative writing and notions of complexity and difficulty, however these are defined.

For both 11- and 15-year-olds, the mean scores of girls were higher than those of boys: primary girls 4.2, primary boys 3.9; secondary girls 4.6, secondary boys 4.4. However, while proportionately more boys congregate in low-scoring groups at both age levels, we note that taking the two highest-score bands together (impression marks of 6 and 7) suggests a greater equality of performance.

In order to see more precisely what the components of this global performance were, we need to refer to the analytic marks awarded on the task. (Note that a 10 per cent sub-sample of scripts is assessed analytically for each survey.)

Commenting on the distribution of scores at primary level, we can say that for 11-year-old girls this task produced scores that were very little different from the average distribution across all tasks, when marks in the two top-score bands were considered. However, it appeared to be slightly more difficult for them to score full marks in the categories of appropriateness and style than on some other tasks. Boys' scores, although generally lower than girls' in all categories, were also closer to their average performance in the category of content and organisation; like girls, they seemed to have experienced more difficulties with appropriateness and style, and grammatical conventions on this task.

The analytic scores for 15-year-olds showed an interesting trend with respect to sex differences. While the proportion of pupils scoring top marks for content (just over 30 per cent) was higher than the average for all tasks, slightly more boys' than girls' scripts fell into this category. (We note, in passing, that high though these proportions may seem, they are still lower than those regularly noted on a task involving the invention of a story for children on which between 40 and 50 per cent of 15-year-olds score top marks for content.) A similar pattern was evident in the marks awarded for organisation, and for appropriateness and style. Boys did better than average with respect to both these categories; girls slightly less well. Both sexes' marks for grammatical and orthographic conventions showed that fewer of them scored highly on this task. On average, at least one-third of girls scored top marks in these categories; on this task the proportion doing so fell to one-quarter, while boys' lower average scores showed a decrease of similar proportion with respect to grammatical conventions. In sum, although fewer boys' scripts were highly rated in impression-marking than were girls', it is clear that the small number of boys whose work was highly rated in both systems of marking were responding well to this task, as is shown by their scores on the salient dimensions of content, organisation and style.

To establish a view of the particular achievements of each age group, the scripts were read with a view to selecting the top- and bottom-scoring groups. This selection was made in both samples by extracting all scripts given above-average impression marks (6 and 7), and all those scoring below-average marks (3, 2 and 1). While the proportions at the top and bottom of the scale were only slightly different at primary level (9.6 per cent and 12.7 per cent), amongst 15-year-olds almost four times as many pupils achieved high marks as low marks.

We begin by looking at the writing of high performers at age 15, on the assumption that this group will define what it is possible to achieve in argumentative writing within the constraints of a specified task, place and time. When we come to look at the nature of low performance on the same topic, a concept of what might have been achieved will enable us to determine both how far the poorer writers have still to develop and whether they have anything in common, in terms of potential, with their more successful peers. Discussion of high performance at age 15 is followed by high performance at age 11; two highly rated scripts from each age group are then compared. Low performance is dealt with in inverse order: age 11 followed by age 15.

8.3 High performance at age 15, persuasive writing task

What did 15-year-olds write about?

The same general topics were selected by both girls and boys in this group, but not in equal numbers. These were the most popular topics:

(i) health (smoking, abortion, contraception, exercise, natural childbirth);

(ii) social issues/environment (pollution, facilities for young people, white weddings, television, sexual equality, racism, pop music and youth, old age);

(iii) animals (vivisection, fox hunting, tail docking, dog fouling, experimentation);

(iv) politics (nuclear weapons, CND, voting age, American foreign policy, present British government, democracy).

Each of these general topics was represented by between 10 and 20 scripts. Smaller groups of pupils wrote on law and order, school rules and uniform, religion, transport and computers. Amongst high-scoring boys, almost half chose to write about political topics, whereas only a fraction of girls' scripts were in this category, with the first three subject areas listed above appearing most frequently. Judging by the results of analytic marking, it would appear that boys' choice of controversial, overtly political subject matter impressed markers. Such themes are not amongst those canonised by examining bodies and therefore stand out as original points of view.

The elements of stereotyping shown in the pattern of subject choice at age 15 need to be considered in relation to pupils' reading habits as well. Each of the surveys of reading performance carried out by the APU has documented the general orientation of girls towards reading matter based on socio-psychological issues, dealing with home and family concerns. The subjects about which many girls felt they had strong opinions were drawn from this domain. By contrast, boys' preferred reading of a wider range of technical, discursive literature may well be linked with subject choices of another kind. However, it

must be admitted that only a few boys, relatively speaking, produced writing of a high standard on this topic and for each of the boys' scripts dealing with a theme of political importance there were many more which at various levels of coherence not only opted for more conventionally 'taught' topics, but also wrote from within a personal, domestic framework.

Characteristics of high-scoring scripts (age 15)

This group of scripts had in common many of these commendable features:

– subject matter explored in some detail and depth, at least as far as the writer's state of knowledge could take it.

– use of paragraphing as a means of segmenting and highlighting information, points of view, and qualificatory statements.

– ways of keying the reader in, for example by use of a descriptive title, a clear opening statement, or an introduction which set the context for what was to follow.

– varied sentence lengths and types which increased the readability of the argument.

– ways of entertaining and adjusting to opposing points of view.

– an ability to pursue a line of thought to a desired conclusion, withholding clinching information or attitudes till the end, in order to make a final point memorable.

– a confident use of personal experience to illustrate a case of potential concern to more than one person.

– writing which was free of almost all errors in grammatical and orthographic convention.

Not all of these characteristics were present all of the time. The following extract from a highly rated script shows a writer in the process of visible management/mismanagement of several aspects of text production:

Introducing to you this topic: the deployment of Cruise Missiles and their true meaning in Britain. You may have a different point of view to me but I urge you to read my views, not totally against cruise missiles and their meaning but neither in total favour of them.

Do we need Cruise? Before we can answer this question we consider their use and purpose. a) Use. The use of cruise missiles is to effectively knock out the opponents by positions that is if what I read and see is correct; b) Purpose. The purpose, well I suppose, it is based on the principle of, if I can't beat you and rule you, you can't beat and rule me! resulting in the total destruction of all things living. So do we need Cruise? Yes! if we are to carry out the above opinion. No! if we want to live but maybe under varying states of governments. The choice is purely individual, live without strong beliefs or die for your opinion.

continued

Let me bring something else to mind after considering the above, the state of the countries economy at the present...

The above script has an introductory move, but it is awkwardly written; moreover the scope of the topic is not well defined despite the after-thought, and repetition, of the phrase 'and their meaning'. While it is clear that the writer wishes to look at pros and cons, the verbal parallelism isn't quite exact ('not totally against ... neither in total favour'). The use of questions to raise and focus issues ('Do we need cruise?... So do we need cruise?') was a device common to other writers in the whole survey: here it is used to introduce an overview of necessary information under two heads: use and purpose of cruise missiles. Although the layout of these points could be improved spatially, their function is clear. Unfortunately, the opposing answers which are allegedly given to the question of need do not exactly spring from the information so far presented and despite their dramatic antithetical heads ('Yes!' 'No!') these contain less precise alternatives than their argumentative force promises ('The above opinion' reads as a vague reference to the position of confrontation; 'varying states of government' is an equally vague phrase for a state of affairs implicitly undesirable).

Other scripts managed their openings better, finding apposite titles: *The Plight of the Non-smoker*; *Nuclear Weapons – A Preventative Measure?*; *Animals Can't Fight Back*; *The Death Game*; *Should they be Ostracised?* (subject, old people); *My Advice to Teenage Smokers*. As might be expected from more able writers, few scripts were content to start where the question left off with statements of 'I think', 'I personally believe', 'I feel'. Typical openings contained either a question or a general statement, or both in combination. From the outset, better writers freed themselves from overt reliance on the topic as set. Examples of good beginnings were as follows:

How many young girls imagine their wedding to be large and grandiose and in a church?

* * *

In the 'eighties with international relations worsening, should Britain be making herself a target for annihilation because of the beliefs of a head-strong, retired movie star and an ageing lady who would dispense with the National Health Service just because her kind can afford to pay the price?

* * *

When adults talk about politics and religion, they never seem to realise that their kids are interested too, but adults seem to dismiss kids opinions as a load of rubbish, which is unfair. Just because we're under 18, why shouldn't our views be taken seriously?

* * *

There are very few people around today who can honestly say that they realise what pains innocent animals have to suffer for the benefit of human beings. Many times, I have asked myself the question, 'How humane are humans?' and every time I have never found the answer.

In all such openings there is evidence of definite overture to a reader, varying in tone from aggressive passionate persuasion to a more reflective examination of the scope of the opinion held, on the assumption that once a reader has been taken through the details, agreement on the general proposition will follow. The influence of an older rhetorical tradition of argument seemed to lie behind some of these openings and also carried through to a powerful conclusion.

Throughout this high-scoring group there was constant evidence of reader awareness shown in the ability to imagine an audience and to work through the known beliefs of others, whilst keeping in mind the direction of the argument. Few pieces were written as an exposition of a topic which offered neither point of view (except that this was a worthy subject, as for example, 'exercise', 'democracy', 'balance in TV viewing'), nor inducement to share it. A striking instance of persuading a skilfully defined reader came in the script entitled *My Advice to Teenage Smokers*. Part of this script is reproduced below.

My advice to teenage smokers.

As a member of the teenage 'gang' I already know about all the problems and stresses of becoming fifteen. Parents don't seem to understand at school teachers seem to be against you, and you feel you need something to get you noticed, to calm your nerves and to make you feel good. Some teenagers turn to drugs which I strongly advise you not to and others turn to smoking and this is the topic I'd like to discuss.

I know it is easy to get caught up in the whirlwind of smokers because it happened to me. Luckily I managed to remove myself from that group of friends and stopped, but you might not be so lucky.

Management of argumentative structure

Nearly all of the highly rated scripts were long (three closely written A4 pages). At times problems in argumentative structure were caused by the volume of subject matter, but more typical of 'breakdowns' was the sudden appearance of illogically placed information, gaps in knowledge, wildly exaggerated statements, or passages of semi-confusion possibly hinging upon the misuse of a word or phrase. Almost every script provided one or more examples of these fractures. We quote from several which typify the category:

An American official when questioned on why the British Government did not have a say in the invasion of part of her realm, this official comes out with the reply that it was nothing to do with Britain even though the Queen of Britain and the Queen of Grenada are the same woman. Then this official goes on further to comment that Britain did not consult America on the recapture of the Falkland Islands even though the Islands were British crown territory. Also American intervention in Vietnam when the Americans bombed civilian villages because they may have been Terrorists in the villages.

* * *

Fifty years ago, women and children felt safe when walking along the street at night and on their own. However, today, many people are murdered or raped, just yards away from their homes. Surely, everyone must consider this wrong, and be willing to support any action to stop these horrible crimes.

* * *

There are plenty more of the animals used in experiments. If the animals used for experiments were set free the whole world would be overrun by animals and disease. There would be no cures for these diseases and everybody would die a horrible death.

* * *

Knowledge of grammatical conventions

As can be seen from the above examples, lack of logical clarity sometimes coincided with errors in grammaticality. Given how few and far between such errors were in this group of scripts, they are probably better attributed to lapses in concentration rather than to a lack of basic knowledge as to the conventions of sentence structure. Nevertheless, both the punctuation and co-ordination of complex written sentences still appear to be causing problems even at this level. While more time spent on drafting and redrafting could tidy up such lapses, it is clear that problems in this area are not confined to weak writers nor to younger pupils.

Teachers are the worst offenders. It seems to be that, although girls are not allowed to wear make-up, which I dont, Teachers wear make-up ten time worse than any schoolgirl. We are then asked not to wear over two inch heels shoes. Although teachers are allowed to wear five inch heel shoes.

* * *

A recent enquiry showed that for a dog licence it costs a mere thirty seven and a half pence. The child or children are then presented with a dog for their birthday, or christmas which will probably be mawled and tormented to death.

* * *

He does this against the wishes of the British Government who the country is part of her commonwealth.

8.4 High performance at age 11, persuasive writing task

The extraction of scripts in the 6 and 7 impression score bands produced fewer examples than had been obtained at secondary level: approximately 12 per cent of the total number, as contrasted with the 24 per cent of 15-year-olds in this category. As we have already suggested in relation to work collected from schools, primary pupils who are given practice in argumentative writing in school appear to be converging on many of the best known topics set for GCE/CSE examinations. It will come as no surprise to learn that in a 'free choice' situation, 11-year-olds elected to voice strong opinions on cruelty to animals, blood sports, school uniform, games and organisation, playing facilities, litter, arming the police, sport and environmental pollution, and nuclear weapons.

Other areas of overlap between the two age groups were in positive strengths in writing, although when we look in more detail at the ways 11-year-olds addressed their subject matter, certain differences are apparent. Briefly their common strengths are these:

– coherent presentation of a substantial amount of subject matter

– stylistically varied writing, which monitors a reader response while elaborating a personal case

– relatively few grammatical or orthographic errors.

We pointed out that not all of the highly rated secondary scripts possessed all such strengths, item by item. Such a qualification is even more necessary to make in relation to the 11-year-olds. Fewer scripts used paragraphs in a consistent way, for example; few provided distinctive titles or contextualised openings, beginning instead, 'I am going to tell you about ...', 'I feel that ...'. 'I think that we shouldn't ...', 'I am writing to say about ...' etc; length of script was associated with repetition more than density of subject matter; quite cogent arguments were found to contain digressions in subject matter, or had their impact lessened by an overuse of non-signifying vocabulary items; finally, as is the case with younger writers generally, errors in grammatical and orthographic conventions were more frequent, and not so easily attributed to lapses in concentration.

Methods of argumentation

In this area we find most difference between the two age groups. Much of the best of 15-year-olds' work has a familiar shape; it echoes current forms of journalism, commentary and reportage. For example, the 15-year-old pupil who wrote 'This article is going to put forward to you my feelings about using animals for experimental work' had in mind a model of writing which was implicitly shared by others of her age group. The writing of 11-year-olds, however cogent or thought provoking, rarely achieves (or even aspires to?) that kind of publicity. The work of 11-year-olds shows a variety of structures being tried out for argument, despite the commonality of themes.

Many of these structures seem to derive directly from children's experience of how arguments are managed in *spoken* exchanges, and their search for an interactive audience leads them not only into experiments with graphic presentation (capital letters, underlining, exclamation marks, all of which help to capture some of the prosodic features of spoken language), but also into outbreaks of dramatic dialogue in the midst of standard prose paragraphs.

One writer who wished to express an opinion about the infrequency of PE lessons at school began her writing like this: 'Mary, I think you are wrong about P.E.' and concluded, 'Now Mary do you think I'm right?' 'Yes I do Caroline because you have made a few good points'.

Another writer, after outlining her disapproval of the fur trade, suddenly made a direct address to the Prime Minister: 'Are you listening to me Mrs. Thatcher!'

Personal force was exerted on the reader by use of capitals, leaving one in no doubt as to the strength of the writer's opinion:

So Hunters go get another job like farming (vegetable farming) or helping animals on their way. Un less you want to get clobbered over the head BY ME!!!! So leave animals alone and go jump in a lake or have your brain tested. BE KIND TO ANIMALS. They woht hurt you unless you harm them.

Capitalisation was widely employed to emphasise a concluding statement, 'DO NOT SHOOT!'; 'put this simply – June 9th CONSERVATIVE X'; 'PLEASE HELP!!', and to stress antithesis:

Disquiet at the practice of fur trading prompted one pupil to end her case with a letter to the Queen:

If ever I get to write a letter to the Queen I would put in it exactly what I feel strongly about. I would speak as if I was there in front of her.

I would say "Dear Queen I feel very strongly about the killing of animals for their fur, and I would like your opinion on the subject. I will try my best to stop it but I don't know whether I will succeed or not, please write to me with your opinion'.

Yours sincerely (name given). That is what I would put in a letter to the Queen.

It seems not too far-fetched to suggest that a generative source for the deployment of varied scripts and address modes is to be found in comics, newspaper headlines and typography, and TV commercials. At any rate, the proliferation of such characteristics gave these arguments an informal quality, which could on occasion combine with a direct, colloquial use of language, establishing an 'issue' with speed and clarity:

I wish people would realise that whale killing is not much fun to whales, because I'm sure they would not like to be shot at with arrows and hauled up so that it is impossible to breath.

* * *

I am going to tell you what I feel strongly about, 'swimming'. I like swimming very much, and it angers me when people say, 'I can't swim'. What they really mean is, they won't swim.

* * *

Our school assemblies are very boring. We hear stories over and over again, and the hymns are even worse. Occasionally we learn new hymns but these are just as bad. The agenda for our assemblies are nearly always the same 1) The Lords Prayer 2) A Boring hymn 3) A story read by our headmaster 4) Another boring hymn 5) Prayers 6) The recorder band plays a march whilst we all walk out.

We will not detail here the nature of grammatical errors found in the high-scoring scripts at primary level: essentially they repeat those mentioned at secondary level, except that they occur more frequently and commonly include dislocation of subject/pronoun reference systems as well as sentence-co-ordination problems. These are errors which lower-scoring 11-year-olds fall into even more often, and the extent of the problem will be more fully discussed in that context. The same may be said about orthographical errors, with the proviso that the further down the mark scale we go, the more likely we are to find, in addition to spelling errors and incomplete punctuation sets, errors in the control of upper/lower case conventions. Errors of the latter type are rare amongst high-scoring pupils.

To conclude this section on high-scoring pupils, we reproduce two scripts, one by a pupil aged 15 and one by an 11-year-old. They illustrate two different approaches to argumentative writing. It would be simplifying the evidence to suggest that the scripts typified the performances of 11- and 15-year-olds respectively. Nevertheless, there was more writing of the kind represented by the 11-year-old's script in both age groups than there was of the kind produced by the 15-year-old in either age group.

Example 1. High performance, age 11, persuasive writing task

I feel very strongly about Nuclear bombs. I think they are just used by countries to shoe their might. There are many kinds of bombs. Pershing, trident, cruise, these are only some of the horrible machines man has invented, machines that will destroy the world if manufacture is not stopped. Atomic or nuclear bombs are made with Uranium which is a rare mineral. As you probably know there is what people call a arms race going on. I observe this a silly childish game, and as you well know children fall out, and fight. Is this to be the world's future?

What about the money spent on arms? Do you know that one fifth of the British arms budget alone can provide pumps to pump fresh water (two every) all over the world, and one third of the United States' budget. Costs of giving the third world plentyful food is about as much as the world spends on arms every two weeks. Did you know that?

But of course you say you now have Nuclear bunkers. Do you know that even if you survived the blast and the radiation in a Nuclear bunker there would be no soil, it would be contaminated and so would the sea, so you wouldn't be able to live.

I think that we should give all the Uranium to power satelites such as HW pioneer ten which has just passed pluto.

That is why I don't approve of nuclear bombs.

MPs who approve Nuclear bombs call them deterrents, but the only thing they can and will deter is life itself.

Example 2. High performance, age 15, persuasive writing task

The deployment of cruise missiles in Britain has caused an outcry by women belonging to the campaign for nuclear disarmament. They have set up camp at many American air bases, particularly Greenham Common, to show the world how strongly they feel about this threat to humanity.

Many people feel that these women are zealots who have not thought seriously about the issue. But do the ordinary people really know the full implications of nuclear war?

Hiroshima and Nagasaki were devasted thirty-five years ago by an A-bomb. People are still slowly dying of an horrific form of cancer.

Nowadays the nuclear bombs are terrifyingly more powerful. Within two hours of both 'super powers'

launching all their missiles, most of the world would be dead. The fire from the blast would use up most of the oxygen in the atmosphere so anyone surviving in a nuclear fall-out shelter would suffocate anyway.

Do not forget that nuclear war could begin by accident! For example, last November 9th, a man plugged a war games cartridge into the supposedly infallible computer at a control room in America . The computer took the game to be real. Stations were alerted and aeroplanes took off – loaded with nuclear bombs. Fortunately the mistake was discovered and World War III was averted.

However, next time could be for real, because in two years a satellite will have been completed by America which will detect a nuclear launch in Russia – be it real, accident or a mistake. The satellite will 'push the button' of all missiles in America. No human will be able to stop it! Maybe nuclear power is here to stay – but it has great potential to improve life not destroy it.

CND supporters, especially women, are looking to the future. They want to secure a peaceful, safe, natural world in which their children can live. All power is not in the hands of Mr. Reagan, Mrs. Thatcher and Mr. Andropov. Ordinary people share this world as well and can have a say in how it is run. Remember! World War III will be won by no-one!

These two scripts have in common the schematic structure typical of argumentative writing, to the extent that each opens with a position-taking statement, then proceeds by a process of exemplification and persuasion to win the reader over to the same point of view. The subject matter in both is comparable (the threat of nuclear war), and their attitude towards this similarly coincident. Yet it is in their methods for conveying this attitude that differences between the two scripts emerge which characterise differences between the 11- and 15-year-olds' approaches to the writing of argument. These differences can be specified in terms of the linguistic choices made by the two writers: as should be clear from the discussion that follows, the distinguishing features of the 15-year-old's script depend on the conventions of written language, while many of the characteristics of the way the 11-year-old writes show an overlap with the conventions of speech.

Thus the 11-year-old begins with an overt, direct statement 'I feel very strongly...' and the text continues with repeated references to the writer's state of mind ('I think' (twice), 'I observe', 'I don't approve'). Linked with the directness of personal reference is an equally straightforward address to the reader, 'you' appearing eight times in the subject of questions or assumptions. The main principle of topic development in this text, given the frequency of the pronouns 'I' and 'you' in sentence initial position, is the interactive one of statements and questions on which so much of actual conversation depends.

This principle gives a sense of immediacy to the persuasion but does not necessarily make for the most efficient or coherent way of developing a written text. It forms a sequence of observations and (rhetorical) questions, which are used in turn to make way for the speaker's comment, which then exhausts the topic. Where it breaks down, as happens in paragraph three, it does so because one element is left out (in this case either a question or an assumed interjection), thus resulting in an isolated fragment.

Also in line with conventions of conversational exchange, this text uses vocabulary which is either very general ('countries', 'all over the world', 'MPs') or very familiar ('horrible', 'silly', 'childish', 'bombs').

Casual connectives are left implicit, to be inferred from juxtapositions of sentences rather than being given lexical realisation. (Were the writer to attempt to insert the connecting links between each sentence it is possible that the floating remark about uranium in paragraph one might be deleted, and placed in the context of the later point concerning exploratory satellites.) Items of contemporary knowledge appear and disappear throughout the text without the writer feeling any need to explain them more fully. Thus we have 'the blast', 'the radiation', 'just passed Pluto'.

The linear organisation of speech seems to account for the loosely appended reference to the United States arms budget in paragraph two, and the similarly loose structure of paragraph three, 'there would be no soil, it would be contaminated and so would the sea, so you wouldn't be able to live.' At other points, however, the writer appears well in command of the tighter organising methods typical of writing (subordination and deliberate repetition):

these are only some of the horrible machines that man has invented, machines that will destroy the world

MP's who do not approve nuclear bombs call them deterrents, but the only thing they can and will deter is life itself.

The 15-year-old leaves us in no doubt about the strength of personal feeling on nuclear arms, nor about the intensity of designs on the reader, but never once uses the personal pronouns 'I' or 'you'. Rather, these attitudes are conveyed by a complex patterning of language. For example, it is not until the last line of paragraph one that the writer's attitude towards cruise missiles is indicated in the phrase 'this threat to humanity'. The implications of 'threat' are picked up and extended throughout the text by emotive descriptions: 'devastated', 'slowly dying', 'horrific form of cancer', 'suffocate', to be contrasted finally with a 'peaceful, safe, natural world ... in which children can live'.

Instead of questions, the script deals in imperatives ('Do not forget!' 'Remember!'), more appropriate perhaps when addressing the vast audience of 'ordinary people', as distinct from 'you'. The development of the notion of 'ordinary people' throughout the text is quite skilful. It first makes its appearance as the 'many people' who might object to the actions of Greenham Common peace protesters, then becomes the 'ordinary people who might not really know the implications of nuclear war'; such innocent persons might be assumed to have a kinship with the victims of Hiroshima; no ordinary human could intervene in a system of satellite communication designed to launch a nuclear attack, and finally all power cannot be vested in just three individuals (by naming them the writer isolates and weakens them), when the mass of 'ordinary people' is considered.

Scepticism about the morality of armed nations is conveyed through use of historical reference, by quotation marks ('super powers') and by qualificatory asides ('supposedly infallible'), rather than by use of an everyday analogy.

The closely reasoned pattern which this text exemplifies can be seen in any strand extracted for analysis. We can look for instance at the manner of handling temporal reference, by which present, past and future are interwoven through flashback and prophecy, each springing from a contemplation of the current state of affairs. The writer's choice of verb tense and aspect also works to emphasise notions of a 'threat to humanity'. Frequent use of the passive serves to place items of weaponry in sentence-subject position, creating a sense of the fragility of human control, the 'fire from the blast' is represented as an active consumer of people's oxygen; modal and future tenses build up a sense of urgent prophecy ('would be dead', 'could begin', 'could be for real', 'will be able'). Urgency and emphasis are also conveyed by the linking of words in lists: 'be it real, accident or mistake'; 'a peaceful, safer, natural world'; 'Mr. Reagan, Mrs. Thatcher, Mr. Andropov'.

These then are some of the ways in which the writer forges a tight attitudinal web around the subject matter of the argument: such techniques are more readily deployed in writing than in speech. The greater time for reflection and planning possible in writing has been used to good account and the result is in fact a text that manages to 'read' with the forcefulness of speech while being constructed along most un-speech-like lines. The combination of text-forming devices noted above was more typical of the highest performance at age 15 than at age 11, and presumably is in part to be traced to older children's greater familiarity with written modes of argument. From the survey of evidence above there would seem to be no doubt about the similarity of intention, or designs on the reader, shown in the written arguments of the two age groups, but there is a difference in the linguistic means available to realise those intentions. The difference is not always to the disadvantage of the younger age group, in whose work there is much potential for strongly persuasive writing. Nor is there a clear-cut distinction between ages 11 and 15, as this necessarily selective discussion perhaps suggests.

8.5 Characteristics of low performance: 11-year-olds, persuasive writing task

With the characteristics of the best work produced by primary and secondary pupils in mind, we turn now to a discussion of low performance at age 11 on the assumption that this will provide evidence about the most rudimentary approaches to written argument in the sample as a whole. We will also be looking for evidence of where the work of the low-scoring pupils contains positive strengths of the kind identified in the work of a higher standard.

The scripts of all pupils who had received low impression marks on the task requiring the persuasive expression of a strong opinion were extracted for closer analysis. As can be seen from Table 8.1, the proportions of girls and boys whose impression scores fell into the bands 1, 2 and 3 on the 7-point scale were very different: almost 40 per cent of boys' writing was in this category, compared with 25 per cent of girls'.

Immediately visible characteristics which all these scripts shared to a greater or lesser degree were the following:

- poor letter formation, at times resulting in illegibility of words or lines.

- inconsistent use of upper and lower case letters.

- uncertain spelling.

- punctuation, if used at all, serving to mark off speech-like units, rather than the sentences of standard written language.

- relatively short amounts of writing (8–15 lines of A4) for this particular topic.

- repetitive use of content words.

- limited choice of vocabulary.

Having isolated these scripts as exemplifying low performance on the basis of an impression (i.e. 'global') score, we are interested in diagnosing that low performance further. Is it the case that pupils whose writing so quickly reveals so many flaws are incapable of producing a written argument, perhaps because of the plethora of technical difficulties they have still to overcome? Or is it the case that despite their shaky hold on the writing system they are nevertheless able to communicate their ideas with some purpose? For the teacher of writing, answers to these questions are important indicators about the relative emphases which different aspects of a language programme might receive: should the stress be on the technicalities of writing generally or on techniques of and scope for argumentative writing? Our evidence suggests that the latter approach is likely to be the more constructive.

It was possible to sort the scripts on the basis of the way the topic was addressed in each. We asked: is the pupil able to articulate an opinion and give any account of its significance? Six distinctive groups of scripts were formed, as outlined below. Over half of the scripts sampled showed that the writer was able to articulate an opinion and at least attempt a persuasive move on that basis. A minority of scripts revealed a failure to conceptualise the task adequately, or displayed deep-seated problems in both language and thought which made interpretation difficult.

In other words, it appears that many children who might appear to be not yet secure enough in their handling of the conventions of written language to be ready for exposure to more than a few supposedly simple functions of writing (typically, story, report, description) are in fact already launched in the direction of persuasive argument on topics ranging from eliminating violence in Northern Ireland to promoting compulsory swimming lessons.

Analysis of low-scoring scripts (11-year-olds): approach to task

Group one: potentially argumentative writing, accounting for about 80 per cent of the sub-sample.

1. Scripts which were able to communicate in writing the substance of an opinion and its signifcance to a wider group. This group contained in roughly equal proportions both scripts which contained an argument in outline (i.e. scripts which introduced an opinion, explained something of its scope, put forward a reason for its acceptance, and concluded by restating the opinion), and those which began with some stated opinion but did not progress beyond illustration or exemplification of it.

2. Scripts which ran up a list of opinions without either emphasising any one of them, or indicating their possible relevance to others. (Multi-statement responses.) Opinions in this group and the one above were based on a variety of public as well as personal topics.

3. Scripts which appeared to be in the throes of developing an opinion but which resisted comprehension in whole or in part *either* because of the combination of confused ideas and lack of grammatical coherence *or* because of illegible handwriting, which very likely concealed deeper confusion.

Group two: non-argumentative writing (wishes, narratives, statements), accounting for about 20 per cent of the sub-sample.

1. Scripts which dealt with one topic, but whose reading of the word 'opinion' translated it as personal desire or wish. A clue to this misreading of the topic was given by the pupil who wrote 'I have a strong opinion to become a Karate expert'.

2. Scripts which were written in the form of a narrative account of an event which was recognisable as a moment of argument or disagreement, caused by a conflict of wishes between the writer and a friend/parent (e.g. reading in bed after lights out, having the record player on a loud volume). A clash of views was implicitly present in these 'stories' though it was not generalised into a framing opinion. Scripts in this group and the one above contained a majority of personally focused topics.

3. Scripts which comprised simple statements, no more than a few lines in length, about the *interest* of a particular topic or the existence of a constraint which may have been controversial. These topics were stated flatly and not generalised into abiding or significant opinions.

As stated above, boys' scripts outnumbered girls' in this sample as a whole; most of the girls' scripts were found in the category of potentially argumentative writing, with fewer examples of girls' writing appearing in all other listed categories.

Looking at the categories listed above it appears fair to say that even amongst the least proficient 11-year-old writers, there exists some productive concept of what it means to argue for or explain an opinion in writing. Over half the sample produced some form of argument in support of their opinions; and a further group were able to communicate a variety of opinions, although these were not well ordered as argumentative texts. The group of scripts classified as least easy to make sense of (group one, no. 3) were also written with a discernible attempt on the part of their writers to respond to the demands of the question. They were not writing at random, however idiosyncratic their texts ultimately appeared. We will look more closely at the problems and successes revealed in this group later, but the first main point we wish to stress is that help given to these pupils needs to take account of the major discovery they have all made: writing can be used as a means of defining and explaining beliefs and opinions; it can also be used as a means of influencing others to share these. Just how they have arrived at this point of knowledge – whether by assiduous teaching or casual osmosis – we cannot tell. It would be unfortunate if, on the basis of the obvious global shortcomings in their writing, they were to be excluded from specific practice in this genre due to its being thought too difficult.

Potentially argumentative writing

(i) Rudimentary or proto-arguments

The scripts which we describe (as a group) as being launched in the direction of argument were so with varying degrees of success: while each one began with a position-taking statement and followed this by reasons given in support or illustration, only about half of this number seemed sufficiently in control of the overall shape of their case to refer back to the original idea, or suggest a desirable change, as a consequence of its validity.

We have informally characterised the more complete scripts at this level as 'rudimentary arguments', and less complete ones 'proto-arguments'. The latter tended to get stuck in the illustrative phase, were simply unfinished, or, more disappointing, introduced irrelevant or contradictory material right at the end, thus dissipating whatever persuasiveness had been built up.

As far as choice of topics was concerned, a range of public and personal issues were aired. These comprised:

opposition to the using and killing of animals/whales/seals; opinions about the danger of nuclear war/Ban the Bomb campaign/Greenham Common women; a case for the introduction of summer football; others for the prevention of skinhead styles, for compulsory swimming lessons, for ending violence in Northern Ireland, for providing improvements to the local pool and for building a local hospital; opinions were expressed about the insufficiency of jobs, the excessive price of postage stamps, the need for government to be more humane, and the advantages of leaving one's PE kit at school.

Examples of these two types of scripts within the potentially argumentative category are given below:

> It would be wonderful if the IRA, INLA, and the UDA, would stop booming people's home's and other people's proparty and to stop killings and kidnapping like the two year old gril who was kidnapped from her home on friday night she was in her caught sleeping.
> She was found some miles away from her home dead.
> and that's whey I would like Ireland to be peateful then more people would come too Ireland than there would be no villiss to fear.

> The subject that I have a strong opinion is throwing rubbish on the sand at sea-shores. I have a strong opinion against it because every time I go to the sea I do see rubbish on the sand and I see people and children throwing rubbish on the sand like crisps packets and biscit wrappers and orange drinck bottles been thrown on the sand. Sometimes I see children picking up glass bottls and smashing them all against the rocks and stones. If Innsent people were walking along happily ready for a swim bear-footed and then suddenly the child or a small baby or it could be one of the parents putting their foot on a sharp peice of glass and have a veory bad cut on their foot and porhaps if the baby steped on it the baby might have to go to hospital because a baby's babies skin is much much softer then peoples skin and it could be serious If small babies were brought to the beach about a year old and say (one a two) a wrapper or something or a peice of glass and picked it up and put it in their mouth without the mother or father weching the baby.

152

As can be seen from the two scripts quoted above, there is already a basis on which to build in helping these writers to develop further. Were they in the same class, it might be useful to set them the challenge of improving each other's arguments, since strengths are at present distributed between them. Thus the author of the rudimentary argument, although able to structure his text overall, has only a minimal amount of evidence to support and explain his point of view. The writer of the proto-argument has really too much illustrative comment and runs the risk of being sidetracked by the vision of accidents which could overtake an unattended child. Most readers could fill in for themselves a notion of what 'litter' comprises; nevertheless, a good case for its nuisance value is built up through the series of observations made by this writer. By contrast, the organisations referred to by the first writer are unlikely to be known to any but a local audience. He could be encouraged to use the greater time and space afforded by writing to give more information about the context. Both writers have more to learn about how to bring their writing to a successful conclusion. The rather jumbled, skeletal ending provided by the first writer suggests a possible starting point for discussion. (What are the main things to stress at the end? Are there new ideas to introduce? How is back-reference to be made to the opening? etc.)

(ii) Multiple-statement responses

These scripts comprised clusters of opinions, many of which were delivered with forcefulness but remained at the level of single statements. Within these scripts there was no necessary logic in the selection of opinions, except where these related to a series of personal *bêtes noires,* as, for example, in the case of the pupil who stated his beliefs that the school could do with a new headmaster, bigger premises, different play areas, better dinner ladies and more games. These opinions were not combined in a general case about, say, general improvements to schooling.

Pupils in this group seemed to have a basic awareness of the use of writing to state a case, but no ready means to develop it persuasively. In this respect what they wrote demonstrated a commonly remarked feature of young children's writing, namely the modelling of written statements on 'conversational turns' in which each participant has typically the space to deliver just one item or segment of thought at a time, before the turn passes to another speaker. When this principle is applied to individually composed written texts, it results in either very short pieces, or longer ones extended by accretion. The capacity to generate more information about one's own ideas without the support of others demands both reflective abilities and a measure of confidence in the efficacy of writing as a medium for thinking. Consequently, for the writers in this particular group, further development would appear to depend on the acquisition of a greater awareness of how writing can be used as an instrument for thought in a more concentrated way than is shown in scripts like the following:

> I don't like girl's play foot ball because there weak and fat ondif it was male v felmale well would have to be very gentle.
>
> Why do men have more sports then boy an girl.
>
> I think that boy's sehald nat play With dall's because bay's schald play With Aton men and girl's play with dolls.

> I do not like blood sports I thing it Should be band becaues. If you were a fox a Hair you would nog like it If you were being chast by some Hous and some men on houses and it you were course and killit will be hard & hunibell It Shoud be band. School uniform must be ban becaues some people mite nat have anthes money I don't see & why they can't were acher dooths like Jerse and a tea-shirt. It will save a lot of money for people.

Non-argumentative writing

A minority of the sample of low-scoring 11-year-olds (about one fifth) were not launched in the direction of argumentative writing as it is traditionally understood (i.e. the selection of a viewpoint which is then explored/defended/elaborated and restated with the intent to persuade others to share it). Obviously we can only speculate as to whether this group of pupils *chose not* to respond 'appropriately' to the question set, or *could not* do so because it called upon unknown skills (skills of writing, of understanding or both). We look in more detail at these below.

(i) Wishes

Pupils who interpreted the phrase 'strong opinion' as strong desire or wish proceeded to use their writing as a way of communicating personal likes and dislikes at the level of circumstantial detail. The subject areas were as follows: 'I like swimming', 'I would like to be a rugby manager', 'I do not know why I have to go to school', 'I wish I was mascot for Newcastle', 'I would like to be a karate expert', and 'I wish people would not mess my bedroom up'. In so far as these feelings related only to the life of the individual writer, the second element of the topic was ignored – there was no specific element of persuasion for anyone else to share these points of view. Often these scripts were interspersed with narrative episodes, filling out the origins of the wish fulfilment impulse. For example, an account of the delaying tactics employed to avoid going to school; a 'story' about the association of a football mascot and his team. An extract from the would-be truant is quoted below:

Example of non-argumentative writing – **Wishes, age 11**

> I do not now wre I have got to go to school. because I don't like it. But ever day I have do got to go to school because my mother tills me to go to school. In the monin it pretend to sleep because I do not wont to go to school. But went my mother gets up she wakes my up to. went she go down than I pretened to go back to sleep. Then my mothers keep calling my so in the end I have go to go down down. I get dressed sloely and Then I go up to wash. I come back down and get my shous on Then I got my coot on and stat walking down sloely. went I get in school then I sed to myself wie down I have to go to school. At the end of school I came home and asked my mother "wie do I have to got to school man. you go to school to lern.

(ii) Narrative

There was obvious overlap between the narrative content of the 'wish fulfilment' scripts and a smaller group of examples which were wholly narrative in structure, without any generalising concept. The themes of these stories, however, were, as stated earlier, implicitly connected with moments of disagreement or constraint. Each one of them could have been further conceptualised to the point where the 'tale' served to illustrate the significance of an opinion (the desirable volume of a record player, the hour for lights out) but, as the following example shows, this stage was far from being achieved:

> The football match Woll cup savis on today I said to my mum 'can I go yes said my mum I will get my football hat and satch on

> and I said to my brother will you tack me to the football match and he said no and I went and told my mum and she said the my brother tack him to the football match so he said OK I will tack him to the football match so my brother but is hat and satch on and we went. my brother said to me. I wen wunt are you going to the macth and I said Liverpool are playing my team. Is that over you are going to to watch. Liverpool and were we got to Half time my brother said the macth is good Liverpool are wining but cor can win in the over Half but Liverpool won and we went home-

The use of narrative in our culture as a vehicle for persuasion is a mode of such long standing, and potential sophistication, that it would be a mistake to conclude that young writers are backward because they respond to an argumentative task by producing a story. We do need to ask questions however about the ways in which such stories are conceptualised, and whether the same writers have any capacity to abstract from the narrative frame such key points of the episode as would serve to shape the logical underpinning of a general belief. If neither of these 'revisions' can be undertaken, it may well be that such children are for the moment stuck in one mode of written discourse, unable to exploit even that one for anything other than a recounting function.

(iii) Statements

The story tellers and the 'wish-fulfilment' writers had in common with another small group (those who made straightforward observations on topics of interest such as fish, netball, and penalties for breaking windows) one characteristic which, more than any other, possibly suggested that in total these pupils' writing was at a less developed stage than others even within the low-scoring group. This characteristic was a seeming innocence of the scope which writing gives not just to *tell* other people about personal feelings but to affect the feelings and beliefs of others. The following script is quoted as typifying many features of this category:

> Fish ale very intuisting You can halle many kinds of fish you can halle a fat fish and you can halle a pleath and a hering and you can halle soked hering wish a isa copath and you can halle a gold fish. and you can halle very many fish they ale all dent cant cant onef fish

154

In the domain of orientation to reader, or audience awareness, all these scripts were deficient. Those who wrote about their strong feelings did so without pausing to consider how best to key the reader in to this state of affairs, or what the point of the revelation might be; those who recounted incidents of personal argument did so without being able to clarify for the sake of non-participants why the altercation remained memorable; while those who wrote briefly about the interest of a particular topic could quite well have justified the selection of non-controversial subject matter, provided the reader's participatory interest had somehow been accommodated.

Scripts which presented multiple problems

The scripts in this category have already been described as *in the throes* of constructing an argument in writing, yet because of the severe difficulties they present to the reader we discuss them as a separate category. The lowest performance on the topic, assessed as '1' in impression-marking, was the following script, which both at the level of deciphering and at the level of comprehension resists attempts at a coherent reading:

> ~~Bridge~~ Driving
> I Thig the Driving at Sud Be put den too 15.
> The peftl at 15 or Sn5B a nof to drive cor tach
> mght Brutle in Irand Brov. a cor to QuBolin.
> tro monoha taykn yfea in food feet. 18 in deed

We stated earlier that linguistic and cognitive elements were equally implicated in the writing of good arguments. The diversity of problems in both these areas which we encounter in reading this selection of scripts seems to underline the inextricable relation of language and thought: we do not find evidence to suggest that linguistic factors are more under control than cognitive processes or vice versa. Passing from script to script at the bottom end of the range, the diagnosis is one of a breakdown in both areas, but in ways that differ from pupil to pupil. In the following script, for example, a pupil moves from an argument (*not* a clear one) about the role of game-keepers to a proposal for a wider ban on guns. The handwriting is clear, with few spelling errors; there is some concept of sentence division as marked by full stops, but serious fractures in grammatical structures coincide with an unclear line of thought to make the text very confusing:

> My opinion is seeing the gamekeepers shooting down
> all the bird because. I go bird watch and I can
> see the gamekeepers shooting down pigeons. crows
> magpies and lots other birds. I would not mind
> the gamekeepers guard the lakes and woods because
> I reported them for shoot magpies to the RSPCA.
> and its horidle seeing the dogs carry them back to there
> owners. All the guns should bea thrown out of Brittian.
> To only keep pistols meddys for police station or
> practise.

By contrast, we cite a problem script of a different sort. Here the handwriting is very uncertain, and the hesitant use of non-cursive script with an inconclusive revision in the opening statement seems to parallel the incomplete movement of thought we are left with. Yet in the most minimal terms, there is here the basis for an opinion about the killing of wild animals: did the writer stop short because he could not think any more or because the effort of writing was too much?

> In my opinion I should like
> to put my opinion on killing ~~with a dbute then~~
> wild life to keep yus varmin
> the winter and killing rabbits
> to keep us alive. and killing birds
> for a sport

Lastly, we reproduce a longer script concerned in some way with bad drivers and/or penalties for rule infringements. Multiple problems are apparent here: sentence division is employed but in an arbitrary way, making the reader's job in some ways more difficult than if no full stops had been inserted. The script itself contains wild and unsupported assertions making any attempt to follow a line of reasoning extremely difficult.

> I have a very strong opinion that there
> is some drivers on the road who with out
> braking the rules of the road. And some
> people brake the rules very much. The
> people who drive quikwell. And there are
> some people who are very bad drivers.
> The people who are good drivers are useally
> blamed for most of the crashs that there
> are today. some the youg ones think they
> are the best drivers. The pblice never
> go after the bad drivers who railey casse
> all the crashes. I think this is not fair
> bo other good drivers on the road today.
> The yougg bad drivers on the road
> should be caught and be learned a
> lesson and if they do not abay it they
> should be put in Jail.

8.6 Characteristics of low performance: 15-year-olds, persuasive writing task

A selection of data was made in the same way as had been done for the primary survey, namely all scripts with impression marks of 3, 2, 1 combinations were extracted for closer analysis. The first difference noted was that we had fewer scripts to deal with: 92 as compared with 124 at primary level. Of these, 58 were written by boys and 34 by girls, indicating yet again that more boys than girls are to be found in low-scoring groups.

In terms of choice of subject matter and methods of presentation there was considerable overlap between the two groups (11- and 15-year-olds), with the topics of school uniform, cruelty to animals, hazards of smoking, nuclear weapons and Northern Ireland figuring in both samples. New topics introduced by 15-year-olds related to their immediate experiences: school leaving age, youth centres and jobs.

The main difference to emerge on reading the sample was that the proportion of scripts which were recognisably argumentative in force and structure was greater. Looking back at the categories used to classify primary scripts, we can say that at secondary level just one of these categories accounted for the majority of scripts: rudimentary or proto-arguments were written by about two-thirds of the 15-year-old lower performers. These were scripts which began with the statement of an opinion and then proceeded to attempt a demonstration of its validity. Within this group, the proportion of those who successfully pursued a line of argument (sketchy or non-existent connections aside) to a concluding statement was similar to that noted at primary level (i.e. about half of the total). However, given that in general most of these scripts were much longer and more impassioned than their primary counterparts, the argumentative force of their persuasion was in some respects little affected by this structural incompleteness.

The remaining scripts bore some resemblance to those from the younger age group in approach if not in quality, except that the category of purely narrative writing was not represented. The use of anecdote for illustrative purposes was evident in many scripts but not one script was written entirely as a 'story'. The closest approach to story writing was in one script which cast an argument about the merits of a pop group as a dramatic exchange, and moreover imported into the dialogue the threat of physical aggression, as seemingly the most efficacious argumentative technique:

Five scripts contained more than one topic; two scripts approximated to the 'I wish' category. One was written

in the form of a personal plea: 'I wish I was 18 . . .' (in order to escape the trials of family life); the other an outburst to a parent figure: 'I feel very strongly about the way you nag and nag at me . . .'. These scripts were among those which drew on narrative techniques to explain their desires.

Similar to our findings at primary level, we noted a small group of scripts which were written about strong *interests* in a topic. These were about school subjects such as Human Biology, CDT and History. By comparison with the 11-year-olds, these writers were more adept at retailing their interests with a view to persuading others to share them, or at least to recognise their validity. (For example, the CDT students stressed its usefulness for job prospects.) Methods of persuasion, as in the knock-down argument quoted above, showed signs of recourse to spoken language exchanges, as can be seen in the following scripts, in which the writer began to enact a conversation with unconvinced friends ('I would tell them to change their minds quick') about the benefits of studying Human Biology. We note in passing the similarity of this speech-based tactic to argumentative styles employed by *high-scoring* 11-year-olds.

Only one script was (virtually) illegible, and in so far as it could be deciphered, it showed a more deep-seated weakness in the handling of grammatical conventions, together with a confusing presentation of content. This script was over a page in length, suggesting perhaps that although only the closest associates of this pupil would be able to decode it, for the pupil herself the task of putting pen to paper did not appear to pose a problem of stamina. Lest it be thought that stamina necessarily increases with age, we quote one script in its entirety which would pass without surprise in a collection from primary school:

8.7 Methods of argumentation: low performers aged 11 and 15

Granted that amongst the lowest-scoring pupils at age 15 a majority seem able to write some kind of argumentative essay, we can ask some questions about the kind of writing they produce. Is it the case that their skills or argumentation show clear advances over the 11-year-olds, so that what we have at the bottom end of the range are script of a higher standard on many counts than those produced by 11-year-olds? Or is it the case that the major sign of 'development' from 11 to 15, at this level of performance, is the demise of indirect, less focused responses to a set topic, as evidenced in the greater number of stories and circumstantially constrained texts written by 11-year-olds?

As with the 11-year-olds in the lowest-scoring groups, we have to conclude that the variation in types of weak writing affords evidence for answering each of these questions in the affirmative. Amongst the low-scoring 15-year-olds are more pupils who have the ability to exploit writing for its affective potential: they can represent their strongly held views persuasively, with evident design to convince another to share these. Similarly there are numbers of others who can see in which general area of task demand the topics fall, and so are able to produce 'an argument' rather than a tangential response to isolated elements of the topic; the degree of conviction either felt by the writer or communicated to the reader is less certain.

In about half of the secondary sample identified as argumentative in intent there was evident overlap between 11- and 15-year-olds in terms of the ways of approaching a chosen topic. These were scripts which were able to nominate a strongly held opinion, to give some reasons/ illustrations for its being so, but which failed to pursue a line of thinking through logically developed points. These scripts 'reasoned' by association (one point growing out of the previous one), or by setting down a number of reflections related to the general topic, in no special order and without interconnections; they were inconclusive and at moments contradictory, without the means to accommodate qualificatory information. Such scripts had much in common with the 'proto-argument' described at primary level.

However, as stated above more of the scripts in low-scoring categories at secondary level had an effective argumentative structure. As with the entire low-performing sample, these scripts as a group displayed some confusions in the management of grammatical and orthographic conventions, and were also equally prone to breakdowns in logical organisation. However, an important strength in these rudimentary arguments was connected with two features of organisation and style: each one began with either a title or a title sentence, and ended with an address to the reader, or a reprise of the starting point.

Additionally, the presence of paragraphs in these scripts, though a sign of structure seen in others of the sample, served more consistently to define stages in the argument. This combination of features is sometimes insisted on in a mechanical way ('you must have an opening, a middle and an ending'); in the context of writing development, however, the occurrence of this type of structure, plus reader-awareness, suggests both a level of text-monitoring and a productive concept of the function of writing as a communicative statement. Where neither of these concepts is apparent, the result is, as we have seen, writing which addresses itself to no one and has no purpose in view.

Admittedly some of the ways of realising an audience were informal and incomplete, such as the adoption of a letter format at the end but not at the beginning of a script; pragmatism combined with desperation produced the following 'conclusion':

Well, there are a few points. I can think of many more but would like to get on with the rest as we have only an hour to complete this booklet.

Likewise, pupils' means of summing up were minimal, depending on 'so' or 'because', as prelude to a single final sentence. We chose two scripts to exemplify performances within the low-scoring group; both of these scripts have some of the essential elements demanded by this task under control.

Low performance: argumentative task: age 15

Low performance: argumentative task: age 15

happening. Scientists dont experiment on animals just the once but hundreds and hundreds.

There are hundreds of people who share my view of this outragous slaugtering. I dont know how they can sit there and push one of those great big neddles in a Animals and then sit there and see it die.

How someone could wear a coat made from an animal I dont know there ever making coats out off hourse and even cats.

I was siting in the house one day watch Wild Life and it was showing you the rabits life it was called run rabit run the rabits looked so bueatiful runing around in fields and on the beach. It Snowed you two rabits playing and then all of a sudden one of the rabit was dead then came along a man with a gun hed shot the rabits head off I was so furious I could neave rung his neck and all he wanted the rabit for was to feed his dogs.

I think the fox is one of the most beautifull creatures on this eath and they are gradualy becomeing extinct because of men and women who think its fun to hunt a fox and then kill it and all they do is cut its nail of and thrown the rest to the dogs.

The worst Killing of all is the seals I dont know how some one could stand there and beat a seal with an hammer till it was dead I could never forgive my self if I did that I dont even think I could do that if I was starving to death this kind of thing really makes me sick and all of it is not really nessecery.

Concluding note

The above examples show how easily instances of low performance from 15-year-old writers merge with those from pupils four years younger. While we may feel that there is considerable scope for development in the case of an 11-year-old pupil who responds to the task of writing a persuasive argument with a minimally productive concept of what a written argument entails, confusion in logic and language notwithstanding, it is less easy to feel optimism on behalf of the 15-year-old who almost certainly has not another four years' full-time education to look forward to. Without being able to document the stages of growth between 11 and 15 we can only guess about whether 'poor' writers aged 15 have remained at much the same level since primary school. Is the group of low scorers at age 15 populated by pupils who at a younger age were producing writing more along the lines of the least able 11-year-olds? (That is, the pupils who were earlier characterised as the writers of unfocused narratives, wishes and statements, plus those whose writing was scarcely penetrable at any level.) On the other hand, low scorers at age 15 may be pupils who would have been assessed as slightly below average at age 11, and have not extended their capacities in writing since that time.

As far as concerns 'development' in this genre of writing, our evidence suggests that there is an extended period of growth and change in the way pupils approach the task of writing persuasively. Some of the best writing from 11-year-olds gains force and immediacy from the adaptation of interactive spoken language exchanges; more evident in the 15-year-old sample is an ability to achieve the desired persuasive force through the exploitation of the conventions of written language. Overall, it would appear that while there are few pupils who are not alert to the use of writing to argue a personal case, most would benefit from a systematic study of the great variety of linguistic techniques which speakers and writers draw upon when taking an authoritative stand on matters of controversial interest. Additionally, the content of many written arguments could be improved if pupils were encouraged to draw upon a wider range of source material than is customarily assumed by public examinations in English. At present, the influence exerted by such examinations appears to extend far down the school system where the teaching and practice of argumentative writing is concerned.

9

Work sampling: a discussion of samples of written work under normal classroom conditions

Synopsis

The work sampling component of the surveys provides a means of obtaining access to a wider range of written work than would be possible under normal survey procedures. A sub-sample of pupils aged 11 and 15 was asked to provide examples of writing concerned with planning practical work or investigations, and for their personally chosen 'best' work. Eleven-year-olds were also asked for examples of argumentative/persuasive writing, while the third category requested from 15-year-olds was the longest piece of writing completed in the school week prior to the main survey. A total of 1,617 pupils were involved in the work sampling component.

Each piece of written work was accompanied by a questionnaire, on which were recorded details concerning the genesis of the writing, revisions it had undergone, and its place and purpose in a scheme of study or longer-term plan for writing development for the pupil(s).

This chapter illustrates in some detail the work gathered from primary schools, making comparisons with the secondary sample where relevant:

– the contexts in which practical work and writing are associated

– the nature and source of revisions undertaken

– the ways in which pupils conceptualise their best work

– the prominence of the English department in defining what writing is.

The evidence presented concerning the practice of writing in classroom conditions suggests that it is rare for schools to have a policy of writing across the curriculum. Writing is predominantly used to reinforce subject knowledge rather than as a means to explore an area of new learning. The writing chosen by many pupils to exemplify their best work generally comprises narrative fiction written on themes of mystery or adventure from titles suggested by the teacher. Teachers' input to writing appears to be highly directive and concentrates upon questions of subject matter, length and surface features. Relatively little guidance is offered concerning matters of style or readership. The increasing provision of notes, worksheets and instructions for writing in the secondary school (in the service of looming public examinations) may not be in the long-term interest of pupils' development as writers. APU surveys of reading have shown that pupils perform less well when they are required to extract relevant information from texts, to recast this in different forms and to identify shifts of attitude. It also appears to be the case that as writers they are rarely set the task of developing and practising these skills on their own initiative or in collaboration with others.

9.1 Introduction

As part of the 1983 primary and secondary surveys, writing was obtained from schools in the work sampling component. The purpose of this component was to obtain evidence of the way pupils write in normal classroom conditions, as well as to include a wider range of written work than it would be feasible to require under survey conditions. The genesis and rationale behind this component of the language surveys has been fully discussed in previous reports, one of which contains a description of data from the 1982 secondary survey. (This was the first occasion when work sampling had been carried out as part of a main survey.)

In the 1983 surveys, slight modifications to the administrative procedures were devised, with schools being asked to complete separate forms ('context questionnaires') for each category or type of written work requested. This was done in preference to the use of a single questionnaire form, in an attempt to clarify as definitely as possible exactly what was being requested in the way of writing. Previous discussions of pilot trials have indicated the amount of overlap there has sometimes been in the way written samples are selected.

In devising the questionnaires for the 1983 surveys, care was taken to provide areas for comparison both in terms of pupils aged 11 and 15 for that year, and in terms of descriptive links with previous collections. Thus both 11- and 15-year-olds were asked, personally, to select examples of their 'best' work, and given an opportunity to explain the reasons for selection. In the 1982 survey, pupils' best work was also collected, but through the agency of teachers, and without the option of written comments from the pupil. A continuing interest in obtaining evidence of writing from diverse curricular areas led us again to request writing concerned with planning or devising an investigation (secondary level). It was particularly stressed on the age 15 questionnaire that the focus of this writing should be planning or problem solving, rather than straight reporting or writing up of completed experiments, since in 1982 it had been found that writing of the latter type predominated in this category. Because argumentative writing at both ages 11 and 15 was to be analysed in the course of this report, we asked for examples of this form of writing from primary pupils. (We had already obtained such evidence from the 15-year-olds in the 1982 survey.) Lastly, as a snapshot means of collecting evidence characteristic of writing practices in school, we asked for the longest piece of writing done by 15-year-olds in the course of the week preceding the main survey.

Other points of comparison between the collections made in 1983 at both age levels concern specific questions asked about the circumstances in which writing was produced (its origins, time taken, revisions made, collaborative or individual work). Teachers were also asked, where possible, to indicate with what frequency the particular form of writing was undertaken, and whether it had any particular place or purpose in an overall scheme/syllabus of language development for the pupil(s) concerned.

The following discussion outlines the results of the work sampling exercises at both primary and secondary level. The number of pupils involved was in each case a sub-sample of those involved in the main survey: 645 primary pupils from 73 schools (1545 samples); 972 secondary pupils from 66 schools (2292 samples).

9.2 Categories of work requested from pupils aged 11 and 15

Primary teachers were asked to submit samples of their pupils' classwork under the following categories:

CATEGORY A: writing based on practical work

CATEGORY B: argumentative/persuasive writing

CATEGORY C: 'best' work chosen by pupil.

Secondary teachers were asked to submit samples of written work as follows:

CATEGORY A: writing concerned with planning or devising practical work or an investigation

CATEGORY B: pupils' longest piece of extended writing done in the past school week

CATEGORY C: 'best' work chosen by pupil.

Practical work/planning an investigation

The samples received from 11-year-olds for category A consisted mainly of accounts of science experiments, excursions/field trips, sections of project work, textbook work and a few pieces describing models/works of art created by the pupil. Writing from 15-year-olds showed, as before, the strong influence of the sciences and home economics, with these areas of the curriculum accounting for almost two-thirds of the work. Certain humanities subjects were also represented, often on rather dubious grounds ('poetry appreciation'; '"Pip and the convict": different types of short stories'). Surprisingly, technical subjects were not much in evidence: ten or fewer scripts came from CDT, woodwork and metal-craft.

Argumentative/persuasive writing at primary level

This category (B) was largely composed of discussions on familiar controversial topics (cruelty to animals, vivisection, smoking, political issues) or on subjects of particular personal interest to pupils (school rules, restrictions enforced by parents).

As indicated above, a completed questionnaire about the origin and production of the work was to be attached to each piece. Specific items from the questionnaire are discussed in detail below. Teachers were asked to tick the appropriate box or write a brief comment. Responses to the common items on questionnaires A and B are discussed below.

1. Was the work represented here done as part of:

general   group work   or work by
classwork   individual pupil?

The majority of the work at primary level (60 per cent category A, 72 per cent category B) was done as part of 'general classwork', with slightly more pupils working in small groups or entirely alone when writing accounts of practical activities. In this type of assignment it is common for pupils to work first in whole class groups and later to break up into smaller groups or to work alone – consequently many teachers commenting on category A writing marked more than one possibility in response to this question.

At secondary level, writing concerned with planning or devising practical work was handled as often as general classwork as individual work (40 per cent in certain cases), with the percentage for group work unchanged (20 per cent).

2. What led up to the writing? (Please give brief details as to input in form of discussion, reading, resource-pack, etc.)

At primary level the most frequent response was 'discussion' both for practical work (34 per cent) and for the argumentative piece (61 per cent). Approximately 5 per cent of the argumentative pieces were based on a formal debate. The next most popular starting point (11 per cent) was the provision of a title. Surprisingly only 33 per cent of the scripts sent in for category A were said to follow practical work involving pupils actively. 20 per cent had either conducted or observed an experiment, 13 per cent had visited a place of interest or participated on a field trip. Of the remainder in most cases the work was based on a more passive experience: viewing a film, TV programme, reading a text.

At secondary level, at least two-thirds of practical work had been preceded by 'discussion', or 'reading and discussion'. Course work requirements or examination demands were cited as specific justification for about one-sixth of the work, with exam practice being particularly a feature of work done in home economics. Something of the nature of the discussions can be inferred from teachers' comments about 'review of previous work', 'methods and expected results', 'theory and methods', 'rules for —'. The reading done as a preliminary exercise was reading of the associated textbook(s). It seems that what is being called 'discussion' in these circumstances was actually general class teaching of the 'talk and chalk' variety. A tiny proportion of teachers referred simply to 'class teaching', 'general lesson' or 'talk' as leading into the practical work. Overwhelmingly, the practical work presented was directed and prescribed, with little scope or place for planning work on the part of the pupils. A handful of pupils had been involved in a process described as 'research, investigation and decision making', or had had the experience of working with materials in order to 'get to grips with it themselves'. Varied inputs such as photographs, films, videos and documentary material or visits to sites of geographical or historical interest were likewise mentioned by a minority of schools.

3. *Was any outline guidance for the work given?*
   notes   plan   theme
   readership   length   expression

Primary teachers appeared to give different kinds of guidance according to the nature of the work assigned. For the writing up of practical activities, especially experiments, 39 per cent of pupils were given an outline plan. A few teachers (4 per cent) commented that their pupils used a standard structure known to them from previous lessons. A considerable proportion (32 per cent) completed the work with no guiding framework. A small group of teachers added that pupils were deliberately allowed to respond freely and to structure and present their work in any way they wished.

In the argumentative category, the most common guidelines offered by teachers concerned theme (53 per cent) and length (24 per cent); between 17 per cent and 22 per cent provided a ready-made plan or set of notes; 8 per cent referred pupils to books or other written sources.

At secondary level, as may have been predicted from the information obtained about the purposes for which practical work was set, teacher input into the writing was of a specific, directive kind. Thus, at least two-thirds of the

pupils were given an outline plan to work to used notes (copied or dictated), or work sheets, or combinations of all these aids. Elsewhere teachers commented that the work followed the 'standard format' of experiments, the 'specific rules' for the subject concerned, or was done 'as set by the exam board'. The influence of GCE/CSE boards was evident in a remark about 'notes laid down as for 'O' level'. Teachers' suggestions were also given concerning graphic and tabular layout, design format, techniques of measurement and sequencing of procedures. Despite the frequent reference to consulting textbooks in responses to question one, fewer than ten teachers indicated that 'outline guidance' for writing was derivable from those sources. An isolated teacher reported that 'group ideas were reported to the class', that 'little framework was given – most was suggested by the pupils', and that 'pupils' input was discussed'.

4. *About how much writing-time was taken?*
   One lesson   several lessons   longer

The majority of 11-year-olds' work submitted under both categories was completed within the period of one lesson (87 per cent of category A; 92 per cent of category B). A small proportion of practical-based writing took longer presumably because the activity itself consumed time attributed to the task.

Figures for secondary pupils showed similarly that writing based on practical work was in about one-third of cases more likely to extend over two or more lessons.

5. *Process of redrafting: has this work undergone revisions?*
   If 'YES', how were the changes determined?
   by the pupil working alone ....
   following discussion with classmates ....
   following suggestions/advice from teacher ....

Teachers gave information about the extent and source of alterations made to the piece. At primary level, for the most part, the submitted script was in its original form. Only 29 per cent of the pieces in both categories had been redrafted or corrected in any way. In those instances where amendments had been made, more were initiated by the teacher than by the pupils themselves (18 per cent of category A; 23 per cent of category B). The responses also revealed that corrections were made by the individual pupil or by classmates to practical work with somewhat greater frequency than to argumentative writing.

At secondary level a similar proportion of work was submitted in unrevised form. There was a change in the proportion of revisions carried out by the pupil working alone when compared to those done under the direction of the teacher. Thus, pupil revisions showed an increase of about 10 per cent and teacher-directed revisions a decrease of about the same amount. The process of collaboratively revising written work was still carried out only by a tiny minority of pupils (2 to 3 per cent).

Questions about the frequency of this type of written work:

How often does this pupil do writing in relation to practical work? Please specify.

on a regular basis ....

whenever appropriate to general theme or area of work

rarely ....

About how much experience does this pupil have in argumentative writing? Please indicate whether this activity is:

a) rare for the year group in your school   specify ..

b) done on a regular basis   specify ....

c) sometimes done   specify ....

It appears that neither argumentative writing nor writing based on practical work is a regular feature of the 11-year-old's classroom. Only 27 per cent of teachers assigned the type of work associated with practical activities with any regularity although 62 per cent stated that work of this kind was done whenever appropriate to the theme or area. Argumentative writing seems to occur even less frequently: only 8 per cent produce this type of work regularly, 55 per cent 'sometimes' and 31 per cent rarely.

For secondary pupils, writing in relation to practical work occurs with greater frequency; 41 per cent of pupils are reported to undertake this type of writing on a regular basis, and 52 per cent whenever appropriate.

Secondary pupils' longest piece of written work

Teachers of 15-year-old pupils were asked to submit the longest piece of written work completed by the sub-sample of pupils in the school week preceding the survey. Over 900 samples were sent in, and a breakdown by subject origin showed that English/English Language/English Literature classes accounted for the major proportion (two-thirds) of the work; History classes produced one-ninth of the samples, while Geography, Religious Education/Studies/Knowledge and Home Economics were represented by about 30–50 scripts apiece. Considering the range of purposes for which extended writing may be used as an aid to learning, it would appear that a relatively narrow range of goals could be served by the concentration of written work in these curriculum areas.

Teachers of all subjects (they totalled 277) were asked in addition, 'How does this particular piece of writing exemplify the relation between writing and learning in the school subject concurred?' With great unanimity, 28 per cent gave answers to do with the use of writing as a synthesis for reading or class discussion, for example, 'writing ensures that some material lodges in the memory', 'consolidates oral classwork', 'crystallisation of concepts'.

The second largest group of replies (21 per cent) saw writing as geared to examination requirements: 'we are dominated by O-level'; 'note-taking and key points are the only way to cover the syllabus'. Possibly in the same category were replies which characterised the purpose of the writing done in terms of its usefulness as a revision aid (8 per cent), or as providing feedback for the teacher (4 per cent).

Replies that might be construed as relating more to the process of a pupil's development as a writer were made by the teachers who noted that writing helps in understanding (11 per cent), or that the writing undertaken was an exercise in the selection of relevant materials (11 per cent), or as an aid to help the organisation of ideas and planning essential for good writing (7 per cent). 2 to 3 per cent of teachers made comments regarding pupils' use of imagination, their enhanced enjoyment of learning or the possible spin-off for 'logical reasoning' as a result of the particular writing assignment.

The majority of the writing had been completed in one or several lessons and had been set as general classwork. In at least 40 per cent of cases, notes had been given by way of guidance, and pupils were similarly directed as to plan, theme and length. Less attention was given to questions of readership or expression; approximately 20 per cent of pupils had received some guidance on these matters.

Discussion of category C: pupils' 'best' work

For category C, pupils themselves were requested to send the piece of written work they considered their 'best'. In most cases the pieces chosen by 11-year-olds consisted of compositions of imaginary or descriptive writing, occasionally poems and parts of, or entire projects.

Secondary pupils chose as their best work writing done in English/English Language/Literature classes in about 60 per cent of cases. Next in popularity came work from the sciences, History and Geography, but altogether writing from these subjects amounted to less than half that taken from English classwork. These findings replicate all previous studies of work sampled from classrooms, which have shown the prominence of the English department in shaping pupils' ideas about what constitutes 'writing'.

1.   Why do you think this is your best written work?

The majority of 11-year-olds justified their choice by referring either to the high quality of the work itself or to the pleasure derived from its production. About 50 per cent of pupils gave more than one reason for selection of best work: in such cases neatness and corrections were generally mentioned as important features. 22 per cent selected their 'favourite' script and commented on its successful content, style or vocabulary, 14 per cent claimed that their chosen composition was interesting, exciting or humorous and a few added that its excellence had resulted in its being read aloud to the rest of the class. Others (20 per cent) maintained that they had enjoyed the work because it formed part of their favourite school subject or because they particularly liked writing stories, poems, projects. Just over 10 per cent selected their piece because it had won their teacher's approval and praise or had been awarded a good grade. A further 13 per cent had sent their 'neatest' work, evidently giving more importance to appearance than to content. Finally, a group of 12 per cent emphasised the fact that they had invested much time and effort in the piece or that they had produced it entirely alone, developing their own ideas unaided. Marginally less than 2 per cent of the sample gave no reason for their selection.

Fifteen-year-old pupils gave similar reasons for their selection of best work. While there was less emphasis on presentational feature *per se* (with only 13 per cent of pupils indicating that this was a major criterion), in the frequent combining of reasons for selection, the following two accounted for over one-third of replies: firstly that the work was selected on grounds of enjoyment or interest, and secondly that it was judged by the teacher to be good (either by means of a grade or comment). 21 per cent referred only to their individual judgement on the high standard of the work, saying it was creative, lively, clear, or that they felt satisfied about it. In view of the highly directive policies for writing evident in teachers' comments discussed earlier, it is worth emphasising that 10 per cent of pupils had selected work with which they had been personally involved, because they had been given an opportunity to express their *own* ideas and point of view and because they had had *no* help from the teacher. Also, in defiance of the prevailing approach to writing in preparation for examination consumption, only a small percentage of pupils selected work specifically for its usefulness as revision aid (3 per cent) or for its connection with an eventual examination or course work folder (2 per cent).

Quite high on pupils' lists of priorities for good writing were qualities which are generally not enhanced by examination procedures, namely having enough time to write without being rushed, and being able to devote time to preparation, research and study in the evolution of the work. Approximately 15 per cent of pupils emphasised these qualities in their replies, and about half their number also appreciated the fact that the work they had done was very comprehensive, accurate and detailed.

2. *About how long did it take you to do the work you have selected?*

    one lesson   several lessons   longer ....
    (Please say how long)

It seems that more time was spent on 'best' scripts than on the type of work submitted under the other categories. 25 per cent reported that they had taken more than one lesson to complete the task, and 52 per cent of 15-year-olds took several lessons or longer.

3. *Did you do this work along with the rest of the class or were you the only one?*

    worked with the whole class
    worked with group   worked alone

Responses indicated that 25 per cent of 11-year-olds' 'best' work and 70 per cent of 15-year-olds' was done by the pupil independently (i.e. not with the rest of the class). This exceeded the proportion who worked alone on work presented under categories A and B for both age groups, although the general trend was for 15-year-olds to work alone.

4. *What started you off on this writing?*

    class/group discussion
    reading books, magazines, etc.
    suggestions from your teacher
    notes on the blackboard or work sheet
    your own ideas   a topic or title was set

When asked about the origin of the piece, most primary pupils (51 per cent) responded that they had been following suggestions made by the teacher. A further 14 per cent made use of teachers' notes on the blackboard or on a work sheet. 25 per cent stated that they had developed their own ideas or had elaborated upon thoughts exchanged in a classroom or group discussion. Naturally, many pupils took advantage of more than one source of ideas.

Secondary pupils likewise made use of more than one source in generating their writing. From the broad grouping of replies we can infer a general shift of emphasis in starting points for writing between the two age groups. Teacher-direction is still the main input, not in the form of 'suggestions' but in the less personalised provision of a 'set topic or title'. A slight decline in the importance of class or group discussion (18 per cent) is perhaps compensated for by a rise in the reported influence of reading matter (17 per cent); the use of blackboard or work sheet notes was mentioned by similar numbers of primary and secondary pupils (14 per cent), while half as many 15-year-olds felt that their own ideas had been the main inspiration for their writing (13 per cent).

5. *If you have re-written this work once or more, can you say something about the changes you've made by ticking any of the boxes which are true for you:*

    Did you start from rough notes or rough work?

    Did you make changes after showing it to your teacher?

    Did you make changes after reading it through to yourself?

    Did you make changes after showing it to some of your friends?

    OR is this exactly as you wrote it the first time?

Scripts falling into the 'best' work category were more highly polished than those in the other groups from primary and secondary pupils alike. First a greater percentage were corrected or amended in some way. Only 40 per cent of primary scripts and 46 per cent of secondary ones were in their original version (as compared to 70 per cent of categories A and B). Second, it seemed that a greater percentage were altered by the pupils themselves: over one-third had rewritten the piece from a rough trial and over half had made changes once the piece was completed. 25 per cent of 15-year-olds had revised with the teacher's aid. Revisions carried out in consultation with classmates were extremely rare at both age levels.

In brief, more time and attention had been devoted to 'best' work than to the sample in the other categories.

9.3 General characteristics of the sample from 11-year-olds

A closer examination of the scripts submitted reveals that the teacher's guidance influences classwork in a major way. There are numerous indications that the advice offered by teachers (as indicated in the questionnaires) was acted upon by pupils. A preferred organisational structure can frequently be detected by looking at several scripts from one class. For example, a series of steps for making a cup of tea were followed in all the scripts from a particular class. Likewise, the guidance of the teacher, as well as the mutual influence of pupils on one another, is apparent in the choice of vocabulary when the same words or phrases occur in the work of several class members. The examples below were accompanied by a comment that the assignment had entailed a collaborative compilation of a pool of vocabulary:

> Our class went down by the Ouse on a stormy day to describe the river. We all took a pool to write words we best thought of.

The River Ouse in Flood.

When we went to the River Ouse a few days ago, we found that it was in flood. It was a very gloomy day: the water was a dirty brown colour, damp and muddy, and it looked very uninviting. There was no noise, but a strong breeze making the water run swiftly on it's way, wherever it was going to.

There was no human life at all, nor was there the ripple of fish. Only the occasional twig or sweet wrapper being swept along.

It was very cold, and the slippery, muddy banks were easy to slip and fall into the water, and drift away, with the swirling current of the water.

The weather was cold, and there was not much light. You could just and so see the sun in the distance, but where we were, there were just clouds, as black as thunder, ready to bring a shower of rain down, at that moment. There was not even enough sun to see a reflection of either me or the trees.

There were many different little things to see on the muddy shore, such as sweet papers where the water had risen and left them behind.

Waves rippled smoothly and quietly along, and in places, looked like a small whirl pool.

At one time, the water rose to 16ft 7 inches, and to prove it was a water mark.

The clouds were beginning to look blacker than ever, so we hurried back to school, very glad that we weren't drenched.

The Ouse in Flood.

What a swirling, whirling, uninviting sight met our eyes as on Tuesday May 3rd our form went down to see the frightening river Ouse in flood.

It had a swift, harsh current, whirlpools whirled with all their might, torrents of freezing water swept along the river taking with them anything, living, or dead, that got swept into that deadly current!

Gushing, rushing, and racing along noises drowned those of the traffic on the bridge above. Deep, muddy water went sweeping along. The edges of the water were calmer.

Water eddying and lapping quietly against the river bank was quite a contrast to the rapids of the river. There were no signs of life, and reflections mingled with the dirty water.

The calm rippling water had twigs and rotting branches in it which gave off a nasty smell.

The flood level was quite high when we went down, I'm glad we did not go down when it flooded in 1982. At that time it was sixteen feet seven inches above normal level!

The Ouse In Flood.

The river was a swirling torrent of dirty grey water. The current was strong and the bank was still flooded in some areas. The water-free ground was muddy and sand had been deposited on the grass. If you ventured too near the mass of eddying water the bank grew perilous and soft.

164

> A white chalk line marked the waters highest level, in 1982, where elevated waters had reached sixteen feet seven inches above normal height.
>
> No sign of life showed, only weeping willows brushing the water like fairies dangling from a moonbeam and Poplars still towering high above the gloomy river, despite the flood.
>
> The noise was of the river gliding swiftly along. Not calmly gliding as you would have thought, but gliding like water just fallen off a waterfall.
>
> Whirlpools acted like water draining out of the bath, down the plughole. The wind was also racing along, pushing the water on, faster, faster whispered the trees swaying in the wind. A sudden slash of wind stirred the river even more and the ripples expanded. The murky water never seemed to halt for a moment, even to take a breath. It never seemed to tire, I was tired even looking at it.
>
> The bridge under which we stood was not enough to stop our ears from being pierced by the wind. The bushes on the opposite bank were nearly left leafless after the wind had ended. At last we left the rushing river behind us and all the trees and bushes, and mud.

It is possible to deduce from the comment and from the compositions that the teacher had intended the task as a vocabulary-building and stylistic exercise and had taken measures to systematise the content.

Features of argumentative/persuasive writing (category B) 11-year-olds

The effect of class or group discussion prior to written work is also seen in the argumentative writing category. Exposure to conflicting points of view is evident in many scripts where writers have enumerated the pros and cons of the issue.

> Should computers be in schools? I think this is a good question. I can think of many things against and many things for computers. Here are some of the things against computers.
>
> How can some schools have the money to get computers when they are short of paper, books and pens. The staff at schools will not know how to use the computers. Kids will use the computer as an easy way out of work as computers do not shout at you when you go wrong. Using computers will cause bad eyesight from whatching the television. If the computer is damaged in any way it will be more expence and who would be in charge of the computer.
>
> But there is good things about computers as well such as, With computers in school all the records of children, lists of payment and other paper work can be kept easily on floppy disks. Children should learn about computing now because as they grow up there will be so many computers around them. The computers can be used as reward for good work (if you do good work you are able to use it) A computer would also help teacher to learn of new things to do with computing.
>
> With computers in schools someone will have to teach about them this should mean more jobs but in other places people will be losing there jobs to computers such as in building cars, ships and areoplanes Indeed already already computers are building cars instead of people.

This example was written by a pupil who had either participated in or attended a classroom debate on the topic. A characteristic of this and many similar pieces is that there is no development of the argument beyond the discussion, and no attempt to convince the reader of the writer's own view. There is no 'reader' suggested or implied. The writing takes the form of a *record* of an argumentative/controversial discussion. In certain instances, class groups sent in compositions, each divided into three sections under headings: (1) for, (2) against; (3) my opinion. In some cases only the first two headings were employed. The outline, usually provided by the teacher, lends itself to a balanced representation of view and focused attention on content, but it does not encourage pupils to adopt a persuasive stance, nor does it allow for a direct confrontation of ideas where the writer is free to differentiate between the importance of conflicting points. In a minority amongst scripts in this category, pupils have made an attempt to present a diversified argument, airing contradictory opinions, while giving greater weight to their own views and therefore soliciting the agreement of the reader.

> ### Cruelty To Animals.
>
> I very strongly disagree to experiments on animals, especially when you see them pinned down on pieces of wood. I think it is all right to distroy animals for food, or if they are in pain, but not just for experiments.
>
> The people who do the experiments should be brought to trial, and be fined a hundred and fifty pounds, or more.
>
> I would prefere, that I die than animals to die. The poor helpless creatures, why can't they live free, with-out being injected almost every day.
>
> I think the R.S.P.C.A. should have some sort of reaction against the cruelty to animals.
>
> There should be a compain against it, and best of all there should be a to LAW against the killings.

The overall impression is that argumentative writing is not of top priority in the 11-year-old's classroom. First, as shown by the questionnaires, it is not practised with any regularity. Second, over one third (36 per cent) of the schools contributing to the sample did not submit a single script under this category. Third, a large proportion of the pieces were not sustained arguments, but consisted rather of a comparative listing of alternative points of view.

Features of writing based on practical activities (11-year-olds)

The writing up of practical work in the classroom appears to be a highly structured exercise. A large proportion of the sample consisted of experiments in the physical sciences and usually followed a standard format: aim, method, results, conclusion. Most of these were also accompanied by a diagram illustrating the apparatus used. In general, the pieces constituted a record of a past event, which was seen in person or read about in a text. By contrast, accounts of experiments or biology investigations actually carried out in class frequently included the pupil's personal reactions as part of the record. Feelings of wonder or disgust revealed obvious enjoyment or involvement. The following exemplify cases where the writers were evidently interested in the exercise and followed each step closely.

> open some more, as he done it clear stuff came out all over the paper which we had put down before we had started Then I got the scissors and got out the pupil after that Nigel turned it outside in and we could see the blind spot which was a brown colour then we spoted a blue and green colour at the back of the eye the we wrapped it up in the paper and put it in the bin.

> ### Rearing Eggs
> About a week ago Mrs. Semple brought in an incubator. The incubator acts as a mother to the eggs. There is a light in the incubator which flashes on and off. This is why. Our body temperature is about 98·4 °F but the temperature of a chicken is 104 °F. If we tried to rear the the chicks we would kill them because of our weight and coolness. When we are sick our temperature is over 104 °F. The light flashes because when the temperature is over 104°F it goes off but when it is below 104°F it goes on.
> There are twenty four eggs altogether. They were brought in by Reginald and Billy both of them brought in a dozen each. The eggs are Bantams. The eggs are turned every day mainly twice. This is done because we don't want any side of the egg getting too much heat. We have one side of the egg with a circle on it and the other with a cross. We do this then we know it has been turned and not been turned. We should have the chicks before the Easter Holidays if all goes well.

> ### The bullseye
> One Thursday Mr. Gibson got a butcher to bring in some bullseyes for us to cut up for Nature study. Mr. Gibson cut a small hole first and left us to do the rest. Nigel who was my partner at the time cut it

There were, however, other scripts – based either on practical activities or on more passive learning – in which writers maintained a formal, more objective style making no reference to teachers, classmates or to anything other than the particulars of the experiment.

> Experiment :- To make carbon dioxide.
> Apparatus :- gas jar, flask, funnel, tubing, trough, bee-hive shelf, marble chips, hydrochloric acid.
>
> Diagram: -
>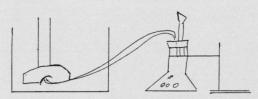
>
> Method:- We emptied some marble chips (Calcium Carbonate) into a flask. We then poured some hydrochloric acid down the funnel onto marble chips. The mixture then sent of Carbon dioxide down the tube, through the bee hive shelf and into the gas jar. We could see the carbon dioxide enter the gas jar because the water level in the gas jar kept on descending. We then slid a glass disc under the gas jar so that the carbon dioxide would not escape.
>
> Conclusion :- We found out that when we put a burning flame into the gas jar the flame went out. This was because of carbon dioxide.

Other work contributed in this category included accounts of how to perform certain practical tasks: how to repair a puncture, how to construct a doll's house, how to build a camp fire. These were written either in the style adopted for experiments – a step-by-step description of a past event – or delivered as a set of instructions to the reader.

Features of 'best' writing (category C: 11-year-olds)

Scripts offered as examples of 'best' work consisted overwhelmingly of imaginative and creative writing of narrative types: mysteries, thrillers, adventures, science fiction and fairy-tales. Very little, if any, of the work was 'picture-based' in the same way as the survey-task **Rainbow**. Many pieces, however, were illustrated or decorated and therefore had a distinctive and individual appearance.

It was noticeable that the same themes tended to recur throughout the sample and that these came from a traditional stock, including variations upon: 'Shipwrecked', 'In the Forest', 'Spy Story', 'Firework Night', 'Haunted House', 'The Wish' – titles which lend themselves particularly to adventure or mystery stories. There was, however, little evidence to suggest that this genre of story-writing constituted one part of a wider writing programme in which different types of writing would be practised. First, because very little work other than narrative was submitted. Second, because very little attention seemed to be directed to the processes or craft of story-writing. In the main, concern lay with the theme and content of the composition and not with the characteristics of the genre itself. This interest in theme was revealed by the fact that 26 per cent of compositions were written in response to a title proposed by the teacher with no other preparatory guidance offered. The majority of pupils did state that written notes had been provided or that a discussion had taken place. Pupils did not elaborate on the content of these preliminaries. Revisions or comments made by the teacher on finished stories indicated that at this stage their greatest concern was with surface features: spelling, punctuation, presentation, while the story – its organisation, plot development, expression – remained unaltered.

The characteristics of these scripts did not differ radically from those found in survey-produced story writing. The best scripts (two examples below) genuinely sustain the interest of the reader through well developed plots and original ideas. There is a sense of control and direction giving the impression that the composition was planned to achieve the effect of mystery and surprise, which is essential to the genre chosen by most pupils. There seems to be no uniformity in the conditions surrounding the production of good scripts. Some were written by individuals working alone and drawing largely on their own resources (example 1), whereas others were the result of joint efforts, discussions or suggestions from the teacher (example 2).

The Severed Head.

There was once a traveller who was on a journey when he came across a severed-head, he passed no remarks on it but when he had passed it spoke to him and said, "keep your mouth closed" and when he looked around he saw that the head was talking to him and ran away in fear. Then he went to the palace and asked for the chief for he had urgent news to tell him. When the chief came and the traveller told him about the head the chief said, "If this is true you shall have a reward if not you shall get your head chopped off."

Then he sent the traveller, the executor and some other men to see if the story that the Traveller had told was true or false. They walked along the road through many fields and hills until they came to the spot where the bush that had the head on it was, the traveller stopped and so did all the men who were tired of walking all the way. The traveller looked up but the head was not there, then he started to look all around the other trees and on the ground but the head was just not there. The executor stood up and said "the head is not here and you shall be punished for telling false tales."

So the traveller was taken back to the palace and executed that evening.

A few days later when the king was walking down his garden he heard a voice saying "keep your mouth closed" and then the king saw the head and rushed into the palace thinking how cruel he was to kill the traveller when the traveller was right.

Victoria Veda

I'm very tired. I think I'll go to sleep. Oh what is this big silver thing cutting me. The pain is agonising and I'm terrified. I'm very sore and I've been cut of from my family. Help me someone. Mum tried to hold on to me but it was no use.

Something lifted me up. Goodness what is this greasy yellow stuff it's putting on top of me Yuk this red stuff is worse, it's all sticky. Oh my legs have disappeared and my arms. The crunching thing is eating me. There is nothing left of me. I've disappeared

I'm going down a long, narrow, dark tunnel. I tried to grab some hairs but I couldn't get hold of them. The tunnel was all dark I went down it slowly at the start but and it got faster at the end.

I landed with a splash in middle of something orange which looked like orangeade. Then I saw bits of chips also floating in the orangeade I saw a potato and some peas. The crunching

> thing must have eaten all these thing
> I looked at the red Substance around me.
> I touched it. Itt was Soft and fleshy. I
> wondered where I was. That brown Stuff
> looks like chocolate and over there is my
> cousin Carol crusty

As indicated previously, signs of teacher suggestions or intervention surfaced when several scripts written in response to a common assignment were sent in. Uniformity of style and theme seemed to depend on the extent of joint preparation and the rigidity of the teacher's instructions. The similarity between the subject matter and choice of simile in the two poems below could be due either to consultation between the two pupils or to influence exerted by the teacher. In fact, both stated that they were given advice by the teacher.

> ~~Lonely~~
>
> Lonely and Sad sitting here.
> I can hear the wind whistling.
> I'm as lonely as a lamb that has lost its mother.
> Lonely as a cloud sailing along in a sky so plain
> and so clear.
> Nobody to talk to.
> I'm so Lonely

> ## Lonely.
>
> I am all alone
> Nobody to love me
> Nobody to care
> Only the leaves to rustle
> And the wind to blow

By contrast, there are also instances of diverse work being produced in the same circumstances.

The following pieces entitled 'Bird's Eye View' were two of four written after co-operative deliberation and discussion between class members and the teacher. Nevertheless they differ widely in their treatment of the topic.

> A bird Eye View of Life.
> One day I was day dream.
> I dreamt. that I had a
> wife, and some children too,
> and have a big car and
> I was very wealthy and I
> lived in U.S.A. and lived in
> a, very big house and I
> had maids and Ihave any
> thing I wanted I would live
> in a ranch and I had horses
> bulls and cows. I would ride
> the horses throught the fields
> and I would have more
> than one car. And I
> had an oil well. And I
> was selling it for a
> lot of money. Mummy awoke
> me and said take your
> dinner. And after two years
> it I came through I told daddy
> about the dream and daddy
> said you had a bird eye
> view of Life.

> A Birds Eye view
> My name is "Brenda the black
> bird" I like my furry feathers
> but the best place I like
> is my eyes because I can
> see a birds eye view when
> I am flying up in the
> sky in ffming I can
> see the other birds
> building their nests because
> the cuckoo has destroyed
> them. They were dumb they
> didnt even think of the
> "cuckoo I have got mine
> camouflaged so the cuckoo
> wont see it in Winter
> I see a birds eye view
> of good children put-
> ing bread out for men
> and bad boys and men
> trying to shoot me in
> winter sometimes I go
> to Austrialia to lie in
> the sun. I think a
> birds eye view is
> terrific.

Weaker scripts tended to be characterised by rambling and disconnected narratives, lack of focus or climax and predictability of outcomes. In some cases these problems were aggravated by length, regarded by many pupils as a good quality and frequently quoted as a justification for the presence of a piece in the 'best' writing category. This emphasis on length appears to be nurtured by some teachers. In one case, a ten-page closely written, unstructured, repetitive, plodding 'adventure' was postscripted by a complimentary mark from the teacher. It is noteworthy that all three pieces by this writer were similar in style and narrative dis-organisation and failed to distinguish between the different kinds of writing requested under the categories A, B and C. Likewise, some compositions which were not successful in content and organisation achieved a good standard in orthography, grammar and surface features and consequently their authors considered them suitable for the 'best' category.

9.4 General comments on the work sampling exercise

A major aspiration in incorporating the work sampling component into the APU language surveys was to obtain evidence about what pupils could 'really' do in writing, outside the constraints of a testing situation. Over the years of surveying it has become clear that the completion of a test booklet in writing has not been a constraining experience for many pupils, nor associated in their minds with the public examination system. Conversely the analysis so far carried out of the work sampled from classrooms has shown that though we have indeed acquired some written work which could not have been done without the support, resources and energies associated with the best classroom teaching, we have also documented a less cheering picture of the state of writing practice in many schools, at both primary and secondary level, than might ideally have been expected. Some general observations made about school writing in a previous report are repeated here.

1. Few schools appear to have anything like a policy for *writing across the curriculum* which would ensure that a diverse range of occasions for writing were provided, drawing upon, as distinct from 'reinforcing', the subject knowledge of many areas of study.

2. The English lesson remains the central focus for writing in the eyes of many pupils who, when looking for a good example of their written work, turn automatically to their English folder.

3. In all parts of the curriculum represented in our sample, there was a heavy emphasis on didactic learning: pupils seemed to have few occasions on which a legitimate use of writing might be to question or genuinely research some area of their learning.

On the basis of the work considered in this chapter, it does not appear that primary pupils are being given a substantially different experience of writing from their secondary peers. Emphases may differ, and more flexibility of approach may seem to be encouraged, but whatever positive strengths are glimpsed in the primary school sample it would be hard to say that these amounted to a different curriculum for writing. Where there are contrasts in the data, such as, for example, the change in teachers' approach from 'suggesting' how a written task might be done to simply setting a title or topic for writing, we can only guess at whether this change is gradually phased over the intervening school years or whether it is an instant effect of secondary schooling. (If the latter, how do pupils react to the decline in negotiability?) We might also speculate on the greater degree of independence shown by pupils in revising their work (where they revised at all). While evidence from the surveys demonstrates that pupils aged 15 are able to write relatively 'correct' first drafts, there are still outstanding questions of text-construction for them to consider. Should teachers have withdrawn from the consultative process to such an extent, and is their assumption of a more prescriptive role the most appropriate response to an older age group?

The discussion of teachers' comments concerning the purposes for which writing was set, and its place in the general scheme of pupils' learning, drew attention to, firstly, the scant awareness shown by many teachers that these matters could be connected ('I've no idea. Has any science teacher?'), and secondly to the highly directive nature of teachers' input into the majority of written assignments. Hardly any work it would seem is written without reference to a body of notes, work sheets, outline plans or instructions about form and layout – all provided *by the teacher*. Paradoxically, when reviewing pupils' *reading* performance, general areas of weakness were noted precisely along the lines of greatest teacher intervention in *writing*. Thus, pupils find reading difficult when they are required:

– to recast information in a different mode

– to read selectively for salient points and record these succinctly without irrelevancies

– to assess the satirical or ironical tone of a passage, or understand the attribution of particular viewpoints to fictional characters.

(see Chapter 2 of this report)

Obviously, one method of coping with weaknesses in such areas is to plug the gap by assiduous provision of pre-digested structures and interpretations. Another method which might in the end prove more efficacious would be to entrust to pupils more of the responsibility for their own learning, and for their development as writers. Pupils and many 'subject' teachers alike need to know more about how writing and learning interrelate and draw upon a complex of language functions. Some of the pedagogical implications of these observations are discussed in Chapter 13 of this report.

10

Attitudes to reading and writing

Synopsis

In the attitude surveys information was obtained about pupils' views on reading and writing, their preferences for different activities involving reading and writing and the extent of their voluntary involvement in those activities. This information is of intrinsic interest but its relevance to monitoring can be seen in the fact that there is a clear association between attitudes to language and performance on the tests.

The attitude surveys at primary level established that most pupils enjoyed reading, particularly the reading of stories. Approximately nine out of ten 11-year-old pupils belong to a library and they are willing to read most materials, including poetry, for enjoyment. There are however some sex-related differences such as a more marked preference among boys for reading materials that have a practical or informational function. Despite the generally encouraging picture, approximately three out of ten pupils are prepared to say that they are not interested in books; nor do they find it easy to concentrate for a long time when using them. A slightly lower proportion only read what they have to.

At secondary level the general pattern is similar, though there is some decline in the pupils' enthusiasm for reading fiction, particularly among boys. Boys are more likely than girls to be reluctant readers. Among both boys and girls the extent of use of public libraries falls, though approximately half of the 15-year-olds sampled still claim to make use of the system.

The first survey of pupils' attitudes to writing at primary level was carried out in 1980. A smaller proportion of pupils (approximately six out of ten) tend to find writing an enjoyable experience than enjoy reading. According to information obtained in the 1983 survey just under half of the pupils found it easy to write clearly and neatly. Just under five out of ten pupils still have some difficulty in dealing with the intricacies of grammatical and non-grammatical punctuation and with spelling. A remnant of not less than one in ten pupils have an active dislike of writing and endeavour to write as little as possible.

In general, pupils at secondary schools hold slightly more favourable views about writing and its applications. A smaller proportion of older than younger pupils admit to having recurrent difficulties in handling the surface features of written language. As at primary level, boys are more likely than girls to endorse statements expressing negative attitudes to writing or indicating reluctance to write. Their responses also reflect a greater preference for expository writing or writing that has a practical or informative aim. Among pupils in secondary schools negative attitudes to writing tend to be more strongly focused towards particular classroom activities such as extended note-taking or the writing of long essays and 'comprehension' exercises.

10.1 Introduction

In the course of the surveys of language performance we have been concerned to establish not simply whether pupils can read and write effectively for a variety of purposes but whether they do such reading and writing voluntarily. We have also tried to establish which school activities involving language they preferred and enjoyed. It is possible to show that such attitudes have a bearing on performance, though not always a direct one.

The uses to which pupils put language depend in part on their opinions and feelings about the utility and value of reading and writing and their perceptions of their own abilities as readers or writers. These perceptions are strongly influenced by their experience at school and at home.

In the surveys, different methods were used to investigate pupils' attitudes to reading. The methods are not detailed here as they have been discussed in earlier reports. Essentially, however, two main techniques were used. One was to ask pupils to indicate whether or not they agreed or disagreed with a series of statements, most of which had been made by pupils of their own ages. Their responses to these statements were of educational interest in their own right but they also allowed for the development of attitude 'scales' in which pupils' responses on selected questions were related. Secondly, pupils were asked to respond to a series of open-ended questions: an exercise which provided an opportunity for pupils to describe their views and experiences in their own words.

In the following discussion some of the findings from a series of surveys will be outlined, with a focus on those which provide an indication of differences in attitudes and behaviour between boys and girls and between pupils of different ages. As the enquiry into attitudes to reading was undertaken earlier than the enquiry into attitudes to writing, there is somewhat more evidence available about the former, and this is reflected in the structure of this chapter.

10.2 Reading at age 11

Reading as a source of pleasure and enjoyment

The findings from all primary surveys suggest that nine out of ten 11-year-olds enjoy reading and that they particularly enjoy the reading of stories. When pupils are asked to refer to books they have enjoyed reading, the great majority refer to works of *imaginative fiction*. Their answers indicate that the majority of pupils enjoy particularly stories with an element of adventure or mystery in the plot and an element of humour in narration and dialogue. The books referred to most frequently in this context were books by Enid Blyton, whose popularity with this age group is unchallenged. C. S. Lewis and Roald Dahl were the other authors referred to most frequently.

Enid Blyton stories continue to be cited by a substantial number of secondary pupils, particularly girls, as being those they have most enjoyed reading. In the report on the 1980 secondary survey we discussed some of the reasons for the popularity of the authors selected by a substantial number of pupils.

With regard to other types of reading, most pupils were able to refer to a work of *non-fiction* that they enjoyed reading. It was a consistent finding that a significantly higher proportion of boys than girls enjoyed reading works related to hobbies or which involved finding out how things worked. A higher proportion of boys than girls also preferred to read comic books and annuals at home rather than stories, the 'Beano' being the comic most preferred.

In the majority of primary surveys, between four and five pupils out of ten agreed with the statement: 'I like reading *poetry*', while about three out of ten pupils expressed emphatic disagreement with the statement. In each case the proportion of boys with negative views about poetry was significantly greater than that of girls. There were clear indications that some pupils whose reading performance was lower than the average nevertheless enjoyed reading poetry and preferred it in some cases to other kinds of reading. The types of poems that pupils in general tended to prefer were short, humorous rhyming verses which were relatively easy to understand. When pupils were asked to write down one or more lines from a poem that they had enjoyed reading, the majority wrote down examples of light verse, nursery rhymes or limericks. It was noted in the report on the 1982 primary survey that the majority of 'serious' poems referred to by pupils were verses written in Victorian or Edwardian times.

Reluctance to read

In a number of surveys approximately four out of ten pupils indicated that they did not usually read at home; and about two out of ten indicated 'that they only read what they had to'. The same proportion tended to agree with a statement to the effect that they had too little time to read at home. In a number of surveys about three out of ten pupils indicated a dislike for tasks that involved using books, particularly for reference purposes.

Library use

Nearly three-quarters of the pupils, and approximately the same proportion of boys and girls, claimed to belong to a public library and to borrow books from it. Approximately six out of ten pupils said that they also had frequent recourse to a school or class library. As far as could be determined, school libraries appeared to constitute the main source of supply of books that pupils enjoyed reading. An analysis of open-ended responses relating to this issue indicated that school libraries supplemented or made up for the apparent lack of reading resources in the majority of pupils' homes. While school libraries tended to be the main *source* for books they enjoyed reading, the preferred *place* for reading for the majority of pupils was at home, particularly in the comparative peace and quiet of a bedroom.

School activities associated with reading

Talking about books was by far the most popular activity as a follow-up to reading; whereas writing about books they had read was only enjoyed by about four out of ten pupils. Nearly half of the pupils had an active dislike for reading aloud in class. The majority preferred silent independent reading. However, one out of ten pupils preferred reading aloud in class to independent reading. These pupils tended to perform less well in reading than the others.

Attitudes and performance

Each year, the scores of pupils who took the reading tests were correlated with their responses to attitude statements. Pupils who were reluctant to read extensively and, as was noted above, those who preferred reading aloud to silent independent reading tended to do less well than did others. In general, the performances of pupils who expressed positive attitudes to reading were significantly higher than those who expressed negative attitudes but the levels of correlation between attitudes and performance were low, though consistent. This finding indicates that many pupils who are not good readers, in terms of their measured performance on the reading tests, nevertheless enjoy reading. This finding is borne out by other evidence from the attitude surveys.

The most important general point to emerge from the surveys of pupils' attitudes is that a large majority of children, including a number of poor readers, claim to enjoy reading, at least in some circumstances. The evidence also seems to show that, in many schools, pupils have encountered a varied and interesting range of reading materials in fiction if not in poetry. It was, however, a consistent finding that just under half of the pupils in each sample indicated that they experienced difficulty in finding books that they wanted to read. This finding must be set against the evidence from the findings of pupils' performance, which appears to indicate the relative success of most reading programmes in schools.

To illustrate the relative stability of a number of the findings and to indicate some of the differences between the responses of boys and girls, the percentage of pupils agreeing with questions asked both in the 1979 and 1983 surveys are shown below. In these two surveys, the first and last in the first phase of the monitoring programme, a substantial number of common questions were introduced for purposes of comparison.

Responses to questions showing positive views of reading (primary level)

| | Proportion in agreement (%) | | | | | |
| | TOTAL | | BOYS | | GIRLS | |
	1979	1983	1979	1983	1979	1983
I like reading stories	95	90	93	84	98	95
I don't like it when I haven't got anything to read at home	56	55	53	51	61	58
I like reading poems	62	65	53	57	71	72
I like going off and reading by myself	91	83	88	81	93	86
I enjoy using a library to find things out	81	77	79	77	83	77
I know how to use a library to find things out	87	86	86	86	87	86

Responses to questions showing negative views of reading (primary level)

| | Proportion in agreement (%) | | | | | |
| | TOTAL | | BOYS | | GIRLS | |
	1979	1983	1979	1983	1979	1983
I don't usually read at home	41	41	43	44	39	39
I am not interested in books	34	35	35	34	33	35
I can't often find a book I want to read	54	60	60	62	49	60
I can't concentrate for long when I read by myself	30	37	34	36	26	37
Some of the books we use in class are too difficult for me	29	35	31	36	28	34
I don't like having to look things up in books	38	36	40	37	37	35

Responses to questions about reading activities (primary level)

| | Proportion in agreement (%) | | | | | |
| | TOTAL | | BOYS | | GIRLS | |
	1979	1983	1979	1983	1979	1983
I like talking about books I've read	70	62	68	60	72	65
I like writing about books I've read	39	36	37	30	41	40
I prefer reading about my hobbies to reading stories	32	35	42	44	22	26
I prefer reading comic books and annuals to other sorts of books	45	51	56	59	35	42
I like reading to myself better than reading aloud	92	91	94	92	90	91
I like reading best when I am reading aloud to somebody	12	15	8	13	16	17
I know how to use a library to find things out	87	86	86	86	87	86

10.3 Reading at age 15

As at primary level, there was a substantial degree of consistency about the findings in successive attitude surveys. This can be illustrated in part with reference to pupils' responses to some of the statements used in the 1980 and 1983 surveys, which are given in the tables at the end of this section.

There is no evidence for a substantial change in attitudes to reading between primary and secondary level, with the possible exception of attitudes to reading poetry and to a more negative view of some classroom activities associated with preparation for examinations.

One of the recurrent findings was that approximately eight out of ten pupils said that they enjoyed reading; one in ten did not. However, in the majority of the secondary surveys about one in four pupils agreed that they seldom saw books that they wanted to read. A similar proportion affirmed that they rarely read books at home. The same proportion indicated that they only read if they wanted to find out something, apart from school work. In more than one survey, about one in four pupils claimed not to have read any books other than those relating to school demands in the month preceding the survey. For about a quarter of the 15-year-olds, therefore, reading, though it may be enjoyed, is decidedly not a regular source of pleasure.

Fiction

While a majority of pupils of both sexes claimed to enjoy reading *fiction*, there was an indication of a somewhat diminished enthusiasm for the reading of stories among pupils of both sexes, as compared to 11-year-old pupils. However, approximately two out of three pupils said that they had enjoyed reading a particular work of fiction in the year of the survey. Just over half were willing to identify a favourite book or author. Over the period of the survey there appeared to be relatively little change in the popularity of authors named. For girls, these included Enid Blyton, Agatha Christie, Catherine Cookson and Virginia Andrews, the latter having apparently become more popular in recent years. Among boys, the names of James Herbert, James Herriot and J. R. R. Tolkien figure frequently, followed by William Golding, Alastair MacLean, Neville Shute, Gerald Durrell and Enid Blyton.

Non-fiction

In a number of surveys just under half of the sample indicated that they had enjoyed reading a particular work of *non-fiction* in the year of the surveys. The general indication was that more boys than girls preferred reading non-fiction to fiction.

Drama

Three out of four pupils enjoyed reading *plays* and about half were generally able to name a play that they had read in the year of the survey. The range of plays referred to was, however, limited. Most frequent references were made to Shakespeare's works. Arthur Miller (*The Crucible*) and J. B. Priestley (*An Inspector Calls*) were the other playwrights referred to most frequently. For the majority of pupils, plays were likely to be encountered as reading material only in school-related tasks. The most 'popular' plays, therefore, tended to be those that were selected as examination texts.

Poetry

The general trend was for there to be a significant decrease in the proportion of responses indicating an enjoyment of *poetry* reading from both boys and girls at secondary level. In the 1979 survey, for example, whereas only a quarter of the 11-year-old girls (28 per cent) expressed a negative attitude towards reading poetry, the negative response among 15-year-old girls in that year was much more emphatic. In the same year, 46 per cent of the boys in the 11-year-old sample expressed negative attitudes towards poetry and 67 per cent of the boys in the 15-year-old group.

It could be inferred from answers given to a number of the open-ended questions that the pupils' attitudes towards poetry had been influenced primarily by the types of poetry they had read at school and by the difficulty they had experienced in understanding the poetry read. In general, the range of poems referred to was relatively limited, many poets being mentioned only in relation to isolated, well-anthologised verses. Relatively few pupils made reference to poets who were active after the First World War.

Purposes for reading

It was noted earlier that there was also a difference of perception between boys and girls with respect to the purposes for which they preferred to read. Three times as many boys as girls preferred reading about their hobbies to reading fiction (41 per cent as opposed to 13 per cent), and seven out of ten boys, as opposed to almost five out of ten girls, liked to read to learn how things work or how to do things. Over half of the boys, as opposed to over a third of the girls, said they preferred books which gave accurate facts; and just under two-thirds of the girls, as opposed to one-third of the boys, said that they liked to read to help understand their own and other people's personal problems.

While the questions were not designed to provide detailed evidence about the types of fiction that pupils preferred, one distinction did evoke significantly different responses from boys and girls. In 1980, six times as many girls as boys said that they liked reading 'love stories'.

Magazines and newspapers

Some information was obtained about pupils' reading of magazines and newspapers. The pupils' own tastes were reflected in the choice of magazines but they were less evident in their choice of newspapers. In general, they read those encountered at home. In the 1980 survey they were asked to comment on the newspapers they read and say why they read them. It was noted in the report on the survey that relatively few pupils seemed aware that different newspapers represented different stances and that they might be read critically or used to stimulate thought. 'Enjoyable, simple news' told from a 'human viewpoint' was appreciated by the majority in conjunction with features such as the letter pages, competitions, jokes and sport. 'Sport' appeared to be the principal area in which accuracy of information was required.

Library use

In the 1980 and 1983 surveys just under 50 per cent of the secondary sample agreed that they enjoyed using a library to find things out. In general a lower proportion of secondary than primary school pupils responded positively to the question, and, at secondary level, boys tended to respond less positively than girls. In the 1980 survey, in response to an open-ended question, pupils indicated that they used the school library primarily as a reference source for specific information related to school work. Those pupils who indicated that they rarely if ever used the school library justified their attitude on the grounds of a lack of inclination or stimulation to make use of it; a lack of time; reservations about the relevance of the books available; and use of alternative sources, particularly a public library.

School activities

Girls were significantly more positive than boys with regard to school activities associated with reading, including the study of novels, plays and poetry. The study of books in class was perceived by both boys and girls as being connected principally with an increase in understanding rather than enjoyment. Talking about books studied was very much more popular than writing about them or making notes on them. In general, the findings reflect the influence of examination pressures on older pupils and their relative dislike of some of the activities associated with the detailed classroom study of set texts.

Some further differences in responses of boys and girls

In each of the secondary surveys significantly more girls than boys endorsed statements indicating that they obtained a great deal of pleasure from reading, while the converse was true with respect to statements expressing reluctance to read. For example, in the 1982 secondary survey, twice as many girls as boys responded positively to the statement 'I like to read long thick books' (31 per cent as opposed to 16 per cent). Just over 60 per cent of the girls as opposed to 35 per cent of the boys agreed that they liked reading by themselves for hours. Twice as many boys as girls responded affirmatively to the statement 'I get bored reading silently to myself' (27 per cent

as opposed to 13 per cent). Similar proportions were reflected in the pupils' responses to the statement 'I only read what I have to' (26 per cent of the boys as opposed to 12 per cent of the girls).

While there is no evidence for a marked decline in enthusiasm for reading among secondary pupils nor is there any evidence for substantial growth or development in this area. While many secondary pupils have learnt to appreciate and enjoy fiction, for most of them the ultimate aim of literature teaching, as this was summarised in the Bullock Report, does not seem to have been attained. (The Committee suggested that whatever else pupils take away from their experience of literature in school, they should have learnt to see it as a source of pleasure, and as something that will continue to be part of their lives.)

In the following charts, the proportion of pupils agreeing with statements implying positive or negative views of reading in the 1980 and 1983 secondary surveys are given. In the main, these illustrate the relative stability of such attitudes and perceptions with respect to the questions asked.

Responses to questions showing negative views of reading (secondary level)

	Proportion in agreement (%)					
	TOTAL		BOYS		GIRLS	
	1980	1983	1980	1983	1980	1983
I seldom see a book I want to read	26	26	33	34	20	17
I only read what I have to	16	19	22	27	10	11
I prefer reading short books	49	56	54	62	44	51
Apart from school work I only read if I want to find out something	22	27	32	41	12	13
It takes me a long time to read most books	38	36	46	46	30	26
I prefer reading comic books and annuals to other sorts of books	30	25	31	29	28	21
I wish that books had less writing and more pictures	11	14	16	18	7	10
I prefer to listen to something being read out to reading it myself	29	37	37	48	21	28
My life outside school is too full for reading	23	28	29	31	17	24

Responses to questions showing positive views of reading (secondary level)

	Proportion in agreement (%)					
	TOTAL		BOYS		GIRLS	
	1980	1983	1980	1983	1980	1983
I enjoy reading	80	76	72	65	88	81
I like reading fiction (stories)	75	73	69	67	80	79
I like reading non-fiction	52	55	56	61	48	49
I like using books to find things out	69	68	70	73	68	64
I like reading by myself for hours	46	42	34	27	58	57
I like reading at home	79	75	70	63	88	87
I enjoy using a library to find things out	50	48	48	48	53	52
I like to read to learn how things work or how to do things	59	57	72	70	48	44
I like to read to help me to understand my own and other people's personal problems	44	47	30	33	58	61
I like going off and reading silently by myself	58	59	49	48	60	70

10.4 Writing at age 11

Preferences for types of writing

The first detailed enquiry into pupils' attitudes to writing at primary level occurred as part of the 1980 survey. One of the open-ended questions related to the type of writing that pupils had most enjoyed doing at school and at home. The largest group of pupils (38 per cent) said that they had most enjoyed story writing or writing imaginatively. Boys and girls made this selection in approximately equal proportions, but they differed significantly in their preferences for other types of writing, such as factual writing arising out of a specific project, letter writing and writing poetry. Boys were more inclined to favour the former and girls the latter two activities.

The analysis of a 60-statement questionnaire used in the 1980 survey showed that boys were generally more likely than girls to endorse statements expressing reluctance to write or lack of confidence in writing. For example, significantly higher numbers of boys agreed with statements indicating that they found difficulty in organising writing time and in the management of the written language.

A preference for story writing was also indicated by pupils in the 1982 primary survey when they were asked to say what they thought was the best piece of writing they had ever done and to give reasons for their answer. An analysis of a selection of their responses again showed that by far the highest proportion of pupils (42 per cent) referred to stories that they had created; and a further 7 per cent referred to narratives of personal experiences. About 12 per cent referred to topics that they had written about in connection with project work, and 9 per cent referred to poems that they had written.

There is some indication, however, from pupils' answers to questions about the varied content of the APU writing booklets, that their expressed preference for narrative is, at least in part, a reflection of the fact that this type of writing bulks large in their experience at school, at least in English lessons.

In the 1982 primary survey a series of questions probed aspects of pupils' perceptions of themselves as writers. The responses given tallied in general with those given in other surveys. There was evidence, for example, that the majority of pupils enjoyed writing, but nevertheless, just over 20 per cent of the sample or one in five of the pupils said that writing was not something that they tended to enjoy or spontaneously undertake. Between 20 and 25 per cent indicated that when they wrote they tried to write as little as possible, and that they frequently found difficulty in finishing what they wrote because of the time it took them. A quarter of the sample felt that they were asked to write too much at school. Approximately the same number anticipated that they would not need to write much when they left school. However, 90 per cent considered that writing would be important in later life.

At least half the pupils in the sample were confident that they were good at written work and just over a third were equally sure that they had mastered any problems relating to surface features of written language. In the 1980 report it was noted that these findings agreed generally with evidence gathered independently about the pupils' mastery of different aspects of writing. In that year, for example, just under 40 per cent of pupils were judged by assessors to have a relatively good control of the orthographic conventions of written English and almost half of the sample (47 per cent) were judged to have mastered the grammatical conventions of written English. (Such pupils were assigned ratings of 4/5 on a 5-point scale in relation to these criteria.) However just under 20 per cent of the sample were assigned ratings of 1 or 2 in relation to these criteria and this result tallies with the pupils' own responses referred to above.

One of the ways in which the perceptions of pupils in primary schools differed from those of older pupils is that a larger proportion claim to have difficulty in mastering surface features of writing and matters of presentation. For example, in the 1983 surveys, 47 per cent of primary pupils as opposed to 29 per cent of secondary pupils agreed in the 1983 survey that they were bothered by having to think about questions to do with punctuation and grammar when they wrote. There is other evidence also that many pupils at primary school lay exclusive emphasis on the importance of features of presentation, neatness and spelling when asked to identify qualities of good writing. For example, in the 1982 survey, pupils were asked to answer the following question: 'What do you think a good writer needs to know in order to do well?' Of the selection of scripts analysed over half made reference to matters to do with aspects of presentation, handwriting and qualities associated with neatness. Just over a quarter in contrast referred to qualities involving imagination or ideas. It was noted that the mean score of the pupils who emphasised the need for good writers to have qualities or capacities associated with imagination or sensitivity was, in that survey, significantly higher than that of pupils who emphasised the importance of presentational features.

10.5 Writing at age 15

In responding to questions about dislikes in writing almost two-thirds of the sample of secondary pupils in the 1979 survey expressed a dislike for writing long essays, copying notes, written exercises and comprehension work. We noted in the report on that survey that these complaints reflected the situation observed by HM Inspectors in the 1979 report in which they commented on 'the tedium of much written work in schools'. They noted that the pattern most frequently found could be described as 'one of notes and essays interspersed with the practice of answering examination questions alongside drills, exercises and tests' (DES, 1979).

We noted above that the judgements of many pupils in primary school about 'good writing' tended to reflect a strong emphasis on the importance of matters relating to neatness and of presentation. This is less obviously the case at secondary level, though such views are still prevalent. In the 1980 secondary survey, for example, pupils were asked to complete the following open-ended question: 'I think the most important thing about writing is . . .' Approximately one-third of the secondary pupils completed the statement by identifying as most important surface features of writing, including spelling, neatness or tidiness, punctuation and correct grammar. These accounted for the largest single group of responses. In this survey also, a significant difference between mean performance scores was associated with statements emphasising such features. In general, pupils' writing performance was lower when they responded this way than when they did not. Approximately one in ten pupils gave replies which indicated that for them the most important feature of writing was that it was a means of self-expression (12 per cent) or that its main aim should be communicative (12 per cent). A further 10 per cent of the sample regarded the enjoyment of the writer as being the most important consideration. The mean scores of pupils in each of these groups was found to be significantly higher than those not voicing such opinions.

Differences were again found in the preferences of boys and girls for types of writing. For example, girls were more inclined to enjoy writing about their families and writing from personal experience than were boys (just under 60 per cent of the girls as opposed to just over 40 per cent of the boys). Throughout the surveys, such differences in patterns of response were found. For example, a divergence of opinion had been reflected in the 1980 secondary surveys in the pattern of replies given to the question: 'Of all the things you've written at school/home which was the one you most enjoyed doing?'. The preferences expressed by boys tended to cluster round explanatory/expository types of writing,

while girls were in the majority where imaginative writing was concerned. Although approximately the same proportion of boys indicated a liking for some instance of imaginative writing as for one of factual writing, far more girls nominated imaginative/creative writing as their favourite type of writing; and significantly fewer girls expressed a particular liking for expository writing (e.g. writing in relation to projects, and the use of resources dealing with factual subject matter etc.). In that survey, again, a higher proportion of boys than girls said that they enjoyed writing about their hobbies, sports or recreational interests, that is writing with a practical, informative bias.

Views about writing at both primary and secondary level

While the influence of negative attitudes should not be over-emphasised, these have particular relevance to teaching. The following chart illustrates the incidence of such attitudes among boys and girls at both age levels. It shows the proportions of pupils at primary and secondary level who responded affirmatively to a number of statements expressing negative views of writing.

While it is not possible to make direct comparisons between the answers given by pupils in the different age groups, the general indication is that, for this set of questions with one exception, the overall proportions of pupils agreeing with the negative views expressed is *lower* at secondary than at primary level. However, the relative difference in attitudes between boys and girls prevails at both age levels, as does the difference in levels of performance.

The following charts show the extent to which pupils in the 1983 surveys responded to questions relating to positive views of writing. The charts are self-explanatory. Those results that indicate a marked contrast between the performance of boys and girls or of older or younger pupils are of some pedagogical interest.

Responses to questions showing negative views of writing (primary and secondary level)

	Proportion in agreement (%) primary			Proportion in agreement (%) secondary		
	TOTAL	BOYS	GIRLS	TOTAL	BOYS	GIRLS
I hate writing	17	22	12	12	18	6
I cannot remember writing anything I have enjoyed	13	14	13	10	13	8
Whenever I have to write something I try to write as little as possible	18	24	13	10	15	6
Apart from school work I only write if I have to	38	46	30	43	57	30
I do better in subjects when I don't have to write a lot	42	50	34	23	30	16
I look forward to the time when I won't have much writing to do	40	47	34	38	48	30

The findings illustrate the relative stability of some of the views held by pupils. At both primary and secondary level, for example, boys are less inclined than girls to enjoy writing that involves the discussion of family or personal matters, and any form of poetic expression. However the enjoyment of writing that fully engages the imagination evidently cuts across divisions of age and sex; whereas writing that involves the gathering of facts and information is less popular among older pupils. The results also appear to show that older pupils come to see writing as being a more important vehicle for the expression of personal opinion than do younger pupils.

It should be noted, finally, that although performance scores of pupils with negative attitudes towards writing tend to be significantly lower than those of other pupils, attitudes towards writing are not necessarily connected with performance in writing itself. For example, most pupils are able to name something that they enjoy or have enjoyed writing at some time even though not all perform equally well in writing. It will be apparent that many factors besides a positive disposition towards writing or towards a specific writing task have a role to play in accounting for achievement.

Responses to questions showing positive views of writing: 1983 (primary and secondary level)

	Proportion in agreement (%) primary			Proportion in agreement (%) secondary		
	TOTAL	BOYS	GIRLS	TOTAL	BOYS	GIRLS
I enjoy writing	63	55	70	61	48	72
I find it easy to write clearly and neatly	46	41	51	53	45	60
Writing helps me to express my ideas clearly	56	55	56	54	49	58
I like writing poetry	42	31	53	26	17	33

Responses to questions showing preferences in writing: 1983 (primary and secondary level)

	Proportion in agreement (%) primary			Proportion in agreement (%) secondary		
	TOTAL	BOYS	GIRLS	TOTAL	BOYS	GIRLS
The writing I enjoy most is writing which allows me to use my imagination fully	69	70	68	72	71	73
I like writing which involves the gathering of facts and information e.g. project work	64	64	63	45	49	41
I like writing about my family and personal experiences	41	37	45	41	29	50
I regard writing as a good opportunity for stating my own views on a subject	49	47	50	67	63	71

11

Language performance in relation to background variables

Synopsis

This chapter reports the data from all ten surveys (ages 11 and 15, 1979–83) for all three language modes (reading, writing, oracy) against 12 background variables. Where statistically significant differences between sub-samples of pupils emerged, the results are presented in Figures which give the data both graphically and numerically. The scores are expressed numerically in standardised form, i.e. on a scale with a mean of 100 and a standard deviation of 15.

The data given in this chapter investigate only differences between sub-samples of pupils on a survey-by-survey basis. That is, every survey has the same mean score and standard deviation, so that only the recurrence (or non-recurrence) of statistically significant differences can be traced across a series of surveys. The data in this chapter do not permit any analysis of significant changes in absolute levels of performance over time: that issue is investigated in Chapter 12. Details of sample sizes are given in the Annex to the chapter.

Perhaps the most interesting results concern the pupil variables of sex and English as a first or second language. Non-native speakers of English in England mostly achieved lower mean scores than native speakers: but in Wales the two groups did not differ. Girls consistently performed better than boys in reading and especially in writing: but in oracy the differences, though statistically non-significant, tended to be in favour of boys.

11.1 Method of reporting

Standardised scores

In all six of the previous reports on language performance, the scores reported against background variables were 'performance estimates' based on a scale with a mean of 50. In this report, a change has been made. The scores reported against background variables here are based on a scale with a mean of 100 and a standard deviation of 15; that is they are 'standardised' scores. This approach was also taken in the final report on the first phase of mathematics monitoring.[1]

---

[1] D. Foxman et al. *A Review of Monitoring in Mathematics, 1978 to 1982*. London: DES, 1985.

The reasons for the change are: (1) the greater familiarity of standardised scores; (2) the need to compare sub-categories of variables across years. For instance, if differences in performance between, say, native and non-native speakers of English in reading are to be compared within each of the five years of surveys, it has to be ensured that like is being compared with like, i.e. that the differences are expressed in the same units on the same scale. Conversion to standardised scores achieves this, and makes it possible to say, for example, 'Pupils aged 11 who were native speakers of English achieved a significantly higher mean score than non-native speakers in reading every year from 1979 to 1983'. It is then justified to interpret this as a robust finding which explains a proportion of the variation between individual pupils.

What survey-by-survey conversion to standardised scores does not achieve, however, is any basis for detecting trends or changes in absolute performance across years, since by definition the scores for each reading survey have exactly the same mean and standard deviation. The same is true for writing, and for oracy surveys.

In order to detect trends it is necessary to adopt statistical procedures which allow the detection of changes in the difference between sub-groups across years. For instance, the gap in average performance in reading between native and non-native speakers aged 11 might have remained roughly constant across the five years, or increased, or diminished: but standardised scores cannot be used to test this, and such issues will not be pursued in this chapter. However, they will be pursued, with the aid of other statistical techniques, in Chapter 12.

Linking performance across tests

Even before one survey can be compared with another, it is necessary to ensure that the various tasks used within any one survey are being assessed on the same scale. The raw scores reported in previous chapters cannot be used for this purpose, since the mean score and distribution of scores on each task are specific to that task. Obviously, some tasks are more difficult than others, and a scaling procedure therefore has to be applied to the raw scores for each task before the scores on all tasks can be aggregated and mean scores calculated across the entire sample of pupils in a survey.

In the case of scores on reading test booklets, the raw scores (percentage of questions answered correctly) need to be adjusted by reference to only one parameter, the difficulty of each booklet compared to the others used in the same survey. This is done by means of a common test included in every one of the booklets in a survey.

In the case of writing and oracy, the raw scores have to be adjusted by reference to two parameters: the relative ease or difficulty of the task, and the relative leniency or severity of the two markers. Because all the markers mark similar samples of all the tasks, the double-marking system ensures that all the markers can be compared to each other, and each marker's scores adjusted accordingly.[1] When allowance has been made for this factor, the characteristics of the tasks can be calculated and allowed for; and finally a standardised score can be attributed to each pupil who was given a particular raw score on a particular task by a particular pair of markers.

It should be noted that these procedures only ensure comparability within each aspect of the language surveys (reading, writing, oracy). Even though the scores on all three modes are converted to the same standardised form, this is no basis for comparison of scores across modes. Such comparisons would only be possible if the same sample of pupils had taken tests in more than one mode and if the scores had been processed accordingly: this remains a task for the second phase of the project.

The background variables used

In the rest of this chapter, pupils' performance in reading, writing and oracy will be discussed in relation to certain variables which serve to differentiate the whole sample. These variables can be classified as pupil, school and geographical variables. The variables which will be discussed in this chapter are included in the following list. Since some of the variables were not used in every survey, the years in which each variable was used are also shown.

Pupil variables	sex	1979–83
	speaker of English as a first or second language	1979–83
	(age 15 only) number of public examination entries	1981–83
	science subjects studied	1980–81
School variables	proportion of children taking free school meals	
	– England	1979–80
	– Wales and N. Ireland	1979–83
	pupil/teacher ratio (England and Wales)	1979–83
	(age 15 only) size of English teaching group	1981–83
	single-sex or co-educational school	1979–81
Geographical variables	school catchment area (urban, rural, etc)	1981–83
	metropolitan or non-metropolitan county (England only)	1979–83
	region (England only: North, Midlands, South)	1979–83
	country	1979–83

For maintained schools, information was obtained on all these variables in the relevant years (except that no data were available on pupil/teacher ratios in Northern

---

[1] This procedure relies on individual markers being consistent, and would begin to break down if some markers were not. Fortunately, no marker's scores have yet had to be discarded on these grounds.

Ireland). For independent schools, information was obtained only on sex of pupils and on region and country: scores from pupils in independent schools therefore enter into the calculation of means only for those three variables.

Presentation of results

A mean score was calculated for each sub-category of each variable. Associated with each mean is a standard error of measurement, and from the standard error 95 per cent confidence limits were calculated for each mean score. These confidence limits lie two standard errors either side of the mean, and represent the limits within which there is a 95 per cent probability that the 'true' mean score lies. (The 'true' mean score is that which would have been obtained if the entire population of relevant pupils had been tested instead of a sample.) In the Figures in this chapter, whenever the numerical value of a mean score is quoted, the standard error (s.e.) is shown in brackets either beside or below the mean. Also, when mean scores are displayed graphically, the confidence limits are shown as horizontal bars projecting from the short vertical bar representing the mean. As a rule of thumb, it can be assumed that where confidence limits relating to two mean scores within a variable do not overlap, or overlap to only a small extent, the difference between the mean scores is likely to be statistically significant at the 0.05 level or better. This can be taken to imply that there are no more than five chances in 100 that the difference occurred by chance.

Where the number of pupils contributing to a mean score is less than 25, the calculation of the mean score and standard error would be unreliable. In such cases, therefore, these data are not presented, either numerically or graphically. Instead, the number of pupils in the relevant category is shown in brackets (e.g. N = 18), in place of the mean score.

11.2 Pupil variables

Differences in performance between girls and boys

The results for this variable are shown in Figures 11.1–11.6. The findings can be summarised as follows.

In all ten surveys (five at age 11, five at age 15) girls achieved significantly higher mean scores than boys in *writing*. In *reading*, the trend was always in the same direction, but the difference attained statistical significance in only half of the surveys. Trends over time in these differences are analysed in detail in Chapter 12.

In *oracy*, none of the four surveys in 1982 and 1983 produced a significant *overall* difference in performance between boys and girls, though there were such differences on particular tasks, as discussed at the end of Chapter 6.

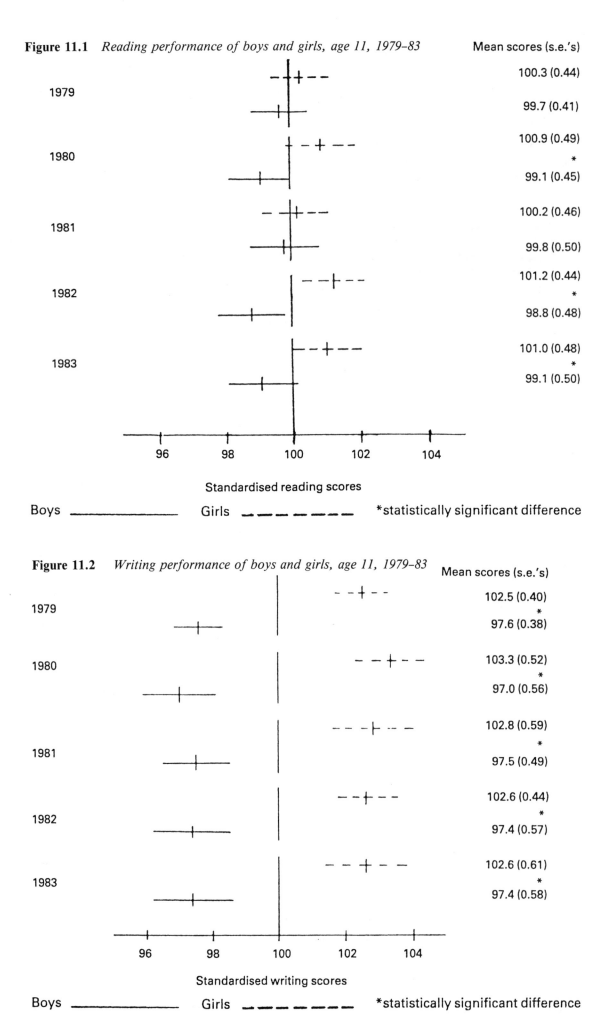

Figure 11.1 *Reading performance of boys and girls, age 11, 1979–83*

Mean scores (s.e.'s)

1979	100.3 (0.44)	99.7 (0.41)
1980	100.9 (0.49) *	99.1 (0.45)
1981	100.2 (0.46)	99.8 (0.50)
1982	101.2 (0.44) *	98.8 (0.48)
1983	101.0 (0.48) *	99.1 (0.50)

96   98   100   102   104

Standardised reading scores

Boys ——————— Girls — — — — — — *statistically significant difference

Figure 11.2 *Writing performance of boys and girls, age 11, 1979–83*

Mean scores (s.e.'s)

1979	102.5 (0.40) *	97.6 (0.38)
1980	103.3 (0.52) *	97.0 (0.56)
1981	102.8 (0.59) *	97.5 (0.49)
1982	102.6 (0.44) *	97.4 (0.57)
1983	102.6 (0.61) *	97.4 (0.58)

96   98   100   102   104

Standardised writing scores

Boys ——————— Girls — — — — — — *statistically significant difference

Figure 11.3 *Speaking performance of boys and girls, age 11, 1982–83*

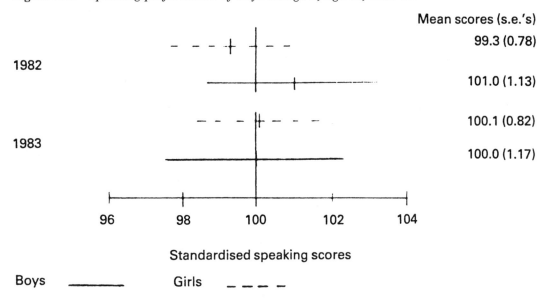

Mean scores (s.e.'s)

1982	99.3 (0.78)
	101.0 (1.13)
1983	100.1 (0.82)
	100.0 (1.17)

Standardised speaking scores

Boys —————— Girls — — — —

Figure 11.4 *Reading performance of boys and girls, age 15, 1979–83*

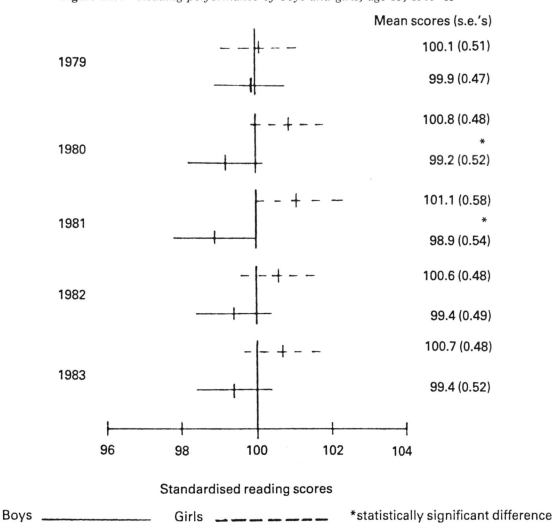

Mean scores (s.e.'s)

1979	100.1 (0.51)
	99.9 (0.47)
1980	100.8 (0.48)
	*
	99.2 (0.52)
1981	101.1 (0.58)
	*
	98.9 (0.54)
1982	100.6 (0.48)
	99.4 (0.49)
1983	100.7 (0.48)
	99.4 (0.52)

Standardised reading scores

Boys —————— Girls — — — — — — *statistically significant difference

Figure 11.5 *Writing performance of boys and girls, age 15, 1979–83*

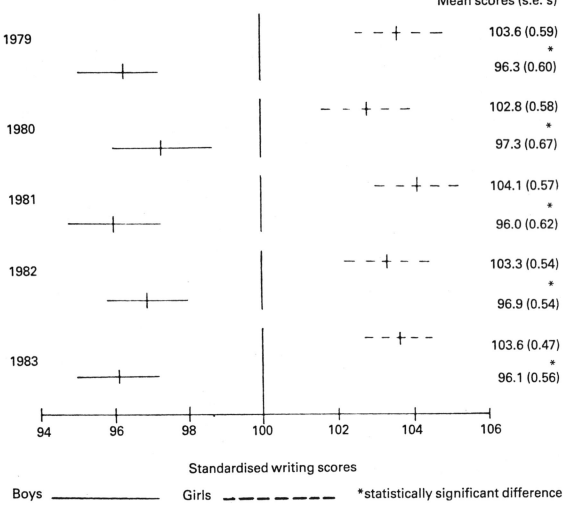

Standardised writing scores

Boys ——————   Girls — — — — — —   *statistically significant difference

Figure 11.6 *Speaking performance of boys and girls, age 15, 1982–83*

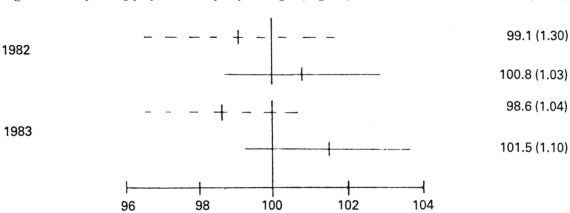

Standardised speaking scores

Boys ——————   Girls — — — — — —   *statistically significant difference

Speakers of English as a first or second language

In most of the ten surveys there were no non-native speakers of English at all in the sample in Northern Ireland, and the total number over five years did not reach double figures. Discussion of this variable is therefore limited to England and Wales. Even in England and Wales, the numbers of non-native speakers of English in the oracy samples were always below 25, and therefore no meaningful comparisons can be made on this variable for oracy.

Considering only the results for reading and writing for England and Wales, the findings for the two countries differed sharply, as can be seen from Figures 11.7–11.10.

In reading and writing in England, native speakers of English achieved higher mean scores than non-native speakers in all ten surveys. All the differences in reading were significant at both ages, as were four of the five differences in writing at age 11. In writing at age 15 only the 1981 difference achieved significance.

In Wales, there were no significant differences in either reading or writing at either age in any year, and the mean scores for second-language speakers of English (all but a handful of whom were native speakers of Welsh) were sometimes fractionally higher than those for monolingual English speakers.

This pattern of results seems to show that at age 11 second-language speakers are on average at a disadvantage in both reading and writing in England. By age 15 they seem to have largely closed the gap in writing, but not in reading.

In Wales, on the other hand, Welsh speakers seem to be at no disadvantage in either mode at either age.

These differences in reading and writing between England and Wales are quite clearly robust. It seems unlikely that inherent qualities of Welsh as a language compared with the principal minority languages of England (Urdu, Punjabi, Hindi, Gujarati, Bengali) are responsible. All five of those languages of the Indian sub-continent just mentioned are members of the same Indo-European family of languages to which Welsh and English also belong; and Welsh does not seem 'closer', in any linguistic sense, to English than those Indian languages.

It may be more likely that social and/or cultural factors lie behind the different L1/L2 patterns in England and Wales. In Wales, Welsh speakers are sociologically indistinguishable from monolingual English speakers, i.e. their distribution across the socio-economic scale is the same. They are also culturally almost indistinguishable from monolinguals. In England, on the other hand, second-language speakers are disproportionately concentrated in the lower bands of the socio-economic scale and are culturally fairly distinct: these may be two of the major underlying causes of the different effects of first- and second-language status in the two countries.

Figure 11.7 *Reading performance of speakers of English as a first or second language, England and Wales, age 11, 1979–83*

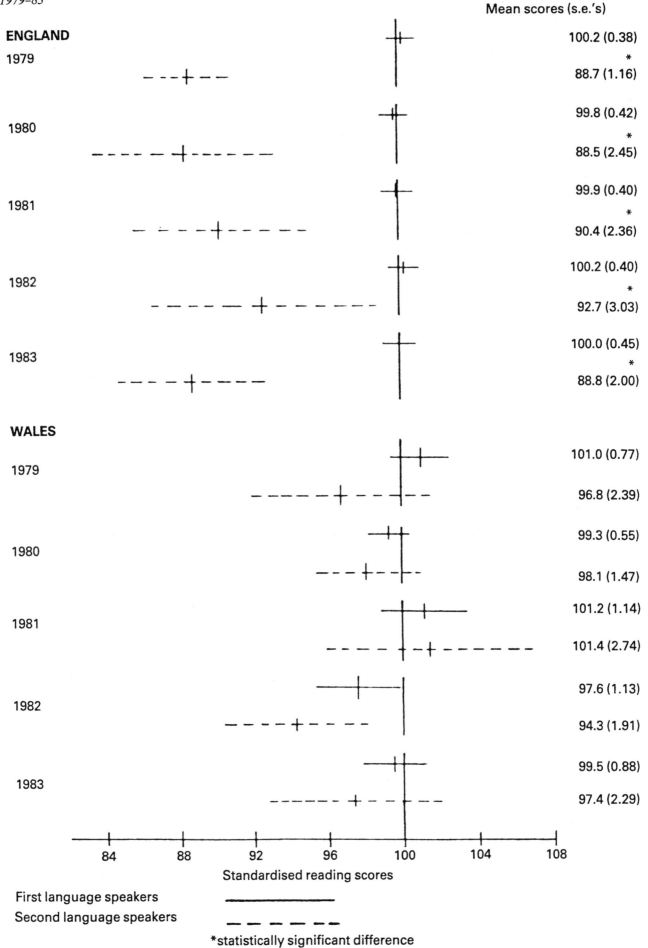

Mean scores (s.e.'s)

ENGLAND

1979
100.2 (0.38)
*
88.7 (1.16)

1980
99.8 (0.42)
*
88.5 (2.45)

1981
99.9 (0.40)
*
90.4 (2.36)

1982
100.2 (0.40)
*
92.7 (3.03)

1983
100.0 (0.45)
*
88.8 (2.00)

WALES

1979
101.0 (0.77)
96.8 (2.39)

1980
99.3 (0.55)
98.1 (1.47)

1981
101.2 (1.14)
101.4 (2.74)

1982
97.6 (1.13)
94.3 (1.91)

1983
99.5 (0.88)
97.4 (2.29)

84   88   92   96   100   104   108

Standardised reading scores

First language speakers ⎯⎯⎯⎯⎯⎯

Second language speakers ⎯ ⎯ ⎯ ⎯ ⎯

*statistically significant difference

184

Figure 11.8 *Writing performance of speakers of English as a first or second language, England and Wales, age 11, 1979–83*

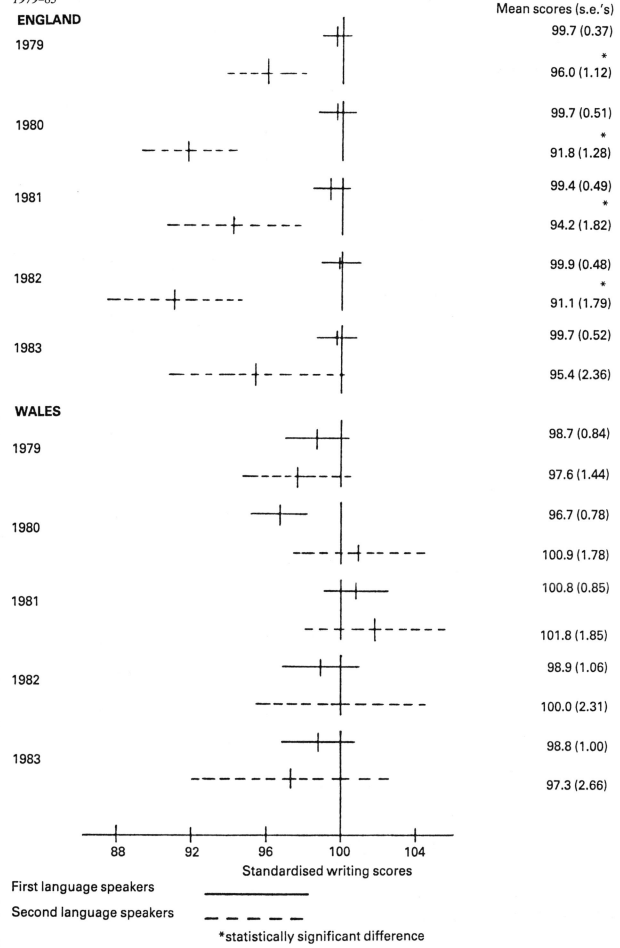

Mean scores (s.e.'s)

ENGLAND

1979
99.7 (0.37)

*
96.0 (1.12)

1980
99.7 (0.51)

*
91.8 (1.28)

1981
99.4 (0.49)

*
94.2 (1.82)

1982
99.9 (0.48)

*
91.1 (1.79)

1983
99.7 (0.52)

95.4 (2.36)

WALES

1979
98.7 (0.84)

97.6 (1.44)

1980
96.7 (0.78)

100.9 (1.78)

1981
100.8 (0.85)

101.8 (1.85)

1982
98.9 (1.06)

100.0 (2.31)

1983
98.8 (1.00)

97.3 (2.66)

88   92   96   100   104

Standardised writing scores

First language speakers ———————

Second language speakers – – – – –

*statistically significant difference

185

Figure 11.9 *Reading performance of speakers of English as a first or second language, England and Wales, age 15, 1979–83*

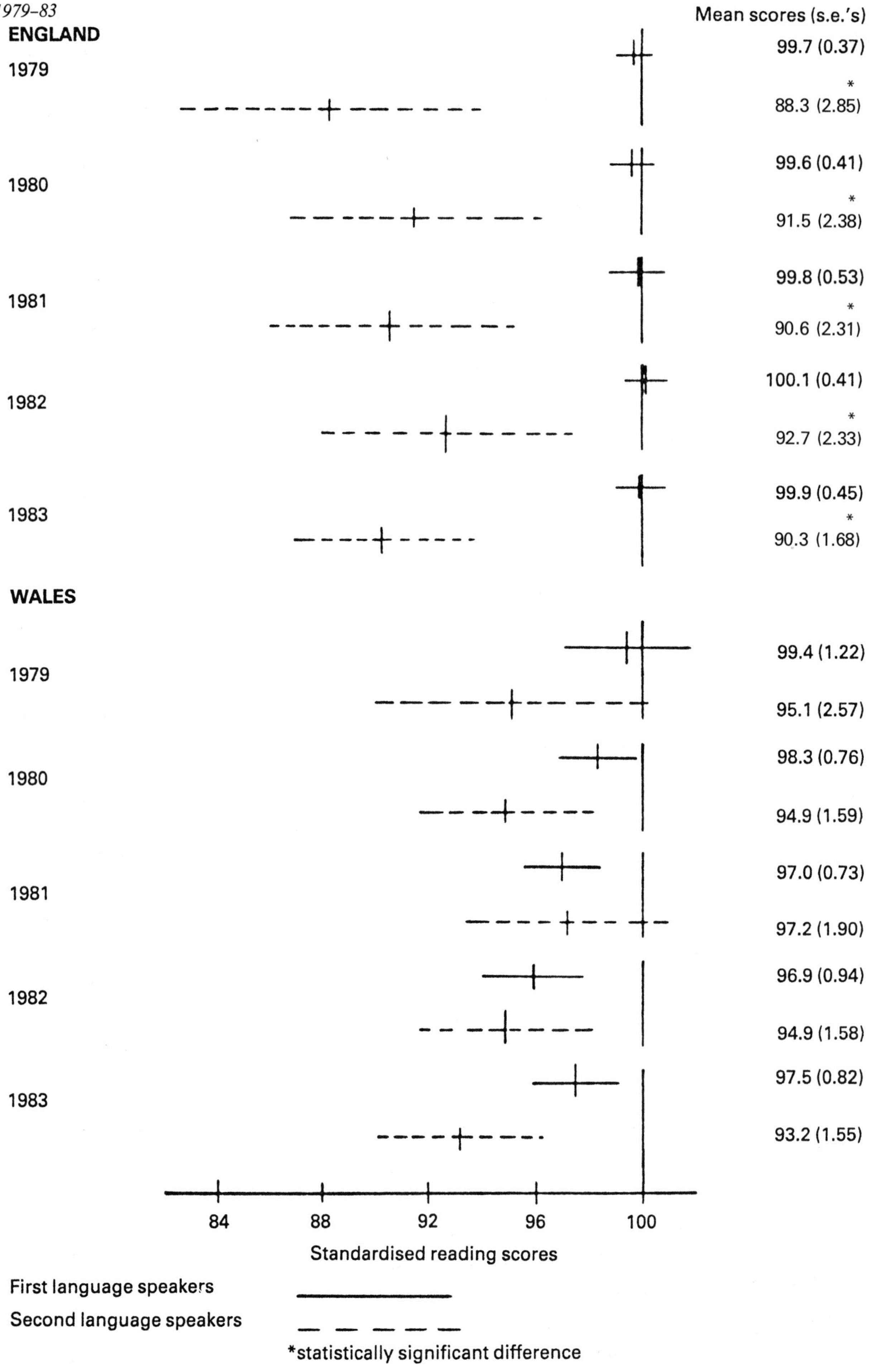

	Mean scores (s.e.'s)
ENGLAND	
1979	99.7 (0.37)
	*
	88.3 (2.85)
1980	99.6 (0.41)
	*
	91.5 (2.38)
1981	99.8 (0.53)
	*
	90.6 (2.31)
1982	100.1 (0.41)
	*
	92.7 (2.33)
1983	99.9 (0.45)
	*
	90.3 (1.68)
WALES	
1979	99.4 (1.22)
	95.1 (2.57)
1980	98.3 (0.76)
	94.9 (1.59)
1981	97.0 (0.73)
	97.2 (1.90)
1982	96.9 (0.94)
	94.9 (1.58)
1983	97.5 (0.82)
	93.2 (1.55)

Standardised reading scores

First language speakers ——————

Second language speakers — — — —

*statistically significant difference

Figure 11.10 *Writing performance of speakers of English as a first or second language, England and Wales, age 15, 1979–83*

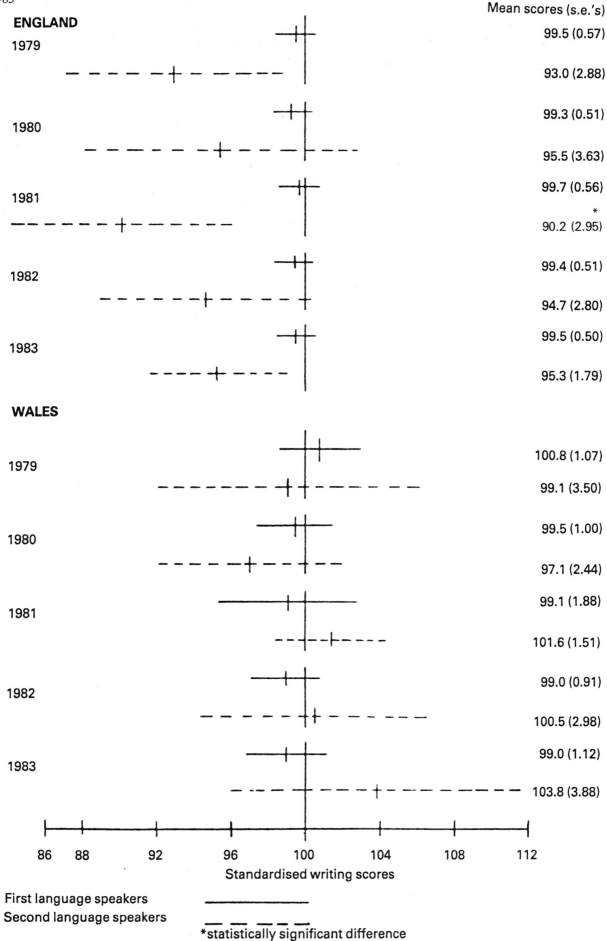

Mean scores (s.e.'s)

ENGLAND

1979
99.5 (0.57)
93.0 (2.88)

1980
99.3 (0.51)
95.5 (3.63)

1981
99.7 (0.56)
90.2 (2.95) *

1982
99.4 (0.51)
94.7 (2.80)

1983
99.5 (0.50)
95.3 (1.79)

WALES

1979
100.8 (1.07)
99.1 (3.50)

1980
99.5 (1.00)
97.1 (2.44)

1981
99.1 (1.88)
101.6 (1.51)

1982
99.0 (0.91)
100.5 (2.98)

1983
99.0 (1.12)
103.8 (3.88)

86   88   92   96   100   104   108   112

Standardised writing scores

First language speakers
Second language speakers

*statistically significant difference

187

Number of public examination entries (age 15)

In the age 15 surveys of 1981–83, which occurred in November, i.e. early in the school year, information was obtained about the number of GCE 'O' levels and/or CSEs each pupil was thought likely to be entered for the following summer. Five sub-categories of this variable were used in 1981, and in 1982 and 1983 one of these was sub-divided to make a sixth, as follows:

1981	**1982–83**
1. 6 or more 'O' levels	1. 8 or more 'O' levels
2. 3–5 'O' levels	2. 6–7 'O' levels
3. 1–2 'O' levels	3. 3–5 'O' levels
4. 5 or more CSEs	4. 1–2 'O' levels
5. 4 CSEs or less	5. 5 or more CSEs
	6. 4 CSEs or less

The results for this variable for reading, writing and oracy respectively are shown in Figures 11.11–11.13.

Most of the differences shown in these categories were statistically significant, except that in oracy, because of the smaller numbers of pupils involved, differences between immediately adjacent categories were rarely significant.

Science subjects studied (age 15)

In the 1980–82 surveys at age 15, at the request of the Science Monitoring team, information was obtained on the science subjects which the pupils in the samples were studying. Representative results on this variable were given in the report on the 1980 survey,[1] and will not be repeated here.

---

[1] *Language Performance in Schools: Secondary Survey Report No. 2.* London: HMSO, 1983.

Figure 11.11 *Reading performance by number of public examination entries, age 15, 1981–83*

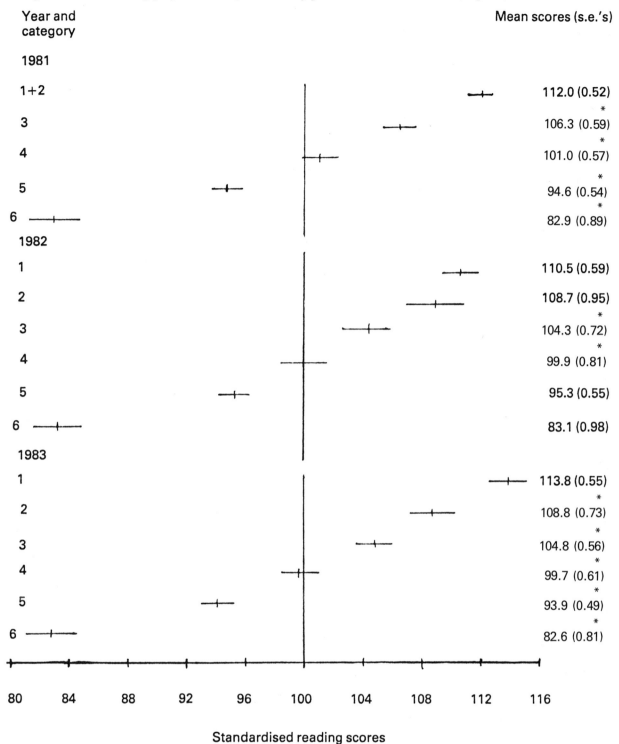

Standardised reading scores

Key: Category 1   8 or more 'O' Levels
           2   6–7 'O' Levels
           3   3–5 'O' Levels
           4   1–2 'O' Levels
           5   5 CSEs or more
           6   4 CSEs or less

*statistically significant difference

Figure 11.12 *Writing performance by number of public examination entries, age 15, 1981–83*

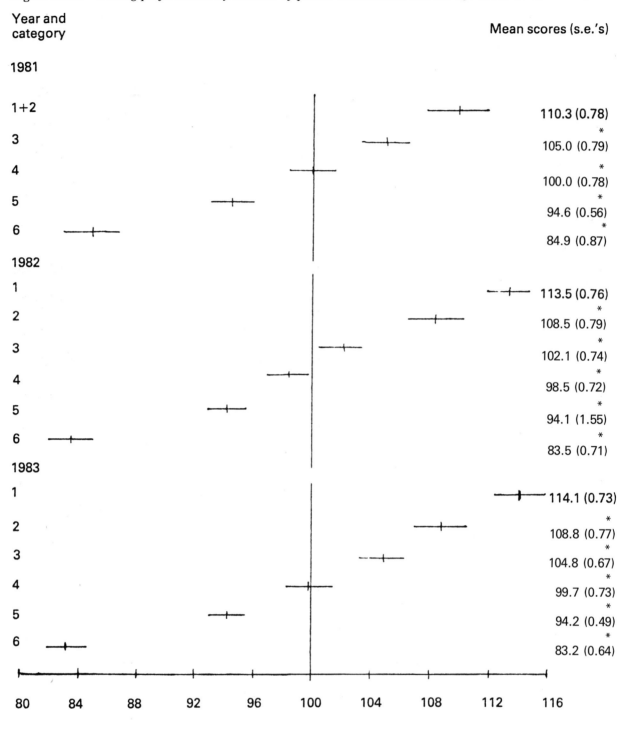

Year and category

Mean scores (s.e.'s)

1981

1+2	110.3 (0.78)
3	* 105.0 (0.79)
4	* 100.0 (0.78)
5	* 94.6 (0.56)
6	* 84.9 (0.87)

1982

1	113.5 (0.76)
2	* 108.5 (0.79)
3	* 102.1 (0.74)
4	* 98.5 (0.72)
5	* 94.1 (1.55)
6	* 83.5 (0.71)

1983

1	114.1 (0.73)
2	* 108.8 (0.77)
3	* 104.8 (0.67)
4	* 99.7 (0.73)
5	* 94.2 (0.49)
6	* 83.2 (0.64)

80   84   88   92   96   100   104   108   112   116

Standardised writing scores

Key: Category 1   8 or more 'O' Levels
2   6–7 'O' Levels
3   3–5 'O' Levels
4   1–2 'O' Levels
5   5 CSEs or more
6   4 CSEs or less

*statistically significant difference

Figure 11.13 *Speaking performance by number of public examination entries, age 15, 1982–83*

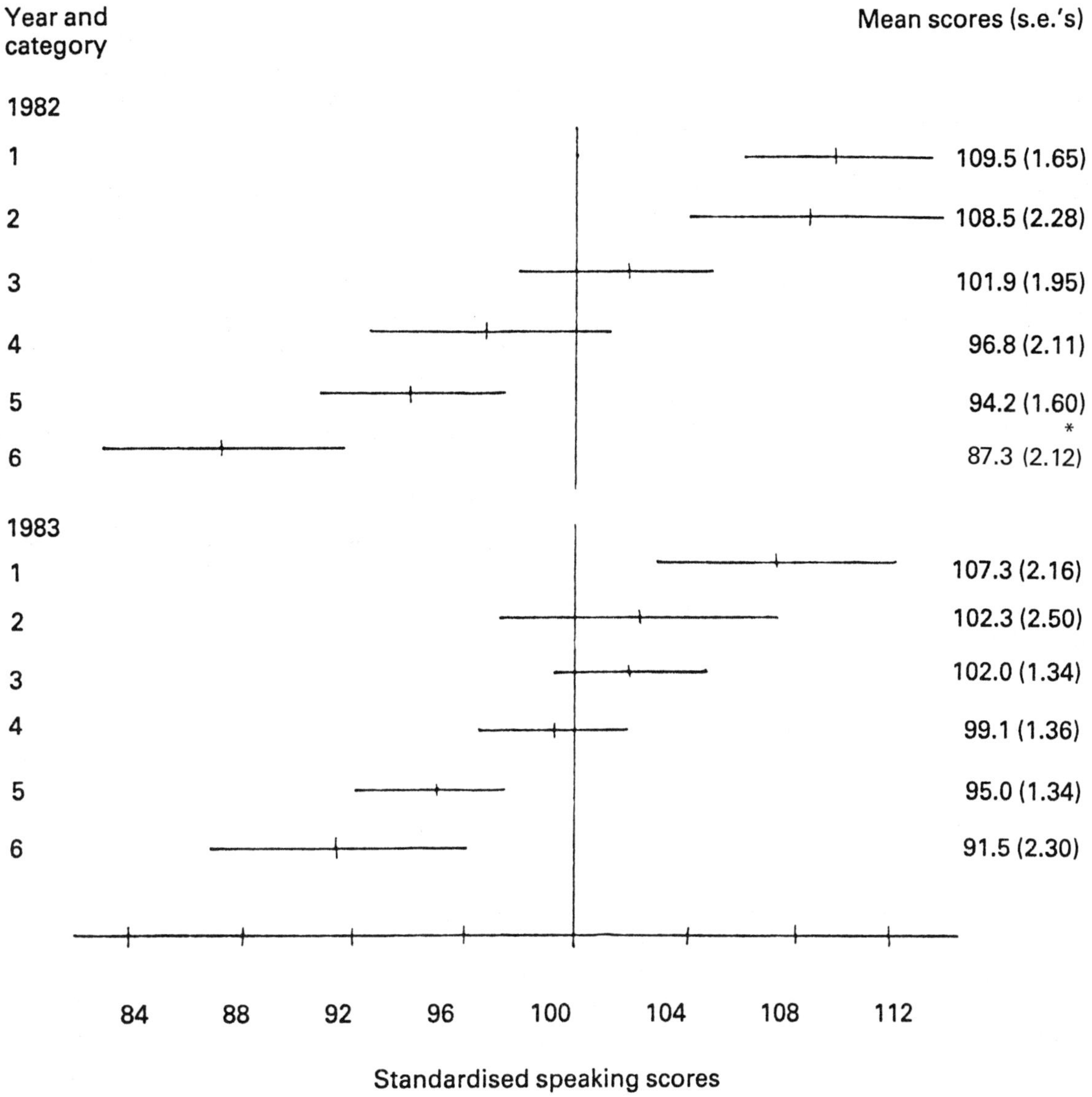

Year and category

Mean scores (s.e.'s)

1982

Category	Mean score (s.e.)
1	109.5 (1.65)
2	108.5 (2.28)
3	101.9 (1.95)
4	96.8 (2.11)
5	94.2 (1.60)
6	87.3 (2.12) *

1983

Category	Mean score (s.e.)
1	107.3 (2.16)
2	102.3 (2.50)
3	102.0 (1.34)
4	99.1 (1.36)
5	95.0 (1.34)
6	91.5 (2.30)

84   88   92   96   100   104   108   112

Standardised speaking scores

Key: Category 1 8 or more 'O' Levels
2 6–7 'O' Levels
3 3–5 'O' Levels
4 1–2 'O' Levels
5 5 CSEs or more
6 4 CSEs or less

*statistically significant difference

11.3 School variables

Free school meals

It may be suspected that socio-economic status is a powerful determinant of educational performance. However, there are technical problems in the definition of 'class', and objections in principle could be raised to asking schools to label their pupils according to this factor. Therefore no information was gathered on individual pupils' socio-economic background.

Instead, information was gathered on the proportion of pupils in a school receiving free school meals, and this acted as a surrogate socio-economic variable, allowing the classification of all the pupils in a *school* as belonging to more or less affluent social strata.

However, difficulties arose with the use of this variable early in the five-year cycle of surveys. Up to 1980, criteria for pupils' eligibility for free meals were laid down by central government, and were applied uniformly by all LEAs. But the 1980 Education Act empowered LEAs to define their own criteria, and since 1981 authorities in England have operated quite different policies. For 1981–83, therefore, data on this variable for England would be meaningless. Authorities in Wales and Northern Ireland, however, have continued to operate the pre-1980 criteria.

Another difficulty about using data from all five years even in Wales and Northern Ireland is that the method of calculating the proportion of free-meal-takers was changed between 1979 and 1980. (The change was made because of a sharp drop in the total number of pupils taking school meals.) In 1979 the proportion was calculated as the number of pupils receiving free meals expressed as a percentage of the total number of pupils in the school *taking meals* on a given date. From 1980 onwards, the proportion was calculated as the number of pupils receiving free meals expressed as a percentage of the total number of pupils *on the school roll* on a given date. Therefore the 1979 results cannot be directly compared with those for later years.

What can be said, however, is that in England in 1979 and 1980, despite the different methods of calculation, performance varied inversely with the proportion of pupils receiving free meals. That is, pupils in schools with a high proportion of free-meal-takers achieved significantly lower mean scores than those in schools with a low proportion of free-meal-takers.

A similar pattern can be reported in more detail for Wales and Northern Ireland for the years 1980–83. The sub-categories used were the following:

Category	Number of pupils receiving free meals as a percentage of total number on roll
1	5.9% and below
2	6–13.9%
3	14% and above

The results for these categories are shown in Figures 11.14–11.19. (Data for pupils aged 11 in 1981 are not available.)

The data show that there was a fairly consistent trend for higher proportions of free-meal-takers to be associated with lower mean scores, even though not all the differences between categories achieved statistical significance. The results were clearest at age 15 in Northern Ireland, where category 1 was significantly higher than category 3 in all four years for reading, and in three out of the four years (all except 1980) for writing. Thus even this indirect and problematic socio-economic indicator suggests that social class does influence performance.

Figure 11.14 *Reading performance by proportion of pupils receiving free school meals, Wales and Northern Ireland, age 11, 1980 and 1982–83*

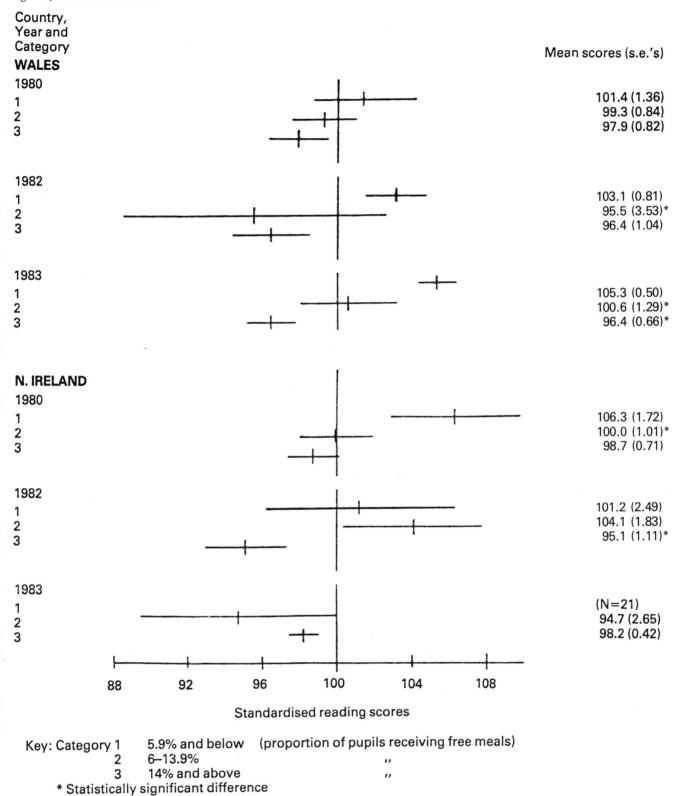

Key: Category 1   5.9% and below   (proportion of pupils receiving free meals)
        2   6–13.9%   "
        3   14% and above   "
    * Statistically significant difference

Figure 11.15 *Writing performance by proportion of pupils receiving free school meals, Wales and Northern Ireland, age 11, 1980 and 1982–83*

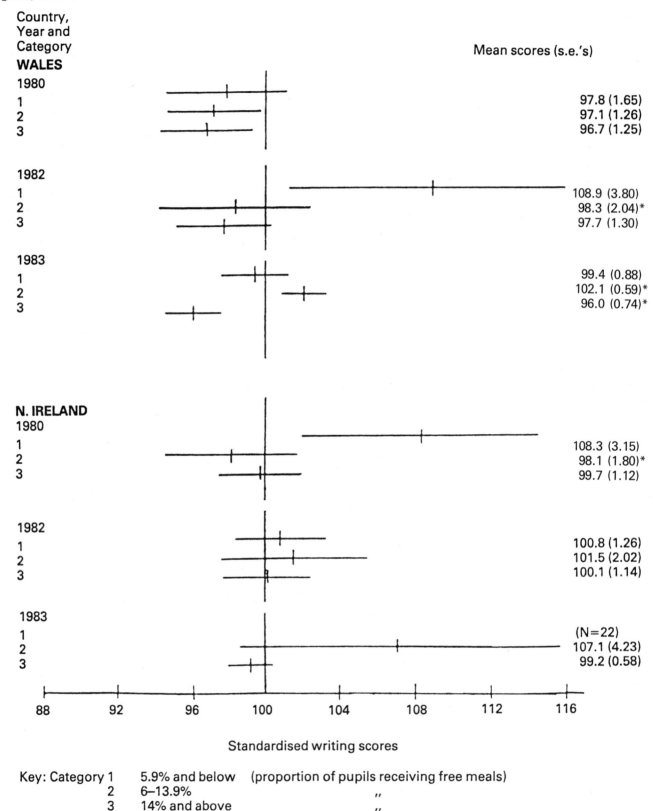

Standardised writing scores

Key: Category 1   5.9% and below   (proportion of pupils receiving free meals)
           2   6–13.9%   ,,
           3   14% and above   ,,
      * Statistically significant difference

Figure 11.16 *Speaking performance by proportion of pupils receiving free school meals, Wales and Northern Ireland, age 11, 1982–83*

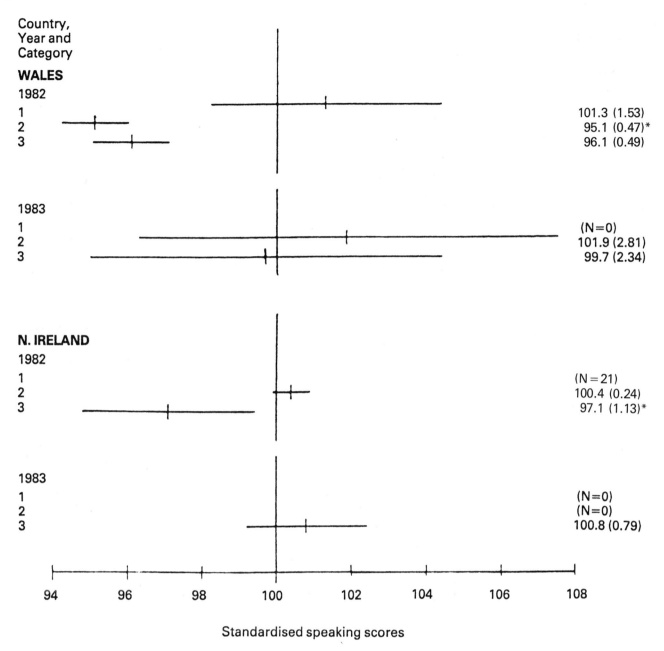

Standardised speaking scores

Key: Category 1   5.9% and below   (proportion of pupils receiving free meals)
          2   6–13.9%   „
          3   14% and above   „
      * Statistically significant difference

Figure 11.17 *Reading performance by proportion of pupils receiving free school meals, Wales and Northern Ireland, age 15, 1980–83*

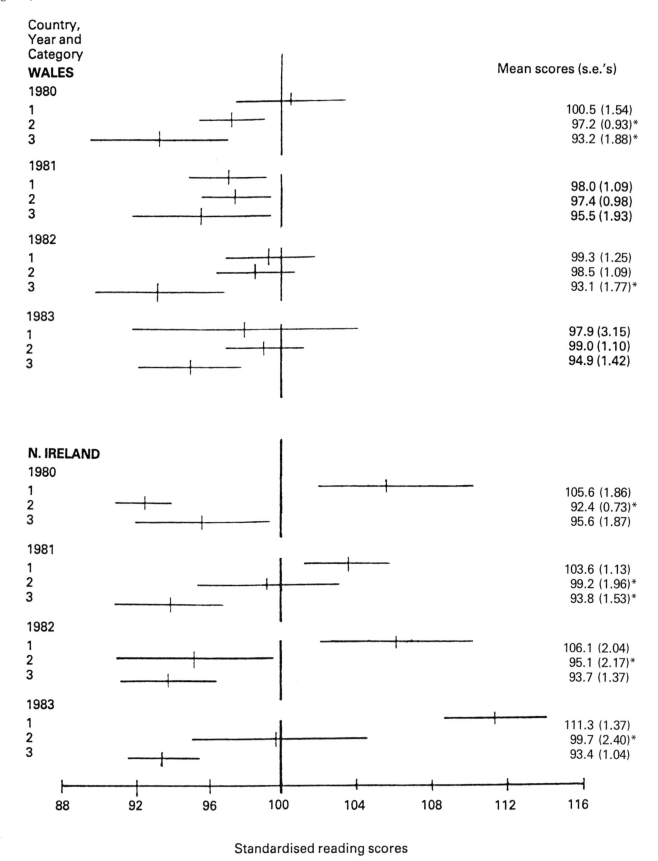

Standardised reading scores

Key: Category 1   5.9% and below   (proportion of pupils receiving free meals)
         2   6–13.9%   ''
         3   14% and above   ''
      * Statistically significant difference

Figure 11.18 *Writing performance by proportion of pupils receiving free school meals, Wales and Northern Ireland, age 15, 1980–83*

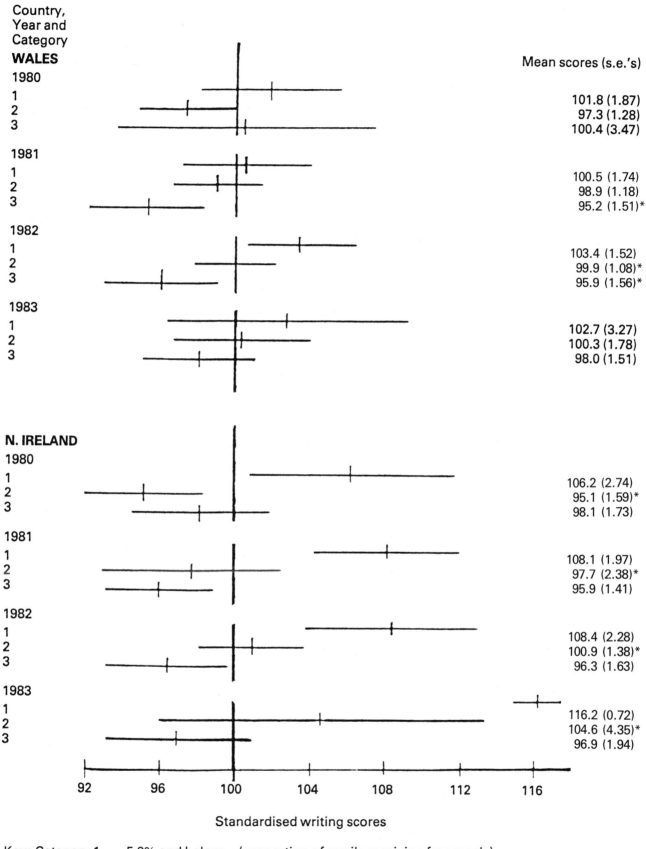

Country, Year and Category

WALES

Mean scores (s.e.'s)

1980
1   101.8 (1.87)
2   97.3 (1.28)
3   100.4 (3.47)

1981
1   100.5 (1.74)
2   98.9 (1.18)
3   95.2 (1.51)*

1982
1   103.4 (1.52)
2   99.9 (1.08)*
3   95.9 (1.56)*

1983
1   102.7 (3.27)
2   100.3 (1.78)
3   98.0 (1.51)

N. IRELAND

1980
1   106.2 (2.74)
2   95.1 (1.59)*
3   98.1 (1.73)

1981
1   108.1 (1.97)
2   97.7 (2.38)*
3   95.9 (1.41)

1982
1   108.4 (2.28)
2   100.9 (1.38)*
3   96.3 (1.63)

1983
1   116.2 (0.72)
2   104.6 (4.35)*
3   96.9 (1.94)

92   96   100   104   108   112   116

Standardised writing scores

Key: Category 1   5.9% and below   (proportion of pupils receiving free meals)
        2   6–13.9%   "
        3   14% and above   "
    * Statistically significant difference

Figure 11.19 *Speaking performance by proportion of pupils receiving free school meals, Wales and Northern Ireland, age 15, 1982–83*

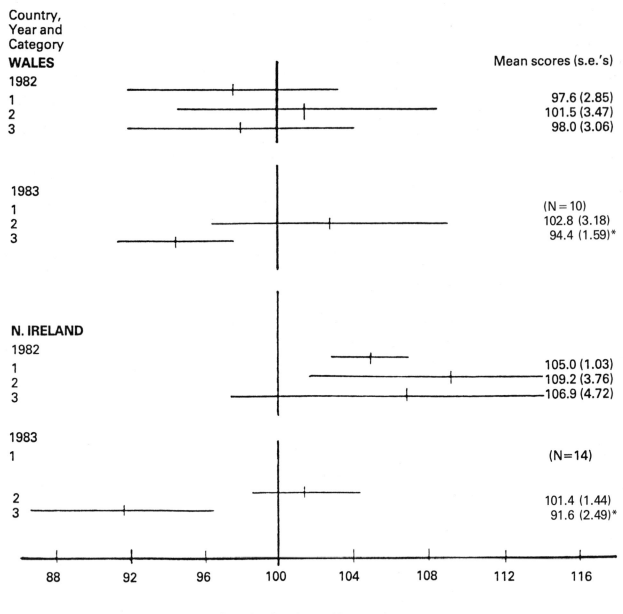

Standardised speaking scores

Key: Category 1   5.9% and below   (proportion of pupils receiving free meals)
           2   6–13.9%   ,,
           3   14% and above   ,,
    * Statistically significant difference

Pupil/teacher ratio (age 11)

Part-time teachers were included *pro rata* in the calculation of results for this variable. It should also be noted that no information on this variable was available for Northern Ireland, and results are reported only for England and Wales. These points apply to both age levels.

Because staffing allowances are calculated differently for primary and secondary schools, the sub-categories of this variable are rather different at the two age levels surveyed, and results for the two ages will therefore be presented separately.

The sub-categories used at age 11 were the following:

Category	Number of pupils per teacher
1	27.5 or more
2	25–27.4
3	20–24.9
4	19.9 or less

The results for Wales produced hardly any statistically significant differences in reading, writing or oracy.

In England the picture was more complicated. In the oracy sample the numbers of pupils in each category were too small for the results to be reliable. The results for reading and writing are presented in Figures 11.20 and 11.21.

These Figures show a largely consistent rank order in both modes across years. Category 4 schools (those with the most favourable pupil/teacher ratio) always had the lowest mean score, and that score was almost always significantly lower than the score in at least one other category.

Thus this variable appears to have some explanatory value at age 11 in England. Its lack of power in Wales may be due to the smaller numbers involved.

Figure 11.20 *Reading performance by pupil/teacher ratio, England, age 11, 1979–83*

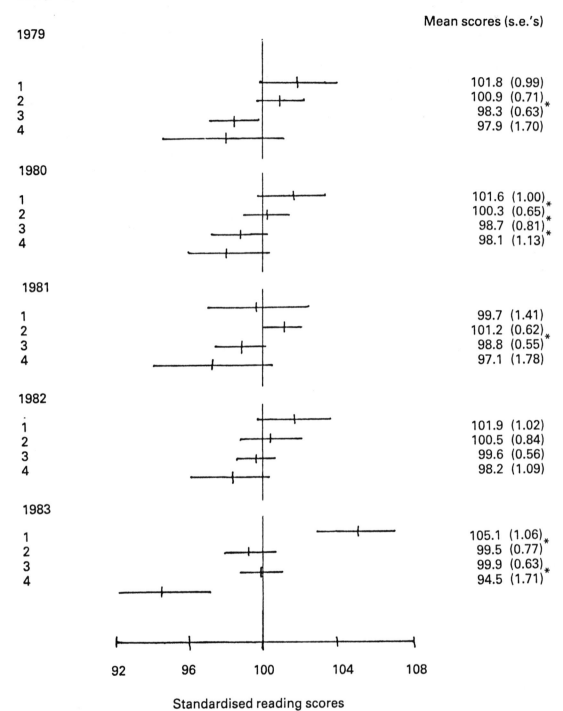

Key: Category 1   27.5 or more (number of pupils per teacher)
          2   25–27.4   "
          3   20–24.9   "
          4   19.9 or less   "

      * statistically significant difference

Figure 11.21 *Writing performance by pupil/teacher ratio, England, age 11, 1979–83*

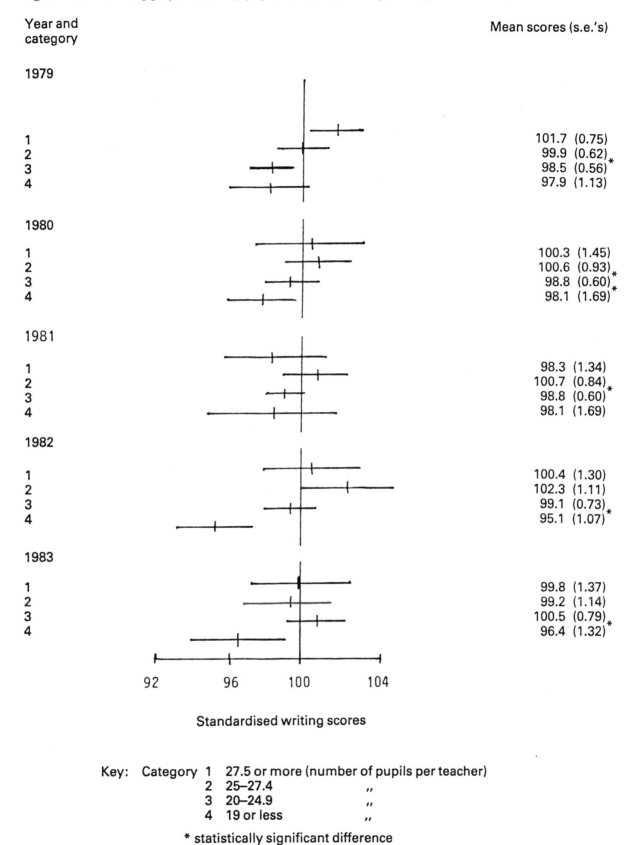

Year and category

Mean scores (s.e.'s)

1979

1   101.7 (0.75)
2   99.9 (0.62)
3   98.5 (0.56)*
4   97.9 (1.13)

1980

1   100.3 (1.45)
2   100.6 (0.93)*
3   98.8 (0.60)*
4   98.1 (1.69)

1981

1   98.3 (1.34)
2   100.7 (0.84)*
3   98.8 (0.60)
4   98.1 (1.69)

1982

1   100.4 (1.30)
2   102.3 (1.11)
3   99.1 (0.73)*
4   95.1 (1.07)*

1983

1   99.8 (1.37)
2   99.2 (1.14)
3   100.5 (0.79)*
4   96.4 (1.32)*

92   96   100   104

Standardised writing scores

Key: Category 1   27.5 or more (number of pupils per teacher)
            2   25–27.4   "
            3   20–24.9   "
            4   19 or less   "

      * statistically significant difference

Pupil/teacher ratio (age 15)

At age 15 pupil/teacher ratio was a less informative variable than at age 11.

The sub-categories distinguished at this level were:

Category	Number of pupils per teacher
1	17.5 or more
2	15–17.4
3	14.9 or less

The results for Wales were again almost entirely non-significant, and the numbers in the oracy sample in England were again very small. In writing in England there were few significant differences, and the rank order was inconsistent. The results for reading in England were broadly similar to those at age 11, as can be seen from Figure 11.22. This shows an almost entirely consistent rank order in which category 4 was always lowest. That is, schools with the most favourable pupil/teacher ratios had the lowest mean scores.

In interpreting the results for this variable at both ages it is necessary to bear two facts in mind. First, pupil/teacher ratio is not necessarily an accurate reflection of size of teaching group. Team-teaching, free periods and the provision of non-teaching heads, etc. mean that teaching group sizes cannot be deduced from the pupil/teacher ratio.

Secondly, it would be unwise to deduce from the apparently counter-intuitive pattern of results that better pupil/teacher ratios *cause* lower performance. Lower pupil/teacher ratios are the *result* in many schools of the deliberate provision by LEAs of extra staff in educational priority areas or other areas of special need. The lower achievement therefore precedes the provision of extra staff; and might have been lower still if that provision had not existed.

Figure 11.22 *Reading performance by pupil/teacher ratio, England, age 15, 1979–83*

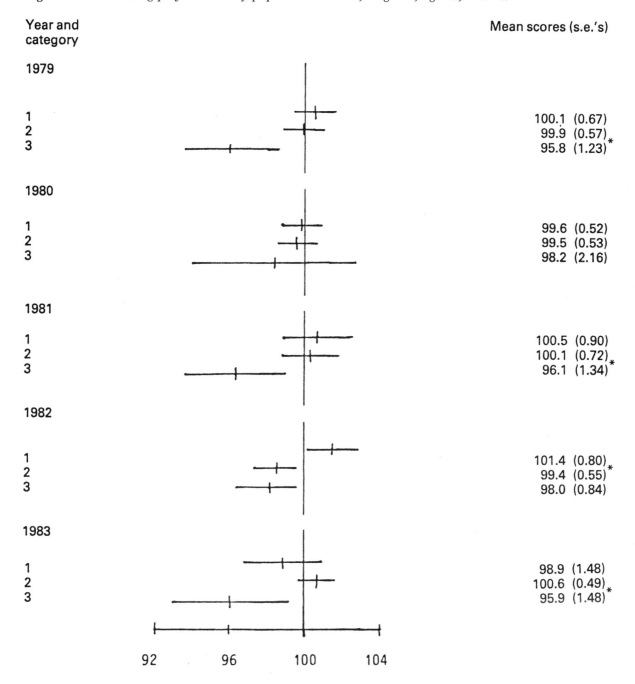

Standardised reading scores

Key: Category 1   17.5 or more (number of pupils per teacher)
2   15–17.4   ''
3   14.9 or less   ''

* statistically significant difference

203

Size of English teaching group (age 15)

By contrast with the uncertainties of the pupil/teacher ratio, this variable was unambiguous. It was a direct measure of the size of the group in which 15-year-old pupils were taught English (or English Language if Literature was separately timetabled). The sub-categories were:

Category	Number of pupils in English group
1	30 or more
2	25–29.9
3	20–24.9
4	less than 20

Information was collected on this variable only for the years 1981–83. The results were mostly clear, as can be seen from Figures 11.23–11.25. In oracy the rank order was not consistent, and hardly any of the differences were significant. In reading and writing, however, the rank order was totally consistent, with higher mean scores always associated with larger teaching groups. All the differences in Figures 11.23 and 11.24 were statistically significant, except that between categories 1 and 2 for reading in 1982.

The clear-cut results need careful interpretation, however. It appears to be the case that many schools have a policy of teaching lower-attaining pupils in smaller classes. If this is the case, then the results on this variable could be interpreted as showing that smaller classes are an effect of low attainment rather than the reverse (cf. the discussion on p. 203).

Single-sex or co-educational school (age 15)

Data on this variable were collected in 1979–81, and representative results were presented in earlier reports.[1] Briefly, they showed that single-sex schools had higher mean scores than co-educational schools: but it was also stressed that this variable was heavily confounded with selectivity, in that most of the remaining single-sex schools are grammar schools. In Northern Ireland, where there are substantial numbers of single-sex secondary modern schools, no single-sex versus co-educational differences were found.

---

[1] *Secondary Report No. 1,* pp. 110–111, 116, 119, 125. London: HMSO, 1982.
Secondary Report No. 2, pp. 106, 111, 117–118, 121. London: HMSO, 1983.

Figure 11.23 *Reading performance by size of English group, age 15, 1981–83*

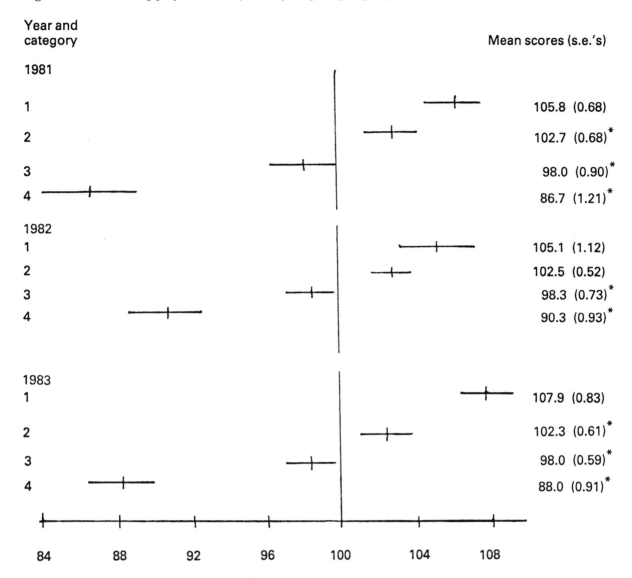

Year and
category

Mean scores (s.e.'s)

1981

1   105.8 (0.68)

2   102.7 (0.68)*

3   98.0 (0.90)*

4   86.7 (1.21)*

1982
1   105.1 (1.12)

2   102.5 (0.52)

3   98.3 (0.73)*

4   90.3 (0.93)*

1983
1   107.9 (0.83)

2   102.3 (0.61)*

3   98.0 (0.59)*

4   88.0 (0.91)*

84   88   92   96   100   104   108

Standardised reading scores

Key: Category   1   30 or more (size of group)
2   25–29.9   „
3   20–24.9   „
4   less than 20   „

* statistically significant difference

205

Figure 11.24   *Writing performance by size of English group, age 15, 1981–83*

Year and
category

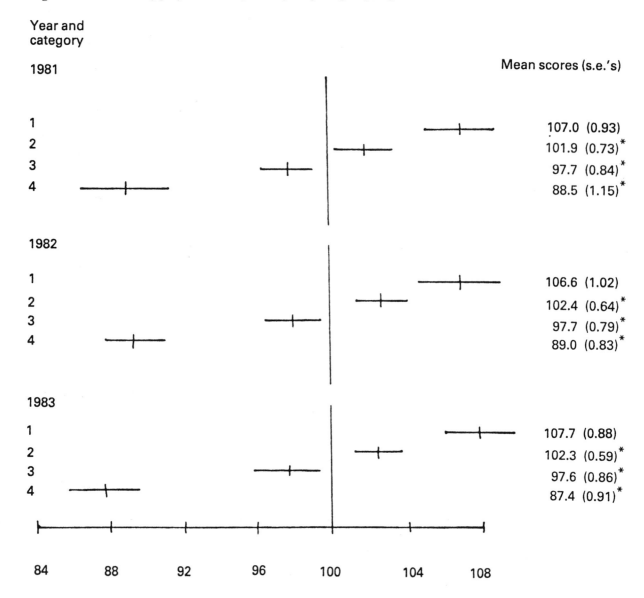

1981   Mean scores (s.e.'s)

1   107.0 (0.93)
2   101.9 (0.73)*
3   97.7 (0.84)*
4   88.5 (1.15)*

1982

1   106.6 (1.02)
2   102.4 (0.64)*
3   97.7 (0.79)*
4   89.0 (0.83)*

1983

1   107.7 (0.88)
2   102.3 (0.59)*
3   97.6 (0.86)*
4   87.4 (0.91)*

84   88   92   96   100   104   108

Standardised writing scores

Key: Category 1   30 or more (size of group)
                 2   25–29.9   ,,
                 3   20–24.9   ,,
                 4   less than 20   ,,

* statistically significant difference

206

Figure 11.25 *Speaking performance by size of English group, age 15, 1982–83*

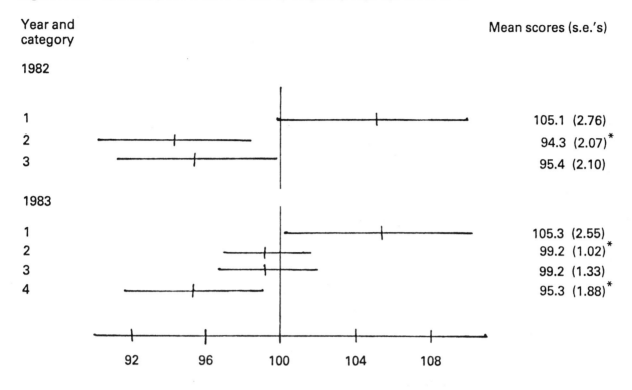

Standardised speaking scores

Key: Category 1 30 or more (size of group)
              2 25–29.9   „
              3 20–24.9   „
              4 less than 20   „

* statistically significant difference

11.4 Geographical variables

School catchment area

Data on this variable were gathered in 1981–83, and the results have also been reported previously.[1] They showed, briefly, that schools in inner-city areas had lower scores than those in the suburbs, etc., and confirmed the picture derived from such other socio-economic indicators as are available.

Metropolitan or non-metropolitan county (England)

This variable served to distinguish the largest conurbations in England from the rest of the country. The areas which were considered metropolitan for this purpose were the counties of Greater London, Greater Manchester,

Merseyside, West Midlands, Tyne and Wear, South Yorkshire and West Yorkshire. No areas were designated metropolitan in this sense in either Wales or Northern Ireland.

The results for England were mixed. In writing at both ages in oracy at age 11 the differences between metropolitan and non-metropolitan areas were consistently non-significant. In oracy at age 15, and in reading at both ages, there was a strong trend for performance to be higher in non-metropolitan counties. The results for reading are shown in Figures 11.26 and 11.27.

All the differences shown were statistically significant, except those for 1983 at age 15 and for 1981 and 1982 at age 11.

These results are difficult to interpret. If they were a reflection of a social or economic factor, differences would also be expected in writing.

---

[1] *1982 Secondary Report*, pp. 176–178, 184, 186. London: DES, 1985.

Figure 11.26 *Reading performance by location, age 11, England, 1979–83*

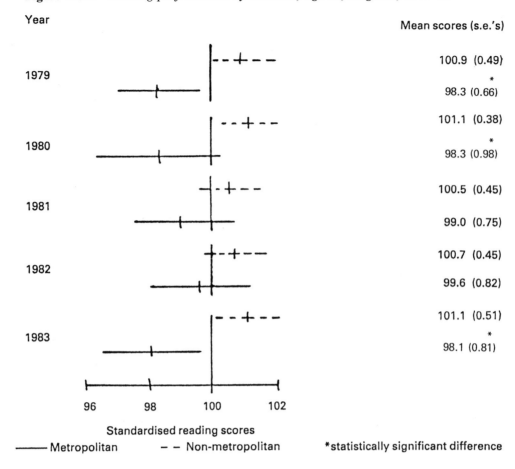

Year

Mean scores (s.e.'s)

1979

100.9 (0.49)
*
98.3 (0.66)

1980

101.1 (0.38)
*
98.3 (0.98)

1981

100.5 (0.45)

99.0 (0.75)

1982

100.7 (0.45)

99.6 (0.82)

1983

101.1 (0.51)
*
98.1 (0.81)

96   98   100   102

Standardised reading scores

——— Metropolitan   – – Non-metropolitan   *statistically significant difference

Figure 11.27 *Reading performance by location, age 15, England, 1979–83*

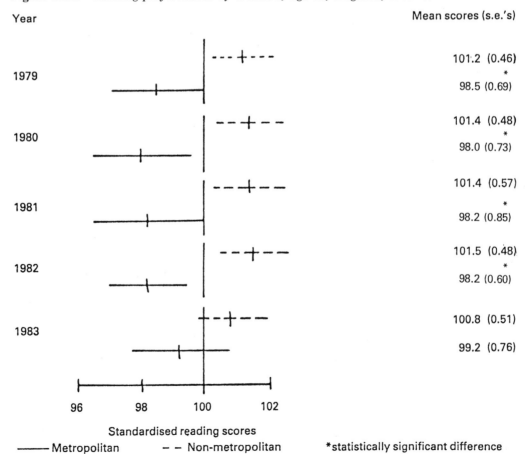

Year

Mean scores (s.e.'s)

1979

101.2 (0.46)
*
98.5 (0.69)

1980

101.4 (0.48)
*
98.0 (0.73)

1981

101.4 (0.57)
*
98.2 (0.85)

1982

101.5 (0.48)
*
98.2 (0.60)

1983

100.8 (0.51)

99.2 (0.76)

96   98   100   102

Standardised reading scores

——— Metropolitan   – – Non-metropolitan   *statistically significant difference

Figure 11.28 *Map showing the three regional divisions of England*

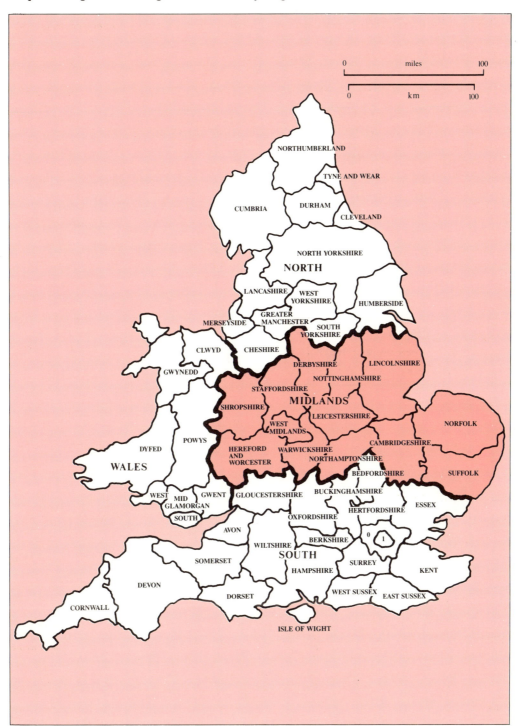

Region (England)

For the purposes of APU surveys, three regions were distinguished in England, namely North, Midlands and South. These are shown in Figure 11.28. Rather few significant differences were found between the three regions in any of the three modes at either age, and the rank order varied from survey to survey.

Country

Comparisons between England, Wales and Northern Ireland also yielded very little useful information.

Northern Ireland was highest in the rank order in all five years in writing at age 11; England was highest in the rank order in all five years in reading at age 15. However, in neither case were the differences between countries always significant, and in other modes and ages there was no discernible pattern.

11.5 Conclusions

Of the background variables discussed in detail in this chapter, the three pupil variables of sex, English as a first or second language, and (at age 15) number of public examination entries, and the school variable of size of English teaching group (age 15) gave the clearest results. On average, lower performance tended to be associated with boys, non-native speakers, pupils with fewer examination entries, and pupils in smaller teaching groups.

For certain other variables the picture was less clear. Metropolitan versus non-metropolitan location (England) produced clear differences only in reading; pupil/teacher ratio seemed to be associated with clear differences only at age 11 in England. Performance data related to country and region appeared to yield little useful information.

The proportion of pupils receiving free school meals yielded fairly clear indications of an association between socio-economic status and performance.

Finally, it should perhaps be said that even if all the variables used in these surveys are considered together, they explain only a relatively small proportion of the differences in performance between pupils, and therefore that the results reported against background variables should be interpreted judiciously.

Annex 11.1

Sample sizes, schools and pupils, by countries

Table A11.1 *Sample sizes, schools and pupils, by countries:*
Primary Survey 1979

	England	Wales	N. Ireland	Total
Number of schools				
Invited to take part	674	173	164	1,011
Actually taking part	628	159	126	913
Number of pupils				
In schools taking part	10,102	2,068	1,688	13,858
Completing tests	9,936	2,044	1,662	13,642
Sub-samples of pupils				
Reading	5,538	1,165	963	7,666
Attitudes	838	196	138	1,172
NS6*	838	196	0	1,034
Writing	2,673	586	454	3,713
Linking Reading	1,087	163	129	1,379
Linking Reading and Writing	637	130	116	884

*National Survey Test 6

Table A11.2 *Sample sizes, schools and pupils, by countries:*
Primary Survey 1980

	England	Wales	N. Ireland	Total
Number of schools				
Invited to take part	463	160	148	771
Actually taking part	421	148	122	691
Number of pupils				
In schools taking part	6,757	1,846	1,413	10,016
Completing tests	6,651	1,817	1,386	9,854
Sub-samples of pupils				
Reading	3,767	1,066	792	5,625
Writing 1, 2, 5–10	2,341	566	485	3,392
Writing 3–4/Reading	543	185	109	837
Total Reading (1 + 3)	4,310	1,251	901	6,462
Total Writing (2 + 3)	2,884	751	594	4,229
Total Linking (3)	543	185	109	837
Attitudes (Approx 20% of reading sample)	753	213	158	1,124

Table A11.3 *Sample sizes, schools and pupils, by countries:*
Primary Survey 1981

	England	Wales	N. Ireland	Total
Number of schools				
Invited to take part	544	154	163	861
Actually taking part	487	146	134	767
Number of pupils				
In schools taking part	5,372	1,314	1,351	8,037
Completing tests	5,262	1,281	1,327	7,870
Sub-samples of pupils				
Reading	2,369	583	596	3,818
Writing	2,632	698	731	4,052
Attitudes	1,307	292	299	1,898

Table A11.4 *Sample sizes, schools and pupils, by countries:*
Primary Survey 1982

	England	Wales	N. Ireland	Total
Number of schools				
Invited to take part	550	141	133	824
Actually taking part	497	134	112	743
Number of pupils				
In schools taking part	7,016	1,880	1,517	10,413
Completing tests	6,887	1,846	1,481	10,214
Sub-samples of pupils				
Reading	3,437	918	747	5,102
Writing	2,706	738	595	4,039
Linking	744	190	139	1,073
Attitudes – Reading	793	197	136	1,129
Attitudes – Writing	784	212	143	1,139
Oracy (approx)*	1,184	304	272	1,760
* including friends not part of original sample	297	51	60	408

Table A11.5 *Sample sizes, schools and pupils, by countries:*
Primary Survey 1983

	England	Wales	N. Ireland	Total
Number of schools				
Invited to take part	436	140	150	726
Actually taking part	391	130	127	648
Number of pupils				
In schools taking part	6,458	1,907	1,743	10,108
Completing tests	6,285	1,867	1,716	9,868
Sub-samples of pupils				
Reading	2,425	732	643	3,800
Writing	2,430	705	651	3,786
Composite	1,430	430	422	2,282
Attitudes – Reading	667	194	172	1,033
Attitudes – Writing	647	164	177	988
Linking 1st and 5th Surveys	948	290	238	1,476
Work sampling	405	148	99	652
Oracy*	824	237	207	1,268
* including friends not part of original sample	258	64	36	358

Table A11.6 *Sample sizes, schools and pupils, by countries:*
Secondary Survey 1979

	England	Wales	N. Ireland	Total
Number of schools				
Invited to take part	335	52	65	452
Actually taking part	288	42	48	378
Number of pupils				
In schools taking part	6,228	1,544	1,870	9,642
Completing tests	5,942	1,445	1,762	9,149
Sub-samples of pupils				
Reading	3,455	812	1,048	5,315
Attitudes	696	156	216	1,068
NS6	702	163	220	1,085
Writing	2,023	471	603	3,097
Linking Reading and Writing	464	162	111	737

Table A11.7 *Sample sizes, schools and pupils, by countries:*
Secondary Survey 1980

	England	Wales	N. Ireland	Total
Number of schools				
Invited to take part	281	73	64	418
Actually taking part	242	58	49	349
Number of pupils				
In schools taking part	7,748	1,923	1,627	11,298
Completing tests	7,387	1,785	1,548	10,720
Sub-samples of pupils				
Reading	4,647	1,137	954	6,738
Linking	583	128	107	818
Writing	2,157	520	487	3,164
Attitudes	755	185	151	1,091

Table A11.8 *Sample sizes, schools and pupils, by countries:*
Secondary Survey 1981

	England	Wales	N. Ireland	Total
Number of schools				
Invited to take part	342	146	148	636
Actually taking part	288	110	101	499
Number of pupils				
In schools taking part	5,225	1,550	1,233	8,008
Completing tests	4,991	1,465	1,176	7,632
Sub-samples of pupils				
Reading	2,461	684	582	3,673
Writing	2,530	781	648	3,959
Attitudes	1,227	99	72	1,398

Table A11.9 *Sample sizes, schools and pupils, by countries:*
Secondary Survey 1982

	England	Wales	N. Ireland	Total
Number of schools				
Invited to take part	445	147	142	734
Actually taking part	367	103	91	561
Number of pupils				
In schools taking part	5,756	1,787	1,302	8,845
Completing tests	5,495	1,694	1,236	8,425
Sub-samples of pupils				
Reading	2,719	818	616	4,153
Writing	2,776	876	620	4,272
Attitudes – Reading	525	133	57	715
Attitudes – Writing	521	144	61	726
Oracy*	592	184	120	896
Work Sampling	237	68	58	363
* including friends not part of original sample	231	78	52	361

Table A11.10 *Sample sizes, schools and pupils, by countries:*
Secondary Survey 1983

	England	Wales	N. Ireland	Total
Number of schools				
Invited to take part	432	112	115	659
Actually taking part	353	85	83	521
Number of pupils				
In schools taking part	7,714	1,762	1,838	11,314
Completing tests	7,328	1,636	1,738	10,702
Sub-samples of pupils				
Reading	3,281	790	787	4,858
Writing	3,199	662	736	4,597
Composite	848	184	215	1,249
Attitudes – Reading	1,044	219	123	1,386
Attitudes – Writing	1,092	169	60	1,321
Work Sampling	759	131	144	1,034
Oracy*	826	180	209	1,215
* including friends not part of original sample	346	81	79	506

12

Reading and writing over the five surveys

Synopsis

This chapter is concerned with data obtained from all ten surveys from 1979 to 1983. It looks at the data in two distinct ways in order to determine whether the performance of pupils in reading or writing has changed over the period. One approach concentrates on data from only the 1979 and 1983 surveys, focusing on identical tests used in both years: this is called the 'constant test' approach. The second approach ('relative difference') uses data from all five years and looks for trends.

The approach using the constant test data produced a number of significant results which are shown in Table 12.1. There were other significant findings but these were judged to result from those given. For example, Northern Ireland pupils did worse in 1983 than in 1979, but this was because both boys and girls did worse. The significant results from the relative difference approach are shown in Table 12.2.

At first sight it appears that there is no particular correlation between the results obtained using the two approaches, and indeed some contradictions. However, it should be remembered that the relative difference approach can only detect relative changes between *sub-classes* of the data over the five years. The constant test approach utilises a very much smaller amount of data than the relative difference approach.

The age 15 writing constant test results indicate that there has been no overall improvement from 1979 to 1983, but with no significant sub-class changes. Consistent with this, the relative difference data show that, on the whole, there is no trend for boys either to catch up with girls or to fall further behind them.

compare the performance of pupils on items and tests directly (see Annex 12.1).

The relative difference approach

The second approach to the analysis of the data has used all the data available from the survey for reading and writing at both ages, and looked for *relative* changes. This approach is described more fully in Annex 12.2, but the basic procedure is to compare the differences between sub-groups of the sample of pupils such as boys and girls, across the five years of surveys. Any change in the performance of boys and girls relative to each other will then be detected from the analysis.

The analysis of the results across the five years has been restricted to two background variables. These are: the sex of the pupils and the country to which the school belongs, i.e. England, Wales or Northern Ireland.

The combination of the data from these two variables has also been analysed. There are several reasons for restricting the analysis to just these background variables. Firstly, as shown in Chapter 11, there are few background variables which have been available for all five surveys. (The interpretation of some variables like 'free school meals' has changed over the five years, and it is important to analyse data using consistent variables.) Secondly, the sex variable is one of specific interest in relation to the performance of pupils in language. The country variable is also of interest.[1]

The significant results on these variables from the two statistical approaches are shown in Tables 12.1 and 12.2, and analysed in the following sections.

12.1 Introduction

The constant test approach

At both ages, though the surveys of both reading and writing have used common material from 1979 to 1983, there are few tests which span all five years in an identical form. However, the 1983 surveys were specifically designed to include some materials for assessment which were identical to those in 1979. These have been assigned the title of 'constant tests'. They make it possible to

[1] It should be remembered that the design of the surveys was such that the sample was not necessarily self-weighting. Wales and Northern Ireland were over-represented as were other sections of the population. All the results in this chapter have had the imbalance redressed with respect to the stratification variables, and are population estimates. The design with respect to reading allowed for all the reading booklets to go to each school; the 'school effect' on individual booklets was thus minimised. However, the overall precision of the reading measure and the writing task measures are affected by the sample design. This effect has been taken into account where necessary except for the comparison of constant tests in writing.

Table 12.1 *Significant results obtained from the comparison of constant tests, 1979 vs. 1983*

Mode and age	Significant Results
Reading, age 11	Boys in England and girls in England performed better in 1983 than they did in 1979.
Writing, age 11	Overall slight improvements, especially for boys in England, between 1979 and 1983, but decline for girls in Northern Ireland over the same period.
Reading, age 15	Girls in Wales and boys in England performed better in 1983 than in 1979.
Writing, age 15	There was no overall improvement in performance from 1979 to 1983.

Table 12.2 *Significant results from all ten surveys using the relative difference approach*

Mode and age	Significant Results
Reading, age 11	Boys in 1983 appeared to be performing less well relative to girls than they did in 1979.
Writing, age 11	In England, boys performed less well than girls, but the gap in performance narrowed across the five years.
Reading, age 15	English pupils did better than Welsh pupils and the level of performance of Welsh pupils was declining, relatively speaking.
Writing, age 15	No significant trends were identified.

12.2 Constant tests – reading

The constant test approach depends on the comparison of identical tests which have been given to comparable pupils under the same test conditions. The comparisons give a direct measure of change from one survey to another, with the test average facility providing an appropriate basis for comparison.

There were four booklets which were used in the age 11 surveys of both 1979 and 1983 (**Whales, King Arthur, Dragons** and **Space**). At age 15, five booklets were used in both years (**Whales** 1 and 6, **The Landlady, Warminster-on-Sea** and **The Flying Machine**).

At both ages, each booklet also contained a sub-test that was common to all the booklets used at that age level. Performance on this common test was analysed across all tests and thus provided a larger basis for comparison. Tables 12.3 (age 11) and 12.4 (age 15) show the mean differences between the 1979 and 1983 results together with the associated standard error and an indication of the significance of the difference. (The test of significance was based on the null hypothesis that there was no difference between the two surveys, i.e. that the difference was not significantly different from zero.)

The percentage point differences are those observed between the average test percentages for the 1979 survey and the 1983 survey. The average test percentages were calculated within a sub-set of the data, e.g. for just the boys or just the girls.

There are considerable fluctuations in the difference in percentage scores from the 1979 age 11 survey to the 1983 age 11 survey, and it is therefore difficult to come to any firm general conclusions about the nature of the change between these surveys. The average changes as indicated in Table 12.3 do, however, illustrate the magnitude of the change in performance between the two surveys, this being about 4 per cent overall, with the largest change relating to girls in England (5.2 per cent).

Table 12.3 *Constant reading tests, age 11, 1979 vs. 1983*

Test		Whales	King Arthur	Dragons	Space	Common
No. of items		37	40	42	45	17
Comparison		Difference in percentage of items answered correctly				
Boys	diff	4.9*	1.3	4.0	4.0	2.3*
	se	2.2	2.2	2.1	2.1	1.1
Girls	diff	4.0	6.5**	5.6**	4.5*	0.5
	se	2.3	1.9	2.1	2.1	1.1
Eng	diff	5.1*	3.7*	5.4	4.8**	2.0*
	se	2.0	1.8	1.8	1.8	1.0
Wales	diff	−4.9	−0.1	0.2	−3.1	−2.6
	se	5.6	5.1	4.8	4.9	2.5
NI	diff	−1.8	4.4	−0.6	−2.3	−2.5
	se	4.5	4.2	3.9	3.9	2.8
B/Eng	diff	5.9	1.9	5.1	4.7	2.9*
	se	2.7	2.7	2.7	2.5	1.3
G/Eng	diff	4.7	7.2**	5.6*	5.1	0.8
	se	2.9	2.3	2.5	2.5	1.3
B/WIs	diff	−6.5	−0.3	0.3	−5.7	−3.9
	se	5.8	5.2	4.7	5.3	2.6
G/WIs	diff	−3.4	1.1	0.0	−0.7	−1.6
	se	4.4	5.0	5.0	4.6	2.6
B/NI	diff	−4.0	9.8	−9.7	−1.4	−2.5
	se	6.8	5.5	5.1	5.4	2.7
G/NI	diff	1.9	−0.1	16.2**	−3.9	−5.0
	se	5.4	6.1	4.8	5.6	2.9

Key: A single asterisk * indicates that we can be 95% certain that the observed difference does not arise by the chance alone. The 1% level of significance is indicated by ** and the 0.1% level by ***.

Table 12.4 gives the differences in the percentages of correct items for the five tests which were common to the 1979 and 1983 age 15 reading surveys. The only significant difference on the individual tests was for boys in England on **The Landlady**. The common test included in all five booklets provided a larger sample-base and, even though there were only 15 items, indicated that boys in England and girls in Wales were performing better in 1983 than in 1979. These results also meant that the boys, girls, English and Welsh samples also showed significant differences in the percentage of correct items from one survey to the other.

Table 12.4 *Constant reading tests, age 15, 1979 vs. 1983*

Test		Whales 1 and 6 combined	**Landlady**	**Warminster**	**The Flying Machine**	Common
No. of items		46	34	59	46	15
Comparison		Difference in percentage of items answered correctly				
Boys	diff	1.8	5.1***	−1.4	1.1	3.6***
	se	1.6	1.8	1.4	1.6	0.9
Girls	diff	−2.1	2.4	2.1	−1.8	2.7**
	se	1.5	1.6	1.6	1.5	0.9
Eng	diff	0.1	3.6*	0.2	−0.3	3.0***
	se	1.3	1.5	1.3	1.3	0.8
Wales	diff	−0.1	6.2	3.9	0.1	6.8***
	se	3.6	3.5	3.2	4.1	1.8
NI	diff	−0.8	1.6	−4.0	−1.8	3.0
	se	2.9	2.6	2.7	2.8	1.6
B/Eng	diff	2.2	5.1*	−1.4	1.1	3.6**
	se	1.9	2.1	1.7	2.0	1.1
G/Eng	diff	−2.6	2.1	2.0	−1.8	2.1
	se	1.8	2.0	2.0	1.9	1.1
B/WIs	diff	−4.5	5.2	−1.1	0.1	2.5
	se	4.4	4.9	4.1	3.9	2.5
G/WIs	diff	3.8	7.2	8.3	0.8	10.7***
	se	3.9	5.0	4.7	4.4	2.5
B/NI	diff	−0.8	1.6	−7.6	−1.9	2.4
	se	5.1	4.3	3.9	4.3	2.7
G/NI	diff	−1.7	−0.4	−2.4	−1.8	2.9
	se	3.4	3.1	3.2	3.7	1.9

Key: See Table 12.3.

Table 12.5 *Constant writing tests, age 11, 1979 vs. 1983*

Task		'Strangest Grown Up'	'Earliest Memory'	'Sammy Rogers'	'Three Interesting Things'	Total
Comparison		Difference in mean scores				
Total	diff	0.35	−0.13	0.23	0.20	0.17*
	se	0.09	0.09	0.10	0.10	0.05
Boys	diff	0.34*	0.21	0.24	0.28	0.26*
	se	0.12	0.13	0.13	0.14	0.06*
Girls	diff	0.32	−0.32	0.32	0.09	0.09
	se	0.13	0.12	0.14	0.15	0.07
Eng	diff	0.32*	−0.03	0.23	0.25	0.19*
	se	0.11	0.12	0.12	0.12	0.06
Wales	diff	0.74*	0.35	0.15	0.01	0.22
	se	0.22	0.25	0.22	0.24	0.11
NI	diff	0.20	−1.34*	0.76*	−0.20	−0.67*
	se	0.26	0.20	0.26	0.37	0.14
Boys/Eng	diff	0.32	0.20	0.25	0.34	0.26*
	se	0.25	0.16	0.15	0.16	0.08
Girls/Eng		0.28	−0.17	0.29	0.14	0.13
	se	0.15	0.15	0.17	0.17	0.08
Boys/Wales		0.58	0.42	−0.09	0.09	0.14
	se	0.30	0.38	0.28	0.32	0.16
Girls/Wales		0.83	0.28	0.47	−0.10	0.27
	se	0.31	0.32	0.29	0.33	0.16
Boys/NI	diff	−0.17	0.44	0.49	−0.63	0.11
	se	0.31	0.37	0.36	0.49	0.19
Girls/NI	diff	0.89	−1.29*	−0.07	−0.39	−0.98*
	se	0.43	0.23	0.35	0.53	0.17

Key: See Table 12.3.
NB * indicates significant at .01

For each task in the above table, the differences are calculated by comparing the distribution of marks in 1979 with that for 1983, for the appropriate sub-set of the samples.

12.3 Constant tests – writing

The design of the age 11 and age 15 writing surveys was such that certain tasks were used in both the 1979 and 1983 surveys. These tasks are designated the 'constant tests' and are the data on which comparisons have been made between the 1979 and 1983 surveys.

At age 11 there were four tasks used in both the 1979 and 1983 surveys. At age 15 there were six 'constant' tasks, one of which was a common task taken by all the pupils in the writing survey. Comparisons between the two surveys were made on each task separately and across all tasks.

At age 11, an overview of the four tasks suggests that pupils performed better in 1983 than in 1979, with the exception of girls in Northern Ireland.

At age 15, while there is some suggestion that certain tasks have become more difficult, no clear pattern emerged across the written tasks, either overall, or in any of the sub-groups considered. Too much should not be made of these results, since the samples are small, particularly for sub-groups, and the tests considered represent only a small part of the curriculum.

It would be prudent to view the significance or otherwise of the differences between the means with some caution.

The results are based on quite small numbers for individual tasks, e.g. about 50 male pupils in Northern Ireland, and so there is bound to be considerable random fluctuation. The significance levels quoted do not take account of the sample design, which is likely to underestimate the standard errors. To make some allowance for the possible effect of this, the statistical-significance test used is more severe than is usual, in that the 99 per cent level is used instead of the 95 per cent level. Such values are marked with * on the table.

The results in Table 12.6 are for the six age 15 'constant' writing tasks including the common task.

It would be inadvisable to make general statements about national changes in writing attainment between the two years from these results. These tests constitute a small and not necessarily representative selection from the manifold writing skills taught in many schools.

12.4 Relative differences – reading

Table 12.7 summarises the results of the relative difference analysis for the age 11 reading data. The 't' test for the constant tests investigates whether there is a significant

Table 12.6 *Constant writing tests, age 15, 1979 vs. 1983*

Task		Rules	Notes for Manual	Acc. of skill	Strong opinion	Story for 4/5 yrs.	Common	Total (not common)
Comparison		Difference in mean scores						
Total	diff	−0.16	−0.36*	0.13	−0.13	0.13	0.04	−0.11
	se	0.10	0.10	0.10	0.10	0.10	0.03	0.06
Boys	diff	−0.13	−0.44*	0.20	0.18	0.23	0.07	−0.03
	se	0.14	0.15	0.14	0.15	0.13	0.04	0.09
Girls	diff	−0.11	−0.33	0.09	−0.28	−0.16	0.00	−0.19
	se	0.12	0.14	0.14	0.13	0.13	0.04	0.08
England	diff	−0.19	−0.32*	0.18	−0.19	0.14	0.05	−0.12
	se	0.12	0.12	0.13	0.12	0.12	0.04	0.08
Wales	diff	0.87*	−0.98*	−0.17	1.10*	−0.33	−0.15	−0.12
	se	0.25	0.26	0.23	0.29	0.22	0.08	0.16
NI	diff	−0.40	−0.64	−0.64*	0.85*	1.37	0.33*	0.11
	se	0.29	0.60	0.21	0.27	0.26	0.08	0.18
Boys/Eng	diff	−0.18	−0.46*	0.28	0.09	0.25	0.07	−0.04
	se	0.17	0.17	0.19	0.18	0.17	0.05	0.11
Girls/Eng	diff	−0.15	−0.24	0.13	−0.30	−0.18	0.00	−0.19
	se	0.15	0.17	0.18	0.14	0.16	0.05	0.10
Boys/Wales	diff	1.29*	−0.61	−0.68	0.83	−0.33	−0.17	−0.05
	se	0.38	0.38	0.33	0.44	0.29	0.12	0.23
Girls/Wales	diff	0.61	−1.27*	0.12	1.44*	−0.22	−0.22	−0.19
	se	0.30	0.35	0.33	0.37	0.31	0.11	0.22
Boys/NI	diff	−0.54	—	−0.74	1.31*	1.07*	0.19	−0.14
	se	0.41	—	0.30	0.46	0.31	0.12	0.25
Girls/NI	diff	0.43	−1.60	−0.66	−0.66	−0.78	0.29*	0.10
	se	0.38	0.59	0.29	0.29	0.52	0.10	0.24

NB *indicates significant at .01 level.

Table 12.7 *Relative differences, reading, age 11, 1979–83*

Survey		Boy - Girl	Eng - Wls	Eng - NI	Wls - NI	England Boy - Girl	Wales Boy - Girl	NI Boy - Girl
79	mean	0.66	−1.04	−2.11	−1.07	−0.78	−0.96	2.45
	se	0.44	0.84	1.13	1.29	0.48	0.79	1.26
80	mean	−1.77	0.68	−0.24	−0.93	−1.67	−2.31	−2.94
	se	0.51	0.71	0.77	0.84	0.56	0.85	−1.11
81	mean	−0.33	−1.11	0.23	1.24	−0.24	−1.24	−0.92
	se	0.64	1.12	0.87	1.30	0.70	1.08	1.12
82	mean	−2.42	2.96	2.56	0.09	−2.32	−2.91	−3.33
	se	0.59	1.10	1.05	1.41	0.64	1.41	1.47
83	mean	−1.90	1.10	−0.91	−2.01	−1.78	−2.50	−4.46
	se	0.54	0.94	1.17	1.36	0.59	0.98	1.37
't' constant		−7.19***	0.95	−0.09	−0.77	−6.40***	−6.26***	−1.94
't' linear effect		−2.32*	1.32	0.91	−0.04	−1.80	−1.67	−1.85

Table 12.8 *Relative differences, reading, age 15, 1979–83*

Survey		Boy - Girl	Eng - Wls	Eng - NI	Wls - NI	England Boy - Girl	Wales Boy - Girl	NI Boy - Girl
79	mean	−0.24	1.05	3.35	2.30	−3.13	−0.43	−3.13
	se	0.67	1.15	0.95	1.38	0.72	1.40	2.53
80	mean	−1.66	1.73	1.18	−0.56	−1.62	−1.21	−3.49
	se	0.66	0.87	0.86	1.08	0.71	1.35	2.35
81	mean	−2.23	2.92	1.03	−1.89	−2.16	−3.00	−2.57
	se	0.67	0.91	0.89	1.10	0.74	1.10	1.96
82	mean	−1.25	3.04	3.59	0.55	−1.06	−4.09	−1.76
	se	0.67	0.91	0.87	1.14	0.73	1.69	1.92
83	mean	−1.30	2.80	1.95	−0.85	−1.31	−0.44	−4.85
	se	0.63	0.89	0.84	1.07	0.67	1.35	2.00
't' constant		−5.84***	11.34***	4.01***	−0.26	−4.86***	−1.66	−2.28*
't' linear effect		−1.44	−2.84**	−0.02	−0.66	0.97	−0.25	−0.23

Key: See Table 12.3.

difference in performance between the categories being compared, e.g. between boys and girls. The 't' test for the linear effect tests whether this difference between categories is increasing or decreasing with time (over the period being considered).

The analysis of the standardised differences in performance between sex, country and sex/country combinations for these data produces only one comparison where there is a significant linear effect. This comparison indicates that the standardised differences in performance between boys and girls increase between 1979 and 1983.

The analysis also shows that there are significant overall differences in performance between boys and girls and between England and Northern Ireland as well as between boys and girls within England and between boys and girls within Wales. The direction of these differences is such that girls perform better than boys, and pupils in England perform better than those in Northern Ireland.

Table 12.8 summarises the corresponding age 15 results. Again, there is only one comparison showing a significant linear effect, but in this case it is for the results for England compared with those for Wales. Pupils in England perform better than those in Wales, and the gap appears to be widening. Table 12.8 also shows significant differences in performance between boys and girls, overall, and within England and within Northern Ireland, as well as between England and Wales and between England and Northern Ireland.

12.5 Relative differences – writing

The analysis of the relative differences with the age 11 writing data between sex of pupil, country and all combinations thereof produces two statistically significant results for the linear effect. These are between boys and girls overall, and between boys and girls within England. Given that the England sample is very influential in the overall sample results, it is considered that the only 'real' result is between boys and girls within England.

It would appear (see Table 12.9) that, even though boys do not perform as well as girls, they are getting better, relatively speaking. (The standardised differences between boys and girls within England was − 7.2 in 1979 but − 4.9 in 1983.)

The results in Table 12.9 indicate very clearly that boys do not perform as well as girls, and this result holds whichever country or survey one looks at. However, it is only within England that the boys are improving relative to the girls. This result is illustrated in Figure 12.1 below.

Figure 12.1 *Relative differences, writing, age 11, boys vs. girls, 1979–83*

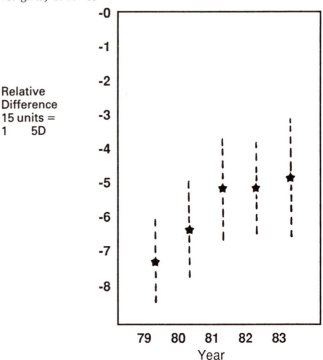

The analysis of the age 15 writing relative differences across the five surveys revealed no statistically significant linear effects. However, as in the primary surveys, there are very clear differences between boys and girls, with the girls performing better than the boys. These results are given in Table 12.10.

Table 12.9 *Relative differences, writing, age 11, 1979–83*

Survey	Boy - Girl	Eng - Wls	Eng - NI	Wls - NI	England Boy - Girl	Wales Boy - Girl	NI Boy - Girl
79 mean	− 7.48	1.37	− 8.12	− 9.49	− 7.23	− 7.68	− 10.47
se	0.66	1.32	2.99	3.18	0.60	1.12	7.47
80 mean	− 6.30	2.54	− 0.48	− 3.02	− 6.36	− 5.18	− 6.53
se	0.63	0.88	1.11	1.24	0.70	1.33	1.47
81 mean	− 5.34	− 1.15	− 4.61	− 3.45	− 5.18	− 5.77	− 7.57
se	0.67	0.91	0.89	1.10	0.74	0.96	1.28
82 mean	− 5.28	1.00	− 1.17	− 2.17	− 5.18	− 5.81	− 6.88
se	0.60	1.05	0.94	1.26	0.66	0.98	1.17
83 mean	− 5.14	1.46	− 1.84	− 3.30	− 4.85	− 8.02	− 7.94
se	0.79	1.12	1.44	1.69	0.86	1.46	0.97
't' constant	− 41.37***	1.40	− 1.44	− 1.75	− 44.03***	− 8.40***	− 4.20***
't' linear effect	5.68***	− 0.38	0.26	0.33	6.84***	0.12	− 0.25

Key: See Table 12.3.

Table 12.10 *Relative differences, writing, age 15, 1979–83*

Survey	Boy - Girl	Eng - Wls	Eng - NI	Wls - NI	England Boy - Girl	Wales Boy - Girl	NI Boy - Girl
79 mean	− 7.30	− 0.95	1.51	2.47	− 7.04	− 8.77	− 11.52
se	0.74	1.14	1.18	1.46	0.81	1.38	2.41
80 mean	− 5.43	0.27	− 0.70	− 0.97	− 5.45	− 6.13	− 3.70
se	0.87	1.31	0.95	1.30	0.94	1.78	2.81
81 mean	− 8.08	1.03	− 0.25	− 1.28	− 8.19	− 6.83	− 7.30
se	0.75	0.95	1.00	1.17	0.81	1.24	2.03
82 mean	− 6.40	0.57	0.25	− 0.31	− 6.37	− 7.11	− 6.17
se	0.70	0.96	1.16	1.35	0.77	1.06	1.93
83 mean	− 7.46	0.55	− 1.25	− 1.80	− 7.29	− 8.59	− 11.46
se	0.63	1.16	1.22	1.55	0.68	1.23	2.36
't' constant	− 18.20***	1.18	0.42	− 0.63	− 16.75***	− 9.76***	− 2.01*
't' linear effect	− 0.39	1.48	− 1.21	− 1.22	− 0.39	− 0.05	− 0.01

Key: See Table 12.3.

12.6 Discussion

The analysis of the data using the writing tasks and reading booklets which were identical in 1979 and 1983 produced several statistically-significant results. The most consistent rules are highlighted in Table 12.11 below.

Table 12.11 *Constant tests, 1979 vs. 1983: main findings*

Mode and age	Significant Results
Reading, age 11	Boys and girls within England performed at a higher level in 1983 than in 1979. In consequence, boys and girls overall and English pupils also appeared to be performing at a higher level in 1983.
Writing, age 11	Overall there was some improvement (especially for boys in England), but this masks a decline for girls in Northern Ireland between 1979 and 1983.
Reading, age 15	Girls in Wales and boys in England performed better in 1983 than in 1979. As a consequence of this, Welsh pupils, English pupils and boys also appear to have performed better in 1983.
Writing, age 15	No consistent improvement or decline between the two years.

Table 12.12 *Relative differences, 1979–83: main findings*

Mode and age	Significant Results
Reading, age 11	Girls performed at a higher level than boys and the difference was greater in 1983 than in 1979.
Writing, age 11	Boys in England performed lower than girls but the performance of the boys was improving since they were closer to the girls in 1983 than in 1979. A similar result carries through to all boys but this is certainly a consequence of the England results.
Reading, age 15	English pupils performed more highly than Welsh pupils and were improving since in 1983 the relative difference between English and Welsh pupils had increased.
Writing, age 15	No significant trends were detected.

Table 12.12 highlights the results from the analysis of the ten surveys using the relative difference approach.

This chapter has presented results from two types of statistical analysis, for two age groups, for two distinct skills, and it is not easy to summarise or interpret the outcomes.

The limitations of the techniques used must be borne in mind. Only a very small number of tests were used in both 1979 and 1983, so the constant test analysis is based on tasks which may test only a limited number of the multitudinous areas which go to make up the skills of reading and writing. It is also true that several of the common tasks have been discussed in earlier reports, and for some of them the booklets have been published, and this exposure, combined with actually using the same tests in several years, may lead to apparent increases in performance. However, bearing in mind the low sampling rates of pupils and the limited circulation of the published material, this is unlikely to have a marked effect.

The relative difference approach does make use of a much wider range of tests, but this in itself does not make the analysis meaningful. In view of the way that the work of the survey team has changed over the years from 1979 to 1983 it is not unlikely that by 1983 the skills being assessed were rather different from those assessed in 1979. For example, a greater use of tests with a scientific/technological emphasis may in itself change the observed relative difference between boys and girls, even if there is no underlying change in performance, though the results so far suggest that this is not the case.

Summary

With these limitations in mind, the main results are outlined below.

In **Reading at age 11**, there does seem to be evidence that performance levels overall rose during the period 1979–83, but with that for boys rising less than that for girls. It may be, however, that improvement in England, the country from which the major part of each survey sample is drawn, is masking more or less static results in Wales and Northern Ireland.

For **Writing at age 11**, the only noteworthy finding seems to be that boys overall improved (particularly in England hence narrowing the gap between the performance of boys and girls) and that the performance of girls in Northern Ireland declined somewhat.

In **Reading at age 15**, the results suggested that performance is improving in England and Wales, though most evidently in the former, and not declining in Northern Ireland. The improvement in England seems mostly for boys, while in Wales girls seem to be improving more than boys.

In **Writing at age 15**, there is no evidence of overall improvement.

Annex 12.1

The constant test approach for looking at change over time

This annex outlines an approach used for the analysis of data from identical tests which were used in two surveys. The approach is similar for both reading and writing, and provides estimates of absolute measures of change.

The design of the 1983 surveys included a number of reading and writing tests which had also been used in 1979. These tests were identical and so provide a basis for comparison from the first to the last survey. The reading tests used for the purpose each have several items which are marked on a right/wrong basis. Since an individual item does not provide a very reliable measure, it is usual to take all the test items as the measure of interest. The measure used to compare performance from 1979 to 1983 was thus based on several items. Writing tasks are impressionistically marked on a 7-point scale, and the basis for comparison was the mean score in 1979 compared with that in 1983.

The comparisons between 1979 and 1983 for reading performance centre around what is termed the 'average test facility'. The facility for an item is defined as the proportion of correct responses, and the average test facility is the average of all the item facilities for the test. This is an estimate and hence has an associated standard error. The size of the standard error and hence the precision of the estimate is dependent upon the sample size and sample design. The comparisons made using the constant tests are made between sub-classes of the population, defined by the sex of the pupil and the country of the survey. The magnitude of the standard errors thus varies according to the comparison. The most precise

estimate is obtained for England and the least precise for boys within Northern Ireland, since there were only 50 or so Irish boys in the sample.

The analysis involves comparing the mean sub-class average facilities between 1979 and 1983, taking into account the associated standard errors. A 't' test statistic is calculated under the null hypothesis that the means for 1979 and 1983 are the same. If the 't' value is sufficiently large, the null hypothesis is rejected.

The comparison of the writing impression mark distributions is similar in principle to the approach used in reading, but there is just one mark on a 7-point scale per writing task.

A problem encountered with these comparisons was that for individual tasks in any survey the sample size was about 450. This is sufficient to obtain reasonable estimates of the distributions for the whole sample, or for boys and girls, but was not enough when estimating boys in Northern Ireland, for example, on about 50 records. The test statistic took into account the sample size but with only 50 records, as was noted earlier, the standard errors of measurement are likely to be large.

Annex 12.2

The relative difference approach for looking at trends over time

This annex outlines an approach used for the analysis of data from five surveys. The approach is applicable to both reading and writing measures and to age 11 and age 15 survey results. This annex uses for illustration the data from the age 11 reading surveys, but data from other surveys would have been as appropriate.

It is perhaps useful to include a reminder about the survey design employed. A stratified sample of schools was selected from the population of schools in England, Wales and Northern Ireland. Pupils from the age group of interest were then selected from the chosen schools and given a test. The test was designed to provide a measure of how well the pupil could perform a written piece of work, or could read and then answer questions on a booklet. There were generally ten writing booklets and a similar number of reading booklets. The tasks and booklets were designed to cover a variety of different aspects of writing and reading skills or applications. There was, however, a common booklet which all pupils took. It was through the common booklet or task that all the other booklets, or tasks, were linked. By use of the technique of Rasch analysis the performance measures derived for each pupil were rendered comparable, regardless of which booklet or task the pupil completed.

Different surveys included different booklets and tasks, although there were some booklets and tasks which were common between surveys. There has as yet been no linking of surveys through the medium of the common material, though this is technically feasible. In this connection it should be noted that the performance measures from one survey to another so far published in reports are not comparable. In fact the performance measures for any one survey have an arbitrary origin and dispersion. They appear to be similar from survey to survey because similar techniques have been used for the analysis and estimation of the performance measures.

In order to compare performance from survey to survey and examine the data for trends, it is necessary to have data which are comparable. The team of people who devised the test material for the language surveys are confident that they are obtaining a measure of performance in reading or writing, but there is no absolute scale for these measures analogous to the meter scale for height. Within any one survey, the training and experience of markers helps to ensure that all tests are marked on the same scale, but this is less true for different surveys, where the population, the tests and the markers may all have changed.

The so-called relative difference approach to some extent overcomes the lack of an absolute metric by considering the relative differences of standardised measures. We first standardise the performance measures within each year so that the mean for the year is set to 100 and the standard deviation is set to 15. These are arbitrary points, but they have some familiarity for teachers. At first sight a problem resulting from this procedure is that all the surveys subsequently have the same mean, and so any possibility of finding a trend for the population as a whole is lost. However, essentially, the procedure only involves the data within a survey. The rescaled performance measures are on the same metric, and therefore provide a basis for relating the means for all the surveys.

The standardised performance scores cannot be usefully compared, but the differences between sub-classes of the data can. For instance, it is possible to compute the difference between the performance of boys and girls for each of the surveys and compare these.

Table A12.1 contains the standardised scores for boys and girls from the age 11 reading surveys. The final column of the table shows the differences between the boys and girls.

Table A12.1 *Age 11 reading data for boys and girls – standardised scores*

Year	Boys		Girls		Diff	
	mean	se	mean	se	mean	se
79	99.674	0.411	100.338	0.439	−0.664	0.438
80	99.133	0.448	100.903	0.480	−1.769	0.505
81	99.828	0.500	100.155	0.463	−0.327	0.635
82	98.767	0.485	101.187	0.440	−2.420	0.587
83	99.057	0.497	100.955	0.478	−1.898	0.539

The purpose of analysing standardised scores and the differences between standardised scores is to determine if a 'trend' exists. For example, boys might improve relative to girls from the first to the last survey.

The data in Table A12.1 suggests that girls are improving relative to boys, since the difference between the standardised means is increasing. We test for a trend by estimating the linear component within the data. If this is significant, in statistical terms, we say that a trend exists. The 'constant' component in the data is also estimated. If this is statistically significant, we have evidence that the differences are, on average, all in the same direction, e.g. girls are always better than boys at reading, and that these differences are unlikely to be the result of chance alone.

The results in Table A12.1 provide an example where the linear component and the constant component are both statistically significant. Hence, we conclude that girls are always performing at a higher level relative to boys and this difference is increasing.

13

Some pedagogical implications of the principles and findings of APU language surveys

Synopsis

The final chapter considers some of the implications for classroom teaching of the research and findings of the monitoring programme. It is noted that the assumptions underlying the tests embody a view of what is involved in knowing how to use language effectively and that such assumptions have practical relevance to work in the classroom. In particular, the tests take account of the fact that spoken and written language are used for different functions and that different varieties of language are used in different circumstances. Consequently, the conceptual linguistic and communicative demands of different tasks vary.

In commenting on the reading tests it was noted that the tests were designed to allow for the application of reading strategies of specific relevance to the types of texts being read. The questions asked were generally selected to take account of the intentions of the writer and the purposes for which a reader might wish to interpret what was read. One of the findings was that pupils who could understand what they read at one level frequently found it difficult to understand the writer's underlying meaning and intention. The act of reading involves the development of a receptive and enquiring habit of mind and a willingness to modify an initial interpretation. A second finding commented on was the fact that many pupils find it difficult to accept the gist of what they read and to reformulate this for some practical purpose.

In oracy assessment it was also necessary to devise tasks that had a wide range of communicative purposes. The majority of tasks involved both the interpretation and production of talk by pairs of pupils or groups made up of pairs. Some of the possible implications of the work on oracy assessment were considered in the context of the discussions with teachers which are commented on below.

In writing surveys pupils were asked to complete a range of tasks reflecting different demands made on them in school and outside it. Evidence of their writing performance was also gathered through sampling work written in normal classroom conditions. The reports on writing assessment indicate how pupils' mastery of subject matter and of aspects of the written code itself varied according to the requirements of different tasks. The difficulties that pupils had with specific tasks were highlighted by the use

of the analytic scheme of assessment. One of the practical implications of the findings from the writing surveys was that the ability to write is more likely to be fostered if the separable skills required are taught with respect to the demands of specific tasks rather than practised as isolated exercises.

The commentary draws attention to some of the possible advantages of group work in writing and to the apparent need for greater emphasis to be given to exploratory drafting and systematic revision of written work. Some observations are given about possible ways by which teachers might modify their strategies in marking children's writing and in providing feedback or commentary.

Teachers' comments on the implications of the work were sought. A number of experienced teachers tended to agree that they had sufficient experience to sequence writing tasks and tasks involving reading over a number of years, but a less clear view of what would be involved in differentiating between types of talk and in sequencing these. Some teachers drew particular attention to the fact that the collaborative work entailed in oracy assessment had implications for teaching styles.

Teachers at secondary level were particularly concerned about the integration of the teaching of English with that of other subjects including Modern Languages, and it was thought that the cross-curricular approach taken in the selection of tasks in the APU surveys was of some relevance in this respect.

The implications for the teaching of reading and writing of a number of the findings about pupils' attitudes to language and language preferences were also thought to be of general pedagogical relevance.

Finally, while it was thought that it might be helpful if a selection of test materials were to be made available for general use, with accompanying explanatory notes, it was recognised that a direct transfer of the tests into teaching could be counter-productive. It was thought that an acquaintance with particular tests would ultimately be of less assistance to teachers than an understanding of the principles that underlay their construction.

Although the tests and procedures developed for use in the monitoring programme were designed to provide information about the language performance and attitudes to language of nationally representative groups of pupils, it has become clear that there are a number of respects in which the tests themselves, the assumptions underlining them and certain of the findings have implications for classroom teaching.

13.1 The underlying assumptions

It was noted in Chapter 1 that all language tests embody a set of assumptions about the nature of language. They also embody a view of what pupils need to know to use language effectively. Many tests of language reflect a somewhat narrow conception of what is involved in language mastery. The tests used in national surveys of language prior to the establishment of the APU programme, for example, simply required pupils to complete a series of unrelated, incomplete sentences. The APU materials embody a more comprehensive view of language attainment and performance; and this conception is as relevant in certain respects to teaching as to assessment.

A number of the assumptions underlying the tests were referred to in the first chapter. Each has pedagogical implications. They include the following:

(i) In the different modes of reading, writing, listening and speaking, we use language for complementary purposes. In the APU surveys the communicative purposes of each test and of each component within the tests, when a sequence of language activities was involved, was specified in so far as this was feasible. In both teaching and assessment such differentiation is clearly desirable. In some cases it may lead teachers to conclude that pupils are being asked to apply language to a somewhat restricted range of functions in their school work.

(ii) We use language in different modes for complementary purposes. The inter-relationships between spoken and written language, in particular, need to be taken account of in teaching and in assessment more deliberately than is generally the case.

(iii) The fact that language is used for a range of different functions has the consequence that different varieties of language are used in particular circumstances. Pupils need to be made aware, primarily through reading and listening to different varieties of language, of some of the ways in which such variation is achieved. They also need to learn through writing and speaking how to convey their thoughts and feelings about a subject in a way that is appropriate to the intended audience or readership. According to the person addressed the content and organisation of what is conveyed and the style of address will be likely to vary.

(iv) The conceptual, linguistic and communicative demands of different tasks will vary. The ways in which they vary can be clarified if teachers pay close attention to how pupils respond in speech or writing, taking selective account of features of content, organisation and expression. Since such analysis is time-consuming, the adoption of such an approach has substantial implications for classroom management.

13.2 The tests and related procedures

Reading

It was noted earlier that, in content and form, the reading tests were devised to reflect the types of reading materials that pupils might characteristically encounter in the classroom when reading textbooks, works of reference and works of literature. In a limited number of cases, the tests were derived from reading materials that pupils would need to refer to for practical purposes in daily life. Wherever possible, the materials were assembled so as to comprise a coherent, related series of readings.

However, even in an assessment programme as comprehensive as that undertaken by the APU, it was possible to include only a small proportion of the different types of reading materials that pupils would be likely to encounter. It is therefore not so much the specific assessment tasks employed as the principles determining the selection of questions that would seem to have the most pedagogical relevance.

Each of the tests was designed to allow for the application of reading strategies of specific relevance to the type of text being read. The questions asked were generally selected to take account of the intentions of the writer in so far as these could be identified and the purposes for which a reader might wish to interpret what was read. The main consideration in devising questions was that they should reflect those that an experienced teacher would think it appropriate to ask pupils, given the specific form and presumed function of the materials to be read.

A number of general points of pedagogical interest arise from the reading survey findings. Some of these have been discussed in detail in earlier chapters of this report.

One such finding is that pupils who could understand what they read, at one level, frequently found it difficult to understand a writer's underlying meaning and intention. There was a recurring tendency for pupils to interpret what writers said rather than what they meant. Effective reading involves the development of a receptive and enquiring habit of mind through which pupils are prepared to envisage different possible interpretations of what was read. It also entails a willingness to modify an initial interpretation in the light of information subsequently assimilated.

The constraints of the assessment programme allowed for the introduction of only a limited number of tasks involving collaborative discussion between small groups of pupils. It was, however, clear that such discussion, if appropriately structured and supervised, provided a context in which pupils were exposed to different interpretations of what they read and to interpretations at more than one level of meaning.

It was suggested in Chapter 2 that the development of more effective reading strategies depends to a considerable extent on the pupil's exposure to a wide range of interesting reading materials in circumstances in which he or she feels encouraged to try to understand these either for purposes of enjoyment or for practical ends. Evidence from the attitude surveys indicates that while many pupils have been exposed to a wide range of fictional materials, this was not the case in all schools. Many pupils do not have access to a substantial body of reading material that they find interesting or enjoyable to read. Nor do they have the opportunity to read and see plays performed and poetry of contemporary poets read. It seems possible that the practice of early specialisation for examination purposes has the effect in some cases of depriving pupils of the chance to read and enjoy a wide range of literature. At the same time the 'literary' emphasis of many English courses also serves to narrow the range of reading materials to which pupils are exposed.

A second finding from the surveys that has somewhat general implications is the fact that many pupils find it difficult to extract the gist of what they read and to reformulate this for some practical purpose.

Both in the surveys of reading assessment and in oracy assessment, tasks involving such interpretations and reformulation proved to be difficult. In school, one of the consistent demands made is that pupils should read selectively and extract the essence of what they read. Provided that such tasks have a justifiable purpose or application there would seem to be some reason for rehabilitating them, as it were. Similarly, more attention should perhaps be given to the effectiveness with which routine notemaking and recording of what is read is carried out. Despite its vogue in schools it appears to be something that many pupils tend to accomplish relatively ineffectively.

Thirdly, evidence from the assessment of both reading and writing indicated that a substantial number of pupils were not able to distinguish very easily between different styles of writing; nor were they aware of the fact that particular varieties of language or 'registers' are conventionally associated with different applications of language.

One way in which the teaching of reading and writing could be integrated, in part, would be to ensure that pupils are given the opportunity to read materials that have been written for different purposes and for different types of reader and to see that they have the opportunity to reflect on the fact that these differences are likely to be related to the way the language of the text is selected and organised. Naturally, the range of different varieties that pupils will be exposed to receptively will be far

greater than those that they would be expected to produce orally or in writing.

Speaking and listening

In the preparatory work for oracy assessment it became clear that, while many teachers are conscious of the fact that it is important to expose pupils to a range of different reading materials and a variety of writing tasks, there appeared to be less awareness of the desirability or the possibility of differentiating between types of talk. In consequence, in the teaching and assessment of talk there tends to be a reliance on a relatively limited number of types of communicative activity and, more particularly, on tasks involving unstructured 'discussion'.

In the two years during which oracy assessment was surveyed it was possible to devise tasks that had a wide range of communicative purposes. These have been outlined in various reports, but certain salient points can be reiterated here as they have relevance both to teaching and assessment.

The majority of tasks developed involved both the interpretation and production of talk. Listening and speaking were not artificially dissociated and the design of the tasks reflects the fact that listening is seldom undertaken as an isolated activity. Generally, we listen in order to speak next or at some later point, and we speak with listeners in mind. Listening and speaking were, however, assessed independently of one another in appropriate contexts.

Many of the tasks entail a sequence of language activities, including reading or writing, as a prelude to or a consequence of talk. They reflect therefore a normal communicative sequence.

Most of the tasks were undertaken by pairs of pupils or groups made up of pairs. The main reason for this was to avoid rather artificial communication situations, but such arrangements were required in tasks where pupils were asked to convey information or relay instructions to someone else.

The number of participants was limited for assessment purposes. However, teachers working with the research team have found it possible to involve larger numbers of pupils in similar tasks. For example, activities conducted by a pair of pupils or by a small group have been observed and commented on by a whole class.

In oracy assessment, as in the assessment of reading and writing, it has been found that performance varies according to the nature of the task and the communicative purpose being assessed. For example pupils tend to find it more difficult to evaluate evidence, to justify an argument or a point of view in discussion, or to summarise the gist of a discussion, than they do to give instructions, to narrate a story or to relay information that has been acquired through listening. The pedagogical implications of these differences in performance need to be explored by teachers.

Many teachers have expressed interest in the criteria used in the assessment of oracy. These are broadly related to the following areas:

the overall organisation of the talk

the particular ideas or propositions conveyed

the grammatical forms used and the vocabulary employed to express meaning

a range of subsidiary verbal and non-verbal features that are needed for talk to be communicated audibly with appropriate emphasis and pacing.

It is not suggested that these are the only categories that might be taken into account in teaching and assessing talk, but some such framework is undoubtedly required, if the demands of different tasks are to be specified, as would seem to be desirable.

Writing

The model of writing reflects a range of activities that 11- and 15-year-olds might normally encounter in school across the curriculum. The scope and variety of such tasks has been indicated in this and other reports. As was the case in the other areas of assessment, the tasks were related to communicative purposes for which pupils were asked to use writing. They reflected also the different demands made on pupils primarily, but not exclusively, in the classroom.

The reports on writing assessment have shown how the pupils' mastery of subject matter and of aspects of the written code itself, including what are sometimes wrongly considered to be more 'mechanical' aspects of writing, vary according to the requirements of different tasks. In general, the findings suggest that the ability to write, though it reflects the application of separable skills, is more likely to be fostered if such skills are considered with respect to the demands of specific tasks, rather than practised or discussed as isolated exercises.

The demands made by different tasks are highlighted by the use of an analytic system of assessment. For writing, the scheme used relates to the nature of the subject matter or content of what is said and the manner in which what is said is organised or sequenced. The analytical scheme takes account of the way the forms of expression used by the writer reflect the different options available in vocabulary and syntax and the ways such expression varies stylistically in relation to the topic, specific purpose, and the readership envisaged for each task. Finally, the scheme reflects the fact that it is necessary for writing to be comprehensible and legible. In the first case, the focus is on grammatical features such as sentence or clause division, and the manner in which successive units are related. Secondly, the analysis takes account of the range of orthographic conventions, including word division and the systematic use of upper and lower case letters, as well as aspects of punctuation and spelling.

In making assessments and focusing on different aspects of writing it is necessary for each piece of writing to be read several times. If such an approach were to be used by teachers they would find that pupils would not normally be able to assimilate at one time all the information derived from such detailed analysis, because of the amount of information that may be amassed with respect to any piece of writing, judged with respect to different analytical criteria. It would clearly be necessary for teachers using a form of assessment that reflected, even in part, the analytic scheme outlined, to focus their commentary on one or other level or on one or other cluster of features.

Because the amount of time that teachers can devote to individual pupils is restricted and because it has been shown repeatedly that pupils are receptive to constructive criticism or commentary from other pupils, the advantages of group work in writing would seem to be apparent. In the work-sampling component of the writing surveys, the team enquired about the extent of revisions undertaken on particular pieces of written work. A minority of the samples received had been revised and, of these, very few had been carried out by pupils working collaboratively. For collaborative work of this kind to be undertaken, however, classroom management needs to be flexible and backed up by facilities for copying and circulating pupils' work.

Whether or not collaborative work is encouraged, pupils' writing would be likely to benefit from a greater emphasis on exploratory drafting and systematic revision of their written work.

We noted above the need for teachers to bear in mind the possibilities for integrating school work involving reading and writing. A similar point can be made with regard to the integration of talking and writing. The analysis of pupils' written work has indicated how pervasive the influence of spoken language forms is on pupils' writing. We have shown in this report how writing which legitimately draws on styles of speaking and on colloquial usage tends to pose fewer difficulties, at least with respect to the handling of stylistic and grammatical conventions, than writing in which such usage would be judged to be inappropriate, given the subject matter and audience envisaged. One of the reasons for the fact that pupils' handling of stylistic conventions in written language was judged to be inadequate in many cases is that many do not have a clear understanding of the systematic differences between the structure and organisation of writing and talk. When pupils repeat in writing the thinking processes that are habitual in speech, such writing is generally judged to be deficient. They therefore need to be given the opportunity to observe for themselves contrastive patterns of usage associated with talk and writing.

In the enquiry into pupils' attitudes to writing it becomes clear that pupils' own judgements about how their writing might be improved were more often based on concern for neatness and correctness than for issues relating to subject matter, style and purpose. We believe that one reason for this is that the marking schemes employed very often give undue emphasis to surface features of language, such as spelling and punctuation. There are no doubt a number of reasons for this, one of which is the fact that teachers have limited time available for marking. Close, analytic assessment is necessarily a time-consuming business. This being the case, it would seem to be advantageous for teachers who wish to focus attention in greater detail on what was written and to provide systematic feedback or commentary to request less writing overall, but to ask for writing for a wider range of purposes and a more varied readership.

13.3   Teachers' comments

Shortly after the final survey in the first phase of monitoring had taken place, in November 1984, a group of teachers was convened to discuss with the project team their view of the possible implications of the monitoring programme for the classroom. Each of the teachers had participated in some way in the surveys, as assessors of writing or talk or, in one case, as Head of the school in which some of the materials were pre-tested. The group met on two occasions and members had the opportunity to read sections of the reports relevant to the areas in which they were most interested. They provided both verbal and written comments. The following paragraphs summarise a number of the issues raised and suggestions made.

In general, there was a consciousness that it was essential for all teachers to come to a better understanding of what was entailed in language development, both in general terms and in relation to different modes of language and different subject areas. Initially, discussion focused on two main issues: what scheme of progression might be feasible so as to ensure that development took place in all language modes; and how progress might be evaluated over a period of time in such a way as to assist pupils in understanding how to do better the things they do well.

While it was thought that many experienced teachers had worked out an approach to teaching which allowed for the sequencing of writing tasks and tasks involving reading, it was agreed that they had a less clear view as to what would be involved in differentiating between different types of talk and in sequencing teaching activities, a point referred to earlier.

A second theme that emerged at different points in discussion related to the integration of English teaching with the teaching of other subject areas, particularly in secondary schools. The tendency for teachers in secondary schools, in particular, to view their subject as more or less independent of other subject areas was commented on. The groups stressed the importance of teachers coming to an understanding of the ways in which the teaching of

English could be more closely integrated with other subjects, so that pupils' language development could be viewed in the broader context of their academic and personal development. It was generally thought that the emphasis on a cross-curricular approach in the selection of tasks in the APU surveys might serve to encourage teachers, other than those specifically concerned with language teaching, to take account of the cognitive and linguistic skills needed to communicate effectively in specialised subject areas. In particular, a number of practical suggestions were made about how teachers of mathematics, science and language might collaborate in examining the texts used in their areas and in considering the communicative needs of pupils. It was recognised that English and mathematics could be regarded from one point of view as subjects serving other areas, although their autonomy within the curriculum was also recognised.

The implications of the oracy assessment programme were the focus of a great deal of commentary. It was generally agreed that, if activities of the kind used in the oracy surveys were to be incorporated into the curriculum, this would need to be preceded by a change in teachers' attitudes in many cases. It was recognised that the collaborative work between pupils that was entailed in oracy work would necessarily involve changes in teaching style. For such work to be encouraged would need to involve the co-operation of the Head of the school.

Several teachers thought that it would be advantageous for oral work to be specifically scheduled as part of the timetable and explicitly referred to in schemes of work made available to pupils and parents. It was thought that such an approach would help to give oracy work more credibility in the eyes of staff and pupils. At the same time it was recognised that such work should *not* be seen as divorced from work in reading and writing. It would also be unfortunate if the impression were to be given that language work is the sole responsibility of the English Department. On the contrary, oracy teaching needed to be integrated with all aspects of the curriculum.

It was thought that most teachers would need assistance in overcoming the practical problems in implementing oral work as an integral part of the language curriculum. It was also thought that it would be necessary for some structured materials to be provided, such as the materials that have been developed to assist in French teaching. In this connection, it was acknowledged that there was much worthwhile experience to be shared between teachers of foreign languages and those teaching a pupil's first language.

There was considerable discussion also about the significance of a number of the findings about pupils' attitudes to language. It was thought important to look at ways in which teachers could take account of these. The following specific comments were made:

The criteria that pupils applied in selecting work that they thought to be interesting to read should be noted in the choice of class readers, even if the authors suggested were not adopted.

There seemed to be a need for less emphasis to be placed on purely 'literary' texts. In particular, pupils' comments on the reading of newspapers pointed to the need for these to be read and discussed critically.

Pupils' comments on the value of school libraries were of substantial interest. They seemed to suggest that regular visits to libraries might be organised during lesson time, both for information-retrieval activities and for reading, as most pupils seemed not to value the library when they had little opportunity to use it. In secondary schools, the case for making the library available to individual pupils and for class use during the school day, as well as for use during lunch hours and after school, suggested the need for full-time librarians.

Teachers found the persistent differences between boys and girls in terms of their reading habits and preferences illuminating. Related differences in attitudes to writing were thought to have serious implications. There was some discussion about the possibilities of adjusting teacher expectations to take such differences in attitudes and in performance in writing into account.

One implication was thought to be that there should be more emphasis placed on teaching a wider range of written work taking account of the preferences expressed. It was also thought important to provide time and space for groups of pupils to work jointly on writing assignments and to serve as 'editors' for one another, and for a greater emphasis to be placed on preparatory work before writing.

Finally, a number of teachers thought that it would be helpful if a selection of APU test materials could be made available for general use, with accompanying explanatory notes for teachers' use; but it was recognised that a direct transfer of the tests into teaching would be counter-productive. In oracy work, in particular, the measures used might be inappropriately applied in a context in which continuous assessment was called for. There seemed to be general agreement that an acquaintance with particular tests would ultimately be of less assistance to teachers than an understanding of the principles that underlay their construction.

Markers' panels for the 1983 surveys

1. Oracy, age 11: on-the-spot assessors

England

Mrs. F. Bacon	Mr. G. Keith
Mrs. D. Barnes	Mrs. C. Munt
Mrs. S. Bartholomew	Mr. G. C. Nicholson
Mr. T. Dimmer	Mr. L. Parmar
Mrs. M. Hadley	Mrs. M. Port
Mrs. K. Hammond	Mrs. C. Ridge
Ms. M. Hargreaves	Ms. A. Tate
Mr. G. Hierons	Mrs. E. Woolf

Wales

Mrs. Baker	Mrs. M. Evans
Mrs. P. Dixon	Mr. M. Rhys

Northern Ireland

Miss C. M. Devine	Mr. T. Stewart
Mr. G. McConnell	

2. Oracy, age 11: second-impression markers

Mrs. N. Beaumont	Mrs. M. Harris
Mrs. M. Fenwick	Mrs. G. Hopkins
Mr. J. Gager	Dr. M. MacLure
Mrs. D. Hamilton	Mrs. C. Shore
Miss M. Hargreaves	Ms. S. Tranter

3. Oracy, age 11: analytic markers

Ms. M. Hargreaves	Mrs. C. Munt
Miss A. Kispal	Mr. D. H. Richards
Mr. C. Luckin	Mr. A. L. Smith

4. Oracy, age 15: on-the-spot assessors

England

Mr. James Cragg	Mr. Stuart Priestley
Miss Elizabeth Howard	Mr. Ed Purcell
Ms. Maggie Iles	Mrs. Anne Rex
Mr. Rob Joslin	Mr. Jim Sweetman
Mr. John Latham	Mrs. Rosemary Tong
Miss Margaret Lawton	Mr. Peter Walker
Mr. Malcolm Lee	Mr. J. Stanley Worthington
Miss Jill Mitchell	

Wales

Ms. Diana Boulton	Mr. Keith Toy
Mr. Barry Childs	

Northern Ireland

Miss Geraldine McClory	Mr. Graeme Thomson
Mr. Glenn Reilly	

5. Oracy, age 15: second-impression markers

Mrs. Dodie Brooks	Mr. Chris Odell
Mrs. Olive Collins	Mrs. Jenny Parry
Mr. Arnold Fletcher	Mrs. Dilys Preece
Mrs. Jenny Hastings	Mr. Michael Preece
Mr. John Heslop	Mrs. Olive Quirie
Mrs. Margaret Hoyle	Mr. Paul Robinson
Mr. John Jackson	Mrs. Ann Soo
Mrs. Stella Lamond	Mr. Rob Summers
Mrs. Judith Meekings	Mrs. Christine Urquhart
Miss Una Murray-Wood	Mr. Chris Walton

6. Oracy, age 15: analytic markers

Dr. Greg Brooks	Mrs. Margaret Hoyle
Mrs. Elizabeth Freeth	Mr. Peter Keatings
Mrs. Miriam Hagan	Mrs. Judith Meekings
Mrs. Jenny Hastings	Mr. Chris Odell

7. Writing, age 11: impression markers

Mrs. V. Astles	Mr. D. Collins
Mrs. J. Baxter	Mr. I. Hunter
Mrs. C. Berezai	Mrs. D. Holmes
Mr. B. Brooks	Mr. R. E. Howe
Mrs. G. Burrows	Mr. D. H. Iles
Mr. R. Brook	Mrs. S. Tiffery
Mrs. A. Maddern	Mrs. B. Kirkpatrick
Mrs. J. Ellis	Miss E. Ellett
Mrs. P. M. Connor	Mr. B. W. Little
Mr. J. Cooper	Mrs. A. Lees
Mrs. K. J. Culley	Mr. C. Luckin
Mr. H. Dawson	Mrs. C. M. Shore
Mr. M. J. Degnan	Mr. D. H. Richards
Ms. J. Gubb	Ms. A. Tate
Mrs. M. Fenwick	Mrs. A. Brinicombe
Mr. R. Free	Ms. M. Hargreaves
Mr. M. D. Furse	Mr. J. White
Ms. C. Kay	Mr. L. Lancaster
Mr. R. Hall	Mrs. M. T. Hunter
Mr. A. Harrington	Ms. J. White

8. Writing, age 11: analytic markers

Ms. A. Kispal
Mrs. M. Manners
Mrs. E. McEwen
Mr. R. Addison

9. Writing, age 15: impression markers

Mr. R. Addison	Mrs. Blundon
Mr. A. Matthews	Mr. D. Bryan
Ms. J. Baker	Mrs. J. Cooper
Mrs. M. Hawkes	Mrs. M. Dobson
Mr. D. Bennett	Mrs. S. Craddock

Ms. S. Dunkley
Mrs. J. Foy
Mrs. S. Gibson
Mrs. S. Burridge
Mr. J. Gubb
Ms. M. Hargreaves
Mrs. S. Harris
Mr. I. Harman
Ms. C. Hallahan
Mr. J. White
Mr. J. Hicks
Mr. J. Winter
Ms. R. Johnson
Mr. P. Lawrence
Mrs. A. Maddern

Mrs. M. McDonald
Mrs. E. McEwen
Mrs. E. Thomas
Mr. G. Moss
Ms. H. Seddon
Mr. L. Warner
Mr. B. Rosser
Mrs. A. O'Rorke
Mrs. B. Stone
Mr. L. Tombs
Ms. L. Wheaton
Ms. T. Parry
Mr. T. Morgan
Mrs. S. Arden
Mrs. G. Bowes

10. Writing, age 15: analytic markers

Mr. L. Tombs
Mr. D. Bryan
Mr. R. Addison
Mrs. E. McEwen

Membership of Groups and Committees

1. Membership of Language Monitoring Team at NFER

Researchers

Dr. T. P. Gorman (Project Director)
Ms. J. White (Deputy Project Director)
Dr. G. Brooks
Dr. M. MacLure (to September 1984)
Ms. M. Hargreaves (full-time to December 1984, 10% from January 1985)
Ms. L. Lancaster (to December 1984)
Ms. A. Kispal (to December 1984)

Secretarial staff

Mrs. B. Peasgood
Mrs. M. Mason (to December 1984)
Mrs. D. Merritt (to December 1984)

2. APU Steering Group on Language

Mr. D. G. Buckland, HMI (Chairman to July 1985)	APU
Mr. P. J. Silvester, HMI (Chairman from August 1985)	APU
Mr. D. G. Brook	Adviser for English, Derbyshire
Professor G. Brown	Department of Language and Linguistics, University of Essex
Dr. C. Cullen	Department of Linguistics, University of Hull
Mr. I. Enters	Stocksbridge School, Sheffield
Mr. P. Gannon	Her Majesty's Inspectorate
Dr. T. P. Gorman	Head, Department of Language, National Foundation for Educational Research
Mr. M. J. Law	HM Inspectorate (Wales)
Mrs. A. Sanderson	Sheffield City Polytechnic
Ms. S. Tyas	Deputy Head, Barugh Green Junior & Infants School, Barnsley
Mrs. M. L. Watson	Department of Education for Northern Ireland

3. Monitoring Group (NFER)

Dr. C. Burstall (Chair)
Mrs. B. A. Bloomfield
Mr. P. Dickson
Mr. D. D. Foxman
Dr. T. P. Gorman
Dr. P. Murphy (observer APU Science team)
Mr. D. Hutchison
Dr. E. Price
Mr. B. Sexton (to January 1985)

4. Monitoring Services Unit (NFER)

Mrs. B. A. Bloomfield (Head of Unit)
Mrs. A. Baker
Miss E. Elliott
Mrs. M. Hall
Mrs. J. Cowan (Secretary)

5. Members of the APU Consultative Committee (at 1.1.86)

Professor J. Dancy (Chairman)	School of Education, University of Exeter
Miss J. E. L. Baird	Joint General Secretary, AMMA
Dr. P. Biggs	Senior Adviser, Wiltshire LEA
Mrs. M. J. Bloom	Project Leader for Building and Civil Engineering, National Economic Development Office
Mr. P. Boulter	Director of Education, Cumbria (ACC)
Dr. C. Burstall	Director, National Foundation forf Educational Research
Professor C. B. Cox	Department of English Language & Literature, University of Manchester
Mrs. J. Davies	Howbury Grange School, Bexley
Mr. G. Donaldson	Flint High Comprehensive School (NUT)
Mr. I. Donaldson	NAS/UWT
Mr. H. Dowson	Deputy Headmaster, Earl Marshall School, Sheffield (NUT)
Councillor G. Driver	Councillor, Leeds City Council (AMA)
Professor S. J. Eggleston	Department of Education, University of Keele
Mr. A. Evans	Education Department (NUT)
Mr. D. Fox	Accountant, Chairman of National Education Association
Mr. C. Gittins	Longsands School, St. Neots (SHA)
Dr. A. Grady	Middlesex Polytechnic
Mr. P. L. Griffin	Windsor Clive Junior School (NUT)
Mr. K. S. Hopkins	Director of Education, Mid-Glamorgan (WJEC)
Mr. C. Humphrey	Director of Education, Solihull (AMA)
Mr. S. A. Josephs	Macmillan Education Ltd
Mr. J. A. Lawton	Kent County Council (ACC)

Mr. G. M. Lee	Doncaster Metropolitan Institute of Higher Education (NATFHE)
Mr. J. M. Leonard	General Inspector, Walsall LEA (AMA)
Mr. M. J. Pipes	Headmaster, City of Portsmouth School for Boys (NAHT)
Mr. G. R. Potter	Director of Education, West Sussex LEA (ACC)
Miss C. L. Richards	(CBI) Understanding British Industry Project, Birmingham
Mr. R. Richardson	Advisory Head, ILEA (NUT)
Professor M. D. Shipman	School of Education, Roehampton Institute
Mr. P. Smith	Springfield Lower School, Bedford
Mr. S. C. Woodley	The Kings School, Canterbury

6. Members of the APU Statistics Advisory Group

Mr. M. D. Phipps (Chairman)	APU
Professor V. Barnett	Department of Statistics, University of Sheffield
Professor D. J. Bartholomew	Department of Statistics, London School of Economics and Political Science
Mrs. B. Bloomfield	National Foundation for Educational Research
Mr. T. Christie	Department of Education, University of Manchester

Mr. J. Gardner	Chief Statistician, DES
Mr. D. Hutchison	Chief Statistician, National Foundation for Educational Research
Mrs. S. Johnson	Centre for Studies in Science Education, University of Leeds
Professor T. Lewis	Faculty of Mathematics, Open University
Professor R. Mead	Department of Applied Statistics, University of Reading
Mr. A. Owen	Her Majesty's Inspectorate
Mrs. V. Scott, HMI	Welsh Office Education Department
Dr. A. S. Willmott	University of Oxford Delegacy of Local Examinations

7. APU Management Group

Mr. M. D. Phipps	Administrative Head of the Unit
Mr. A. G. Clegg, HMI	Professional Head of the Unit
Mr. M. E. Malt	
Mr. P. J. Silvester, HMI	
Mr. D. Sleep	
Miss H. Bennett	
Mrs. M. L. Pooley	Secretary to Language Steering Group
Miss N. E. Mitchell	
Miss T. Pilborough	

Related APU publications

Language Performance in Schools: Primary Survey Report No. 1
London: HMSO, 1981

Language Performance in Schools: Primary Survey Report No. 1
London: HMSO, 1982

Language Performance in Schools: Primary Survey Report No. 2
London: HMSO, 1982

Language Performance in Schools: Primary Survey Report No. 2
London: HMSO, 1983

The above reports on the 1979 and 1980 surveys may be purchased from Her Majesty's Stationery Office, 49 High Holborn, London WC1V 6HB, or through booksellers. No reports on the 1981 surveys were published. The following reports on the 1982 surveys have been produced in limited numbers:

Language Performance in Schools: 1982 Primary Survey Report
London: DES, 1984

Language Performance in Schools: 1982 Secondary Survey Report
London: DES, 1984

Copies may be consulted at educational libraries and at the library of the Department of Education and Science, Elizabeth House, York Road, London SE1 7PH.

In addition, a series of short reports for teachers has begun to appear. The first four titles are:

Margaret MacLure and Mary Hargreaves **Speaking and Listening: assessment at age 11**
London: DES, 1986

Janet White **The Assessment of Writing: pupils age 11 and 15**
London: DES, 1986

Tom Gorman **The Framework for the Assessment of Language**
London: DES, 1986

Greg Brooks **Speaking and Listening: assessment at age 15**
London: DES, 1987

Index

facility, average test, 218
feelings, difficulty in expressing, 48
fiction, enjoyment of reading, 171, 172
flexibility in handling different types of task, 24–6
Flying Machine, The (Bradbury), 9, 10
foreign languages teaching, techniques useful in teaching English oracy, 224
form, sense of, 56
free response writing, based on pictures, 125–31
functions of writing, 124

GCE guidelines for English argumentative writing, 142
    see also O-levels
GCSE English (Language) examination, oral component, 123
geographical variables in language performance, 207–8
Glossary, using, 26, 28
Golding, William, 173
Gorman, T. P., 74n
Gott, R., 101
grammatical conventions in written work, 137, 143, 147, 223
    analytical marking of, 13–14, 17–18
        age 11, 14–15
        age 15, 17
    mastery of and attitude to writing, 175, 176
graphic experimentation, 143
graphical layouts *see* diagrams; map
group work, advantages
    in oracy, 222
    in reading, 221–2
    in writing, 223
growth and argumentative writing, 141, 142, 158
Gulls oracy task, 93, 96

handwriting and attitude to writing, 175
Herbert, James, 173
Herriot, James, 173
HMI (Primary) remarks on argumentative writing, 141
HMI (Secondary) 1979 report on 'tedium of much written work in schools', 175–6
hobbies, reading relating to, 171, 172, 173
Holbrook, D., 57
holistic marking *see* impression-marking
Horse and Two Goats, A (Narayan), 45, 51–3, 56, 60–61
humorous perspective, author's, recognition of stylistic choices in, 52, 57
Huxley, Aldous, 53
hypothetical situations, ability to adapt information to, 24–5, 38

ideas, ability to co-ordinate, 141
illustrations, matching information with, 26
images, use of
    alertness to, 48
    interpretation in satirical prose, 52, 55
imaginative writing, 124, 125
impression-marking, 4
    of oracy performance, 64, 74, 99–101
        distribution of scores (age 11), 18; (age 15), 18
    of writing performance, 11–13, 125, 133, 144–5
        distribution of scores (age 11), 11; (age 15), 12
Index, use of, 8, 11, 26–8
information, oral
    organisation of content, 84
    relaying of, 65, 92
information, written
    direct transference of, 23
    location of specific, 8, 11, 26, 38
    reassessment, 23, 31–3, 38
    reformulation, 23, 33–7, 38

retrieval, 21–38
    use of and attitude to in preference statements, 23
inner city schools *see* metropolitan area schools
Insects, written comparison task, 132–9
instructions
    oral, 222
    writing for someone else to follow, 142
integration
    of all aspects of language performance, 223
    of English teaching with other subject areas, 224
interactive tasks, oracy, 95–123
internal action in story *see* empathy
interpretation of narrative, 49–63
    differences between good and poor readers, 7–8, 56–7
    literal, 9
investigation, planning, work sampling, 159, 160
Ireland, Northern, free school meals and language performance, 192–8
    language performance in writing (age 11), 209, 212
    sample sizes (1979–83), 210–11
irony, recognition of, 54, 56
Island oracy task, 66, 71–2, 84–9

Jobs oracy tasks, 19, 20, 78–84, 93, 95
judgements about character *see* opinions
    making based on evidence, 31–3

King Lion 9

Landlady, The (Dahl), 9, 45, 46, 56, 58–9
language development
    how teachers can promote, 224
    place of writing in, 159
language performance, 178–211
    data on reading and writing, 212–18
    integration of all aspects, 223
learning, interrelation with writing, 169
LEAs *see* local education authorities
Lessing, Doris, 45, 49
Lewis, C. S., 171
lexico-grammatical features of oracy, 75, 78, 80, 84, 86, 90, 113, 123
library use, 171, 172, 173
    pupils' comments on, 225
'like/alike' confusion, 138
list of books for further reading *see* bibliography
listening and speaking
    age 11, 64–92
    age 15, 93–123
    ages 11/15 comparison, 120–23
    assessment of, 5–6, 65, 222–4
    performance in, 18–20, 75–8, 79–85, 87–9, 90–92
        conclusions, 92, 123
        1982–3 (age 11), 181, 195; (age 15), 182, 191, 198, 207
        results of impression-marking, 74
        scoring, 178–9
    tasks, 65, 67
    tests and related procedures, 222–3
literacy, basic, on leaving primary school, 10
literature
    assessment of response to, 45–63
    interpretation of, 45–6
    see also drama; narrative; poetry
local education authorities (LEAs)
    and free school meal eligibility, 192
    and lower pupil/teacher ratios, 202
location of school and language performance, 207–8
logical thinking and argumentative writing, 141
longest piece of written work (age 15), 160, 161

MacLean, Alastair, 173
magazines, reading, 173
map aids, use of, 8, 113
Map oracy task, 19, 97, 98, 113–20
markers, consistency of individual, 179, 219
marking *see* analytical marking; impression-marking
mathematical commentary, correlation with language, 113–20
Mathematics Monitoring Project, 98, 178
meals, free school
    eligibility criteria, 192
    and language performance, 192–8, 210
    method of calculating percentage, 192
meaning
    aspects of, 8, 11
    of words deduced from literary context, 8, 11
metaphor, alertness to use of, 8, 11, 48, 127
metropolitan area schools, 207, 210
minority languages of England, 183
moral issue, collaborative exploration of, 97
motivation
    deduction of, 8, 9, 10, 11, 31, 47
    understanding of, 52

Narayan, R. K., 45, 51
narrative
    analyses of responses to, 49–63
    oracy test, 65, 222
    preference for writing, 175
    writing, 126, 128
negative, errors in forming, 137–8
newspaper articles, 29
    need for critical study of, 225
    pleasure in reading, 173
    viewpoint in, 57
non-fiction, enjoyment of reading, 171, 173
notes
    making from reading, 222
    presenting information in form of, 10
nuclear weapons writing task, 149–50

O levels, number of entries and language performance, 188–91
objectivity, constraints of, in written comparison, 132–9
open-mindedness in interpreting character and action, 11, 56
opinions
    forming personal, 8, 11, 23–4
    revising first, 23, 32–3, 38, 48, 56, 222
oracy
    surveys, 18, 64, 123
        implications for the classroom, 225
    tasks (1983), 18–20
        primary, 65–7
    see also listening; speaking
organisation, overall oral, 90, 92, 123
organisation of written content, 132, 133, 134–6, 143
    analytical marking of, 13, 18
        age 11, 13
        age 15, 15
orthographic conventions, 132, 138, 223
    analytical marking of, 13, 17
        age 11, 15
        age 15, 17
    mastery of related to attitude to writing, 175–6

paragraph
    finding main ideas of, 11
    writing a, 132, 135–6
part-time teachers in pupil/teacher ratios, 199
performance features, oracy, 75, 78, 80, 84, 86, 90, 113, 123
performance, language, 178–211
    background variables, 179

232

Printed in the United Kingdom for Her Majesty's Stationery Office
(2546/87) Dd289264 C38 1/88 G443 10170